S0-AMP-859

Studies in Church History

44

REVIVAL AND RESURGENCE IN CHRISTIAN HISTORY

REVIVAL AND RESURGENCE IN CHRISTIAN HISTORY

PAPERS READ AT
THE 2006 SUMMER MEETING AND
THE 2007 WINTER MEETING OF
THE ECCLESIASTICAL HISTORY SOCIETY

EDITED BY

KATE COOPER

AND

JEREMY GREGORY

PUBLISHED FOR
THE ECCLESIASTICAL HISTORY SOCIETY
BY
THE BOYDELL PRESS
2008

First published 2008

A publication of the Ecclesiastical History Society
in association with The Boydell Press
an imprint of Boydell & Brewer Ltd
PO Box 9, Woodbridge, Suffolk IP12 3DF, UK
and of Boydell & Brewer Inc.
668 Mt Hope Avenue, Rochester, NY 14620, USA
website: www.boydellandbrewer.com

ISBN 978-0-95468-094-7

ISSN 0424-2084

A CiP catalogue record for this book is available
from the British Library

Details of previous volumes are available from Boydell & Brewer Ltd

This book is printed on acid-free paper

Typeset by Pru Harrison, Hacheston, Suffolk
Printed in Great Britain by
Antony Rowe Ltd, Chippenham, Wiltshire

CONTENTS

PREFACE

Professor David Bebbington chose the theme of 'Revival and Resurgence in Christian History' for his Presidency of the Ecclesiastical History Society in 2006–7. Perhaps not surprisingly the topic proved to be particularly popular for those researching modern-day revival movements and especially those connected with the Evangelical Revival. This volume contains six of the main papers given at the EHS Summer conference held at Cardiff University in 2006, and at the January meeting in 2007, as well as a number of the communications delivered at the Summer Meeting. As usual, we would like to thank those members of the Society who peer reviewed the articles, and our authors for responding to our requests for revision.

The Society would like to thank Cardiff University, and especially staff at its conference centre, for accommodating us for the Summer Meeting, and Dr David Wykes and his colleagues at Dr Williams's Library for providing us with a congenial space for the Winter Meeting.

As Editors, we would like to thank Dr Hannah Williams for her care and hard work in copy-editing this volume, and we are grateful to the Society for funding Hannah's Editorial Fellowship. Hannah has been a model of calm efficiency, and her grace and good cheer have been a source of inspiration to us and to our authors. During the production of this volume we have both had periods of sabbatical leave, and we are grateful to Hannah for steering the volume through the successive stages of consultation and correction.

Finally, we would like to offer our congratulations to Gemma Betros, who has been awarded the Michael Kennedy prize for the best essay by a postgraduate student published in *Studies in Church History*.

* * *

We have reached the end of our term of office as Editors of Studies in Church History, having taken over from Robert Swanson, who remained a valuable font of advice. We have seen five volumes to completion (SCH 40 to 44). It has been an immense privilege to have worked alongside a distinguished succession of Presidents, and to have come to know so many outstanding colleagues, both through their work and through the process of collaboration. *Studies in Church History* rightly enjoys an international standing for its distinctive contribution of drawing out continuities and contrasts across the full chronological span of the history of Christianity, and our period as Editors has been an education as well as a pleasure. One of the great strengths of these volumes over the years has been their bringing together the work of senior scholars with that of new researchers, several of whom have had their first publication in SCH, and many of whom, have, in time, become senior scholars themselves. We have particularly enjoyed working with the rising generation of researchers, and look forward to seeing their careers progress.

We wish every success to Peter Clarke and Tony Claydon, the incoming Editors, and are delighted that SCH is in such capable hands.

Kate Cooper
Jeremy Gregory
University of Manchester

CONTRIBUTORS

D. W. BEBBINGTON (*President*)
Professor of History, University of Stirling

Andrew ATHERSTONE
Tutor in History and Doctrine, and Latimer Research Fellow, Wycliffe Hall, Oxford

Gareth ATKINS
Research Student, Magdalene College, University of Cambridge

Gemma BETROS (*Michael J. Kennedy Postgraduate Prize; EHS post-graduate bursary*)
Research Student, Peterhouse, University of Cambridge

Janet BURTON
Professor of Medieval History, University of Wales, Lampeter

Alister CHAPMAN
Assistant Professor of History, Westmont College, Santa Barbara, California

Gary DICKSON
Honorary Fellow, School of History and Classics, University of Edinburgh

Dominic ERDOZAIN
Lecturer in the History of Christianity, King's College, University of London

Keith A. FRANCIS
Associate Professor of History, Baylor University

Geordan HAMMOND (*EHS postgraduate bursary*)
Research Student, University of Manchester

Margaret HARVEY
Retired Senior Lecturer in History, Durham University

Scott Fitzgerald JOHNSON
Assistant Professor of Classics, Washington and Lee University

David Ceri JONES
Lecturer in History and Welsh History, Aberystwyth University

David KILLINGRAY
Emeritus Professor of Modern History, Goldsmiths College, University of London

Anne KIRKHAM (*EHS postgraduate bursary*)
Research Student, University of Manchester

Hannah LANE
Assistant Professor of History, Mount Allison University

Peter B. NOCKLES
John Rylands Library, University of Manchester, and Visiting Fellow, Oriel College, University of Oxford

Patrick A. PRESTON
Visiting Fellow in Church History, University of Chichester

Ian M. RANDALL
Tutor, Spurgeon's College, London, and Senior Research Fellow, International Baptist Theological Seminary, Prague

Alec RYRIE
Reader in Church History, Durham University

Darren SCHMIDT (*EHS postgraduate bursary*)
Research Student, St Mary's College, University of St Andrews

Mark SMITH
University Lecturer in English Local and Social History, University of Oxford

Rowan STRONG
Associate Professor of Church History, Murdoch University

Kevin WARD
Lecturer in Theology and Religious Studies, University of Leeds

Peter WEBSTER
Editorial Controller, British History Online, Institute of Historical Research, University of London

Martin WELLINGS
President, World Methodist Historical Society, Kidlington, Oxfordshire

Eryn M. WHITE
Senior Lecturer in History and Welsh History, Aberystwyth University

Emma WILD-WOOD
Tutor, Cambridge Theological Federation

John WOLFFE
Professor of Religious History, The Open University

ABBREVIATIONS

AHR	*American Historical Review* (New York, 1895–)
BJRULM	*Bulletin of the John Rylands University Library of Manchester* (Manchester, 1903–)
BL	London, British Library
CCSL	*Corpus Christianorum, Series Latina* (Turnhout, 1953–)
CSEL	*Corpus Scriptorum Ecclesiasticorum Latinorum* (Vienna, 1866–)
EHR	*English Historical Review* (London, 1886–)
HistJ	*Historical Journal* (Cambridge, 1958–)
JEH	*Journal of Ecclesiastical History* (Cambridge, 1950–)
MGH	*Monumenta Germaniae Historica inde ab a. c. 500 usque ad a. 1500*, ed. G. H. Pertz et al. (Hannover, Berlin, etc., 1826–)
NF	Neue Folge
ns	new series
ODNB	*Oxford Dictionary of National Biography* (Oxford, 2004), available at: *http://www.oxforddnb.com/*
PG	*Patrologia Graeca*, ed. J. P. Migne, 161 vols + 4 index vols (Paris, 1857–66)
PL	*Patrologia Latina*, ed. J. P. Migne, 217 vols + 4 index vols (Paris, 1841–61)
SC	*Sources Chrétiennes* (Paris, 1941–)
SCH	*Studies in Church History* (London, Oxford and Woodbridge, 1964–)
SCH.S	*Studies in Church History: Subsidia* (Oxford and Woodbridge, 1978–)
Speculum	*Speculum: a Journal of Medieval Studies* (Cambridge, MA, 1925–)
TRHS	*Transactions of the Royal Historical Society* (London/Cambridge, 1871–)

INTRODUCTION

Revival and resurgence have punctuated Christian history at frequent intervals. There have been moves to renew failing institutions; there have been efforts to rekindle an earlier flame of devotion; and there have been attempts to restore the pattern of the Church discerned in the pages of the New Testament. All these developments, and others like them, have been provoked by a sense that not everything was well, perhaps that existing methods were proving ineffectual or that the Church had lost its first love. A new vitality was sought after a perceived period of neglect or decay. In the period since the early seventeenth century revivals have sometimes taken a distinctive form in the more evangelistically inclined sections of Protestantism. Revivals in the classic Evangelical sense were defined by an American Methodist in the mid-nineteenth century as 'those outpourings of the Spirit, which result in the quickening of the church and the conversion of sinners'.[1] They were conceived to be divine in origin, rousing those who were already Christians and bringing others to faith for the first time. Many of the papers in this volume relate to such happenings, but they are by no means its only subject. The volume also takes in revitalization movements from earlier periods and a variety of quests for recovery from the later period. The common thread running through the papers is the Church being stirred into fresh life.

A thematic outline of the contents may help the reader. There is only one paper on a classic Evangelical revival covering a long period, Kevin Ward's survey of the twentieth-century East African Revival, which, he points out, has now proceeded for more than three-quarters of a century. Other contributors, however, deal with aspects of protracted movements. Emma Wild-Wood considers a radical branch of the same East African Revival and Dominic Erdozain examines a dimension of the Welsh Revival of 1904–5, the last major movement of this kind in the British Isles. Four papers address dimensions of the Evangelical Revival that arose in the eighteenth century: Darren Schmidt looks at John Wesley's understanding of the historical loca-

1 *Christian Advocate* quoted in *Wesley Banner* (London), February 1849.

tion of the movement of which he was a leader; David Ceri Jones studies the conversion narratives produced in the Calvinistic section of the revival community; while Gareth Atkins and John Wolffe both explore aspects of the self-understanding generated in its Anglican sector. These contributions are complemented by three papers that deal with particular revivals: Eryn White gives an overview of the crucial 1762 revival in Wales, Hannah Lane turns to a series of episodes on the Canadian–United States border in the earlier nineteenth century and the presidential address confines itself to a Cornish Methodist revival of 1849. It may be suggested that, while there is certainly future need for broad treatments of the phenomenon of revival in this specific sense, there is also scope for further scrutinies of particular aspects of larger awakenings and for detailed local studies that will bring out what actually happened more clearly than we have hitherto understood.

Several contributors ask whether their subjects can properly be called revivals. Peter Nockles decides that, in the case of the Oxford Movement, the answer should be no; David Killingray suggests that the Pleasant Sunday Afternoon movement of the late nineteenth century should be seen as similar, rather than identical, to a revival; but Keith Francis concludes that the recent large-scale growth of Seventh-Day Adventism on Grenada does qualify for the label. Another group of papers shows that the concern for revival, deeply ingrained in the Evangelical psyche, was central to three post-war English denominational groups. Martin Wellings discusses the Methodist Revival Fellowship; Ian Randall analyses the encounter of its Baptist counterpart with early charismatic renewal; and Alister Chapman reveals the ambiguities of the Evangelical Anglican attitude to the subject of revival. Geordan Hammond shows that there were signs of flexibility within the Church of England even before the eighteenth-century revival and Gary Dickson demonstrates that something very similar to the phenomenon of later revivalism was to be found in fifteenth-century Italy.

Episodes of resurgence took many forms. There are two medieval instances in this volume. The monastic reformers in the eleventh- and twelfth-century Cistercian order, Janet Burton demonstrates, were consciously evoking the past when insisting on the strict observance of the rule. Francis of Assisi was depicted as repairing church buildings, Anne Kirkham points out, in order to illustrate his role in ecclesiastical renewal in the thirteenth century. There are two early modern cases.

In the resurgence of Catholic interests marked by the Counter-Reformation, as Patrick Preston explains, the Dominicans played a leading part. Margaret Harvey's study takes for its subject a Renaissance figure, Robert Ridley, who was opposed not only to the Reformation but also to Erasmus's Catholic reform, so reminding us that resurgence was often resisted for carefully thought out reasons, and not just because of inertia. From the later modern period there are two nineteenth-century pieces. Gemma Betros shows that under Napoleon the restoration of female monasticism in post-Revolutionary France was far from easy. The equally demanding task of reasserting the role of the Church of England in the empire, Rowan Strong relates, was no longer undertaken from the 1840s by the British state but by an ecclesiastical organization. The twentieth century furnishes two case-studies of Evangelical Anglicanism. Vigorous parish life, Mark Smith demonstrates, played its part in the post-Second World War return of the party to prominence within the Church of England; and Andrew Atherstone studies the reinvigoration of Wycliffe Hall, Oxford, an Evangelical Anglican theological college, after a collapse in the 1960s. Resurgence was clearly as multifarious as it was common.

There remain three papers on revivals of something much more specific than a reinvigoration of the Church after earlier torpor. The contribution covering the earliest period, by Scott Fitzgerald Johnson, analyses the fourth-century reawakening of interest in the historical apostles through travel literature. Alec Ryrie considers the reinvention of piety during the Reformation by early English and Scottish Protestants, laying bare the outlines of the simple devotional forms they recommended. And Peter Webster discusses the renewal of art patronage in the Church of England by an alliance of clergy and artists during the twentieth century. Each of these developments, though in one sense a revival in itself, was conceived as a means of promoting further life in the Church.

To generalize on the basis of so diverse a body of material is hazardous. Yet in several papers there is a sense that the memory of past episodes of vitality in the Church tends to generate more of them. That was true of the fourth-century author who sought out sites associated with the apostles of Jesus, of the twelfth-century monks who wanted a return to earlier rigour in the rule they followed and of the Methodist and Baptist fellowships that tried to foster the spirit of revival in the twentieth century. The theme may be discerned in many of the other contributions too. The record of the Church enjoying spiritual prosperity in the past appears to have had the effect of encouraging attempts to reproduce it in later years. In that sense, revival and resurgence turn out to have been self-replicating.

David Bebbington
University of Stirling

REVIVING THE MEMORY OF THE APOSTLES: APOCRYPHAL TRADITION AND TRAVEL LITERATURE IN LATE ANTIQUITY

by SCOTT FITZGERALD JOHNSON

IN this essay I aim to consider the association of place with apostolic personae.[1] The imaginative worlds generated between the time of the apostles in the first century and the rise of the medieval Christian world in the seventh and eighth centuries can be seen as an integral part of what we now label 'late antiquity'.[2] The period of late antiquity, roughly from 300 to 600 AD (from Constantine to Mohammed), is substantively a period of consolidation and reorientation: knowledge from the ancient Greco-Roman civilizations was queried, repackaged, and disseminated; classical literature was copied, commented upon, and imitated; Roman law was collected, rearranged, and declared authoritative.[3] What has been less studied in this period is the reception of the apostolic world as a realm of knowledge in its own right.

The theme of revival offers a valuable framework in which to consider this resurgence of devotion. The awakening of historical interest in the apostles and their geographical associations can be linked to the advent of the Christian pilgrimage movement. This movement, beginning in earnest in the early fourth century, appropriated classical genres of writing, such as the *itinerarium* and the *periplous*, for the purposes of describing the topography of the Holy Land and other

1 This essay takes inspiration from treatments by Peter Brown in *The Making of Late Antiquity* (Cambridge, MA, 1978), esp. ch. 1, and *The Cult of the Saints* (Chicago, IL, 1981). This essay also expands arguments made in Scott Fitzgerald Johnson, *The Life and Miracles of Thekla: a Literary Study* (Washington, DC and Cambridge, MA, 2006).

2 On the use of apocryphal legends in late antiquity, see Averil Cameron, *Christianity and the Rhetoric of Empire: the Development of Christian Discourse* (Berkeley and Los Angeles, CA, 1991), 89–119. See also Scott Fitzgerald Johnson, 'Apocrypha and the Literary Past in Late Antiquity', in Hagit Amirav and Bas ter Haar Romeny, eds, *From Rome to Constantinople: Studies in Honour of Averil Cameron*, Late Antique History and Religion 1 (Leuven, 2007), 47–66.

3 On this picture of the intellectual character of late antiquity, see Hervé Inglebert, *Interpretatio Christiana: les mutations des savoirs (cosmographie, géographie, ethnographie, histoire), dans l'Antiquité chrétienne, 30–630 après J.-C.* (Paris, 2001).

sacred locales.[4] The link between this topographical literature and the revival of writing on the apostles in late antiquity has not yet been explored in detail. I hope to offer in this essay some evidence of this link as well as some attempts at explaining why these two Christian phenomena might find their earliest expression in the fourth and fifth centuries AD.

A vast amount of literature – some of it orthodox, much of it heterodox at best – was produced in the aftermath of the first- and second-century writings that came to be included in the canon of scripture. These non-canonical texts of the second, third, and fourth centuries are almost solely devoted to investigating and expanding the memory of the apostles and they often depend on the canonical writings for their imaginative reconstructions. As much as the history and institutions of the classical past, this apostolic inheritance of imagined worlds became a foundation of late antique Christian culture.

At the beginning of the period under consideration Eusebius of Caesarea wrote his famous *Ecclesiastical History* documenting the rise of the early Church: he is, of course, credited with being the first Church historian, and many followed in his vein.[5] Eusebius felt keenly the importance of the apostolic inheritance. He tried to link the existing patriarchies directly back to the apostles through a line of unbroken succession, a method of research which was integral to later arguments over patriarchal supremacy.[6] He also connected the question of which books accurately communicated the gospel of the Church with the question of which ones were authentically apostolic.[7] This has remained a strategy of Protestant and Catholic apologetics until today. Further, some of the books that Eusebius includes under the category 'spurious' (νόθος) – that is, non-canonical but not necessarily heretical – are apocryphal Acts of the apostles (e.g. the *Acts of Paul*).[8]

A few generations later, in the year 400, the first set of patristic sermons on the canonical Book of Acts was produced by John

4 See Jaś Elsner, 'The *Itinerarium Burdigalense*: Politics and Salvation in the Geography of Constantine's Empire', *Journal of Roman Studies* 90 (2000), 181–95.

5 Though (significantly and explicitly), the later historians never attempted to rewrite the terrain he covered; see Socrates Scholasticus, *Historia Ecclesiastica*, 1.1 and Sozomen, *Historia Ecclesiastica*, 1.1.

6 For example, on the 'Pentarchy', Henry Chadwick, *East and West: the Making of a Rift in the Church, from Apostolic Times until the Council of Florence* (Oxford, 2003), esp. 115–16, 164–5.

7 Eusebius, *Historia Ecclesiastica*, 1.24–5.

8 Ibid., 1.25.

Chrysostom.[9] Chrysostom began this series during Easter week in Constantinople and preached the fifty-five long homilies of the series throughout the rest of the year, making it all the way to the twenty-eighth and final chapter of Acts. At the beginning of the first sermon, he chides his congregation for not knowing Acts well, and even for not knowing that it is in the Bible.[10] Judging from comments such as this and from a second extant series of historical sermons, the *Panegyrics on Paul*,[11] Chrysostom seems to have considered apostolic knowledge to be confined primarily to the canonical books: he does not produce similar sermons on apocryphal themes.[12] Yet, clearly demonstrated in his exegetical writing is what we might like to call the cognitive value of the apostolic inheritance: that is, Chrysostom and others were stimulated by a revival of interest in apostolic traditions to produce more writing which commented upon and publicized Christian history.

This awareness of the value of the history of the apostles is an important example of revival writ large. It offers an early example of reaching back into the historical past of the Christian Church for

9 *In Acta apostolorum homiliae* (ed. M. Geerard, *et al.*, Clavis Patrum Graecorum, 7 vols (Turnhout, 1974–) [hereafter: CPG], 4426, PG 60, 13–384). See also the study by Amanda Lee Berry Wylie, 'John Chrysostom and his Homilies on the Acts of the Apostles: Reclaiming Ancestral Models for the Christian People', unpublished Ph.D. thesis, Princeton Theological Seminary, 1992. On the manuscript tradition and printing history of these sermons, see E. R. Smothers, 'Toward a Critical Text of the Homilies on Acts of St. John Chrysostom', *Studia Patristica* 1 = *TU* 63 (1957), 53–7.

10 *Homiliae in Acta apostolorum*, 1.1. See also the comment in his fragmentary *Homiliae in principium Actorum* (CPG 4371, PG 51, 65–112), dating from AD 387: 'We are about to set before you a strange and new dish ... strange, I say, and not strange. Not strange, for it belongs to the order of Holy Scripture; and yet strange, because perhaps your ears are not accustomed to such a subject. Certainly, there are many to whom this book is not even known (πολλοῖς γοῦν τὸ βιβλίον τοῦτο οὐδὲ γνώριμόν ἐστι).' Chrysostom goes on to note that the book of Acts is traditionally only read during Holy Week.

11 See the edition and French translation by Auguste Piédagnel, ed., *Jean Chrysostome: panégyriques de S. Paul* (Paris, 1982). See also his sermons on the New Testament books of Titus and Philemon, books which very rarely received dedicated treatment in patristic exegesis: *Homiliae in epistulam ad Titum* (CPG 4438, PG 62, 663–700); *Argumentum et homiliae in epistulam ad Philemonem* (CPG 4439, PG 62, 701–20). See also the study of these sermons by Blake Goodall, *The Homilies of St. John Chrysostom on the Letters of St. Paul to Titus and Philemon: Prolegomena to an Edition* (Berkeley and Los Angeles, CA, 1979). And see, more generally, Margaret Mary Mitchell, *The Heavenly Trumpet: John Chrysostom and the Art of Pauline Interpretation* (Tübingen, 2000).

12 Most of the homilies on apostles besides Paul which are attributed to Chrysostom are generally held to be spurious: e.g. the sermon on Thomas (CPG 4574, PG 59, 497–500; see also J. M. Sauget, 'Deux homéliares syriaques de la Bibliothèque Vaticane', *Orientalia Christiana Periodica* 27 (1961), 387–424, at 408) and the sermon on Thekla (CPG 4515; see M. Aubineau, ed., 'Le Panégyrique de Thècle attribué à Jean Chrysostome (BHG 1720)', *Analecta Bollandiana* 93 [1975], 349–62).

inspiration in the present. It also provides a precedent for future revivals. Thus, the theology of the 'patristic period' – one traditional way of naming late antiquity – is often revered in today's churches as promoting the cause of apostolic Christianity. In terms of religious practice, a historian might prefer to point to the cult of the martyrs and the models that the apostles provided for perennially important late antique saints (e.g. Antony). I would like to add to this discussion the example of travel literature, which had an important role to play in the revival of apostolic history.

Travel Narrative and Apostolic Geography

In the year AD 686 (or perhaps 688), Adomnan, abbot of Iona and author of the famous 'Life of St Columba', presented King Aldfrith of Northumbria with a copy of his work *De locis sanctis* ('On the Holy Places').[13] This work was a long, systematic account in three books of pilgrimage sites in the Holy Land, concentrating in the first book on Jerusalem, but branching out in the second and third books to include places further afield, such as the Galilee, Samaria, Damascus, Tyre, Alexandria, and finally Constantinople. The work was not without some pretensions to style and has been studied in modern times for its Latinity.[14] The Venerable Bede thought so much of the work that he used it as the basis for his own *De locis sanctis* of 702/3.[15] Despite all of these salutary qualities, it is worth noting that Adomnan himself had never travelled to the Holy Land. Rather, as he makes plain in the preface to the work, he was prompted to write his book by the Holy Land pilgrim Arculf, who came to Iona in 683, after having shipwrecked off the coast of Britain.[16] This fortuitous shipwreck provided Adomnan with the raw material he needed to write his work. Less a pilgrimage account than a topography firmly in the vein of Eusebius's

13 See the introduction, edition, and translation by Denis Meehan, *Adamnan's De locis sanctis* (Dublin, 1958), at 3–4 for the presentation to Aldfrith. See also the edition by Ludwig Bieler, ed., *Adamnani de locis sanctis libri tres*, CCSL 175 (Turnholt, 1965), 175–234. For the context of this work in seventh-century Europe, see Peter Brown, *The Rise of Western Christendom: Triumph and Diversity, AD 200–1000* (2nd edn, Oxford, 2003), 318–19 and 329.

14 Ibid., 5 and n. 2.

15 For Adomnan's text, see the critical edition by L. Bieler, CCSL 175 (Turnholt, 1965), 249–80. Peter the Deacon, librarian of Monte Cassino, in 1137 wrote a book on the holy places, based on Bede, Egeria (see below), and a third otherwise unknown text.

16 Bede tells us Arculf was a bishop from Gaul; but Iona is far out of his way if returning to Gaul from the Mediterranean. On this issue, see Meehan, *Adamnan's De locis sanctis*, 7.

and Jerome's *Onomastica*,[17] Adomnan's *De locis sanctis* evocatively describes how he copied down notes from Arculf onto wax tablets (*tabulae*), which he then set into a succinct narrative (*brevi textu*) written on parchment (*in membranis*).

The value of this literary-historical episode for the present essay is that it exemplifies the vibrant genre of topographical writing in late antiquity and its firm connections to the practice of Christian pilgrimage. Adomnan's *De locis sanctis* comes at the very end of the period under consideration, yet as such it encapsulates a number of principal themes of the topic at hand. First, Arculf is the earliest pilgrim after the Arab conquest of the Holy Land whose account has come down to us. The Arab conquests of the mid-seventh century dramatically affected the social and political landscape of the Mediterranean and are understandably considered by many to mark the beginning of a new age.[18] Arculf notes that the religious topography of urban areas had already changed by the time he made his journey in 679–82: he identifies numerous 'churches' (mosques) of the 'Saracens' (Arabs) in Jerusalem and elsewhere.[19] Second, despite this changed landscape, Arculf's journey illustrates the continued relative ease with which a pilgrim might make his way from West to East via Constantinople in the seventh century. In contrast to so easy a journey – which had been the case since the early fourth century – Willibald of Eichstätt in the eighth century was imprisoned twice by Muslim authorities while attempting to visit holy

17 There has been considerable interest of late in the work and tradition of Eusebius's *Onomasticon*: see now R. Steven Notley and Ze'ev Safrai, ed. and trans., *Onomasticon: the Place Names of Divine Scripture, including the Latin edition of Jerome* (Leiden, 2005); Susan Weingarten, *The Saint's Saint: Hagiography and Geography in Jerome* (Leiden, 2005); Stefan Timm, *Das Onomastikon der biblischen Ortsnamen: Edition der syrischen Fassung mit griechischem Text, englischer und deutscher Übersetzung* (Berlin, 2005); and finally, G. S. P. Freeman-Greenville and Joan E. Taylor, *The Onomasticon: Palestine in the Fourth Century A.D.* (Jerusalem, 2003).

18 Though the trend in late antique studies has been to see late antiquity extending much later than previously thought up to and including the Umayyad world, at the least. See the introduction to Glen Bowersock, Peter Brown, and Oleg Grabar, eds, *Late Antiquity: a Guide to the Postclassical World* (Cambridge, MA, 1999), vii–xiii; and more aggressively, Peregrine Horden and Nicholas Purcell, *The Corrupting Sea: a Study of Mediterranean History* (Oxford, 2000), 32–4 (on Henri Pirenne).

19 Ibid., 28–9, for the Church of John the Baptist at Damascus, partially converted into a mosque. Furthermore, while there is no explicit evidence for this beyond the date of his journey, Meehan (the editor of Adomnan's text) thinks it likely that Arculf was involved in the Third Council of Constantinople in 680–1, which attempted to resolve the question of Monothelitism, a question in which the Dyothelite western churches felt they had a high stake. See Chadwick, *East and West*, 59–70.

sites.[20] Finally, and most importantly for our purposes, every step of Arculf's journey was imbued with religious significance, principally the significance of places associated with Jesus and the apostles. In Alexandria, for instance, Arculf visited the Church of St Mark, which contained the valuable relics of the saint: these relics were stolen by Venetian traders in 828, just a hundred and fifty years later (forming the spiritual nucleus of today's San Marco).[21] The tradition that Mark had evangelized and finished his life in Alexandria still held sway in Arculf's time and directed both the journey and the narrative: not insignificantly, Alexandria provides the climax of the second book and marks the end of Arculf's sojourn in the Holy Land.

Writing that was stimulated by the revival of apostolic history came in many forms. Travel narratives are one of the most intriguing because they often attempt to connect that history with places on the ground. The most fundamental aspect of this interaction between narrative and place is that, according to the received apocryphal tradition, the apostolic world was not of a piece: rather, it was segmented into what might be termed an 'apostolic geography'. A particular scene is repeated a number of times in apocryphal literature from the second and third centuries. The apostles receive from Jesus a commission – not simply the general 'Great Commission' of Matthew 28: 18–20 – but specific commissions to specific regions of the Mediterranean and further afield.[22] This scene underpins the image of motion out from the centre upon which nearly all the Apocryphal Acts depend: from the earliest *Acts of Peter* and the *Acts of Paul* in the mid-second century, to the highly significant *Acts of Thomas* in the third, and to the fourth- and

20 The account of Willibald's travels, called the *Hodoeporicon*, was written by his biographer Hugeburc (Hygeburg/Huneberc) of Heidenheim, a nun and member of Willibald's family. See the study by Eva Gottschaller, *Hugeburc von Heidenheim: philologische Untersuchungen zu den Heiligenbiographien einer Nonne des achten Jahrhunderts* (Munich, 1973). The text of Willibald's *Vita* (Société des Bollandistes, *Bibliotheca Hagiographica Latina Manuscripta*, 3 vols [Brussels, 1898–1901 and 1986] [hereafter: BHL] 8931), including the *Hodoeporicon*, can be found in Oswald Holder-Egger, ed., MGH Scriptores 15.1 (Hanover, 1887). See also the discussion in Michael McCormick, *Origins of the European Economy: Communication and Commerce AD 300–900* (Cambridge, 2001), 129–34.

21 On the theft of the relics of St Mark, see McCormick, *Origins of the European Economy*, 237–40. On the authenticity of the *Translatio S. Marci* (BHL 5283–4), see idem, 238 n. 2.

22 See Jean-Daniel Kaestli, 'Les scènes inventoriés d'attribution des champs de mission et de départ de l'apôtre dans les actes apocryphes', in François Bovon, ed., *Les actes apocryphes de apôtres: christianisme et monde païen* (Geneva, 1981), 249–64. A similar scene appears in Eusebius, *Historia Ecclesiastica*, 3.1, ostensibly quoting Origen; see Eric Junod, 'Origène, Eusèbe et la tradition sur la répartition des champs de mission des apôtres', ibid., 233–48.

fifth-century Acts which are written afresh, such as the *Acts of Philip*. This is one of many points of contact between these two epochs in Christian literary history – early Christian literature and late antique Christian literature – and is worth exploring in more detail.

This partitioning of the world generated pilgrimage sites dedicated to those apostles who claimed that particular pilgrimage city or region. In such cases, the apostle's presence at that site, either because it was associated with his biography (or hers, in the case of Thekla), or because his remains were *in situ*, provided the motivation for the journey in the first place. I have already mentioned how Arculf went out of his way to visit Alexandria and St Mark's sepulchre. Another site of apostolic importance (in Jerusalem itself) was Mount Sion where a shrine arose to the (proto)martyr Stephen (Acts 7). The 'discovery' (*inventio*) of this site seems to have occurred in the early fifth century, and the empress Eudocia (wife of emperor Theodosius II) founded a major basilica there in 460.[23] Due to her efforts at monumentalizing the shrine, numerous pilgrimage accounts from the fifth and sixth centuries note the shrine of Stephen: for instance, the fifth-century *Breviarius* of the Holy Land lists a shrine (*sacrarium*) on the site where Stephen was stoned, containing *the* stone (*ille lapis*) which was used.[24] Likewise, the *Holy Land Topography* of a writer named Theodosius in the early sixth century claims that the church was founded on the site of Stephen's martyrdom, 'outside the Galilean gate' (*foras porta Galilaeae*), and he names the empress Eudocia as its founder.[25] Later pilgrims, such as the Piacenza pilgrim in the late sixth century and Arculf in the seventh, also mention the shrine and emphasize that the stones (plural) were open to view at the site.[26]

Also in the seventh century, the bishop Sophronius of Jerusalem

23 Eudocia made a pilgrimage to the Holy Land in 438 and eventually made her home there after being exiled from the capital in 443/4 (A. H. M. Jones, J. R. Martindale, J. Morris, *Prosopography of the Later Roman Empire*, 3 vols [Cambridge, 1971, 1980, 1992], 2: 408–9). According to Gerontius's *Life of Melania the Younger* (ed. D. Gorce, SC 90 [Paris, 1962], 57–8,), the pilgrim Melania the Younger made so great an impression on Eudocia that she decided to visit the Holy Land in person. Melania seems to have initiated Eudocia into devotion to Stephen: both Melania and the empress were present at the dedication ceremony of the original shrine in 439. On Melania, Eudocia, and the shrine of Stephen, see E. D. Hunt, *Holy Land Pilgrimage in the Later Roman Empire, AD 312–460* (Oxford, 1982), 230–44.

24 *Breviarius*, 4.93–5 (ed. R. Weber, CCSL 175 [Turnhout, 1965], 111).

25 *Theodosii de situ terrae sanctae*, 8 (ed. P. Geyer, CCSL 175 [Turnhout, 1965], 118).

26 Piacenza Pilgrim: *Antonini placentini itinerarium*, 22 (ed. P. Geyer, CCSL 175 [Turnhout, 1965], 140–1). Arculf: 1.18 (ed. Meehan, *Adamnan's De locis sanctis*, 62–3).

(himself a former pilgrim and traveller) wrote a poem in anacreontic metre on the Christian city of Jerusalem, which weaves together tradition and imagination in its praise of Mount Sion:

> And speeding on,
> May I pass to Sion,
> where, in the likeness of fiery tongues,
> the Grace of God descended;
> where, when he had completed
> the mystic supper, the King of All
> teaching in humility
> washed the disciples' feet.
>
> Blessings of salvation, like rivers
> pour from that Rock where Mary,
> handmaid of God, childbearing for all men,
> was laid out in death.
>
> Hail Sion, radiant Sun of the universe!
> Night and Day I long and yearn for thee.
> There, after shattering hell,
> and liberating the dead,
> the King of All, the Shatterer
> appeared there, the Friend.[27]

While there is no mention of Stephen in this passage, Sophronius's poem is striking for the way it uses a holy place to associate a wide range of textual allusions. From Pentecost to the last Supper to the Resurrection and even Mary's own death, the site of Sion takes on the role of the Christian Jerusalem as a whole, both in its biblical or literary resonance and as a pilgrim's destination. In fact, we can see in the account of the Piacenza pilgrim that the site was, by the seventh century, overwhelmed with associations, biblical and apocryphal alike: for instance, the house of James, the crown of thorns, and the column upon which Peter's cross (brought from Rome) had stood are only a few of the relics associated with the site.[28]

Mount Sion and the memory of the martyr Stephen, of course, have biblical warrant, and perhaps owe more to a renewed interest in the

[27] Sophronius, *Anacreontica* (ed. M. Gigante [Rome, 1957], 125–6); trans. John Wilkinson, *Jerusalem Pilgrims before the Crusades* (Warminster, 2002), 158–60.

[28] *Antonini placentini itinerarium*, 22 (ed. P. Geyer, CCSL 175 [Turnhout, 1965], 140–1).

history of the Gospels and Acts – like Chrysostom's sermons – than they do to apocryphal tradition. Looking elsewhere, however, one of the earliest pilgrim narratives also happens to be one of the richest for tracing the value of specifically apocryphal legends in travel literature. Travelling to the Holy Land in the years 381–4,[29] the Spanish matron Egeria made her remarkable journey in the generation between the first flowering of Constantinian pilgrimage and the era of massive building campaigns of Eudocia and the fifth-century emperors.[30] Like the anonymous 'Bordeaux Pilgrim' before her (our earliest pilgrimage narrative, from AD 333), Egeria's text is dominated by the resonance of the Old Testament and the Gospels. There are, in fact, so many references to Old Testament sites in these early pilgrimage narratives that they have led scholars to postulate an established system of Jewish pilgrimage prior to Constantine's reign.[31] Unlike the 'Bordeaux Pilgrim', however, Egeria includes extended descriptions of places visited outside the Holy Land.[32] In particular, there are two specific incidents in Egeria's text

29 The dates of her pilgrimage were established by Paul Devos, 'La date du voyage d'Égérie', *Analecta Bollandiana* 85 (1967), 165–94. For questions of authorship – the text as it stands is truncated and anonymous – see Pierre Maraval, *Égérie, journal de voyage (Itinéraire): introduction, texte critique, traduction, notes et cartes* (2nd rev. edn, Paris, 2002).

30 Constantine's mother, Helena, famously visited the Holy Land in the last years of her life before returning home to Rome and dying there as an octogenarian. Legend has it, of course, that Helena discovered the True Cross in Jerusalem, on the site of today's Church of the Holy Sepulchre. While oft-cited, this particular legend has no strong historical evidence in its favor. What we do know rather well is that Constantine invested heavily in monumentalizing the city of Jerusalem and its environs, just before and coincident with Helena's travels. Moreover, immediately subsequent to Constantine's investment comes our earliest Christian pilgrimage account to have survived, the anonymous 'Bordeaux Pilgrim' from AD 333. The text mentions Constantine by name on three occasions, in relation to the following buildings: a basilica on Golgotha (presumably the Holy Sepulchre church, dedicated in 335), another at Bethlehem (dedicated in 339), and a church at the Oak of Mamre (*quercus Mamris*; dedicated in the late 320s). Golgotha: *Itinerarium Burdigalense*, 594.1–4 (ed. P. Geyer and O. Cuntz, CCSL 175 [Turnhout, 1965], 17); Bethlehem: *Itinerarium Burdigalense*, 598.1–7 (ed. idem, 19–20); Mamre: *Itinerarium Burdigalense*, 599.3–6 (ed. idem, 20). All these are mentioned also by Eusebius in his *Life of Constantine* and elsewhere and were well known in the Christian East. See Eusebius, *Vita Constantini*, 3.25–47 and 51–3 (ed. Friedhelm Winkelmann, *Eusebius Werke*, Die grieschischen christlichen Schriftsteller der ersten drei Jahrhunderte, 1.1 [2nd edn, Berlin, 1975], 94–104 and 105–7). See also the translation and commentary by Averil Cameron and Stuart G. Hall, *Eusebius: Life of Constantine* (Oxford, 1999), 132–43 and 273–301.

31 See John Wilkinson, 'Jewish Holy Places and the Origins of Christian Pilgrimage', in Robert Ousterhout, ed., *The Blessings of Pilgrimage* (Urbana, IL, 1990), 46–53; and also Joan E. Taylor, *Christians and the Holy Places: the Myth of Jewish-Christian Origins* (Oxford, 1993), esp. 318–32.

32 Whereas the 'Bordeaux Pilgrim' follows rather strictly the ancient genre of the Roman *itinerarium* outside of Palestine – only breaking away from that model while visiting

(outside of the confines of Jerusalem) which testify to the role of apocryphal legends in her journey. Their value for the historian is not limited to the social evidence of cultic activity on the ground; rather, they should have a voice in our evaluation of her narrative and in our understanding of the rise of Christian travel literature in late antiquity.

Egeria and Apostolic Legends

The two incidents I would like to discuss are Egeria's visits to the shrine of St Thekla at Seleukeia in south-eastern Asia Minor (modern Silifke in Turkey) and her visit to St Thomas's shrine at Edessa in the Roman province of Osrhoëne (modern Urfa, also in Turkey, further to the east). Both these visits are described by Egeria as being off the beaten path; she emphasizes the special care she took to visit them in person. Moreover, in both cases there is a textual component to her pilgrimage. Stories she has read about these saints motivate her to seek out the places where they are honored. Furthermore, in both cases she either produces a text that she owns related to the apostle or takes away a text to add to her collection. Her visits to these shrines were brief, only a few days at each, and both of them occurred on the way back home to Spain via Constantinople, but they both engage much larger imaginative worlds than their brevity suggests. Egeria's accounts are prime examples of the revival of interest in late antiquity in the historical apostles. Coincident with the birth of Christian pilgrimage in the fourth century, this historical or antiquarian spirit is at the forefront of Egeria's narrative.

Chronologically, Egeria's visit to Thekla's shrine in Seleukeia occurred after the visit to the city of Edessa, but I shall consider the Thekla visit first since it provides a helpful introduction and since her account of Edessa is more elaborate. Thekla's shrine was located along the coast of south-eastern Asia Minor, just to the south-west of Tarsus, the birthplace of the apostle Paul. Egeria notes that she had visited Tarsus on her way to Jerusalem but had not taken the time to visit the shrine at Seleukeia. The Seleukeia visit probably took place in May 384 on her way back to the West.

the most sacred sites in Jerusalem and nearby – Egeria's text could be read as demonstrating an acquaintance with a broader range of travel literature from the ancient world (e.g. *Onomastica*, the ancient novel, etc.). On the 'Bordeaux Pilgrim' and *itinerarium* genre, see Elsner, 'The *Itinerarium Burdigalense*'.

Some background is necessary on Thekla – a woman not named in the canonical New Testament, yet one who had achieved considerable prominence by Egeria's day. According to the legend, Thekla was a female companion of St Paul. All that we know of her is contained in the mid to late second-century apocryphal text entitled simply the *Acts of Paul and Thekla*.[33] This text is romantic and novelistic in style and can hardly be considered a trustworthy source for the historical Thekla, if there was one at all.[34] The *Acts of Paul and Thekla* was a best-seller by early Christian standards and contributed greatly to the social formation of a cult of Thekla, which saw its peak in the fifth century.[35] About a hundred years after Egeria, in the 470s, the Roman emperor Zeno monumentalized the cult site with at least one major church, and perhaps as many as three.[36] At Egeria's time the site was not so developed, but important early Christian writers such as Gregory of Nazianzus had special attachments to Thekla, and Egeria herself notes a significant amount of activity at the shrine. She describes the monastic communities there, both men's and women's, which seem to have been substantial. The women's ascetic community was headed by a woman named Marthana, whom Egeria claims she had known well when she was in Jerusalem. One could suppose that Marthana planted the idea to visit the site in Egeria's mind when they were both in the Holy Land.

Once Egeria arrived at Seleukeia she went straight to the *martyrium* located near, or under, the main church. Upon entering the shrine she said prayers and, as she says, 'read the entire *Acts* of holy Thekla.' When

33 There is currently no complete critical text for the *Acts of Paul*, of which the *Acts of Paul and Thekla* comprises the middle third. The best edition is R. A. Lipsius and M. Bonnet, eds, *Acta Apostolorum Apocrypha*, 3 vols (Hildesheim, 1891, rpt. 1972), 2: 235–72, though reference must be made to the 'critical translations' of E. Hennecke and W. Schneemelcher, eds, *New Testament Apocrypha*, trans. R. M. Wilson, 2 vols (rev. edn, Louisville, KY, 1992), 2: 213–70, and J. K. Elliott, *The Apocryphal New Testament: a Collection of Apocryphal Christian Literature in an English Translation Based on M. R. James*, (rev. edn, Oxford, 1999), 350–89. Lipsius and Bonnet made use of eleven Greek manuscripts for their edition, but over forty are now known to be extant. There are also numerous versions in almost all the ancient Christian languages. Willy Rordorf's new critical edition of the *Acts of Paul* for the Corpus Christianorum Series Apocryphorum is thus eagerly anticipated.

34 Even though some have tried: W. M. Ramsay, *The Historical Geography of Asia Minor*, Royal Geographical Society's Supplementary Papers 4 (London, 1890), 375–428.

35 On the late antique cult of Thekla, see Stephen Davis, *The Cult of Saint Thecla: a Tradition of Women's Piety in Late Antiquity* (Oxford, 2001); see also the introductions to Gilbert Dagron, *Vie et miracles de Sainte Thècle: texte grec, traduction, et commentaire*, Subsidia Hagiographica 62 (Brussels, 1978) and Johnson, *Life and Miracles*.

36 On the archaeology of the hilltop site, see the references at Johnson, *Life and Miracles*, 5 n. 17.

finished she exclaims, 'I gave heartfelt thanks to God for his mercy in letting me fulfill all my desires so completely, despite all my unworthiness.' She stayed for two more days praying and communing with the male and female ascetics.[37]

I would like to concentrate on Egeria's reading the 'entire *Acts* of holy Thekla' at the shrine. It is unlikely that the text she read there is anything but the famous *Acts of Paul and Thekla*, given what we know about the popularity of this work in the broader late antique world (and given the lack of any *comparandum*).[38] But whose text was it: was it hers from home? Did she purchase it in Jerusalem? Was there a library at Seleukeia? All these things are possible. However, there is evidence that Egeria may not have known much Greek,[39] and we know from Tertullian that the *Acts of Paul and Thekla* had been translated into Latin at a very early point, perhaps even within 20 years of its original composition.[40] So, the most likely explanation is that she had a copy in Latin with her.[41] This text travelled so widely in the period that it is also entirely possible that she acquired it on her journey, perhaps after meeting Marthana in Jerusalem and once she knew she would visit the site on her return to Constantinople.

Another way of interpreting this event in Egeria's narrative is that the text itself prompted her visit to the shrine. Whether or not Egeria personally owned a Latin copy of the *Acts of Paul and Thekla*, she was clearly anticipating her visit to the site, and she feels no need to explain to her readers (perhaps fellow nuns or lay women in Spain?)[42] who Thekla was or what she accomplished alongside her companion Paul. According to the *Acts of Paul and Thekla*, Thekla was commissioned by Paul to teach and baptize in her home city of Iconium after having narrowly escaped two attempts on her life and having baptized herself in the process. She spent her final days, however, at Seleukeia. Thekla's legend is apocryphal both in the sense of being non-canonical and also

37 Egeria, *Itinerarium*, 23.1–6 (ed. A. Franceschini and R. Weber CCSL 175 [Turnhout, 1965], 66).

38 On the popularity of this work in late antiquity, see Johnson, *Life and Miracles*, 1–14.

39 Egeria, *Itinerarium*, 47.3–4 (CCSL 175, 89).

40 See Johnson, *Life and Miracles*, 3 nn. 5–6. Admittedly, Tertullian read Greek and could be reading the Greek original rather than a Latin translation (ibid.).

41 In the absence of any archaeological evidence of a library: *contra* Dagron, *La Vie et Miracles de Thècle*, 33.

42 See Hagith Sivan, 'Holy Land Pilgrimage and Western Audiences: Some Reflections on Egeria and her Circle', *Classical Quarterly* ns 38 (1988), 528–35; eadem, 'Who was Egeria? Piety and Pilgrimage in the Age of Gratian', *Harvard Theological Review* 81 (1988), 59–72.

in the sense of belonging to the imaginary worlds of Christian *Acta* from the second century. This legend was conveyed by the text of the *Acts* and thus had a discernable impact on the decisions Egeria made in determining her course.

The fact that Egeria inserted the act of reading this text into her own book says much about the archival value of the apocryphal legends in late antiquity and how collecting the texts went side by side with the experience of visiting the shrines. Travel literature can thus profitably be read as archival, and these two practices of collecting sites and collecting texts are mutually reinforced in much travel literature from the period: as in the example of Arculf, whose experiences are incorporated into Adomnan's text of the *De locis sanctis*, experiences which Adomnan deftly refines and organizes with the help of other texts open at his desk.[43] Similarly, Egeria assumes a knowledge of the Thekla legend, or at least access to it, among her readers, and these readers share her experience of reading the text on site through Egeria's encapsulation of this event.

A similar episode from Egeria's narrative is her visit to the city of Edessa, where there was a shrine to the apostle Thomas that contained his relics.[44] Unlike Thekla, Thomas *does* appear in the New Testament, in the Gospels and Acts. He is named among the twelve disciples in Matthew 10: 3, Mark 3: 18, and Luke 6: 15. He is called Thomas Didymus ('the twin') at John 11: 16 and 21: 2 and he famously doubts the resurrection at John 20: 24–8.[45] Thomas is, in fact, very prominent in the Gospel of John (e.g. 14: 5–7) and has even been offered by one scholar as a candidate for the so-called 'beloved disciple' (13: 23, 19: 26, 21: 20–4), in place of that title's traditional attribution to John.[46] The name Didymus means 'twin' in Greek, as does the name 'Thomas' in Aramaic and Syriac (the Christian Aramaic spoken at Edessa). In addition, at a very early point in the tradition the apostle Thomas was

43 Meehan, *Adamnan's De locis sanctis*, 5, 11–18. See also Brown, *Rise of Western Christendom* (2nd edn), 329.

44 See the article by Paul Devos, 'Égérie à Édesse: S. Thomas l'apôtre, le roi Abgar', *Analecta Bollandiana* 85 (1967), 381–400. Devos is, however, unwilling to allow Egeria's account of Thomas to stand in contradiction to Eusebius's account (see below), thereby short-circuiting questions regarding the reception and availability of these legends (382).

45 The motif of 'Doubting Thomas' is a highly successful one in medieval and early modern art and literature. See Glenn W. Most, *Doubting Thomas* (Cambridge, MA, 2005), Pt 2.

46 James H. Charlesworth, *The Beloved Disciple: Whose Witness Validates the Gospel of John?* (Valley Forge, PA, 1995).

conflated with Judas or Jude, the brother of James and Jesus (Matt. 13: 55, Mark 6: 3) and also the titular author of the small letter of Jude just before Revelation in the New Testament.[47] This conflation appears to have taken place with only the materials of the canonical New Testament at hand.[48] Let us now turn briefly to the highly significant extra-canonical expression of Thomas's apostolic persona.

One of the earliest apocryphal gospels (and one which has received a lot of attention recently) is the *Gospel of Thomas*, a text which clearly has a relationship both with the synoptic gospels and with the Gospel of John: its connection to the synoptics concerns the *Gospel of Thomas's* knowledge of 'Q' (the sayings source behind Matthew and Luke). As for its connection with John, that depends on one's definition of the conjunction of religious groups rather inconveniently labelled as 'Gnostic Christianity'.[49] Conventional wisdom has it that the *Gospel of Thomas* was written in northern Mesopotamia in the second century, after the Gospel of John and in reaction to it.[50] More recently, some scholars have attempted to argue that the *Gospel of Thomas* is earlier than the Gospel of John, the latter being written in reaction to the former.[51] The scholarly debate is too detailed to go into here, but suffice it to say that, if the conventional model is chosen for the emergence of Thomas literature in second-century Mesopotamia, then the testimony of Egeria in the fourth century that Edessa was a city devoted to Thomas begins to make more sense.

While the earliest traditions about Thomas have nothing explicit to say about Edessa in particular, literature concerning Thomas seems to have been centred on this region from an early point. Edessa is the capital of a large, Syriac-speaking province of Osrhoëne, just to the

47 The author of Jude names himself in the first verse and claims he is the brother of James.

48 This conflation appears in the *Gospel of Thomas*, the *Book of Thomas the Contender*, and the Old Syriac version of John 14: 22. See the references in Han J. W. Drijvers, 'The Acts of Thomas', in Wilhelm Schneemelcher, ed., *New Testament Apocrypha*, trans. Robert McLachlan Wilson, 2 vols (rev. edn, Louisville, KY, 1992), 2: 324.

49 On Gnosticism and labels, see Michael Williams, *Rethinking "Gnosticism": an Argument for Dismantling a Dubious Category* (Princeton, NJ, 1996), and Karen King, *What is Gnosticism?* (Cambridge, MA, 2003).

50 See Han J. W. Drivers, 'East of Antioch: Forces and Structures in the Development of Early Syriac Theology', idem, *East of Antioch: Studies in Early Syriac Christianity* (London, 1984), no. I: 15–17.

51 See Elaine Pagels, *Beyond Belief: the Secret Gospel of Thomas* (New York, 2003), esp. ch. 2. Compare Most, *Doubting Thomas*, 242–4.

north-east of the province of Roman Syria and across the Euphrates. Thus the *Gospel of Thomas* (surviving complete only in Coptic),[52] the *Book of Thomas the Contender* (also surviving in Coptic),[53] and the *Acts of Thomas* (originally in Syriac and Greek)[54] have all been read as betraying a specifically Syrian (or more precisely Syriac)[55] brand of Christianity, one that shares a taste for theological dualisms, ascetic renunciation, and other quasi-Gnostic elements.[56] This 'Thomas Christianity', as it has been called, remains a debated epithet, and I do not want to minimize the complexity of the problem.[57] However, the imaginary role of Thomas in Syriac Christianity is strong, and in many ways he becomes the spiritual founder of Christianity both within Syriac speaking regions and far to the East of them.

It will be profitable at this point to give an account of Egeria's experiences in Edessa before exploring the larger significance of the apostle Thomas in apostolic geography. Egeria states that after three years she decided to return home to the West but that, at the same time, God had given her a desire to visit (what she calls) 'Syrian Mesopotamia', that is Osrhoëne.[58] Her desire to visit the city of Edessa, off the beaten path of most pilgrims, is immediately given *gravitas* through a mention of

52 The critical text in Coptic (including an edition of the three surviving Greek fragments) is in Bentley Layton, ed., *Nag Hammadi Codex II, 2–7 Together with XIII, 2*, Brit. Lib. Or. 4926(1) and P. Oxy 1, 645, 655*, Nag Hammadi Studies 20–1, 2 vols (Leiden, 1989), vol. 1. See also the English translation in Layton, *Gnostic Scriptures*, 376–99.

53 The critical text is in Layton, *Nag Hammadi Codex 2*, vol. 1. See also John Douglas Turner, *The Book of Thomas the Contender from Codex II of the Cairo Gnostic Library from Nag Hammadi (CG II,7): the Coptic Text with Translation, Introduction, and Commentary*, Society of Biblical Literature Dissertation Series 23 (Missoula, MT, 1975).

54 For the Syriac text, see William Wright, *Apocryphal Acts of the Apostles*, 2 vols (London, 1871, rept. Hildesheim, 1990), *q'b–šlg*, with the translation on 146–298. For the Greek text, see Lipsius and Bonnet, *Acta Apostolorum*, 2.2: 99–288. For textual issues regarding the original version of the *Acts of Thomas*, see Klijn, *Acts of Thomas* (2nd edn), 1–4 (see also the 1st edn, which has valuable material not included in the 2nd). For an English translation and commentary, see Klijn, *Acts of Thomas* (2nd edn), 17–251.

55 The adjective 'Syriac' is preferable to 'Syrian' because what we are referring to is a cultural and linguistic region larger than the political designation of Roman Syria: Syriac was spoken in the fourth to sixth centuries in parts of what is today Syria, Turkey, Iraq, and Iran. In ancient terms this large cultural region comprised all or part of the following late Roman provinces: Syria, Euphratensis, Osrhoëne, and Mesopotamia.

56 See Bentley Layton, 'The School of St. Thomas', idem, *The Gnostic Scriptures* (New York, 1988), 357–65. For a contrary interpretation, see Drijvers, 'Acts of Thomas', 334–7, where early Syriac Christianity is not quasi-Gnostic at all, but rather 'sophisticated'.

57 See Philip Sellew, 'Thomas Christianity: Scholars in Quest of a Community', in Jan N. Bremmer, ed., *The Apocryphal Acts of Thomas* (Leuven, 2001), 11–35.

58 Egeria, *Itinerarium*, 17.1 (CCSL 178, 58).

Thomas. Egeria disingenuously claims that 'everyone' who visits Jerusalem also goes to Edessa and justifies this prominence through the following statement:

> [I also wanted to visit Syrian Mesopotamia] for the sake of praying at the *martyrium* of Saint Thomas the Apostle, where his corpse was placed intact. The corpse is at Edessa, [the city] to which our God Jesus, after his ascension into heaven, was sending Thomas. [Jesus] witnessed to this in the letter he sent to King Abgar by the messenger Ananias. This letter is preserved with great reverence at the city of Edessa, where is the aforementioned *martyrium*.[59]

Immediately, the reader of this account is thrown into an entire world of Christian associations: the corpse of Thomas the apostle, a letter Jesus wrote, King Abgar, and a messenger Ananias. The King Abgar legend is familiar from Eusebius, who places this story in a very prominent position at the end of the first book of his *Ecclesiastical History*.[60] According to legend Abgar was the king of Edessa at the time of Jesus's ministry, but he was ill with a disease, so he sent a letter to Jesus, asking him to come heal him in Edessa. Jesus declined, but promised to send one of his apostles in his stead. In Eusebius's account, Judas Thomas sends the apostle Thaddeus after Jesus's death and resurrection, and Eusebius quotes letters (translated into Greek from Syriac) to prove this story.[61] Thaddeus, one of the twelve disciples/apostles in Matthew 10: 3 and Mark 3: 18,[62] goes on to heal Abgar and thereby converts the people of Edessa to Christianity.[63] According to Eusebius, these letters between Jesus and Abgar were still preserved in his time (c.325 AD) in the 'Archives' or 'Record Offices' (γραμματοφυλακεῖα) at Edessa, where

59 Ibid.

60 Eusebius, *Historia Ecclesiastica*, 1.13.

61 On the tendentiousness of Eusebius's account, see Sebastian Brock, 'Eusebius and Syriac Christianity', in Harold W. Attridge and Gohei Hata, eds, *Eusebius, Christianity, and Judaism* (Detroit, MI, 1992), 212–34.

62 Also identified with the 'Judas, son/brother of James' in Luke 6: 16 and Acts 1: 13. Could this potentially be a source of the relations (and later competition) between Thaddeus and 'Judas Thomas'? 'Brother' is possible here because in both passages the earliest witnesses do not have a definite article between Judas and James, i.e. Ἰούδας Ἰακώβου. If accepted, then the apostle to Edessa was essentially understood to be a relation of James, no matter whether that meant Judas Thomas or Judas Thaddeus. For comparison, there is extant a curious inscription from the '40 caverns' at Edessa: Θαδδαῖον τὸν καὶ Θωμᾶν (Devos, 'Égérie à Édesse', 398).

63 Interestingly, in some traditions Thaddeus is not the named disciple but 'one of the seventy (or seventy-two)' from Luke 10: 1 and 10: 17.

Eusebius says he extracted (ἀναλαμβάνω) and translated (μεταβάλλω) them from the original documents, which were in Syriac (ἐκ τῆς Σύρων φωνῆς).[64] There is no mention in Eusebius, however, of Judas Thomas himself going to Edessa, nor of a messenger Ananias, as in Egeria's account.[65]

Leaving from Antioch and crossing the Euphrates into Mesopotamia, Egeria arrived at Edessa in April of 384, one month prior to her visit to the shrine of Thekla. Once in the city, Egeria says that she went straight to the *martyrium* of Thomas. There she prayed and read from what she calls 'certain things of holy Thomas himself' (*aliquanta ipsius sancti Thomae*). She describes a large church on the site, built 'in the new fashion', as she says, and she claims to have seen a number of other *martyria* there, among which lived some of the monks present in Edessa.[66]

What is immediately striking about this account is how similar it is to her visit to Thekla's shrine, especially her reading of Thomasine texts immediately upon arrival.[67] What were these writings? It is possible that they were the famous apocryphal *Acts of Thomas*, which had been composed early in the third century AD, probably concurrently in Greek and Syriac versions on our best evidence.[68] But there are other candidates for Egeria's writings about Thomas as well: I have already mentioned the *Gospel of Thomas* and the *Book of Thomas the Contender*, both of which would have been available in Egeria's time.[69] One important consideration is whether the genitive in her description – *aliquanta ipsius sancti Thomae* – signifies authorship or not. If it does, then the *Acts of Thomas* (as it stands today) can be excluded immediately, since it is written in the third person. For the moment I will assume that the genitive does not signify authorship but should be translated 'concerning holy Thomas himself'.

64 Eusebius, *Historia Ecclesiastica*, 1.13.5.

65 Elsewhere (*Historia Ecclesiastica*, 3.1.1), Eusebius claims that Thomas is the apostle to Parthia (i.e. Persia). See Eric Junod, 'Origène, Eusèbe et la tradition', 239–40 and 247–8.

66 Egeria, *Itinerarium*, 19.2–4 (CCSL 175, 59–60).

67 The similarity extends even to the syntax of the two passages, especially the use of the phrase *nec non etiam et* connecting the notices about praying first, then reading the text on site. Compare Egeria, *Itinerarium*, 19.2 with 23. 5 (CCSL 175, 59 and 66).

68 Drijvers, 'East of Antioch'. On authorship, date, and setting, see Jan N. Bremmer, 'The *Acts of Thomas*: Place, Date, and Women', idem, ed., *The Apocryphal Acts of Thomas* (Leuven, 2001), 74–90.

69 The *Book of Thomas the Contender* is available today only in Coptic translation but in all likelihood came from a Greek or Syriac original (or originals in both languages: see previous note).

Let us consider the *Acts of Thomas* first. The apocryphal *Acts of Thomas* is a fascinating text: it describes Thomas's success at evangelism, his miracles, and his eventual martyrdom.[70] However, the *Acts of Thomas* makes no explicit reference to Edessa. Rather, the story takes place almost completely in India or on the way to India. Thomas is the apostle to India, not Edessa.[71] If this is the text that Egeria read at the *martyrium* of Thomas in Edessa in April of 384, then it is strange indeed that she does not mention Thomas's legendary commission to India.[72] The only two references to Mesopotamia in the *Acts of Thomas* come, first, in the 'Hymn of the Pearl', an elegant, Gnosticizing poem ostensibly sung by Thomas while in prison in India: in the poem the protagonist seems to come from somewhere in Mesopotamia, though Edessa (Urhai in Syriac) is never mentioned; second, at the very end of some Greek manuscripts, the *Acts of Thomas* says that his body was transported to Mesopotamia by some of his followers: the Syriac text and other Greek manuscripts merely say that he was transported 'to the West' (εἰς τὰ τῆς δύσεως μέρη).[73]

On this basis, it may be the case that Egeria was reading from the 'Hymn of the Pearl', which is known to have been composed separately from the rest of the *Acts*.[74] The 'Hymn of the Pearl' is written in the first person, which means that the phrase that was noted above (*aliquanta ipsius sancti Thomae*) could be describing this text as a work of Thomas's own. Or, she could have been reading the *Gospel of Thomas*, which claims to be a writing of 'Didymus Judas Thomas', though this work had already come under severe criticism by Egeria's day.[75] Like the *Gospel of Thomas*, the *Book of Thomas the Contender* claims to be secret knowledge imparted to 'Jude Thomas', though written down by the

70 On the text, see n. 52 above.

71 A contemporary reference to 'Judas Thomas' in India is the *Doctrina Apostolorum* of c.250 in Syriac: see Alphonse Mingana, 'The Early Spread of Christianity in India', *BJRULM* 10 (1926), 435–510, at 448.

72 Roughly contemporary with Egeria, however, is Ephrem the Syrian, who makes reference to Thomas in India (*Carmina Nisibena*, 42). Ephrem is not necessarily an independent witness since he clearly knows the *Acts of Thomas* well: see Mingana, 'Christianity in India', 450.

73 See Klijn, *Acts of Thomas*, 250–1. Egeria is the next writer to mention Thomas at Edessa, and from that point on the association appears very widely recognized (e.g. Socrates, *Historia Ecclesiastica*, 4.18; Sozomen, *Historia Ecclesiastica*, 6.18).

74 See Paul-Hubert Poirier, *L'Hyme de la Perle des Actes de Thomas: introduction, texte-traduction, commentaire* (Louvain-La-Neuve, 1981), esp. Pt 2.

75 For example, Eusebius, *Historia Ecclesiastica*, 3.25.6.

disciple Matthias.[76] Neither the *Gospel of Thomas* nor the *Book of Thomas the Contender* seems to be the type of text one would read at a *martyrium*: they are mainly comprised of secret sayings of Jesus and do not have much to do with Thomas himself. And of all of these options, only the 'Hymn of the Pearl' and the *Gospel of Thomas* are written in the first person, making Egeria's claim of reading 'certain things of holy Thomas himself' very difficult to interpret.

After praying and reading this text (whatever it may be) at his shrine, Egeria is given a tour of the city by the bishop. He asks her if he could show her 'all the places Christians should visit here': one gets the sense he has done this before. Their first stop is the palace of King Abgar. Inside are, among other things, marble portraits (*archiotipae marmarae*) of Abgar and his son Magnus (Ma'nou),[77] portraits which Egeria admires for their wise and noble aspect. Next the bishop shows her the river that emerges from a spring under the palace. He tells her the story of a siege by the Persians during which that source sprang up magically when the Persians had cut off their only water supply. The Persians were defeated through the intervention of the letter that Jesus had sent to Abgar. Abgar took the letter to the gate and prayed: 'Lord Jesus, you promised us that no enemy would enter this city.'[78] Immediately a darkness fell on the Persians and they were confounded. Every time afterwards when an enemy threatened, the letter was produced and read at the gate and the city was saved.

Finally, the bishop takes Egeria to this very gate of the city where the letter was first received and repeatedly read out thereafter. When they arrive there the bishop prays and he himself reads out the letter. Egeria notes that the gate is considered holy: from the day that the letter was brought by the messenger Ananias, no one has been allowed to pass through it who is unclean or in mourning, nor has any dead body been taken out through it.[79] The bishop also shows Egeria the tomb of Abgar and his family – 'beautiful,' she says, 'but old-fashioned' (*pulchra, sed facta more antiquo*).[80] At the end of her account Egeria relates one last salient detail, which connects this story with the rest of her narrative

[76] On the text, see n. 53 above.

[77] On the question of which Abgar Egeria was viewing, see Devos, 'Égérie à Édesse', 392–400. On the Edessene dynastic name Ma'nou, see the references at Bremmer, 'The *Acts of Thomas*', 75, nn. 5–6.

[78] Egeria, *Itinerarium*, 19.9 (CCSL 175, 60).

[79] Ibid., 19.16–17 (CCSL 175, 61).

[80] Ibid., 19.18 (CCSL 175, 61).

about Thomas and also with the one about Thekla. She says that she was especially pleased by the fact that she was able to obtain, in her short time there, copies of the letters between Abgar and Jesus. She parenthetically remarks that she already had copies of them at home but that it is much better to acquire them at Edessa. She suspects that the ones she has back home are incomplete because the new ones are longer. She promises her readers – 'dearest ladies' she calls them – that they will be able to read them when she returns home.[81]

Modern scholars have done extensive work on Egeria's travelogue as a whole, a text which was only discovered in the late nineteenth century.[82] However, this aspect of Egeria's account, the reading and collecting of apocryphal narratives about the apostles, has only rarely been noticed, and no one has taken the time to unpack it at length.[83] Egeria's journey touched upon, at various points, an imaginative world far larger than the pilgrimage journey itself would suggest. Most of the sites she visited, as I noted above, concerned the Old Testament or the Gospels, but the prominent examples of Thomas and Thekla on her return journey should give us pause.[84] Most important between these two scenes is the act of reading at the shrines. In both cases she produces texts, either locally acquired or part of her personal library. Moreover, in Edessa we see what must have been a natural habit for her (and others), that of procuring copies of the apocryphal narratives which she then took home. If scholars ever felt the absence of a model for the dissemination of apocryphal narratives, Egeria's account of her own experiences admirably fills that void: we see a devout, no doubt wealthy Christian woman studiously educating herself on apostolic geography, incorporating that geography into her journey, and preserving the knowledge of apostolic wanderings for others. This is the palpable archival quality of Egeria's narrative, and perhaps we could consider her *modus operandi* here indicative of the mental habits of Christian travellers and travel-writers more generally in the period.

81 Ibid., 19.19 (CCSL 175, 62).

82 On the discovery of the text and subsequent editions, see Maraval, *Égérie*, ch. 2.

83 An exception is Paul Devos's article 'Égérie à Édesse', on which see n. 44 above.

84 Sivan only gives passing attention to the sites outside of Jerusalem: 'It would appear, then, that the prime aim of pilgrimage from the circle's point of view was to relive established biblical episodes rather than those narrated in apocryphal writings' ('Egeria and her Circle', 530). The two categories should not be so readily separated, either as destinations for pilgrimage or as literary devices.

Thomasine Christianity and the Geographical Consequences of Revival

I noted above two by-ways among the legends of the apostle Thomas to which Egeria does not refer in her narrative. The first is the story of the apostle Thaddeus (or Addai in Syriac) coming to Edessa and converting its people, having been sent by Thomas in Jerusalem. Egeria, by way of contrast, talks about an Ananias bringing the letter and she claims that Thomas himself came to Edessa, having been sent by Jesus, and is responsible for the conversion of the city. The second by-way which Egeria does not seem to know is the story that Thomas was the apostle to India, which is contained in the third-century *Acts of Thomas.* The *Acts of Thomas* were very popular in late antiquity and have consequently survived in almost every ancient Christian language (Latin, Armenian, Coptic, Ethiopic, Arabic, Slavonic, and Georgian) in addition to its original Greek and Syriac.[85] I shall consider the afterlife of these two stories in order.

Thaddeus takes on an important apostolic role of his own within Syriac Christianity. Interestingly, this career is kept entirely separate from Thomas traditions, such as the one Egeria knew at Edessa in 384.[86] Shortly after Egeria's visit, around AD 400, a text was written, probably at Edessa itself, called the *Teaching of Addai* (usually called by its Latin title, the *Doctrina Addai*). The *Doctrina Addai* mainly comprises a long sermon by Addai to the people of Edessa, performed at the request of King Abgar following his conversion. In the course of the sermon, Addai references a number of important apocryphal legends. For instance, he relates a version of the famous Mandylion story that a likeness of Jesus was supernaturally imprinted on a cloth. In later tradition copies of the Mandylion (literally, 'handkerchief') were venerated and used as prophylactic devices for cities (not unlike Abgar's letter in Egeria's narrative).[87] Addai also makes mention of the tradition that it was not Helena, the mother of Constantine, who discovered the True Cross on Golgotha, but it was Protonike, a fictitious wife of Claudius

85 The most recent critical editions of these versions are collected in Klijn, *Acts of Thomas* (2nd ed.), 4 nn. 6–11.

86 See n. 62 above.

87 See Averil Cameron, 'The History of the Image of Edessa: the Telling of a Story', in Cyril Mango and Omeljan Pritsak, eds, *Okeanos: Essays Presented to Ihor Ševcenko on his Sixtieth Birthday by his Colleagues and Students* (Cambridge, MA, 1984), 80–94 [reprinted in Averil Cameron, *Changing Cultures in Early Byzantium* (Aldershot, 1996), no. XI].

Caesar, emperor from 41–54 AD.[88] In addition to these stories, the *Doctrina Addai* established a legend about Thaddeus – very influential in its own right – which was further elaborated in later saints' 'Lives': thus, the sixth-century Greek 'Acts of Thaddeus' and the Syriac 'Acts of Mari' build their narratives onto the core of the *Doctrina Addai* story.[89]

One way of interpreting these apocryphal traditions about Thaddeus is that they represent a deliberate, creative attempt to provide a legitimate history for ecclesiastical institutions already in existence on the ground. Egeria's travel narrative sufficiently proves this interpretation in her description of the remarkable amount of building and monastic activity at Edessa. Of course, Egeria is aware only of the Thomas tradition and not that of Thaddeus. But even in Thomas's case we see legitimating histories being fabricated (or perhaps, embellished or elaborated) based on some lost kernel of truth. As noted above, in the *Acts of Thomas* the apostle finds his way to India. At first, when a post-resurrection Jesus tells him to go there, he refuses, like Jonah and other Old Testament prophets. So Jesus sells him into slavery and Thomas gets taken by a merchant down the Red Sea and over to India. Along the way he persuades elite couples not to consummate their marriages.[90] Once in India Thomas performs many miraculous acts and converts many to the Christian faith. In some scenes Jesus poses as Thomas and works miracles himself; Thomas too is mistaken for Jesus. These scenes are drawing on the 'Twin' motif of Thomasine literature: not only was Judas Thomas supposed to be the brother of Jesus, he was also (according to apocryphal tradition) supposed to be his identical twin (*alter Christus*). Such recognition scenes introduce elements of

88 See George Howard, *The Teaching of Addai* (Chico, CA, 1981), 21–35 (with facing Syriac text). On the Protonike legend, see Han J. W. Drijvers and Jan Willem Drijvers, *The Finding of the True Cross: the Judas Kyriakos Legend in Syriac* (Leuven, 1997), esp. 14–16. The legend exists only in extant Syriac and Armenian texts (appearing first in the *Doctrina Addai*) and is thus thought not to have travelled outside these traditions.

89 Greek *Acts of Thaddeus*: Lipsius and Bonnet, *Acta Apostolorum*, 1: 273–8. Syriac *Acts of Mari*: see Amir Harrak, *The Acts of Mar Mari the Apostle* (Atlanta, GA, 2005). For a separate tradition about Thaddeus, see the Armenian *Acts and Martyrdom of the Holy Apostle Thaddeus* in S. C. Malan, *The Life and Times of S. Gregory the Illuminator* (London, 1868), 66–98.

90 On 'encratism' and the *Acts of Thomas*, see Han J. W. Drijvers, 'Facts and Problems: Early Syriac-Speaking Christianity', idem, *East of Antioch*, no. VI: 170–1. The *Acts of Thomas* was adopted by the Manichaeans as a foundational text, along with other apocryphal *Acta*: see P.-H. Poirier, 'Les Acts de Thomas et le manichéisme', *Apocrypha* 9 (1998), 263–87.

mystery and comedy to the narrative, in addition to providing a visual reference to distinctively Syriac theological underpinnings.[91]

It is important to note that both the third-century *Acts of Thomas* and the fifth-century *Doctrina Addai* are travel narratives in their own right. They thus amount to important instances in late antiquity of the blending of genres.[92] Just as Egeria travels to Edessa to see the shrine of Thomas and to obtain the Abgar letters, Thomas before her travelled to Edessa on a mission from Jesus himself. I would like to suggest that Egeria's familiarity with the apocryphal Acts affected the way she travelled and the way she wrote about her travels. She was following in the footsteps of the apostles, legendary or not, and she sought out documents of legitimization both for their travels in history and her contemporary travels. The same effect can be seen in her account of Thekla, where she recognizes the significance of Seleukeia for Thekla and the significance of Thekla for the region: as at Edessa, she makes a special trip out of her way to visit the shrine, and her primary act of worship on site is to read the *Acts of Paul and Thekla*. This apocryphal document substantiates her worship. And her own literary product perpetuates the cycle of travel, writing, and archives.

By way of conclusion, I would like to point briefly to the real history of Syriac Christianity in India. In the mid-sixth century an Alexandrian trader called Cosmas Indicopleustes (not his real name) wrote a lengthy account, called the *Christian Topography*, of journeys from Egypt down the Red Sea, around the Persian Gulf, and even to Taprobane (Sri Lanka, Ceylon).[93] His primary motive was to confute the Greek tradition on the point that the earth was spherical: he preferred the idea that

91 On the theological resonance of this theme, see Drijvers, 'East of Antioch', esp. 15–16: 'I believe that Judas the twin brother of the Lord is the most perfect representative of the state of salvation, which implies an identification with the Savior, God's Word and Spirit dwelling in a human being. Who is more like the Lord than His own twin brother?'

92 The blending of genres and experimentation with form can be read as definitive of late antique literature, see Scott Fitzgerald Johnson, ed., *Greek Literature in Late Antiquity: Dynamism, Didacticism, Classicism* (Aldershot, 2006), esp. introduction.

93 Critical edition is Wanda Wolska-Conus, *Cosmas Indicopleustès: Topographie Chrétienne*, 3 vols (Paris, 1968–73). See also eadem, *La Topographie Chrétienne de Cosmas Indicopleustès: théologie et science au VIe siècle* (Paris, 1962). The name 'Cosmas Indicopleustes' (i.e., 'Cosmas the India-sailor') was not attached to this work until the eleventh century. The author was intentionally anonymous, calling himself only 'a Christian'. On questions of authorship and date, see the introduction to Wolska-Conus, *Cosmas Indicopleustès*. As Cosmas notes in the prologue (1–2) to the *Topography*, he wrote two other geographical works, both of which are now lost: these are the *Geography* dedicated to a Constantine, and an *Astronomy* dedicated to a deacon Homologos.

the earth was flat and that the universe was shaped like the Mosaic Tabernacle.[94] Beyond his polemical eccentricities, Cosmas was an accurate observer of flora, fauna, and urban life along his route. He purports to describe Christian churches on the island of Taprobane, off the coast of India.[95] Cosmas himself had become a Christian, a 'Nestorian' Christian, under the tutelage of the katholikos of the Persian Church, Mar Aba (540–552), when Aba visited Alexandria.[96] The churches Cosmas describes in Taprobane are 'Persian' (i.e. 'Nestorian') and 'under a Persian bishop', and he claims there are also Persian churches on the west coast of India, in cities named *Male* (Malabar) and *Kalliana*.[97] There is no embellishment of Cosmas's narrative with apocryphal stories and it even seems that he does not know the tradition that Thomas proselytized in India, which is most surprising considering his own conversion to the 'Nestorian' Church, what we today call the Church of the East (or the Assyrian Church of the East).[98]

What is striking about Cosmas's claims in Sri Lanka and India is that there truly seem to have been Church of the East churches there from at least the sixth century. In fact, we have archaeological evidence from the period which confirms Cosmas's account: 'Nestorian' tomb inscrip-

94 See, e.g., *Christian Topography*, 2.35 (ed. Wolska-Conus, 1: 340–1). Cosmas's principal interlocutor was John Philoponus, a Miaphysite theologian, philosopher, and cosmologist in the sixth century. See Wolska-Conus, *Cosmas Indicopleustès*, 40–1. Philoponus's *De opificio mundi* was a direct retaliation to the *Topography*. See Carl William Pearson, 'Scripture as Cosmology: Natural Philosophical Debate in John Philoponus' Alexandria', unpublished Ph.D. thesis, Harvard University, 1999.

95 Cosmas's discussions of Persian churches in Taprobane are at 3.65 (ed. Wolska-Conus, 1: 502-5) and 11.14 (342–5). It is not absolutely certain from the *Christian Topography* whether Cosmas travelled himself to India and Taprobane or whether he was relying on others' accounts: see Wolska-Conus, *Cosmas Indicopleustès*, 17. On Taprobane, including Cosmas's description, see D. P. M. Weerakkody, *Taprobane: Ancient Sri Lanka as Known to Greeks and Romans* (Turnhout, 1997).

96 On Cosmas and Mar Aba, whom Cosmas calls 'Patrikios', see the *Christian Topography* 2.2 (ed. Wolska-Conus, 1: 306). On the Antiochene tradition of theology to which Cosmas assented, see Wolska, *La Topographie Chrétienne de Cosmas Indicopleustès* (Paris, 1962), 63–85 and Adam H. Becker, 'The Dynamic Reception of Theodore of Mopsuestia in the Sixth Century: Greek, Syriac, and Latin', in Johnson, ed., *Greek Literature in Late Antiquity*, 29–47.

97 *Christian Topography*, 3.65 (ed. Wolska-Conus, 1: 502–3). He also describes such Persian churches on Dioskorides (Socotra, in the Gulf of Aden): ibid.

98 The label 'Nestorian' is today understood to be pejorative and historically misleading: see Sebastian P. Brock, 'The "Nestorian" Church: a Lamentable Misnomer', in J. F. Coakley and K. Parry, eds, *The Church of the East: Life and Thought*, *BJRULM* 78 (1996), 23–35. For the history of the Church of the East, see Wilhelm Baum and Dietmar W. Winkler, *The Church of the East: a Concise History*, trans. Miranda G. Henry (London, 2003), and Christophe Baumer, *The Church of the East: an Illustrated History of Assyrian Christianity* (London, 2006).

tions from India have been dated as early as AD 547, contemporary with Cosmas's narrative.[99] A ancient tradition competing with the Thomasine one is that the apostle Bartholomew was the first one to reach India. Eusebius relates this and tells us that a teacher of Clement of Alexandria, Pantaenus, went to India at the end of the second century and found Christians there with copies of Matthew's gospel written in Hebrew, which Bartholomew had given them.[100] Several scholars have suggested, however, that Pantaenus's 'India' was actually Roman Arabia Felix, or the Yemen, rather than today's India.[101] No matter the precise location of these apostles' supposed wanderings, it is impressive that Christian churches were flourishing so far outside of the Roman empire in the sixth century. And, of course, Syriac Christianity flourishes in India today, especially in the south-west, along the Malabar coast, in the northern portion of the state of Kerala.[102]

I would suggest that the revival of interest in apostolic history and the movements of Christian peoples should be read in tandem as part of a larger movement in late antique history. The link between such a revival and the travels of real Christians – whether Egeria's pilgrimage or Christians settling in India – are the apocryphal narratives from the apostolic past. Egeria and the Thomasine Christians of India are linked through a shared reliance on what I have called 'apostolic geography'. Though separated by a couple of centuries, Egeria and the late antique Christians of southern India both rely on the wanderings of the apostle Thomas for a sense of identity and connection to the apostolic commission. Furthermore, their commitment to the human figures of apostolic history can be linked to other texts from the period, including the sermons of Chrysostom, multiple pilgrimage narratives and breviaries,

99 Weerakkody, *Taprobane*, 134–5.

100 Eusebius, *Historia Ecclesiastica*, 5.10–11. For a separate tradition about Bartholomew (though one which mentions Thomas, India, and Thaddeus), see the Armenian *Acts and Martyrdom of the Holy Apostle Bartholomew* in Malan, *S. Gregory the Illuminator*, 99–103.

101 See Mingana, 'Christianity in India', 449. See also Albrecht Dihle, 'The Conception of India in Hellenistic and Roman Literature', *Proceedings of the Cambridge Philological Society* 190 (1964), 15–23, for a different view, i.e. that Christian writers had a rather precise knowledge of (real) Indian geography. For example, 22–3: 'In early Christian literature the conception of India definitely changed and was adapted to really existing conditions. We are able to prove this change not only by comparing the different size and shape given to India in pagan and Christian literature but also by noting the differences in the ethnographical details attached to the general idea of India.'

102 On the later history of the Syriac churches in India, see Leslie Brown, *The Indian Christians of St Thomas: an Account of the Ancient Syrian Church of Malabar* (rev. edn, Cambridge, 1982).

and of course the apocryphal legends themselves, which continued to be copied, translated, and written afresh in late antiquity. This layering of texts and legends is highly characteristic of late antiquity and provides a new context for the movement of travellers around the Mediterranean and further east, through Persia, India, and beyond.

Washington and Lee University

PAST MODELS AND CONTEMPORARY CONCERNS: THE FOUNDATION AND GROWTH OF THE CISTERCIAN ORDER

by JANET BURTON

OF all the medieval monastic orders the Cistercian has undoubtedly received the most attention from historians, and this engagement with the White Monks shows no sign of abating. In the words of David Robinson in his recent volume on the Cistercian abbeys of Wales, 'to turn one's back on the subject, even for a moment, is to lose the plot'.[1] Current scholarship continues to be concerned with a range of issues. However, much of the most controversial scholarship has centred on the dating of key Cistercian documents: the narratives of the origins of Cîteaux, that is, the *Exordium Parvum* and the *Exordium Cistercii*, as well as various versions of the Cistercian constitution, the *Carta Caritatis*, and successive *capitula*, that is, the pronouncements of the Annual General Chapter. The debate is not new. For over seventy years scholars, including in an English context Dom David Knowles, have sought to unravel the textual and manuscript complexities of the documents relating to the foundation and growth of the mother house itself and of the order.[2] In the last six years two significant contributions to this area of scholarship have appeared, the first more controversial than the second. First, Constance Berman argued that the key Cistercian documents were inventions of the latter part of the twelfth century, designed to create a past for the Cistercian order, an organization which, she argues, did not exist before the mid-twelfth century.[3] Before then, Berman suggests, *ordo Cisterciensis* meant not a formal order, but the way of life (*ordo*) followed at Cîteaux and other reformed houses, initially in Burgundy but gradually spreading more widely. Berman's arguments have not met with

1 David M. Robinson, *The Cistercians in Wales: Architecture and Archaeology 1130–1540* (London, 2006), x.

2 The bibliography is exhaustive. The issues were addressed by David Knowles, 'The Primitive Cistercian Documents', in *Great Historical Enterprises: Problems in Monastic History* (London, 1963), 197–222.

3 Constance Hoffman Berman, *The Cistercian Evolution: the Invention of a Religious Order in Twelfth-Century Europe* (Philadelphia, PA, 2000).

universal acceptance but have forced a reassessment of the evidence.[4] Second, between 1999 and 2002, Chrysogonus Waddell produced in three volumes new editions, with notes and translations, of the *Exordium Parvum*, *Exordium Cistercii*, *Carta Caritatis*, the twelfth-century statutes of the General Chapter, and the *Usus Conversorum*, or Usages of the Lay Brothers, thus providing the basis for future discussion.[5]

It need hardly be stressed that the dates of these documents have important bearings on key questions about the very origins of what is commonly described as the most successful of all new monastic movements to emerge from that great period of revival and resurgence, the eleventh and twelfth centuries. Those questions bear repeating here. What were the intentions of the founders of the New Monastery, as Cîteaux was first known, that is, of Abbot Robert and his band of twenty-one monks who left the prosperous monastery of Molesme in 1098 for the *heremum*, the desert, of Cîteaux? When did the ideologies that we associate with the Cistercians first emerge? And at what point can we detect the beginnings of a Cistercian order, that is, a group of houses bound by both shared aspirations and aims and by a constitution, the *Carta Caritatis*, which held those houses together in a common observance?[6] It is with some trepidation that I put my toe in the still swirling waters of controversy. However, the undoubted impact that the Cistercians had on the monastic world of the Middle Ages seems to invite a reassessment of how far the dynamics behind the enterprise were inspired by the themes of this volume, that is, by notions of revival and resurgence. The aim of this essay is therefore to review in a critical way where scholarship stands on, and what it has to tell us about, the impulse behind the emergence of Cistercian monasticism. Was it a

4 See, for instance, the review articles: Brian Patrick McGuire, 'Charity and Unanimity: the Invention of the Cistercian Order; A Review Article', *Cîteaux: Commentarii Cistercienses* 51 (2000), 285–97, and Chrysogonus Waddell, 'The Myth of Cistercian Origins: C. H. Berman and the Manuscript Sources', ibid., 299–386.

5 Chrysogonus Waddell, ed., *Narrative and Legislative Texts from Early Cîteaux*, Cîteaux: Commentarii Cistercienses, Studia et Documenta IX (1999) [hereafter: *Narrative and Legislative Texts*]; idem, *Cistercian Lay Brothers: Twelfth-Century Usages with Related Texts*, Cîteaux: Commentarii Cistercienses, Studia et Documenta X (2000); idem, *Twelfth-Century Statutes from the Cistercian General Chapter*, Cîteaux: Commentarii Cistercienses, Studia et Documenta XII (2002).

6 Among many articles and papers that treat these questions, see J. Leclercq, 'The Intentions of the Founders of the Cistercian Order', in M. Basil Pennington, ed., *The Cistercian Spirit: a Symposium*, Cistercian Studies Series 3 (Spencer, MA, 1970), 88–133. Editions and translations of the *Summa Cartae Caritatis*, *Carta Caritatis Prior* and *Carta Caritatis Posterior* are included in *Narrative and Legislative Texts*.

movement concerned with past models, and a conscious evocation of history? Or was it prompted more by contemporary concerns of the late eleventh and twelfth centuries? Within a monastic context revival can imply a sense of renewal after a period of decay, as, for instance, in tenth-century England. It can also suggest that those who sought to 'renew' saw weaknesses in existing models, in the case of Cîteaux in the practices of eleventh-century monasticism, and in the past much of the debate has centred on the growth of the Cistercians as a response to crisis and decline in the Benedictine world.[7] In addressing these questions I want to include, but at the same time to cast the net wider than, what are often called the primitive Cistercian documents on which recent scholarship has tended to concentrate. I want to look at some non-Cistercian texts, and to consider how Cistercians within a regional context expressed their ideologies and how they developed them in relation to past models.

There exist two Cistercian narratives of the origins of Cîteaux, the *Exordium Parvum*, and the *Exordium Cistercii*. Chrysogonus Waddell has argued that the earlier of the two – in part at least – is the longer text, the *Exordium Parvum*. This comprises a prologue and eighteen chapters. Waddell's hypothesis is that the prologue and chapters I, II, together with chapters IV to XIV, represent a primitive or early version of the *Exordium*. This early version, he suggests, was composed by Stephen Harding, abbot of Cîteaux from 1109 to 1133/4, probably as a 'postulants' guide' around the time of the foundation of Cîteaux's first daughter house at La Ferté in 1113. This version of the text does not survive independently – it is hypothetical – but Waddell argues persuasively for its existence. Waddell further suggests that the additional material came from the pen of Raynard du Bar, abbot of Cîteaux from 1134/5 to 1150, and was composed around 1147 as a preface to the RIII customary that included the revised version of the *Ecclesiastica Officia*.[8] Waddell was not the first to see the *Exordium Parvum* as a composite document. In 1986 Jean Baptiste Auberger argued that chapters I to X

7 See the important articles: Norman F. Cantor, 'The Crisis of Western Monasticism, 1050–1130', *American Historical Review* 66.1 (1960), 47–67; J. Leclercq, 'The Monastic Crisis of the Eleventh and Twelfth Centuries', in N. Hunt, ed., *Cluniac Monasticism in the Central Middle Ages* (Hamden, CN, 1971), 217–37; John van Engen, 'The "Crisis of Cenobitism" Reconsidered: Benedictine Monasticism in the Years 1050–1150', *Speculum* 61.2 (1986), 269–304.

8 *Narrative and Legislative Texts*, 197–231 (introduction), 233–59 (text), 417–40 (text and translation).

and XIV were the work either of Stephen Harding or an associate, composed before 1123, probably c.1119.[9] The shorter narrative, *Exordium Cistercii,* Waddell also identifies as the work of Raynard du Bar, produced early in his abbacy, probably 1136/7, as an historical introduction to the second revised customary designated RII.[10] It will be appropriate to start by looking at these two texts and isolating the features that seem to point to ideas of resurgence and renewal, and I will begin with the *Exordium Cistercii* as the earlier of the two in its surviving form if not in terms of its original composition.

In the two fairly short chapters of narrative in the *Exordium Cistercii* the monastery of Molesme, from which the famous secession took place in 1098, is described in terms that are far from critical. Molesme was 'of the most celebrated renown, and remarkable for monastic observance', and 'illustrious by the gifts of [God's] grace', 'ennobled ... with illustrious men' and no 'less ample in possessions than resplendent in virtues'. It was the prosperity of Molesme, however, that was the cause for concern 'because association of possessions with virtues is not usually longlasting' and it was for this reason that the founders of the New Monastery began 'thinking upon poverty, fruitful mother of a virile stock'.[11] This is the first manifestation in the *Exordium Cistercii* of the Cistercian theme of revival and resurgence, a return to that poverty which is linked to virtue, the apostolic poverty of the early Church. The author makes a further link between poverty and virtue, for the monks are said to realize that their lives could not without poverty be fully holy and respectable; indeed, that poverty, they 'fell short of their desire and purpose to observe the Rule they had professed'.[12] Here, in this phrase, is the second indication of the evocation of earlier models, in this case the Rule of St Benedict. A third indication comes with the description of the site of Cîteaux, which is called *locum tunc scilicet horroris et vastae solitudinis*, a phrase derived from Deuteronomy 32: 10,

[9] Jean-Baptiste Auberger, *L'unanimité cistercienne primitive: mythe ou réalité*, Cîteaux: Commentarii Cistercienses, Studia et Documenta III (Achel, 1986), 42–52. For further discussion, in particular of the impact of Abbot Stephen Harding on developments at early Cîteaux, see H. E. J. Cowdrey, 'Quidem Frater Stephanus nomine, anglicus natione', in E. Rozanne Elder, ed., *The New Monastery: Texts and Studies on the Earliest Cistercians*, Cistercian Fathers Series 60 (Kalamazoo, MI, 1998), 57–77.

[10] *Narrative and Legislative Texts*, 137–61 (introduction), 179–81 (text), 399–404 (text and translation). Auberger, *l'unanimité cistercienne*, 52–7, argues for a Clairvaux origin for the *Exordium Cistercii.*

[11] *Narrative and Legislative Texts*, 399–400.

[12] Ibid., 400.

the desert through which the chosen people travelled to the Promised Land. The full verse is *Invenit eum in terra deserta, in loco horroris et vastae solitudinis*, translated in the King James version as 'He found him in a desert land and in the waste howling wilderness'. At Cîteaux the monks found their *heremum*, their desert or solitude, a word that evoked not only the biblical wilderness, but the eremitical origins of monasticism in the eastern deserts, and also the opening chapter of the Rule of St Benedict. The narrative in the *Exordium Cistercii* of the settlement of Cîteaux closes with the monks of the New Monastery binding themselves to stability, *firmantibus stabilitatem*,[13] that cornerstone of the Rule of St Benedict, thus firmly embedding Robert and his companions in a Benedictine tradition.

The *Exordium Cistercii* accordingly introduces what we might call three past models, those of apostolic poverty, the Rule, and the desert. Abbot Raynard, in condensing the narrative of Cîteaux's foundation for the *Exordium Cistercii*, evidently saw no reason to paint a picture of Molesme that was anything but good. The features which distinguished Cîteaux from Molesme were its location and its stress on poverty. Historians of the Cistercian order have always been struck forcefully by the difference in tone between the *Exordium Cistercii* and the *Exordium Parvum*, and we must remember that we are comparing one text, *Exordium Parvum*, which was in part a product of the first generation of monks at the New Monastery, with another produced after the death of Stephen Harding, the last abbot to have been a founder father of Cîteaux. The two texts are a generation apart, and a turbulent generation at that. Moreover, if Auberger and Waddell are correct in seeing the *Exordium Parvum* as a dual-layered compilation then we need to look at the nuances of both the primitive and the expanded text.

The primitive *Exordium Parvum*, which we may take to represent or reflect the earlier views on the main issues, is striking for the frequency with which it invokes the Rule of St Benedict. Indeed, it would not be overstating the case to describe the Rule as the dynamic around which the whole text is constructed. Here it does indeed stand in contrast to the *Exordium Cistercii*. The Rule is mentioned in seven of what Waddell sees as the thirteen chapters of the primitive *Exordium Parvum* and in three of the additional five chapters. Let us look first at the chapters deemed by Waddell to represent an early stage of composition, possibly

13 Ibid., 401.

two decades before the *Exordium Cistercii*. In chapter I the monks led by Robert of Molesme are said, without any particular nuance, to have wished to place their lives under the custody of the holy rule of Father Benedict.[14] In chapter II the language is somewhat stronger. The monks had stood before Archbishop Hugh of Lyons and, according to his letter had 'professed that you wished from then on to adhere more strictly and perfectly (*arctius deinceps atque perfectius*) to the Rule of the most blessed Benedict, which till then you had observed lukewarmly and negligently in that monastery'.[15] The same word, *arctus*, is employed in the letter of Archbishop Hugh of Lyons that forms chapter XII: the monks are said to have left Molesme for the sake of a stricter (*arctior*) and more secluded (*secretior*) life. At this point, despite the generally critical tone concerning Molesme, the author strikes a different note. The monks who left, he says, determined to observe the Rule of St Benedict 'having set aside the customs of certain monasteries – judging their frailty (*imbecillitas*) no match to bear with so great a burden'.[16] Here the decision to jettison the heavy liturgical burdens of contemporary monasticism is not expressed in terms of a return to the Rule, but in terms of the stamina of the monks themselves.

But what of those chapters that Waddell sees as much later additions, the work of Raynard du Bar? In chapter III the criticism of Molesme is raised a notch. This describes the departure of the monks from Molesme and their foundation of the New Monastery as the direct result of the failure of Molesme to observe the rule which amounted to perjury (*et ob hoc periurii crimen scienter incurisse*).[17] A key chapter in the *Exordium Parvum* is chapter XV, which Waddell sees as Abbot Raynard's summary of the capitula and statutes agreed by c.1147. Entitled 'The Institutes of the Monks of Cîteaux who came from Molesme', this lays out the ideology of the order in many aspects we have come to see as the distinguishing features of the White Monks.[18] Here the Rule is used in several ways. First, the Cistercians rejected everything that was seen directly to contravene the Rule in matters concerning food and drink and clothing, and determined to adhere to its regulations. This was implicitly critical of current monastic practices parodied so articulately some twenty-five years after the foundation of

14 Ibid., 418.
15 Ibid., 419.
16 Ibid., 430.
17 Ibid., 421.
18 Ibid., 434–7.

the New Monastery in Bernard of Clairvaux's *Apologia*. Second, there is an appeal to the Rule which in reality goes beyond the Rule, and largely derives from the Life of St Benedict by Gregory the Great. By invoking Benedict's life, chapter XV explains the decisions to ban certain types of revenue, to prevent women from entering monasteries, to exclude burials, to found monasteries in lone places, and to establish new foundations with the apostolic number of twelve monks and an abbot. Here the appeal is not to the Rule but to the man himself.[19] Third, chapter XV makes additions to the Rule to achieve what was seen as its spirit. Thus it records the decision to refuse to accept tithes on the grounds that it was inappropriate for monks to do so. It also records the important introduction of the *conversi*, or lay brothers, designed to preserve for the monks their way of life within the cloister 'for without the assistance of these they did not understand how they could fully observe the precepts of the Rule day and night'.[20]

Of the three manifestations of an appeal to earlier traditions mentioned above in connection with the *Exordium Cistercii,* one, the Rule of St Benedict, is dominant in the *Exordium Parvum*, and to the possible reasons for this I will return. The appeal to the desert tradition of monasticism is more muted. The words *heremum* and *solitudo* are used to describe the site of Cîteaux on several occasions, but the phrase from Deuteronomy, used in the *Exordium Cistercii*, which was to pass into Cistercian mythology and form the classic description of a Cistercian site, is not employed.[21] Raynard chose instead to characterize the location of the New Monastery as inaccessible to humans and inhabited by wild beasts. But there is another way in which the antithesis between Molesme and Cîteaux is expressed and that is in terms of the cenobitic and the eremitic. In chapter VI the author recorded Pope Urban II's order for the return of Robert from Cîteaux to Molesme, 'from the desert to the monastery' and that 'both those who love the desert live together there in quiet, and that those in the monastery observe the practices of the Rule'.[22]

19 Gregory the Great, *Dialogues*, Book II, conveniently translated by Myra L. Uhlfelder, *The Dialogues of Gregory the Great, Book Two, Saint Benedict* (Indianapolis, 1967). For Benedict's sister, Scholastica, and her burial in Benedict's monastery, see ibid., 42–4.

20 *Narrative and Legislative Texts*, 435.

21 For the phrase see, for instance, the *Narratio de Fundatione* of Fountains Abbey, printed in *Memorials of the Abbey of St Mary of Fountains*, I, ed. J. R. Walbran, Surtees Society 42 (1863), 2.

22 *Narrative and Legislative Texts*, 423.

What are we to make of the *Exordium Parvum*'s evocation of these past models? The shorter text, the *Exordium Cistercii* of c.1136, expresses none of the concerns, so prevalent in the *Exordium Parvum*, about the poor monastic observance at Molesme, and the failure fully to follow the Rule. It has become common to see the *Exordium Parvum*'s insistence that strict observance of the Rule was the dynamic behind the creation of the New Monastery as a response to criticism of the Cistercians concerning the way in which their monastery came into being as the result of schism.[23] Scholars who have taken chapter XVIII at face value, and dated the text to the early 1120s, have read it in a context of the emerging debate between the Cistercians and Cluniacs, the most famous salvo of which was Bernard's *Apologia*. They have seen the *Exordium Parvum*'s insistence that every aspect of the foundation of Cîteaux was canonical, or in accordance with the Rule, as the apologia of the second generation of Cistercian monks and as a defence against criticism that in abandoning Molesme the monks had also abandoned their Benedictine vow of stability. Constance Berman also sees a defensive tone but one which arose in an entirely different and much later context. She suggests that the *Exordium Parvum* may 'have been composed in response to growing criticism of the Cistercians, particularly a letter of Alexander III dated 1170' and that by the 1170s the *Exordium Parvum* had turned 'the simple familial language of the earlier *Exordium Cistercii* into a piece of rhetoric, a legal brief arguing for the legality of Cîteaux's secession from Molesme'.[24]

The conclusion of this line of argument is that whether the *Exordium Parvum* was written in the 1120s, the 1140s, or the 1170s, its deliberate emphasis on the Rule was a means of recreating or rewriting the origins of Cîteaux. Is this interpretation still tenable in the light of Waddell's hypothesis that the primitive version of the *Exordium Parvum* was composed by Stephen Harding c.1113? Waddell himself rightly points out that the fierce discord engendered by the departure of Abbot Robert from Molesme in 1098 had largely been settled by 1113. Moreover, this date is rather too early to see any real tension emerging between the White Monks and the Cluniacs. If the *Exordium Parvum* does indeed date from the beginning of the Cistercian expansion then its evidence suggests that we should see that desire to return to the Rule

23 See, for instance, Louis J. Lekai, 'The Rule and the Early Cistercians', *Cistercian Studies* 5 (1970), 243–51.

24 Berman, *Cistercian Evolution*, 9–23, esp. 10.

of St Benedict in its primitive form as the dynamic behind the actions of the monks, and not simply as a device employed as polemic or to rewrite origins. We still need, however, to take account of the more explicit criticism of Molesme especially in the additional chapters. This suggests that around 1147, when Raynard revised the *Exordium Parvum* and added chapter III, with its notorious accusation that the failure of Molesme to keep the Rule amounted to perjury, there was a perceived need for more forceful language. The ongoing debate between the Cistercians and the Cluniacs may indeed have brought with it a desire to avoid a charge that in leaving Molesme the monks had subverted a key principle of the Rule, *stabilitas*. I would argue that the *Exordium Parvum*, both in its primitive and in its expanded form, creates for the Cistercians in a way that the *Exordium Cistercii* does not the idea that the Cistercians were preservers and transmitters of the Rule in its strict form, and that in so doing the text records the reawakening of the values of the author of the Rule that motivated Robert and his companions. This was the emphasis in what Waddell sees as the primitive version of the *Exordium Parvum* and it was reinforced by Raynard du Bar through his additions to the text.

A key word to emerge from a study of the Cistercian narratives is *arctus*, the strict, or stricter, observance of the Rule.[25] Did the reputation of the Cistercians as 'strict' upholders of the Rule spread further than the confines of Cîteaux and the Cistercian world? Here it may be instructive to look at views expressed in non-Cistercian writing. Often overlooked in this context is William of Malmesbury's essay on the Cistercians, which from its reference to the archbishop of Vienne, *qui nunc apostolicus est*, was clearly written before 1124, before, that is, the Cistercians had made their first landfall on British soil.[26] That an English Benedictine monk could write with confidence about the Cistercians speaks volumes about contacts between their monasteries and the English Church by the third decade of the twelfth century.[27]

25 On the significance of the word, see Leclercq, 'Intentions of the Founders', 90 and 101–1.

26 William of Malmesbury, *Gesta Regum Anglorum: the History of the English Kings*, ed. R. A. B. Mynors, R. M. Thomson, and M. Winterbottom, 2 vols (Oxford, 1998–9) [hereafter: *Gesta Regum*], 1: 576–85. The pope referred to is Calixtus II, who confirmed the *Carta Caritatis* in 1119. The editors of *Gesta Regum* note the accuracy of William's account of the Cistercians (2: 288–94).

27 Berman, *Cistercian Evolution*, 69, 101, discounts the witness of William of Malmesbury as evidence of the nature of the Cistercian order, stating that he wrote only of Cîteaux and

William's account of the origins of Cîteaux was coloured by his admiration for its third abbot, the Englishman Stephen Harding. William records how Stephen became a monk at Molesme, a monastery described as *novus* and *magnus*, where 'he easily recognized the basic elements of the Rule he had seen long ago'.[28] However, Stephen 'modestly' raised questions 'when other observances were set before him which he had neither read of in the Rule nor seen anywhere'. For William, then, the revival of the original spirit of the Rule was central to his understanding of Cistercian origins. According to his account the debate at Molesme was about the nature of the observance of the Rule of St Benedict, with Abbot Robert proposing 'that they should abandon superfluities and explore the very marrow of the Rule and nothing else' (*sententiam probaret supersedendum superfluis, solam medullam regulae uestigandum*). Ultimately this led to the secession of the abbot and eighteen monks 'declaring that it was not possible to maintain the purity of the Rule in a place where mounting wealth and overwhelming meals stifled even the spirit that fought against them' – and one may hear in this an echo of the *Exordium Cistercii*.[29] The description that William goes on to give of life at Cîteaux could almost have been drawn from the pages of the Rule, and his remark that they kept 'so closely to the Rule that they think it wrong to diverge by one letter, one iota' suggests a close familiarity with the sentiments if not the text of the *Exordium Parvum* and with the *Carta Caritatis*.[30] It would appear that by 1124 the Cistercians had acquired a reputation as upholders of the Rule that had spread to England. They were seen to hold to the Rule not just *arctius* but literally. One may recall here a similar description of the characteristics of Cistercian monasteries by another Benedictine monk, Orderic Vitalis.[31]

The description of a Cistercian community as one which by definition maintained a close observance of the Rule passed into later Cistercian historiography. The 'Life of Ailred of Rievaulx', written by

not of Cistercian monasteries, despite William's evidence that at the time of writing Stephen Harding had founded sixteen abbeys and begun seven more (*Gesta Regum*, 1: 583). The editors of *Gesta Regum* suggest that William's knowledge of the Cistercians came from a French Cistercian house, possibly L'Aumône (2: 291).

28 *Gesta Regum*, 1: 579.

29 Ibid., 1: 581; *Narrative and Legislative Texts*, 399–400.

30 *Gesta Regum*, 1: 580–3 ('ita regulae incubantes ut nec iota unum nec apicem pretereundum putent'); *Narrative and Legislative Texts*, 408–9 (*Summa Cartae Caritatis*), 444 (*Carta Caritatis Prior*).

31 *The Ecclesiastical History of Orderic Vitalis*, ed. and trans. M. Chibnall, 6 vols (Oxford, 1969–80), 4: 312–27.

Walter Daniel following Ailred's death in January 1167, clearly models the early community at Rievaulx on a monastery derived from the Rule. In an early chapter Walter puts in the mouth of a friend of Ailred a description of the infant community.

> A pound of bread, half a pint (*emina*) of drink, a dish of cabbage and one of beans make up their meal. If they sup, the remnants of the previous meal are put back on the table, except that fresh vegetables, if any are available, are served in the place of the two cooked dishes. They sleep girded, one to a bed, in cowl and tunic winter and summer alike. They have nothing to call their own; they do not even talk together, and no-one undertakes anything of his own volition. Their every occupation is begun, or changed, at the superior's nod. Great and small, wise and ignorant, all are governed by the one law, be it at table, in procession, at communion or in other observances and rites.[32]

This summary of the characteristics of the early Rievaulx community is derived from chapters 5, 6, 22, 33, 39, 40 and 42 of the Rule.

This was, of course, a retrospective, an account written in 1167 of an event, Ailred's conversion, that took place in 1134 two years after the foundation of Rievaulx. In other words the Life was written at a time when Cistercian historiography was developing but had not yet reached the heights in England that it would do forty years later. An even greater gap separates the events it describes from the composition of the most sophisticated of English Cistercian foundation narratives, the *Narratio de fundatione* of Fountains Abbey, begun by Hugh, monk of Kirkstall Abbey at the request of Abbot John of Fountains (1203–11).[33] It is now many years since Derek Baker tackled the question of the literary and documentary sources of the *Narratio*, and more recently Elizabeth Freeman has discussed its place in the Cistercian tradition of historical writing.[34] It is clear that although Hugh's preface suggested that his main source was the aged eyewitness Serlo, a monk of Kirkstall

32 Walter Daniel, *The Life of Ailred of Rievaulx*, ed. and trans. F. M. Powicke (London, 1950), 10–13, at 11–12. I have preferred the translation by P. Matarasso, *The Cistercian World: Monastic Writings of the Twelfth Century* (Harmondsworth, 1993), 153–4.

33 Printed in *Memorials of Fountains*, I.

34 L. G. D. Baker, 'The Genesis of English Cistercian Chronicles: the Foundation History of Fountains Abbey', 1, *Analecta Cisterciensia* 25 (1969), 14–41, and 2, *Analecta Cisterciensia* 31 (1975), 179–212; Elizabeth Freeman, *Narratives of a New Order: Cistercian Historical Writing in England, 1150–1220* (Turnhout, 2002), 151–68.

then approaching his one hundredth year, his account of the secession of a group of Benedictine monks from St Mary's Abbey, York, and the foundation of Fountains Abbey, took its inspiration from Cistercian sources such as the *Exordium Parvum*. The parallels are clear. The secession from St Mary's was provoked by the arrival of a group of monks from Bernard's abbey of Clairvaux en route to found the first Cistercian house in the north, Rievaulx. However, they merely fomented discontent within the York abbey caused by a failure to observe the Rule of St Benedict, by a desire to restore primitive Benedictine observances, and by the pull of the 'desert'.

> There were at that time in the monastery of York which is called St Mary's religious men walking in the way of the fathers, following without question the institutes that they had received from their elders. They lived in the manner and custom of the traditions of their fathers, honourably, under a Rule and an abbot, but far from the vow of their profession, far from the perfection of the discipline of the Cistercians. Some of them, having heard of the purity of the order were led by holy instinct to emulate them [the Cistercians]. Their consciences accused them of fulfilling their profession less than they should, and the example of others highlighted for them their own shortcomings . . .
>
> . . . It embarrassed them that they lived this side of perfection, that they had dwelt so long in the land of Moab, and had accepted a heritage beyond the river Jordan. The tumult of the world and the clamour of the city wearied them. They longed with great longing for the desert, for the labour of their hands, for the ways of the prophets.[35]

It may be tempting to dismiss the *Narratio* as designed to create a myth and a past for the English abbey that drew comparisons with the mother house of the order, and allowed Fountains to emerge as the English Cîteaux. But that concern for the Rule was indeed an important dynamic is reinforced by Bernard's letter to Abbot Richard and the monks of the newly founded monastery of Fountains praising their actions: 'you yourselves discovered whether or not it were safe for those who have vowed to observe the Holy Rule to remain in a stage below

[35] Latin text in *Memorials of Fountains*, I, 5–6, my translation. The reference to the land of Moab is to Josh. 13: 32, the division of the land of Canaan.

what is required by it'[36] – they were moved, in other words, by a desire to observe the Rule *arctius*.

A re-reading and re-assessment of the texts, then, suggests to me that we should not see the insistence on the Cistercians' observance of the Rule *arctius* merely as polemic discovered or invented either in the 1120s in the context of the growing debate between the Cistercians and the Cluniacs, or in the 1140s, or even in the 1170s, and recycled by the English Cistercians in the second half of the twelfth century. The Rule was a genuine role model, and the return to it a real attempt to revive what was seen as the spirit of primitive Benedictine monasticism. At the same time the Cistercian view of the Rule was not a static one. Too often critics have been inclined to take the Cistercians to task for creating rules, and then breaking them, and for holding themselves up as followers of the Rule while they selectively altered and modified it.[37] While it is true that the writings from both inside and outside the Cistercian order stress the role of the White Monks as the upholders of the Rule, they themselves saw that in order to maintain the spirit of the Rule, they would have to adapt it.

The more obvious ways in which the Cistercians made additions to the Rule lie in the constitutional arrangements laid down by the *Carta Caritatis* to maintain uniformity and promote *caritas*, and in the mechanisms for regulating the economic activities of Cistercian houses through the *conversi*. There is also clear evidence that the Cistercian insistence on the Rule was more about reinterpretation than literal restoration or revival and that they were adapting the Rule to suit the spirit of the age. One obvious example is the attitude to child oblates. This raised its head early in the growth of the order, when one Cistercian at least was forced to confront the issue. In 1119 Bernard, the young abbot of Clairvaux, wrote to Robert, often described as his nephew but probably his cousin, who had become a Cistercian. Robert then regretted his decision; his conscience evidently troubled him because he had been promised as a child by his parents to Cluny. Bernard, in a view that would be adopted as official Cistercian regulation, condemned the practice of offering children as oblates contained

36 'Professis siquidem sanctam Regulam, an citra eius puritatem sistere gradum tutum sit, ipsi sensistis': *Sancti Bernardi Opera*, ed. J. Leclercq and H. Rochais, vols 7 and 8, *Epistolae* (Rome, 1974–7), 7: 246–7 (letter 96), translated in *The Letters of St Bernard of Clairvaux*, trans. B. Scott James (London, 1953), 240–1 (letter 171).

37 However, see Lekai, 'Rule and the Early Cistercians', 248–51.

in chapter 59 of the Rule of St Benedict, but he did so by appealing to Benedict himself:

> Let them see and judge which has the most force: the vow a father makes on behalf of his son, or the vow a son makes on his own behalf, especially when it is a vow of something better. Let your servant and our law giver, Benedict, judge which is the more in order: a vow made for a child when it is too young to know anything about it, or the vow he afterwards makes for himself when he realizes and understands what he is doing, when he is of an age to speak for himself.[38]

Thus it was that the Cistercians turned their backs on one key chapter of the Rule that was not in harmony with twelfth-century attitudes.[39]

Some five years after he wrote this letter Bernard felt compelled, in his *Apologia*, to deny that he was criticizing other orders, and to condemn Cistercians who might be so doing. In the chapter 'Against Detractors' he insisted on the importance of following the spirit, rather than the letter, of the Rule. He is here addressing those Cistercians who criticize others.

> I have heard it said that you speak of yourselves as the only ones with any virtue, as holier than everyone else, and the only monks who live according to the Rule; as far as you are concerned other monks are simply transgressors.[40]

Bernard insists that no-one should pass judgement on another, contrary to the gospels and the epistles. But not all monks were satisfied with his answer.

> They retort: 'How can these monks be said the keep the Rule? They wear furs and they eat meat and fat. Every day they have three or four different dishes, which the Rule forbids, and they leave out the work it enjoins. Many points of their Rule they modify or extend or restrict as they like.' This is so; no one could deny it. But look at God's Rule, with which St Benedict's regula-

38 Letter 1, Leclercq and Rochais, eds, *Opera*, 7: 1–11, at 6; James, *Letters of St Bernard*, 1–10, at 6.

39 *Narrative and Legislative Texts, Instituta Generalis Capituli*, LXXX (361, 490). This fixed the minimum age for entry into the noviciate at fifteen. It was later raised to eighteen.

40 *Cistercians and Cluniacs: St Bernard's Apologia to Abbot William*, trans. Michael Casey, Cistercian Publications (Kalamazoo, MI, 1970), 45–52, at 45.

> tions agree. It says that 'the kingdom of God is within you', it does not consist in outward things like bodily clothing and food, but in man's interior virtues ... You cast aspersions on the Fathers because of mere outward observances, while you yourself don't bother about the more important spiritual regulations laid down by the Rule. You gulp down the camel and strain out the gnat. How absurd! Great care is taken to see that the body is clothed according to the Rule, whilst the Rule is broken by leaving the soul naked.[41]

Bernard is not, of course, excusing infractions of the Rule, and in the *Apologia* he goes on in a typically robust way to condemn what he sees as manifestations of a decline in observances that would have shocked the great abbots of Cluny as much as anyone. However, in the passage I have just quoted, he is both inveighing against monks judging others, and setting the spiritual against the bodily. To the detractor he states: 'If you think that all those who make profession of the Rule are obliged to keep it literally without any possibility of dispensation, then I dare say you fail as much as the Cluniac'.[42] For Bernard, then, the Rule is to be followed in spirit as much as to the letter.

The same need for adaptation appears in the writings of Ailred of Rievaulx. In the final chapters of *The Mirror of Charity* Ailred turns to musings on the monastic life, prompted by a letter whose author has indicated what, for him, were the essentials of monastic life, that is, stability, conversion of life, and obedience according to the Rule of St Benedict.[43] This is what the unnamed correspondent called the 'essential character' of the monastic profession, as distinct from the practices which sustain it. Ailred admits that what his correspondent describes as those practices – manual work, the quantity of food and drink and so on – can be changed and dispensations allowed. However, Ailred's view of what can be adapted includes even the 'essential character or body' of the monastic life. He argues that even the concept of stability can be modified, for Benedict himself sent Maur to Gaul without compromising his profession, and

> How often monks are transferred by a dispensation from their

41 Ibid., 46–8.

42 Ibid., 50.

43 Aelred of Rievaulx, *The Mirror of Charity*, trans. Elizabeth Connor, Cistercian Fathers Series 17 (Kalamazoo, MI, 1990), III, 35 (279–87).

> abbots, I do not say from monastery to monastery but even from region to region. How then can stability of place susceptible to such frequent dispensations pertain to the body of our Rule and the essential character of monastic profession?[44]

It is clear that for Ailred, as for Bernard, the significance of the Rule lay less in its literal interpretation than in what it represented about the resurgence of the spirit of primitive monasticism. The image articulated in the *Exordium Parvum* and in non-Cistercian texts such as the *Gesta Regum* was one of the Cistercians living strictly according to the Rule. The Rule of St Benedict was clearly of paramount importance to the Cistercians, not only in the way they interpreted the monastic life, but also in their construction of their self image. However, this view needs to be modified in so far as we should recognize that the White Monks themselves admitted that modification might be necessary. They saw in their way of life a restoration of early practice overlaid with concerns for current conditions.

But what of the other indelible image associated with the Cistercians, that of the 'return to the desert' that characterized a number of contemporary movements of the eleventh and twelfth centuries? The Rule of St Benedict itself provides a link with the desert origins of the monastic life, since chapter I articulates Benedict's view that the cenobium, that is, the community, provides the training ground or apprenticeship for the 'solitary combat of the desert'. The Cistercians' own narratives provide powerful evidence on which have been constructed views of the desert associations of the White Monks. As we have seen, the *Exordium Parvum* uses the word *heremum*, that is, desert place, or solitude, to describe the location of the New Monastery, while *Exordium Cistercii* prefers *locum horroris et vastae solitudinis*. The 'Cistercian Institutes' laid down that Cistercian abbeys were not to be built 'in cities, walled towns, villages, but in places removed from human habitation'.[45] The Benedictine monk Orderic Vitalis also understood the secluded nature of Cistercian abbeys when he wrote that 'they have built monasteries with their own hands in lonely wooded places'.[46]

Critics from the twelfth century onwards have accused the Cisterc-

44 Ibid., 282.

45 *Narrative and Legislative Texts*, 408 (*Capitula*), 435 (*Exordium Parvum*), 458 (*Instituta*).

46 Orderic Vitalis, *Ecclesiastical History*, ed. and trans. Chibnall, 4: 327.

ians of using the desert as a myth, both to create an image that was far from reality and to justify the dispossession or relocation of population to create the desert. As the satirist Walter Map put it:

> It is prescribed to them that they are to dwell in desert places, and desert places they do assuredly either find or make . . . they make a solitude that they may be solitaries.[47]

However the desert was not just about physical location. The phrase served two purposes in Cistercian historiography. It served as a link with the founders of monasticism, thus stressing the authentic tradition followed by the Cistercians, and it helped to foster the spiritual or psychological desert which the Cistercians sought in isolating themselves from the world. In Book I of the *Vita Prima* of Bernard, William of St Thierry described his visits to Clairvaux:

> Unworthy though I was, I spent a few days with him [Bernard], and wherever I turned my eyes I was amazed to see as it were a new heaven and a new earth, and the well-worn path trodden by the monks of old, our fathers out of Egypt, bearing the footprints left by men of our own time . . . The first impression of those approaching Clairvaux down the steep scarp was of God's presence in the little huddle of houses, for the dumb valley itself proclaimed, through the poverty and humility of the buildings, that of Christ's poor whose dwelling place they were . . . There was a sense in which the solitude of that valley, strangled and overshadowed by its thickly wooded hills, in which God's servants lived their hidden lives, stood for the cave in which our father St Benedict was once discovered by shepherds – the sense in which those who were patterning their lives on his could be said to be living in a kind of solitude. They were indeed a crowd of solitaries. Under the rule of love ordered by reason, the valley became a desert for each of the many men who dwelt there.[48]

Cistercian writers further evoked the desert by calling on the names of the earliest monks. When in the *Apologia* he condemned excess Bernard appealed to a pre-Benedictine tradition: 'Long ago, when the monastic

47 Walter Map, *De Nugis Curialium: Courtiers' Trifles*, rev. edn C. N. L. Brooke and R. A. B. Mynors (Oxford, 1983), 92–3.

48 Translated in Matarasso, *The Cistercian World*, 30–1. For St Benedict, his cave, and the shepherds who found him there, see Uhlfelder, *Dialogues of Gregory the Great*, 4–6.

Order began, who would have dreamed that monks could become so slack? Oh, how far away we have moved from Anthony and his contemporaries!'[49] And of monks who sought dispensation on the grounds of sickness he wrote: 'Is this the way Macarius lived? Is it Basil's teaching or Anthony's command? Did the fathers in Egypt adopt such a manner of life?'[50] It was not just the desert places sought by the Cistercians that linked them to the founders of the monastic life, but the very evocation of their names.

The witness of texts, both Cistercian and non-Cistercian, argues that the Rule of St Benedict and the desert were twin planks of Cistercian notions of renewal and revival, though the renewal of the Rule was seen both in terms of strict or stricter (*arctus/arctior*) interpretation and a revival of what was seen as its spirit even at the expense of the letter of the Rule. However there was a third dynamic to Cistercian growth, a return to evangelical or apostolic poverty. As we have seen, Cistercian texts stress that poverty was a feature of early Cîteaux, in contrast to the prosperous Molesme, and make clear that monastic virtue and wealth were not easily reconciled. One way in which this poverty was manifest was in the austerity of Cistercian buildings, the *Exordium Parvum*'s 'wooden monastery' at early Cîteaux, and the huddle of buildings at Clairvaux evoked, nostalgically perhaps, by William of St Thierry. However, as early as 1124 William of Malmesbury noted as a feature of Stephen Harding's abbacy that he gave any surplus income to the poor or used it on building further monasteries:

> It is an index of his self-denial that in those houses (*ibi*) you nowhere see, as you do in other monasteries, the glitter of gold or flashing gems or gleaming silver; for as the pagan poet says, 'To what purpose gold in holy places?' The rest of us think our sacred vessels fall short unless a solid sheet of precious metal is outshone by glorious gems . . . But the Cistercians (*illi*) put in second place what other mortals wrongly think most important; their efforts are all spent on the adornment of the character and they prefer pure minds to gold-embroidered vestments, knowing that the best return for a life well spent is the enjoyment of a clear conscience.[51]

William here accurately captured the sentiments of chapter XVII of the

49 *Apologia*, 54.
50 Ibid., 58–9.
51 *Gesta Regum*, I: 584–5.

Exordium Parvum, the institutes or practices said to have been introduced by Stephen Harding, and anticipated the strictures of Bernard's *Apologia* on matters artistic and architectural.[52] Bernard himself was echoed by Ailred in his *Mirror of Charity*.

> Outward curiosity concerns all the superfluous beauty which the eyes like in various forms, in bright and pleasing colors, different kinds of workmanship, clothing, shoes, vases, pictures, statues, or various creations exceeding necessary and moderate utility – all those things which people who love the world seek out to attract the eyes . . . So it is that even in the cloisters of monks you will find cranes and hares, does and stags, magpies and ravens – which are certainly not means used by Anthony and Macarius, but effeminate amusements. None of these things are at all expedient for the poverty of monks, but feed the eyes of the curious.[53]

Those who are attracted by these sights rather than by the poverty of Jesus find only mental anguish, and this thought leads Ailred to an exposition on humility and the need for contemplation on biblical texts which was at the heart of the monastic life.

The Cistercian story continues to intrigue and to invite debate. The sources are rich and complex and do not admit of easy interpretation. However, the paradox remains. The Cistercians created something new: an ecclesiastical organization that was held together through the mechanisms of annual visitation and the general chapter, that insisted on uniformity in all things, and that overrode political boundaries. Yet the novelty of the Cistercian adventure was rooted in the revival of what they claimed to be primitive monasticism, and the evocation of past models, harnessed to their current concerns.

University of Wales, Lampeter

52 *Narrative and Legislative Texts*, 438; *Apologia*, 63–6.
53 Ailred, *Mirror of Charity*, II, 24 (212–15, at 212).

SAINT FRANCIS OF ASSISI'S REPAIR OF THE CHURCH

by ANNE KIRKHAM

AROUND 1230 Burchard of Ursperg, a Premonstratensian canon, writing about the Fourth Lateran Council (1215), reported that 'with the world already growing old, two religious orders arose in the Church – whose youth is renewed like the eagle's'.[1] The success of the Franciscans in contributing to what Burchard saw as the renewal of the Church's youth was simultaneously assisted and celebrated by documenting the life of the founder, Francis (1182–1226), in words and images soon after his death and throughout the thirteenth century.[2] Within these representations, the pivotal event in securing Francis's religious 'conversion' was his encounter with the decaying church of San Damiano outside Assisi. His association with the actual repair of churches in the written and pictorial accounts of his life was a potent allegorical image to signal the revival of the Church and the role of Francis and his followers in this. This essay focuses on how references to the repair of churches were used to call attention to the role of the Franciscans in the revival of the Church in the thirteenth century.

The problems of the Church and the papacy in the late twelfth and early thirteenth centuries are well documented: conflict with the Holy Roman Emperor, heresy, the loss of Jerusalem and threats from Mongols and Muslims, internal strife, and antipathy directed at the inadequacies of the secular clergy.[3] In this context Michael Goodich

1 Quoted in Lester K. Little, *Religious Poverty and the Profit Economy in Medieval Europe* (New York, 1978), 167. The orders were the Franciscans and the Dominicans. I am grateful to my session chair at the EHS Summer Meeting, Prof. R. N. Swanson, and my research supervisor, Dr Cordelia Warr, for their comments which have contributed greatly to the development of this paper.

2 Thomas of Celano's first *Life* of Francis was written in 1229. Celano wrote a second version in 1244–6 and Bonaventure's *Legenda Maior* was written in 1263. Scenes from Francis's life in glass at the Barfüßerkirche, Erfurt have been dated to 1230–5 (see Erhard Drachenberg, *Mittelalterliche Glasmalerei in Erfurt* (Dresden, 1990), 30–4) and the *Berlinghieri Dossal* in San Francesco, Pescia is dated 1235.

3 The problems of the Church/papacy in this period have been widely studied; my indicative list draws on Michael Goodich, 'The Politics of Canonization in the Thirteenth Century: Lay and Mendicant Saints', *Church History* 44 (1975), 294–307, at 294, Colin Morris,

credits Innocent III (1198–1216), Gregory IX (1227–41) and Innocent IV (1243–54) with launching 'a major offensive aimed at both spiritual renewal and organisational efficiency.'[4] The measures included centralizing church bureaucracy, codifying canon law, reducing episcopal power, founding schools and universities, approving mendicant orders and exploiting saints' cults.[5]

These last two measures show how the popes were able to turn potential threats into strengths. Unofficial religious groups led by charismatic, often radical, preachers and the proliferation of saints' cults threatened to destabilize church authority.[6] In approving the Franciscans (1210) and Dominicans (1216) the papacy harnessed to itself the spiritual leadership and flair in preaching displayed by certain of the unofficial religious groups.[7] Bonded to the pope, they became new leaders in the spiritual and pastoral care of the laity whilst countering the appeal of dissident, and even heretical, religious groups.[8] In 1234, Gregory IX asserted formal papal control over canonizations. In reserving to the papacy the conferment of sainthood, Gregory IX was able to exploit the popularity of saints' cults by canonizing those supportive of Rome. That he had already canonized Francis in 1228 and Dominic in 1233 underlines the importance to the papacy of their orders.

The reality was that the popes needed the approved mendicant orders to lead the spiritual revival of the Church, but, with an itinerant lifestyle resembling certain heretical movements, the orders needed the popes' continued support of their irregular religious life. For this relationship to prosper, its messages needed to be communicated. This could be effected through the use of 'images' of Francis repairing or supporting a church. I will begin by considering images concerned with the repair of churches in the fresco cycle depicting the life of Francis in

The Papal Monarchy (Oxford, 1989), 413, and C. H. Lawrence, *The Friars: the Impact of the Early Mendicant Movement on Western Society* (London and New York, 1994), 3 and 7.

4 Goodich, 'Politics of Canonization', 294.

5 Ibid.

6 Lawrence, *The Friars*, 19–25, and A. M. Kleinberg, *Prophets in Their Own Country: Living Saints and the Making of Sainthood in the Later Middle Ages* (Chicago, IL and London, 1992), 24.

7 Little, *Religious Poverty*, 167–9.

8 The role of the two main mendicant orders in the revival of the Church in the thirteenth century has been extensively examined. See Lawrence, *The Friars*, J. R. H. Moorman, *A History of the Franciscan Order* (Oxford, 1968), D. Nimmo, *Reform and Division in the Franciscan Order 1226–1538* (Rome, 1987), and W. A. Hinnebusch, *The History of the Dominican Order*, 2 vols (New York, 1966 and 1972).

the Upper Church at San Francesco, Assisi, the mother-church of the Franciscans.[9]

The cycle of twenty-eight frescoes begins on the north wall of the nave, continues with a single fresco on each side of the east entrance to the church, and finishes on the south wall. On the north and south walls the frescoes are organized into groups of three or four within the architectural bays. Whilst the cycle depicts key events from throughout Francis's life and death, the grouping of the frescoes sub-divides Francis's life into themes so that the viewing of three, or four, images together reinforces particular messages which the cycle contains.[10] A similar thematic device is also found in the structure of the written chapters of Bonaventure's life of St Francis known as the *Legenda Maior*.[11]

The theme of the second group of three frescoes on the north wall of the nave is Francis's repair of the Church. In the first fresco on the left [fig. 1] there is a church with parts of its roof and walls missing. Inside this damaged church Francis, in prosperous civilian dress, prays before an image of Christ on the Cross. In the central fresco [fig. 2] Francis, having handed back his clothes to his father, stands on the right with the bishop and clerics whilst his appalled family and friends stand to the left. In the final fresco of this group [fig. 3], to the left of Pope Innocent III, is a representation of the Pope's dream of Francis, now in a Franciscan habit, holding up the Lateran church. The church leans slightly to the right and Francis's hand and shoulder are pressed to the roof of the portico, though otherwise the church appears intact.

Although questions over the dating of this cycle have not been resolved, there is general agreement that the source of the cycle is the *Legenda Maior* which provides a *terminus post quem* of around 1263.[12] In

9 San Francesco was founded in 1228 and substantially complete by 1239, but its decoration continued throughout the thirteenth century. See John White, *Art and Architecture in Italy 1250–1400* (3rd edn, New Haven, CT and London, 1993), 21–4 and 175–224.

10 Alastair Smart, *The Assisi Problem and the Art of Giotto* (Oxford, 1971), 18–19.

11 Bonaventure, *The Soul's Journey into God; The Tree of Life; The Life of St. Francis*, trans. Ewart Cousins (London, 1978), 183–4 [hereafter: Bonaventure, *Legenda Maior*]. The themes of the grouped frescoes do not correspond precisely to those of Bonaventure's chapters.

12 Smart, *Assisi Problem*, 5. Peter Murray states that an inscription on the 'Dream of Innocent III' is from the *Legenda Maior* in 'Notes on some Early Giotto Sources', *Journal of the Warburg and Courtauld Institutes* 16 (1953), 58–80, at 72. See also Millard Meiss, *Giotto and Assisi* (New York, 1960), Luciano Bellosi, *La Pecora di Giotto* (Turin, 1985), 9–14, White, *Art and Architecture*, 207–24, and B. Zanardi, *Il cantiere di Giotto: le storie di San Francesco ad Assisi* (Milan, 1996).

Fig. 1. St Francis Praying in the Church of San Damiano (fresco)/
San Francesco, Upper Church, Assisi, Italy,
Giraudon / The Bridgeman Art Library

Fig. 2. St Francis Renounces his Father's Goods and Earthly Wealth (fresco)/ San Francesco, Upper Church, Assisi, Italy, Giraudon / The Bridgeman Art Library

Fig. 3. The Dream of Innocent III (fresco)/ San Francesco, Upper Church, Assisi, Italy, Giraudon / The Bridgeman Art Library

the *Legenda Maior* the church with damaged roof and walls is identified as San Damiano where, according to Bonaventure, the painted icon of Christ commanded Francis to 'go and repair my house which, as you see, is falling completely into ruin.'[13] Bonaventure recounts that following this sign from God Francis spurned his family by returning to them his wealth, including his clothes.[14] Francis then embarked on a religious life and attracted followers to him. After a few years he journeyed to Rome and, following Francis's first meeting with the pope, the pope saw in a dream 'that a little poor man, insignificant and despised, was holding up on his back the Lateran basilica which was about to collapse'.[15]

In the written *Lives* Francis's association with the repair of churches is prominent. The episodes found in Bonaventure's *Legenda Maior* and referred to as the 'Speaking crucifix of San Damiano', which bids Francis to repair God's house, and the 'Dream of Innocent III', in which Francis supports the Lateran, are already present in Thomas of Celano's second *Life* of the saint (1244–6), although they are not in his first *Life* (1229).[16] In Celano's first *Life* Francis, who has already been receiving religious visions, comes across San Damiano and is moved by its threatened collapse from age. He urges money on its priest, convincing the priest of his sincerity by praying earnestly.[17] Although there is no speaking crucifix in this early version of Francis's life, it is after this encounter with the decaying church of San Damiano that Francis renounces his family and fortune and embarks on his religious life.

In this first *Life* Francis's encounter with and repair of San Damiano is followed by references to his repair of another dilapidated church close to Assisi and of the ruined Santa Maria in Portiuncula. Since this account was written within ten years of his death, and thus when witnesses were certainly available, it suggests that Francis was involved in some capacity with their actual repair and that the account has a literal basis. In the Middle Ages church buildings were constantly being built, repaired and refashioned. One well-known account is that of the monk Rodulfus Glaber who suggests that relief at surviving the first

13 Bonaventure, *Legenda Maior*, 191.

14 Ibid., 193.

15 Ibid., 206.

16 Thomas of Celano, *The Lives of S. Francis of Assisi*, trans. A. G. Ferrers Howell, (London, 1908) [hereafter: Celano, first *Life* and Celano, second *Life*], 154 and 162.

17 Celano, first *Life*, 10–11.

millennium and an enthusiasm for renewal at the beginning of the second millennium prompted an excess of church building. He writes, '. . . especially in Italy and Gaul, men began to reconstruct churches, although for the most part the existing ones were properly built and not in the least unworthy.' Moreover, this activity covered the whole spectrum of churches: 'Almost all the Episcopal churches . . . monasteries . . . and little village chapels.'[18]

It is not easy to put together a 'condition survey' of church buildings for each century of the Middle Ages, but there is evidence that the reforms underpinning the Church's revival in the thirteenth century were part of a virtuous circle which promoted repairs and improvements to church buildings as well as the building of new churches. Colin Morris writes of the thirteenth century that for 'the reforming bishops the parish church was the keystone to ecclesiastical discipline'.[19] Morris believes that architectural evidence throughout Europe demonstrates wide-spread building activity in local churches in the first half of the thirteenth century and by 1250 'the nature of the church's presence in the countryside had greatly changed. In almost every district there were more parish churches . . . and they were even larger, better built, with a more numerous staff of clergy.'[20] Thus it is certainly plausible to suggest that Francis was involved in the physical repair of churches.

But it is also clear that the repair of churches in Celano's first *Life* was intended to be read allegorically. According to Celano

> the first work which blessed Francis undertook after having been delivered from the hand of his carnal father was to build a house for God: but he did not try to build it anew, rather did he repair the old and restore the ancient; he pulled not up the foundation, but built upon it, ever (though unwittingly) respecting Christ's prerogative, for 'other foundation can no one lay than that which hath been laid, which is Christ Jesus.'[21]

So Celano emphasizes Francis's mission as one of restoration, and that the restoration points beyond the material referent of the ageing physical church of San Damiano to the institution of the Church,

18 Rodulfus Glaber, *Historiarum Libri Quinque*, ed. and trans. John France (Oxford, 1989), 115–17.

19 Morris, *Papal Monarchy*, 536.

20 Ibid., 538–9.

21 Celano, first *Life*, 19.

whose foundation was laid by Christ. It also points associatively to the authority vested in Peter by Christ as recounted in Matthew's Gospel, 'That thou art Peter, and upon this rock I will build my church; and the gates of hell shall not prevail against it. And I will give unto thee the keys of the kingdom of heaven.'[22] Thus this first *Life* establishes the allegorical force of Francis tending to the Church founded by Christ and given by Christ into the guardianship of Peter and his papal successors.

This imagery is extended in Celano's second *Life* and in Bonaventure's *Legenda Maior*. Bonaventure follows Celano's second *Life* closely in his account of Francis's experience at San Damiano[23] but the exhortation of the speaking crucifix to 'go and repair my house' is, significantly, repeated three times in Bonaventure's account.[24] Bonaventure explains that Francis resolves to repair the church materially but also understands that the principal intention of the command related to the institution of the Church and the spiritual practice of Christianity.[25] Bonaventure utilizes the repair of the three churches already recounted in Celano's first *Life* to underline the tripartite nature of the reforms Francis undertook on behalf of the institutional Church. As if in answer to the icon's thrice repeated instruction to make repairs Bonaventure explains, 'For like the three buildings he repaired, so Christ's Church . . . was to be renewed under his leadership in three ways: by the structure, rule and teaching which he would provide.'[26]

In their explanations that the signs which Francis receives from God carry a message other than, though not excluding, a literal one, Celano and Bonaventure access the familiarity with symbolism whereby medieval society was accustomed to interpret the world on a number of levels.[27] There was a long-established set of symbolic associations attached to the Church found, for example, in the writing of Hugh of St-Victor (c.1096–1141) and William Durandus (c.1220–96). Hugh's *Mystical Mirror of the Church* begins:

22 Matt. 16: 18–19.
23 Celano, second *Life*, 153–4.
24 Bonaventure, *Legenda Maior*, 191.
25 Ibid., 191–2.
26 Ibid., 197–8.
27 On the medieval attitude of symbolism, see H. F. Dunbar, *Symbolism in Medieval Thought and its Consummation in the 'Divine Comedy'* (New York, 1961).

> The material church signifieth the Holy Catholick Church, which is builded in the heavens of living stones. . . . All the stones be polished and square; that is, all the Saints be pure and firm: the which also be placed so as to last forever by the hands of the Chief Workman.[28]

This is typical of the explanations of symbolism in the treatise. Here saints are identified as the building blocks of the Church and are connected to its eternal nature. This sanctions and encourages the association of saints with building churches and with the Church. This is apparent in medieval images of saints holding the model of a church as attribute, or of saints participating in building a church. Images of Francis tending to decaying churches extended this iconography.

Durandus identifies the material church as a symbol of the Church Militant (the Church on earth struggling against evil), of the Church Triumphant (that has overcome the world and exists as the Holy Jerusalem) and of the body of Christ.[29] These interpretations emphasize the sacrosanct integrity of the church, whether by reference to the institutional Church or to Christ's body, and the familiarity of such powerful symbolic associations made the imagery of Francis's repair of the church particularly potent.

The art of the Franciscans uses the familiarity with symbolism to present what Bonaventure termed 'the principal intention of the words' about repairing the church.[30] The visual retelling of Francis's involvement with churches in disrepair in the tightly composed group of three images within the Assisi cycle is strikingly effective in announcing its allegorical message. The decaying state of San Damiano, which permits us to see Francis praying before the crucifix through the missing walls, suggests the need for repair and so we understand this as the message of the crucifix. However, Francis's response is to renounce the very means – his wealthy family and merchant career – by which he could have effected the physical repair of the church, thus requiring an interpretation that is not, or not only, concerned with the material fabric of the church.[31] In Francis's response to the plea of the crucifix for repair a

28 From a translation of the prologue of Hugh of St-Victor's *Mystical Mirror of the Church* included in William Durandus, *The Symbolism of Churches and Church Ornaments*, trans. J. M. Neale and B. Webb (Leeds, 1843), 198.

29 Durandus, *Symbolism of Churches*, 18–19.

30 Bonaventure, *Legenda Maior*, 191.

31 In Celano's first *Life* Francis's initial response to the parlous state of San Damiano is to

problem with the Church itself is adduced. The Church is broken, damaged, in need of restoration, and Francis stands with the officials of the Church as remedy. He stands under the protection of the bishop, the protection underlined by the cloth the bishop holds around Francis's naked body.[32] That the mission of his conversion to a religious life is to support and promote the orthodoxy of the Church and papal authority is made even more apparent in the third image where Francis keeps the leaning church from falling. This group of three frescoes uses images of churches in disrepair (the material referent) as a forceful sign of problems perceived within the Church (of which actual churches in disrepair may have been a symptom) and the Franciscans' role in their remedy.

The symbiotic relationship of the papacy and the Franciscans was particularly well illustrated by the 'Dream of Innocent III'.[33] The earliest surviving depiction of the scene is in a severely damaged fresco in the Lower Church at San Francesco, Assisi.[34] Possibly painted before the church's consecration in 1253, it is one of five scenes from the saint's life which Chiara Frugoni has argued were carefully selected by the Franciscans to convey the messages they wished – perhaps in conjunction with the papacy – to promote at the mother-church.[35] In the 1280s the scene is included in a fresco cycle at San Francesco, Gubbio.[36] The earliest known panel including this episode is an eight-scene dossal, dated to c.1280–90, by Guido di Graziano now in the Pinacoteca, Siena, but formerly at San Francesco, Colle Val d'Elsa.[37] Around 1300 it was included in the Upper Church fresco cycle, and in a window, at San Francesco, Assisi,[38] in the fresco cycle at San Francesco, Pistoia (bearing a close correspondence to the image at

urge money on the priest, but Francis then considers this response inadequate leading to his 'conversion', 10–11.

32 Francis's nakedness is discussed in Richard C. Trexler, *Naked Before the Father: the Renunciation of Francis of Assisi* (New York, 1989).

33 The special nature of the relationship between Innocent III and the Franciscans is underlined in Brenda Bolton, '*Via ascetica*: a Papal Quandary?', in W. J. Sheils, ed., *Monks, Hermits and the Ascetic Tradition*, SCH 22 (Oxford, 1985), 161–91, at 188–91.

34 Louise Bourdua, *The Franciscans and Art Patronage in Late Medieval Italy* (Cambridge, 2004), 2.

35 Ibid., 2–3. Chiara Frugoni, *Francesco e l'invenzione delle stimmate* (Turin, 1993), 283–93.

36 Bourdua, *Franciscans*, 3.

37 Murray, 'Giotto Sources', 71. A later date is proposed by James H. Stubblebine, *Guido da Siena* (Princeton, NJ, 1964), 107–9.

38 Murray, 'Giotto Sources', 71–2.

Assisi) and in a small scene below the main image of Francis's stigmatization in the *Louvre Stigmatization* signed by Giotto [fig. 4].[39] This shows Francis applying apparently casual support to the church; one column at the front of the portico is fractured, although, as in the Assisi fresco, the structure appears largely intact.

Although generalizations about 'patterns' in medieval art are prone to distortions owing to the precariousness of the survival of medieval art, or of reliable accounts of the same, the 'Dream of Innocent III' appears to gain popularity in the late thirteenth century. Why? The preference for posthumous miracles on the earliest Franciscan cycles is in keeping with the emphasis on miracles in imagery used to promote saints' cults.[40] J. R. H. Moorman suggests that only later in the thirteenth century did artists move away from representations of Francis the 'wonder-worker' to concentrate on the important events of his life.[41] One factor in this may have been that, despite their mutual need of each other, for much of the thirteenth century relations between the papacy and the Order were not straightforward.

Despite the 'Dream of Innocent III' in which Francis supports the falling Lateran being critical to the success of Francis's petition for approval of the Order in both Celano's second *Life* and the *Legenda Maior*, Jacques Le Goff suggests that the pope had placed limitations on the approval (1210), and that both the pope and Francis and his followers retained misgivings about the nature of the agreement between them.[42] However, in the 1240s the mendicants came under increasing pressure from what C. H. Lawrence describes as 'a hardening of attitude on the part of the secular clergy [which] increasingly debarred friars from using parish churches for preaching.'[43] By the 1250s their need of the pope's protection was intensified by attacks from the academic wing of the secular clergy. In 1253 the mendicants were expelled from the university in Paris for failing to co-operate in action protesting against violent attacks on students by city officials. Although the expulsion was overturned by Alexander IV in 1255, this challenge to the mendicants' authority, powerfully led by William of

39 Julian Gardner, 'The "Louvre Stigmatization" and the Problem of the Narrative Altarpiece', *Zeitschrift fur Kunstgeschicte* 45 (1982), 217–47.

40 Bourdua, *Franciscans*, 2.

41 J. R. H. Moorman, *Early Franciscan Art and Literature* (Manchester, 1943), 353.

42 Jacques Le Goff, *Saint Francis of Assisi*, trans. Christine Rhone (London and New York, 2004), 31–5.

43 Lawrence, *The Friars*, 109.

Fig. 4. The Vision of Pope Innocent III, c.1295–1300 (tempera on panel), Giotto/ Louvre, Paris, France, Giraudon / The Bridgeman Art Library

Saint-Amour, persisted.[44] It is thus possible to see the inclusion of Innocent III's dream in Celano's second *Life* and the *Legenda Maior*, and then gaining popularity in visual cycles, as emphasizing Franciscan orthodoxy and their importance to the papacy in its reform of the Church in response to increasing opposition to the Order beginning in the 1240s.

Certainly the bond between the papacy and the Order was strong in the later thirteenth and early fourteenth century.[45] The first Franciscan Pope Nicholas IV (1288–92) was particularly supportive of San Francesco, Assisi, presenting it with two pieces of precious metalwork.[46] And perhaps his action in explicitly linking his restoration of the Lateran with the 'Dream of Innocent III' in an inscription at the Lateran[47] increased the popularity of the image in the following decades. Julian Gardner makes a strong case for identifying the representation of the Lateran on the *Louvre Stigmatization* as Nicholas IV's rebuilt Lateran, and Peter Murray and John White point to the refurbished portico as identifying the rebuilt Lateran in the Upper Church cycle at Assisi.[48]

One of the most telling pieces of evidence about the importance of the image is its adoption by the Dominicans. In connection with Dominic (1170–1221) the episode of the pope's dream is first recorded in Constantine of Orvieto's *Life* of St Dominic (c.1246–47) soon after its first appearance in connection with Francis in Celano's second *Life*.[49] Joanna Cannon has suggested that the association of the episode with Dominic borrows textually and visually from Franciscan sources.[50] On Nicola Pisano's sculpted *Arca di San Domenico* (1265–67) in San Francesco, Bologna, Dominic faces the viewer with his back pressed up against a church. A late thirteenth or early fourteeenth century panel now in the Museo Nazionale di Capodimonte, Naples, depicts Dominic, to the right of the slumbering pope, effortlessly lifting up one

44 Ibid., 154–9.

45 Gardner, 'Louvre Stigmatisation', 229.

46 Julian Gardner, 'Pope Nicholas IV and the Decoration of Santa Maria Maggiore', *Zeitschrift fur Kunstgeschicte* 36 (1973), 1–50, at 1.

47 Gardner, 'Louvre Stigmatisation', 230.

48 Ibid., 228, Murray, 'Giotto Sources', 72, White, *Art and Architecture*, 220.

49 Michael Goodich, 'Vision, Dream and Canonization Policy under Pope Innocent III', in J. C. Moore, ed., *Pope Innocent III and his World* (Aldershot, 1999), 151–63, at 152.

50 Joanna Cannon, 'Dominic *Alter Christus*? Representations of the Founder in and after the *Arca di San Domenico*', in K. Emery and J. Warykow, eds, *Christ Among the Medieval Dominicans* (Notre Dame, IN, 1998), 26–48, at 31.

end of an apparently undamaged church. On the *Saint Dominic Altarpiece* (1345) painted by Francesco Traini for Santa Caterina, Pisa (now in the Museo Nazionale, Pisa), the fracture half way up the wall of the church is pronounced and Dominic's effort in supporting the upper part of the building is more evident, yet the church is deficient only in respect of the fracture: its roof is fully tiled and the walls otherwise complete.

The image was shared by both saints because their orders were exceptionally supported by the papacy in the mission to reassert religious orthodoxy and spirituality. It seems to be a feature of the images that the imperilled churches are generally intact, suffering little more than a lean to one side which the saint easily resists. Whilst the representations of San Damiano in the fresco cycle at Assisi, and in the closely derived cycle at San Francesco, Pistoia, are of churches in a parlous state, the damage inflicted on the Lateran, the church of the Holy See, seems quite restrained. Any risk posed to the Church, represented by the off-centring of, or small cracks in, the depicted Lateran, is arrested in the image by the combination of the supporting saint and the pope in whose dream the vision occurred. Francis and Dominic are clearly shown as supporting the Church. The allegorical image is powerful because the activity of supporting material structures was well understood, and the repair of actual churches familiar.

Giles Constable discusses the importance of rebuilding and repairing churches to the twelfth century clerical reform movement and sees this being repeated in Francis's actions. Constable highlights the referential significance of the physical activity: 'Behind this need for material repair lay a deeper need of spiritual renewal, both of individuals and institutions'.[51] The wider significance of the image of the 'Dream of Innocent III' may be an association with what I have described as the virtuous circle whereby the spiritual revival of the laity went hand in hand with the building of churches. Lawrence discusses how from the 1240s '[e]ncouraged by their lay benefactors, they [the mendicants] embarked on a programme of enlargement and new building, constructing churches spacious enough to provide an auditorium for the large crowds attracted to their preaching.'[52] On occasion, the bond

[51] Giles Constable, 'Renewal and Reform in Religious Life', in Robert L. Benson and Giles Constable, eds, *Renaissance and Renewal in the Twelfth Century* (Toronto, Ont., 1991), 37–67, at 44–5.

[52] Lawrence, *The Friars*, 109.

between the pope and the mendicants was made explicit in this activity. In 1252, Innocent IV exhorted the faithful to support the rebuilding of Santa Croce in Florence.[53] Colin Morris writes that 'the parish church was a more lively place in 1250 than in 1150 and the laity contributed to its activities more than they had done in the past.'[54] That upsurge in religious feeling had been stimulated in no small part by the Franciscans and the imagery of Francis supporting 'churches' was both a celebration of and a further exhortation to spiritual revival.

University of Manchester

53 Rona Goffen, *Spirituality in Conflict: Saint Francis and Giotto's Bardi Chapel* (University Park, PA, 1988), 4.

54 Morris, *Papal Monarchy*, 539.

REVIVALISM AND POPULISM IN THE FRANCISCAN OBSERVANCE OF THE LATE QUATTROCENTO

by GARY DICKSON

REVIVAL, as this volume shows, has had many different meanings within Christian history, and has taken many different forms.[1] Institutional revitalization, for example, is one thing; popular revivalism is another. Of course, they may be intertwined, as they were in the case of the Franciscan Observance of the late Quattrocento. The 're' of 'revivalism' is usually taken in a retrospective sense – that which previously existed is brought to life once more. Renaissance classicism is an obvious instance. With the Franciscan Observance, it is true, one does get a sense of the desire to restore, to re-institute, the idealized primitive poverty of the order in the days of St Francis. For the Observants, pristine Franciscanism would have been the equivalent of the early Church in the eyes of the Protestant reformers. Yet 'revivalism' can also be thought of as pertaining to remarkable occasions of religious intensity, moments of collective enthusiasm, moments, as Emile Durkheim puts it, of 'general effervescence.'[2] But champagne is too light-headed and celebratory to do justice to the phenomenon. A better symbol of 'revivalism' would be the flames of Pentecost. Here I shall attempt to show how the Observance rose to prominence, and eventually triumphed within the Franciscan order, through the raging fires – creative as well as destructive – of popular, indeed *populist* revivalism.[3]

The term 'populism' in my title also calls for clarification. Often in contemporary Britain it is used in a derogatory sense, abusively, as a

[1] My teacher at Edinburgh, the late Denys Hay, teaches me still; and my former doctoral student, also at Edinburgh, now at the Warburg Institute, Clare Lappin, has kept me up-to-date bibliographically with the Observance, on which she wrote her fine thesis, 'The Mirror of the Observance: Image, Ideal and Identity in Observant Franciscan Literature, c.1415–1528', unpublished Ph.D. thesis, University of Edinburgh, 2000.

[2] Emile Durkheim, *The Elementary Forms of the Religious Life*, trans. J.W. Swain (New York, 1915), 241.

[3] On medieval revivalism, see Gary Dickson, 'Revivalism as a Medieval Religious Genre', *JEH* 51 (2000), 473–96. Also, idem, 'Medieval Revivalism', in Daniel Bornstein, ed., *Medieval Christianity, A People's History of Christianity* 4, gen. ed. Denis R. Janz (Minneapolis, MN, 2008 forthcoming).

way of disparaging illiberal view-points. Here, by 'populist' I mean simply that which corresponds to and enlists prevailing attitudes, both positive and negative – love and hate – held by the great mass of the populace. Observant preachers knew how to appeal to what the populace craved, like civic peace, and what it could be persuaded to crave, like moral reform. They knew as well what the populace loathed, the Jews for example. Most of all, they were also perfectly in harmony with the ardent devotional feelings of the time, especially towards the Virgin and the cult of saints.

With the Observance 'populism' signifies crowds and charismatic preachers as a stimulus to collective enthusiasm. Large crowds addressed by the star-preachers of the Observance were the characteristic 'mixed crowds' of medieval revivalism, which were quintessentially populist. As medieval chroniclers describe them, they cut across social ranks and divisions. The old and the young; men and women; rich merchants and poor debtors; artisans and aristocrats; peasants and townsfolk – all gathered together in the *piazza* to listen to an eagerly anticipated visiting preacher, whose reputation for kindling enthusiasm had preceded him.[4]

The sermons they listened to not only touched on contemporary issues, but also triggered strong emotions rooted in traditional religious values. Preachers spoke; crowds acted on what they heard. The crowd's response was sometimes immediate, as with anti-Jewish riots. At other times, local authorities, acting on the crowd's behalf, translated its moral impulses into puritanical legislation. The waves of theocratic populism which periodically engulfed medieval Italian cities were set in motion by revivalist preaching. So, far from disappearing into empty air, the preacher's words had both foreseeable and unforeseen consequences.

The fact that Observant preachers repeatedly berated their congregations for their moral failings, far from diminishing their popularity, enhanced it. Then, too, during times of plague, when fear and helplessness paralyzed communities, revivalist preachers offered hope by leading processional litanies of supplication. Hence if there was one factor which accounts for the success of the Franciscan Observance in

4 See Gary Dickson, 'The Crowd at the Feet of Pope Boniface VIII: Pilgrimage, Crusade and the first Roman Jubilee (1300)', *Journal of Medieval History* 25: 4 (1999), 279–307, here at 294–6, and 'Medieval Christian Crowds and the Origins of Crowd Psychology', *Revue d'Histoire Ecclésiastique* 95: 1 (2000), 54–75.

mid- and late-Quattrocento Italy, it would have to be the grand preaching tours undertaken by their most charismatic revivalists. These Observant friars – Christian populists through and through – were men of exceptional educational and intellectual attainments. They were the initiators and leaders of the last great Christian revival in Pre-Reformation Europe.

Ineradicable, persistent tensions existed within Franciscanism from Francis's lifetime in the early thirteenth century to the eventual triumph of the Observance. The correct interpretation of Franciscan poverty was a particular sticking point. The fourteenth century, with its battles between the Spirituals and the Conventuals – not to mention the heretical Fraticelli – was a particularly bad time for Franciscanism. Various compromises were attempted between, on the one hand, perfectionism as defined by strict adherence to the image, as well as the rule, of St Francis, and, on the other, accommodation to the pressing realities of the world, changed circumstances, and papal demands. All such compromises failed, and, in 1517, Pope Leo X split the order between the Observants and the Conventuals, with primacy going to the Observants.[5]

Pope Gregory XI's backing for the reforms of the Observant leader Paolo de' Trinci in 1368 and 1373 was a significant first step. But the pace of momentum quickened in the early fifteenth century, when four outstanding friars emerged. They were the so-called Four Pillars of the Observance – Bernardino da Siena, Giovanni da Capestrano, Alberto da Sarteano, and Giacomo della Marca. Their influence on the papacy and the people transformed what was a peripheral reform movement into a powerful force within Franciscanism and Christian society.[6] As a popular preacher, none of these four was more celebrated than Bernardino da Siena. A mere six years after his death, his canonization in 1450 confirmed the fame of his preaching and his reputation for sanctity.[7]

[5] A short selection from an extensive literature would include: John Moorman, A History of the Franciscan Order (Oxford, 1968); Denys Hay, *The Church in Italy in the Fifteenth Century* (Cambridge, 1977); *Il Rinnovamento del Francescanesimo: L'Osservanza* (Società Internazionale di Studi Francescani, Convegni, 11) (Assisi, 1985); Duncan Nimmo, *Reform and Division in the Franciscan Order, 1226–1538* (Rome, 1987); Clare Lappin, 'Mirror of the Observance'.

[6] Moorman, *Franciscan Order*, 371–4, 506.

[7] Of the many, and more recent, studies devoted to Bernardino da Siena, the most readable – if perhaps too affectionate – portrait remains the one drawn by Iris Origo in *The World of San Bernardino* (New York, 1962).

The Observants' most gifted preacher of the next generation inherited San Bernardino's legacy. Martino Tomitano was received into the order by Giacomo della Marca, in 1456, and chose as his new name in religion, one which immediately proclaimed his new identity. Martino became Bernardino. Centuries later the name of Bernardino da Feltre would be added to the list of eight other fifteenth- and early sixteenth-century Franciscans, likewise named Bernardino, all listed as 'blesseds' (*beati*) in the *Bibliotheca Sanctorum*.[8]

But Bernardino da Feltre was more than just an imitator of Bernardino da Siena – in the medieval sense of *imitatio*. He could almost be called a replicant. The Sienese saint, toothless, shrunken, and emaciated, with a ragged and patched tunic, did not just conform to the Franciscan ideal; he embodied it. The charisma of the Sienese saint was therefore visual before it ever became verbal.

Bernardino da Feltre was a small man as well. He was called the 'the very little one' or 'the little saint.' But not only did he resemble his illustrious namesake, he also shared his spiritual vocation. The spiritual calling of the great Bernardino was equally his – preaching, always preaching. In twenty-five years of preaching, Bernardino da Feltre delivered more than 3,600 sermons, sometimes three a day, each lasting up to three hours.[9]

And he was in great demand. Every major city in Italy wanted the best possible preacher for Lent, so the papacy sometimes had to intervene to decide which of Bernardino da Feltre's invitations took precedence.[10] One Umbrian city which often invited him to come and preach was Perugia. The record of expenses gifted to him on 2 May 1486 describes Bernardino as 'that most excellent preacher newly come to Perugia'.[11]

Umbria was the birthplace of St Francis and Franciscanism, as it was the homeland of the Observance, and Perugia was Umbria's crown jewel. Perugia's love affair with Franciscanism did not end when those escorting the dying Francis – already a proto-relic – were forced to take

8 Vol. 2 (Rome, 1962; repr. 1983), col. 1288–1321.

9 Moorman, *Franciscan Order*, 523. Maria Giuseppina Muzzarelli, *Pescatori di uomini: predicatori e piazze alla fine del Medioevo* (Bologna, 2005), ch. 3, 'Bernardino da Feltre', 193–265.

10 Ibid., 210–13.

11 Benvenuto Bughetti, 'Documenti perugini intorno al B. Bernardino da Feltre,' *Studi Francescani* 14 (1942), 32–41, here at no. 16, 36.

evasive action in order to prevent the Perugians from snatching him, thus enabling Francis to die in his native Assisi.[12]

Perugia, however, did manage to retain the body of the Blessed Giles, Francis's third companion, and it was Giles's former hermitage half a mile outside the city at Monteripido, later christened San Francesco al Monte, that was formally given to the Observants on 8 June 1374. This would be the residence and headquarters of the Observance in Quattrocento Perugia.[13] Their choice of location was entirely appropriate. The Blessed Giles, *beato Egidio*, was a staunch advocate of rigorous adherence to the ideals of early Franciscanism. So Giles was a spiritual progenitor of the Observance.[14]

Of the Four Pillars of the Observance, two had especially strong links with Perugia. Giovanni da Capestrano, who died in 1456, and was canonized in 1724, had been a student, then a respected judge in Perugia. After a vision of St Francis, he entered Monteripido as a novice. When the plague struck, Capestrano's moral authority persuaded the Perugians to hold processions to appease God's anger. Like San Bernardino da Siena, Capestrano was regarded as a living saint.[15]

Truly it can be said that the cult of San Bernardino in Perugia began during his lifetime. From the 1420s to the 1440s, he frequently visited the city. Pleased with his moral reforms in Perugia, he told his own Sienese: 'There is as much difference between you and the Perugians as between heaven and earth.' His moral reforms began with peace-making. In his Sienese sermons, he remarks that 'so many reconciliations were made [in Perugia] that I was amazed that there could have been so many enmities as there had been.' The so-called 'Bernardinian Statutes' in the Perugian law-books imposed severe penalties for crimes of blasphemy, gambling, sodomy, brawling, and usury. Thanks to his intervention, Perugia's bloodthirsty game, the 'Battle of Stones,' was abolished. Also in Perugia, he had the 'vanities' of dice, playing cards, wigs, flounces, and baubles worth a considerable sum, heaped up in the

12 See Father Cuthbert, *Life of St. Francis of Assisi* (London, 1927), 435.

13 Nimmo, *Reform and Division*, 408.

14 For an introduction, edition, and translation of the *Vita beati fratris Egidii*, see *Scripta Leonis, Rufini et Angeli*, ed. and trans. Rosalind B. Brooke (Oxford, 1970), 307–49.

15 See M. G. Dickson, 'Patterns of European Sanctity: the Cult of Saints in the Later Middle Ages (with Special Reference to Perugia)', unpublished Ph.D. thesis, University of Edinburgh, 1974, 496.

piazza and burnt.[16] In 1440, he inaugurated a course in moral theology at Monteripido by giving the first lecture himself.[17]

Vast crowds came to hear him preach in the piazza from the specially constructed marble pulpit attached to the façade of the cathedral. The shops were closed so that everyone could attend his sermons. While he was preaching, no one was to be seized for crime or imprisoned for debt. His death in L'Aquila was marked by a lavish funeral service in Perugia; and news of his canonization excited further popular enthusiasm.[18] First, the priors established a chapel dedicated to San Bernardino in the cathedral; then, a magnificent oratory, completed in 1461, was built to perpetuate his memory. On the tympanum he appears in glory, while in the niches on either side of the portals are the statues of two of the city's ancient patron saints. Towering above them is San Bernardino, Perugia's newest celestial protector and advocate.[19] This is one example of how the Observance refreshed the cult of saints in Perugia and throughout Europe.

Our second Bernardino, Bernardino da Feltre, began his revivalist preaching tours in Perugia about forty years after the death of his canonized namesake. From 1485 to 1493 he made at least eight visits to Perugia, some lasting for several months.[20] Like the Sienese Bernardino, he, too, stayed at Monteripido, and like him as well, he preached against usury, and in the process vilified the Jews.

Bernardino da Feltre's anti-usury preaching, while primarily directed against Jewish lending, strongly condemned Christian moneylenders as well – they were Judaizers. That, indeed, was the view of San Bernardino, who regarded lending at interest as a sin against Christian charity which entrapped the poor in their poverty.[21] As an economic thinker, the Sienese saint did not disallow the productive use of money

16 On San Bernardino in Perugia, see Gary Dickson, 'Encounters in Medieval Revivalism: Monks, Friars, and Popular Enthusiasts', *Church History* 68: 2 (1999), 265–93, at 290–1. On his peacemaking activities throughout Italy, including Perugia, see Cynthia L. Polecritti, *Preaching Peace in Renaissance Italy: Bernardino of Siena and his Audience* (Washington, DC, 2000).

17 Nimmo, *Reform and Division*, 592.

18 Dickson, 'Patterns of European Society', 481–2.

19 See the Oratorio San Bernardino in Francesco Santi, *Perugia, guida storico artistica* (Perugia, 1950), 94–9.

20 The most reliable chronology is provided by Bughetti, 'Documenti'.

21 On San Bernardino and the Jews, see Franco Mormando, *The Preacher's Demons: Bernardino of Siena and the Social Underworld of Early Renaissance Italy* (Chicago, IL and London, 1999), ch. 4, 164–218.

in commerce, say, by entering into a business partnership in which risk was shared, but the provision of interest-bearing loans or pawnbroking – both permitted to the Jews – were anathema to him.[22]'Usurers are leeches,' he declared. 'Every Jew, particularly when he is a lender, is the deadly enemy of the Christian.'[23] Jews showed the same lust for gain as 'the most greedy Judas who out of avarice sold and betrayed the Saviour.'[24] The Jews of San Bernardino's Italy were present at the Crucifixion.

Now, neither San Bernardino's anti-Jewishness on religo-economic grounds, nor his Christian anti-Judaism amounts to anti-Semitism in Langmuirian terms.[25] What is missing is a wholly irrational element: myth, in a word. Bernardino, however, did believe in and circulate at least two myths about Jews which must have fanned hatred against them. Jews, he alleged, in order to mock Christians, urinated in the cups or pots they offered to Christians, as well as in the sacramental vessels and chalices that impious Christians pawned to the Jews. What is more, he warned Christians against having recourse to Jewish doctors, for they boasted about how many Christians their medicines had killed.[26] People would be wise to avoid any form of social contact with Jews. Like San Bernardino, Da Feltre believed that Jews should be kept isolated because they posed a threat to Christian society.

In central Italy there were comparatively few rich Jewish bankers. All the great merchant-banking houses were owned by Christians. Primarily, but not exclusively, the Jews offered small loans to people who desperately needed credit and were turned away by other bankers. Such people were prepared to pawn small items as security, and pay

22 Raymond de Roover considers him one of medieval Europe's two great economic thinkers; see his *Bernardino of Siena and Sant'Antonino of Florence* (Cambridge, MA, 1967), 'What was Usury', 27–33.

23 Léon Poliakov, *Jewish Bankers and the Holy See*, trans. Miriam Kochan (London, 1977), 142, citing Bernardino's sermon forty-three, *Opera omnia*, vol. 4 (Florence, 1955), 377–87.

24 Giacomo Todeschini, 'Teorie economiche francescane e presenza ebraica in Italia (1380–1462 c.)', in *Il Rinnovamento del Francescanesimo*, 195–227, at 213, citing Bernardino's sixth sermon from his *Quadragesimale de christiana religione*, *Opera omnia*, vol. 3 (Florence, 1955), 101–2.

25 See Gavin I. Langmuir, *Towards a Definition of Antisemitism* (Berkeley and Los Angeles, CA, 1990), especially part 4, 'irrational fantasies'. Note also the medieval essays, including a contribution by Gavin Langmuir, in Diana Wood, ed., *Christianity and Judaism*, SCH.S 29 (Oxford, 1992).

26 Mormando, *The Preacher's Demons*, 176, 178.

high rates of interest. Jews were offering a social service, although at a price.[27] Debtors, naturally, have little love for their creditors.

The remedy for the burden of debt, as Bernardino da Feltre saw it, was in interest-free loans, which would simultaneously benefit the poor and drive the Jews out of the market, cutting off their major source of income and so hastening their conversion. Hence he became the leading advocate of the *Monti di Pietà*, banks which offered small loans to the poor.[28] Originally, these were intended to be interest free, but when this proved administratively impossible, a charge of 5% was imposed. Of course the idea of a Franciscan-supported institution charging interest caused great controversy in the order – Bernardino da Siena would have had apoplexy. Nevertheless, Da Feltre persevered, establishing his first *Monte* at Mantua in 1484, and ultimately winning the battle with his brethren over interest charges in 1495, and with the papacy in 1515.[29] So while San Bernardino's iconographic attribute is the Holy Name of Jesus, Bernardino da Feltre's is a mountain of coins – the emblem of the *Monte di Pietà*.[30]

The very first *Monte* was founded in Perugia, in 1462, by the Franciscans Michèle Carcano and Fortunato Coppoli. It was able to open its doors thanks to a Jewish loan of 2,000 florins.[31] On the other hand, the Jews of Perugia were rightfully apprehensive whenever Bernardino da Feltre visited the town and preached against Jewish usury. Although his preaching in Perugia provoked no anti-Jewish riots, that was not the case in Florence.[32]

Even more disturbing for the Jews of Perugia, however, is what occurred in Trent. In 1475, Bernardino da Feltre came to Trent as a Lenten preacher. His sermons, fiercely attacking Jewish usury and Christians who associated with Jews, would surely have contributed to a heightening of anti-Jewish feelings. Adding to an atmosphere of hostility towards Jews was anxiety about some unspecified, impending evil connected with them, which, Bernardino predicted, would soon afflict Trent.

27 For general background, see Léon Poliakov, *Jewish Bankers*, ch. 4.

28 Bernardino da Feltre was 'the most effacacious instrument of the preached word to induce the foundation of Monte di Pietà': Maria Giuseppina Muzzarelli, *Il denario e la salvezza: l'invenzione del Monte di Pietà* (Bologna, 2001),13.

29 Muzzarelli, *Pescatori*, 231.

30 For the iconography of the respective saints, note the *Bibliotheca Sanctorum*, vol. 2, and George Kaftal's *Saints in Italian Art*, vols. 1–4 (Florence, 1952–85).

31 Moorman, *Franciscan Order*, 529–30; Muzzarelli, *Il denario*, 18–20.

32 Ibid., 11–12.

Then, as if in answer to prophecy, on Easter Sunday, 26 March 1475, the body of little Simon was discovered. He had been ritually murdered – or so it was alleged – by the Jews of Trent, who were tortured into confessing their crime.[33] The cult of the child-martyr *beato Simonino* of Trent signalled the arrival in Italy of the centuries-old northern European myth that Jews ritually slaughtered Christian boys.[34] Undoubtedly, reception of this classic anti-Semitic myth was facilitated by Observant sermons which engendered an all-encompassing hatred of Jews.

So whenever Fra Bernardino da Feltre appeared in town, the Jews of Perugia could not fail to be reminded of the fate of their co-religionists at Trent. While his preaching in Perugia made the Jews apprehensive, it provoked no expulsions. Yet his sermons probably did contribute to discriminatory legislation in the Perugian statutes of June 1486, which reinstated the Jewish badge.[35]

But opposition to usury by no means exhausted Fra Bernardino's campaign for moral reform in Perugia. Peacemaking played a central role in his evangelical revivalism, as it had done with San Bernardino. Clan vendettas and violent disputes – especially between the respective followers of the Oddi and the Baglioni – resulted in the death and injury of many citizens.[36] While Da Feltre was in the city, there was one such instance of clan warfare. On 13 June 1486, an armed skirmish between allies of the Oddi and Baglioni began in the piazza near the church of San Fortunato. A contemporary chronicler records that 'Fra Bernardino, our preacher, with certain other friars of San Francesco del Monte' walked straight into the midst of the warring factions. 'Fra Bernardino had a great cross in his hand which he planted in the middle [of the piazza, between the two groups of armed men]. Then he went from one side to the other, crying *Pace! Pace!* (peace! peace!) . . .' Many combatants on both sides were wounded, but, aided by the papal vice-legate, Fra Bernardino, cross in hand, succeeded in restoring a brief interval of peace.[37]

33 R. Po Chia Hsia, *Trent 1475: Stories of a Ritual Murder Trial* (New Haven, CT, 1992), 25, 33, and see n. 49 below. Léon Poliakov, *The History of Anti-Semitism, vol 1: From the Time of Christ to the Court Jews*, trans. Richard Howard (London, 1966), 148.

34 The cult was papally abolished in 1965: Mormando, *The Preacher's Demons*, 179.

35 See Ariel Toaff, *Gli Ebrei a Perugia*, Fonti per la Storia dell'Umbria, 10 (Perugia, 1975), 80.

36 General background: William Heywood, *A History of Perugia*, ed. R. Langston Douglas (London, 1910), 299–308.

37 For this incident, Bernardino's hagiographer Bernardino Guslino is cited by Muzzarelli, *Pescatori*, p. 225; but the vivid account quoted here comes from O. Scalvanti,

In addition to peacemaking, as part of his moral crusade Bernardino da Feltre proposed sumptuary laws for Perugia in order to 'correct and reform the bad customs of the citizens.' These ordinances of 1485 probably stemmed from his Lenten preaching.[38] In them, he singled out the vice of 'luxury' – one of the seven deadly sins – a vice associated with lasciviousness, and so with women.[39] The immodest dress of women was a conspicuous example of such behaviour which he urged the communal authorities to address.[40] Whether or not Fra Bernardino or San Bernardino (who was likewise obsessed by female 'luxury') ought to be accused of 'profound misogyny' is for others to judge.[41]

To purge Perugia of its civic vices, Fra Bernardino did exactly what his Sienese master had done. He burnt the vanities.[42] On Sunday 18 June 1486, five days after his courageous exercise in peacemaking, he preached a sermon in the cathedral piazza in front of a huge crowd. According to the chronicler, Fra Bernardino dwelt on many sins – vanities of games and masquerades and the 'false hair' (wigs) that women wore. He spoke as well of homicides and enmities, and of broken pacts of peace.

Beforehand, he had wooden castle constructed. It looked rather like a pavillion, very tall, and covered in canvas. Suddenly, he ordered the canvas raised, and a large horned devil appeared at the top. In the middle of the castle were two swordsmen with swords and shields in their hands. On different tiers, there were books of necromancy; books of love spells; playing cards; dice tables of various sizes; masks; wigs; and vials of cosmetics. When, at Bernardino's command, the castle was set

'Cronaca perugina inedita', *Bollettino della regia deputazione di Storia Patria per l'Umbria* 9 (1903), 246.

38 Bughetti, 'Documenti', no. 6, 34 and n. 2.

39 Medieval equivalents for the sin of *luxuria* included *fornicatio* and *libido*. See Morton W. Bloomfield, *The Seven Deadly Sins* (East Lansing, MI, 1952), 69, 77.

40 Compare L. de Besse, *Le bienheureux Bernardin de Feltre et son oeuvre*, 2 vols (Tours and Paris, 1902), 1: 182–3, and C. F. Black, 'Politics and Society in Perugia, 1488–1540', unpublished B.Litt. thesis, University of Oxford, 1966, 140–1.

41 This is the view of Michele Monaco, 'Aspetti di vita privata e pubblica nelle città italiane centro-settentrionali durante il xv secolo nelle prediche del beato Bernardino da Feltre Francescano dell'Osservanza', in *L'uomo e la storia: Studi storici in onore di Massimo Petrocchi*, Storia e letteratura, raccolta di studi e testi, 153 (Rome, 1983), 120.

42 San Bernardino's burning of the vanities in Perugia in 1425 is best described in the *Cronaca del Graziani*; the relevant passage of which is translated by William Heywood in his *Palio and Ponte* (London, 1913), 154–5.

on fire, the flames shot up instantly, for the wooden castle was filled with gunpowder. Quickly, it and the vanities were burnt to ashes.[43]

It would take a cultural anthropologist as subtle and discerning as Clifford Geertz at the Balinese cockfight to interpret this spectacular burning of the vanities.[44] Whatever its meaning, this was revivalism as ritual and as theatrical performance. Alas, we lack either a report of the crowd's reaction, or a statement of the preacher's intent. So, was this a dramatic illustration of the hell-fires awaiting the sinners whose specific sins were itemized in Bernardino da Feltre's sermon, just as they were objectified in the burning castle of vices? Or was it a symbolic act of communal expurgation, ritually cleansing the city of its impurities? Was it analogous to the burning of heretics? Or was it the cauterizing of a collective wound? Fire, a potent symbol then as now, heals as well as destroys.

Nevertheless, the burning of the vanities was not the climax of Fra Bernardino da Feltre's eventful career as an itinerant revivalist in Perugia. That came when he helped to launch a new devotion in the city, one whose life-span was far longer than that of a combustible wooden castle. Twelve years before Bernardino arrived in Perugia, a German Franciscan, Vinterio di Roberto, came to the city in 1473, bringing with him what became Perugia's greatest civic treasure and religious trophy. Fra Vinterio, betraying the trust of his fellow Franciscans in Chiusi, ran off with their prized relic, the Sant'Anello – the Virgin Mary's wedding ring.[45]

Fra Vinterio's role as a 'pious thief' is undermined somewhat by the fact that he also spirited away his convent's silver votive offerings along with the church plate. Moreover, there are grounds for suspecting that Vinterio was working in collusion with a Perugian gentleman, who obtained the ring, then donated it to the municipality of Perugia, who, in return, paid his many debts and granted him an annuity, which extended to his sons, and their descendants for three generations. As for

43 Scalvanti, 'Cronaca perugina inedita', 247–8. I wish to thank Professor Jon Usher of Edinburgh for helping to clarify a point in this text.

44 Clifford Geertz, 'Deep Play: Notes on the Balinese Cockfight', in idem, *The Interpretation of Cultures* (London, 1993), 412–53.

45 Older accounts of the Sant'Anello are not always free of pious legends; among them is Adamo Rossi, *L'Anello Sponsalizio di Maria Vergine che si venera nelle cattedrale di Perugia. Leggenda* (Perugia, 1857); another is a pamphlet, Ettore Ricci, *Storia del Sant'Anello* (Perugia, 1942). See also Diane Webb, *Patrons and Defenders: the Saints in the Italian City-States* (London and New York, 1996), 227–30.

Fra Vinterio, after a show trial and a short, comfortable imprisonment, he was rewarded with a civic banquet, a handsome annual stipend, and a sinecure. He lies in the chapel housing the Sant'Anello, and a plaque commemmorates his services to the Virgin.[46]

The ring was kept in the cathedral of San Lorenzo, but access to the keys to the reliquary was controlled by the communal authorities, for the Holy Ring was a civic relic. The theft of the relic also had political repercussions. Siena, Chiusi's powerful overlord, threatened war. But Pope Sixtus IV, a Franciscan who had studied at Perugia and been given Perugian citizenship, smoothed things over, and in 1486 Pope Innocent VIII decided that Perugia would be the Sant'Anello's permanent home. As early as August 1474, a year after the arrival of the ring, it was decided to schedule the solemn ostension of the Sant'Anello on the second day of that month, in order to tempt pilgrims on their way to the famous Franciscan Porziuncola Indulgence in Assisi, to stop off at Perugia. Before acquiring the Sant'Anello, Perugia was unable to profit from the lucrative pilgrimage traffic to and from the shrine of St Francis.[47]

Veneration for the Sant'Anello had far-reaching devotional implications, something which Bernardino da Feltre was quick to grasp. For this was the very ring of the *Sposalizio*, the ring by which Joseph espoused Mary. Moreover, in 1474 – the same year that Perugia decreed the ring's exhibition for public veneration – Pope Sixtus IV authorized the cult of St Joseph.[48] As a Franciscan, Sixtus IV was undoubtedly aware of San Bernardino da Siena's ardent promotion of the newly emerging cult of St Joseph, the bridegroom of Mary, and earthly parent of Jesus.[49]

The Quattrocento witnessed a dramatic change in attitudes towards

46 Rossi, *L'Anello Sponsalizio*, pp. 37–38, 88–98. See A. Riccieri, 'Indice degli Annali Ecclesiastici-Perugini', *Archivio per la Storia Ecclesiastica dell'Umbria* 5 (Foligno, 1921), 379–516, at 447–8, 457. Scalvanti, 'Cronaca perugina inedita', 83–5. Note the brief account in Giovanna Casagrande, 'Devozione e Municipalità: la Compagnia del S. Anello / S. Giuseppe de Perugia (1487–1542)', in *Le Mouvement Confraternel au Moyen Âge*, Collection de l'Ècole Française de Rome, 97 (Rome, 1987), 155–83, at 159–60, n. 20. Ricci, *Storia del Sant'Anello*, 26.

47 For the long diplomatic row between Perugia, Chiusi, and Siena, see Rossi, *L'Anello Sponsalizio*, 44–119, and Webb, *Patrons and Defenders*, 227, 229. On the link with the pilgrimage to Assisi, see Casagrande, 'Devozione e Municipalità, 161–2.

48 Joseph Dusserre, 'Les origines de la dévotion à Saint Joseph', extract from *Cahiers de Joséphologie* (Montreal, 1953–4), 82.

49 See Joseph Seitz, *Die Verehrung des hl. Joseph in ihrer gesichtlichen Entwicklung bis zum Konzil von Trent* (Freiburg im Beisgau, 1908), 208–9. Seitz's work is the fundamental study.

St Joseph. He was beginning to shed his early-medieval persona as a decrepit, vaguely comic figure, whose Methuselah-like years were a visible confirmation of Mary's virginity. St Joseph was now being preached as a role model for contemporary fathers and husbands. Prepared to promote St Joseph's growing reputation were eminent men like San Bernardino, as well as the illustrious theologian and churchman Gerson of Paris, who, as early as 1400, wrote a mass for a proposed new feast of the marriage of the Virgin and Joseph.[50] Bernardino da Feltre zealously promoted his cult as well. Here, too, he was the ever-faithful disciple of his namesake. In Da Feltre's sermon on St Joseph, he praises not only the Joseph of Egypt who received Pharaoh's ring, but that other Joseph to whom God gave the ring by which he married Mary. Directly addressing those who painted St Joseph's image, Fra Bernardino thunders: 'O painter I don't want you to depicit him like that, nor sleeping! Make him handsome and agreeable. Never was there a more glorious old man . . .'[51] Glorious, yes; but St Joseph would not always remain an old man. To serve as the socially plausible head of a Christian household, Joseph had to be younger and stronger: that he became.[52]

In Perugia, Bernardino da Feltre showed himself to be a passionate devotee of St Joseph.[53] On 31 May 1486, while he resided in the city, a chapel dedicated to the Virgin and St Joseph was established in the cathedral. This was the same chapel in which 'the most sacred ring of the Virgin Mary' was lodged.[54] Veneration for the Sant'Anello and the

50 K. A. H. Kellner, *L'Anno Ecclessiastico e le Feste dei Santi nel loro svolgimento storico*, trans. A. Mercati (Rome, 1906), 241–2.

51 *Sermoni del Beato Bernardino Tomitano da Feltre*, 3 vols, ed. C. Varischi, (Milan, 1963), 'De sancto Joseph' (Pavia, 1493), 1: 393–402, in which Gerson and St Bernardino da Siena (who 'converted to and renewed the Christian life in all of Italy,' 396) are lauded for praising St Joseph (396–7). The quoted passage appears on 398–9.

52 Compare, for example, the superannuated, humble image of Joseph in an early fifteenth-century German woodcut of the *Holy Family* in Brigitte Heublein, *Der 'verkannte' Joseph zur mittelalterlichen Ikonagraphie des Heiligen in deutschen und niederländischen Kulturraum* (Weimar, 1998), no. 76, with the vigorous, manly, middle-aged Joseph of Raphael's *Holy Family* or *Madonna of the Palm Tree*, c.1506–07 (National Gallery of Scotland, Edinburgh). For the latter, see Carolyn C. Wilson, *St. Joseph in Italian Renaissance Society and Art: New Directions and Interpretations* (Philadelphia, PA, 2001), 230, n. 250. I wish to thank Michael Bury, historian of art, Edinburgh, for alerting me to this title, as he did to Rosso Fiorentino's *Marriage of the Virgin* (1523), in which St Joseph, remarkably, appears as no older than Mary. Wilson, *St. Joseph*, 187, n. 99.

53 For an overview of his efforts in Perugia, note Seitz, *Die Verehrung*, 209–10.

54 See Bughetti, 'Documenti', no. 17, 36–7: 'Provisio obtenta pro capella S. Ioseph fienda

cult of St Joseph were henceforth inseparable. Fra Bernardino was responsible for taking their intertwined devotion a step further.

The next year he founded an important lay confraternity whose members included the civic elite as well as families and individuals from across the social spectrum.[55] Medieval confraternities were often the products of collective enthusiasm. Thus they commemorated as well as institutionalized revivalist populism. The Perugian humanist Francesco Matarazzo was probably himself a confrére of Bernardino's new brotherhood; he writes: 'At this time the Company of St Joseph was organized by Fra Bernardino da Feltre. And among other ordinances he ordained that there should be a torchlight procession on the day of the feast of St Joseph, as may be read in the book of the rules of the Company; and many gentlemen and merchants enrolled their names in that order.'[56] The chroniclers agree that before this the feast of St Joseph (19 March) had never been observed in Perugia.[57] And it was done, says one chronicler, 'for love of the Madonna's ring.'[58]

The relic of the Sant'Anello; the Marriage of the Virgin; the rise of St Joseph – all paved the way for the new cult of the Holy Family. Indeed, new Umbrian images of the *Sposalizio*, in which the wedding ring is a focal point, appear as a direct response to veneration of the Sant'Anello.[59] Unlike the way she was represented in the ubiquitous pictures of the Madonna and Child, Mary could no longer be thought of as a single mother. She was, after all, St Joseph's wife. What the Holy Family gave European society was no less than an idealized religious model of the modern nuclear family.[60]

To conclude: Fra Bernardino da Feltre's preaching and active role in

in ecclesia S. Laurentii: . . . in dicta capella reponatur sacratissimus anulum ipsius Viginis Marie . . .'

55 Casagrande, 'Devozione e Municipalità', 163–4; 168–76.

56 Rossi, *L'Anello Sponsalizio*, 221–2. Francesco Matarazzo, *Chronicles of the City of Perugia, 1492–1503*, trans. Edward S. Morgan (London, 1905), 9.

57 See *Cronaca della Città di Perugia dal 1309 al 1491 nota col nome di 'Diario del Graziani . . .'*, ed. A. Fabretti, *Archivio Storico Italiano* 16: 1 (Florence, 1850), 671.

58 See *Memorie di Perugia dal'anno 1457 al 1540*, in *Cronaca della Città di Perugia*, ed. A. Fabretti, vol. 2 (Turin, 1888), 108.

59 Perugino's 'Marriage of the Virgin' (completed 1503/4) was commissioned for the reliquary chapel in the Perugia's cathedral of San Lorenzo in 1499; Raphael's *Sposalizio* dates from 1504 (Città di Castello). Carolyn C. Wilson, *St. Joseph*, 26–7 (and pl. 12).

60 A perfect example is the intimate, domestic view of the Holy Family, the *Sagrada Familia 'del pajarito'* by Murillo (c.1645–50), in which Joseph, no greybeard, is the right age for a family man. See Diego Anguilo Iñiguez, *Murillo: su vida, su arte, su obra*, 3 vols (Madrid, 1981), 1: 283–4; 2: no.193, 175–6; 3: pl. 51.

the civic and devotional life of Perugia provides a fair illustration, in microcosm, of the social dimensions of Observant populist revivalism, and hence of its success.

University of Edinburgh

REACTION TO REVIVAL: ROBERT RIDLEY'S CRITIQUE OF ERASMUS

by MARGARET HARVEY

CHRISTIAN historians have found it hard to approve those who resist revival and resurgence in the Church and particularly in the period of the Reformation. It is often assumed too readily that sympathy with Renaissance biblical and patristic scholarship (resurgence *par excellence*) should have led honest scholars to Protestantism. Yet it did not always do so. Erasmus outstandingly did not fit this pattern but nor did many others, even among those who benefited from his scholarship and shared some of his concerns. Modern scholars have too often regarded such dissenting voices as at best conservative and at worst benighted or dishonest. Contemporaries were equally (or more) scathing about one another. It is very difficult therefore to give proper value to those who shared some but not all the tendencies which Erasmus epitomized yet were deeply critical of some of the conclusions to which these could lead.[1]

Robert Ridley was such a man.[2] He was of Northumberland gentry background, and paid for the education of his better-known nephew, the leading Protestant Reformer, Nicholas Ridley. He was a Renaissance scholar, who shared many typical traits. He was a careful reader of some of the latest theological scholarship, but also read various Renaissance editions of classical works, probably because he was for a time 'Terence Lecturer' in Cambridge, concerned with classical literature.[3] Marginal notes to his books show that he searched out manuscripts and compared versions. He helped Polydore Vergil with the first printed edition of Gildas's *De Excidio*.[4] All his books show careful corrections of

1 On these issues, see R. Rex, 'The Role of English Humanists in the Reformation up to 1559', in N. S. Amos, A Pettegree, and H. van Nierop, eds, *The Education of a Christian Society: Humanism and the Reformation in Britain and the Netherlands* (Aldershot, 1999), 19–40, esp. 30–1.

2 See R. Rex, 'Ridley, Robert (d. 1536?)', *ODNB*. I owe my list of Ridley's books to Dr Ian Doyle and Dr Rex; I examined all pages for marginal notes.

3 For the significance of this, see D. R. Leader, *A History of the University of Cambridge, vol. 1: The University to 1546* (Cambridge, 1988), 249–51.

4 D. E. Rhodes, 'The First Edition of Gildas', *The Library*, ser. 6, 1 (1979), 355–60; for the

printing errors and some also have notes revealing concern about historical accuracy.

Ridley studied theology at Cambridge where he became a fellow of King's Hall (BA 1496, MA 1500, BTh 1516, DTh 1518) and may have gone to Paris after 1500 for a few years. He almost certainly knew Greek, perhaps learned at King's Hall.[5] The turning point for him must have been becoming secretary to Cuthbert Tunstal when the latter (a relative) became bishop of London in 1521. He stayed with Tunstal when he became bishop of Durham in 1530 and thus was caught up with Henry VIII's (successful) attempt to bully Tunstal into giving the oath of supremacy. In 1534 Cromwell's agents came to Bishop Auckland to search Tunstal's residence for evidence of resistance.[6] They found nothing against Tunstal but there was a copy of *Opus eximium de vera differentia* with hostile marginalia by Ridley, as well as his writing defending church endowment. Ridley was arrested and probably died in prison; certainly he is not heard of again and by 1536 he was dead.

Ridley may have known Erasmus personally from Cambridge; in any event the scholar's work would have been known to him because Erasmus was a friend and correspondent of Tunstal. Membership of Tunstal's household made Ridley part of a very scholarly circle. It also, however, introduced him to the hunt for heretics in which Tunstal was involved as bishop of London. The English campaign against Lutherans in the 1520s has now been thoroughly studied; Ridley was a minor player but was involved in several trials, including the first trial of Robert Barnes, and perhaps shared Tunstal's idea that scholar-heretics should, if possible, be persuaded by sound theology and good argument.[7] Unlike Erasmus, Ridley had practical experience of the pastoral consequences of the new scholarship as well as of the spread of Lutheranism and that may explain in part why his attitude to Erasmus was often hostile.

full history of the text, see T. Mommsen, *MGH auctorum antiquissimorum chronica minora saec. IV–VII*, 13.1 (Berlin, 1895), 10–19.

5 A note perhaps in his hand in D[urham] C[athedral] L[ibrary], D VII. 2 (volumes 5, 6 of the works of Jerome), has Greek in vol. 6, fol. 135r.

6 See Rex, 'Ridley', *ODNB*. The copy of *Opus Eximium* has not been found.

7 Idem, 'The English Campaign against Luther in the 1520s', *TRHS*, ser. 5, 39 (1989), 85–106, references to Ridley, 88, 97, 104; C. W. D'Alton, 'The Suppression of Lutheran Heretics in England, 1526–29', *JEH* 54 (2003), 228–53, references to Ridley, 236, 247; D'Alton, 'Cuthbert Tunstal and Heresy in Essex and London, 1528', *Albion* 35 (2003), 210–28, references to Ridley, 219–20.

We know of Ridley's attitudes chiefly from the marginalia in his books, of which about forty-three remain, now scattered about England.[8] He commented on and cross-referenced his volumes, so that one can discover much about his views, including about Lutherans, but I will here confine myself to his reactions to Erasmus.

Erasmus's patristic editions and commentaries were crucial to the new theology, especially for biblical studies and the history of the early Church. Ridley owned Erasmus's 1516 edition of Jerome's works, together with a copy of Jerome's *Letters* of 1524 and including Oecolampadius's index to Erasmus's scholia on Jerome, as well as Erasmus's edition of Ambrose's works in two volumes and his Augustine.[9] These survive with copious marginal notes. He also owned Erasmus's reply to the censures of Paris, but that copy was not available to me.[10] The views from the margins of these can often be supplemented by notes in other books Ridley owned; clearly he had read more than he is known to have owned. Tunstal had a good library.[11]

Ridley valued Erasmus's scholarship. He evidently knew and better still understood the biblical studies (especially the New Testament scholarship) of which Erasmus was the leading light.[12] He certainly understood some of the scholarly labour involved, partly because Tunstal was a collaborator. For instance, Erasmus rejected a commentary on Hebrews often ascribed to Ambrose. In the preface to his Ambrose he explained that some learned Englishmen had sent him text copied from this.[13] In the margin here Ridley wrote: 'This was Tunstal, then the most learned bishop of London, now of Durham.' And in volume two of the edition, where the text said that a commentary on Hebrews was not included, Ridley noted 'This is not yet printed but it exists in the monastery of Canterbury in England and in the Carmelites of London.'[14]

8 This paper is part of a larger study of Ridley's Library which I am completing.

9 Jerome is now DCL, D VII, 1–4 (the set lacks vols 3 and 4 of this edition); D VII, 5 is the index; D VII, 6–11 is Augustine; D VII, 23–4 is Ambrose.

10 For sale by M. Morton-Smith of Guildford in September 1960, *XVIth Century Books*, list 8, item 56, D. Erasmus . . . *Declarationes ad censuras Lutetias vulgatas* (Froben, Basel, 1532) with Ridley's signature on the title page (as was typical).

11 What may be Tunstal's library catalogue is discussed by W. H. Herendeen and K. R. Bartlett, 'The Library of Cuthbert Tunstall, Bishop of Durham: British Library Add 40,676', *The Papers of the Bibliographical Society of America* 85 (1991), 235–96 with edition 262–96.

12 For this I have found most helpful J. H. Bentley, *Humanists and Holy Writ: New Testament Scholarship in the Renaissance* (Princeton, NJ, 1983).

13 DCL, D VII 23, sig. AA5.

14 DCL, D VII 24, fol. 1r (*fratrum predicatorum* has been erased and *carmelitarum* inserted

Ridley accepted some of Erasmus's views and realized that they involved adjusting contemporary ideas about the received biblical text. For instance, in the margin of the invective of Rusticus against Jerome he marked a passage quoted there about the woman taken in adultery (John 7: 53–8: 11) writing: 'concerning this, which is perhaps an addition (as it seems to Erasmus), see in the new *Annotations* on John'.[15] Ridley is not known to have owned the *Annotations* (published 1516), but sure enough, Erasmus wrote there: 'This is not in some Greek exemplars. In some it is in the margin.'[16] He added that Jerome found it in some codices and he then discussed treatments of it.

One can also observe Ridley struggling with the question of the canon of Scripture, which inevitably arose for anyone who read Erasmus's Jerome with care. He read the new editions and in part used them to collect ammunition in contemporary arguments. He noted in his margins what parts of the New Testament Jerome quoted: 'The book of the Apocalypse was accepted by the Church in the time of Jerome and with the name of John the Evangelist', he wrote next to the letter to Paula and Eustochium where Jerome quoted it.[17] He objected to some of Erasmus's conclusions in his scholia, particularly when Erasmus did not agree with Jerome. In the scholia to book two, where Erasmus says that while Jerome was alive the Romans did not receive the Epistle to the Hebrews nor the Greeks the Apocalypse, Ridley wrote: 'this is false and almost impious, if I am not mistaken'.[18] Erasmus went on to doubt that Peter's Epistles were by Peter, partly on grounds of style. Ridley was outraged: 'as if the apostles preached Christ throughout the world through interpreters and not by the gift of tongues given them by Christ. This is not far from impiety and foolishness.'[19] Clearly one could not judge the Holy Ghost by style. Next to Erasmus's further rejection of 2 Peter Ridley wrote: 'I wonder at this audacious and impudent lie about Jerome', who accepted it.[20]

Ridley was concerned where discussions of biblical authority under-

above); see K. W. Humphries, *The Friars' Libraries*, Corpus of British Library Catalogues (London, 1990), 188: assigned to Ambrose.

15 DCL, D VII 1, part 2, fol. 130r.

16 D. Erasmus, *Opera Omnia*, ed. J. Lerclerc (Leiden, 1705), vol. 6, col. 373; Bentley, *Humanists and Holy Writ*, 147.

17 DCL, D VII 1, part 1, fol. 57r.

18 DCL, D VII 1, part 2, fol. 3r.

19 DCL, D VII 1, part 2, fol. 3.

20 DCL, D VII 1, part 2, fol. 3v.

mined traditional usages and doctrines. There is evidence, particularly in his marginalia to John Eck's work on the Primacy of Peter, that he had read about and pondered on the question of the primacy of the text of scripture over preaching by apostolic authority (a version of the argument about scripture and tradition, and involving papal authority).[21] Evidently here he had read Jacques Lefèvre D'Etaples's commentaries on the four evangelists and seems to have followed Lefèvre's views on whether the evangelists (particularly Luke and Mark who could not be thought to have apostolic authority) had actually seen and heard the Lord. Ridley thought they had.[22]

If Ridley accepted and used some of Erasmus's scholarship, why did he dislike the other scholar so much? Evidently he objected most to Erasmus's tone of voice and particularly to his scornful repudiation of much traditional piety. Ridley owned a number of volumes of traditional biblical scholarship and aids to preaching, including Nicholas Gorran's thirteenth-century *Postilla* on the Epistles, printed in 1502, which also has marginalia showing that he read it carefully.[23] The only substantial manuscripts in his own hands are copies of sermons largely from the central Middle Ages; this style of preaching was regarded as hopelessly old-fashioned by Renaissance scholars.[24]

Ridley seems to have thought that some of what Erasmus was doing simply undermined beliefs without supporting piety. A flavour of his distaste can be seen in his notes in the margin of the preface to the edition of Jerome on the Evangelists. The preface is signed by Amerbach but Ridley did not accept that, being sure that it was really by Erasmus. The preface rejected as spurious a commentary on Mark, 'impudentissime' ascribed to Jerome. The preface thought that some monk or other had ascribed it; monks, says the text, monopolized Bible study 'almost tyrannically'.[25] Ridley commented:

> This preface is without doubt by Erasmus in the person of Amerbach . . . how much he scorns and how hostile he feels about the writings of religious fathers and monks is clear from the

21 Ridley owned Oxford, Bodleian Library, fol. Theta 651(1): J. Eck, *De primatu Petri*; bound in with T. Netter, *Sacramentalia*, both Paris 1521.

22 Ibid., fol. Theta 651(1) Book 1, ch. 1, fol. 41; J. Lefevre D'Etaples (Faber Stapulensis), *Commentarii initiatorii in quatuor evangelia* (Simon Colin, Meaux, 1522), fols 175r/v, 216r/v.

23 DCL, P V 31: N. Gorran, *Postilla..super epistolas* (Henri Gran, Hagenau, 1502).

24 Cambridge University Library, Mss Add 7197, Dd 5 27.

25 DCL, D VII 4, fol. 1v.

> content of this preface and from other innumerable places where he does not call them elucidation but tyranny and oppression. As if only the most arrogant of apostates, Erasmus, ought to be held a worthy interpreter of scripture. Who, I ask, Erasmus, showed you that these commentaries on Mark and on all the epistles of Paul were ascribed by monks to Jerome and that this was not done by ignorant, greedy scribes? Indeed what prevents a great part of them from having been written by Jerome; certainly they are learned and Christian and agree with what Jerome wrote elsewhere.

In other words, for Ridley it was not enough just to establish a text and work out authorship; more general questions of piety and edification should be considered and were probably more important.

Ridley was well read in the controversy sparked by Erasmus's work on the biblical text and was particularly concerned with Erasmus's attack on the Vulgate. He had certainly read Erasmus's new translation into Latin.[26] He had read and quoted with approval Sutor's (Pierre Coustourier's) *De tralatione Bibliae et novarum reprobatione interpretationum,* published in Paris in 1526. Ridley must have read this almost at once after publication because he quoted it in a letter, probably of February 1527.[27] In the work Sutor, with the approval of the Sorbonne, launched the first of several attacks on Erasmus for casting doubt on the accuracy of the Vulgate and on Lefèvre for translation into the vernacular.[28] Ridley also knew Erasmus's reply *Adversus Petri Sutoris … debacchationem Apologia*, which he cited in a margin to elucidate a puzzle from Lamentations, where Erasmus said that Sutor had not understood the meaning of the passage.[29] On the particular point Ridley agreed with Erasmus but in general he agreed with Sutor, who contended that the Vulgate was inspired.

26 See n. 31 below.

27 A. W. Pollard, *Records of the English Bible* (Oxford, 1911), no. XIII, 124.

28 J. K. Farge, *Orthodoxy and Reform in Early Reformation France* (Leiden, 1985), 178–9, 187; see also idem, *Biographical Register of the University of Paris, 1500–1536* (Toronto, Ont., 1980), no. 123; E. Rummel, *Erasmus and his Catholic Critics*, 2 vols (Nieuwkoop, 1989), 61–73; E. Rummel, *The Humanist-Scholastic Debate in the Renaissance and Reformation* (Cambridge, MA, 1995), esp. 103–18.

29 Comment on Lam. 3: 23: *novi diluculo multa est fides tua*, referred to in the margin of Ridley's copy of Denys the Carthusian on the major prophets (Peter Quentel, Cologne, 1534), DCL, P V 5, fol. 276: *novi secundum Erasmum contra Sutor disputantem nomen est non verbum.* For Erasmus I have used Bodleian Library, Antiq.f. GS 1525. 2 (Froben, Basel, 1525), discussion is m3r/v with quotation m4v.

In 1526 these became questions of pressing concern in England because Tyndale produced the New Testament in English and Tunstal had the task of preventing its spread into England.[30] Ridley was involved and wrote the only letter of his which remains, to explain to Archbishop Warham's secretary why Tyndale's Bible would not do.[31] His objections were twofold: scholarly and pastoral. He realized quite rightly that Tyndale's prefaces were Lutheran but he argued that key passages of the translation were also Lutheran, supporting justification by faith, rather than traditional good works. This translation, he said, agreed neither with the ancient translation (the Vulgate) nor with the Erasmian. Not surprisingly one of the passages was Matthew 25: 35, where the Vulgate *penitentiam agite* had been translated 'repent'. He summed up his objections by saying that Christian words like penance, charity, confession and grace were here losing their traditional meanings. This, of course, was perfectly true and for someone of Ridley's viewpoint made the text seriously dangerous to those who read it without a scholarly background.

Erasmus's attitude to papal history also received Ridley's censure. In the editions of the Fathers, Erasmus several times noted that the early papacy did not have the status it claimed later. From 1517 this was a crucial matter and in England after 1529, of course, a life-threatening question. Ridley's books are peppered with marginalia showing his eagerness to find corroboration of papal supremacy in early writings. His copy of Cyril of Alexandria on John, for instance, notes when Peter is called *princeps apostolorum* or is given first place among the apostles.[32] His copy of John Eck's *De Primatu Petri* (1521) has at the beginning of the text:[33]

> This work is clearly very salubrious and full of Christian erudition and cannot not be very much revered by anyone unless he be infected with heretical depravity and too much love of novelty.

The entire book is thick with marginalia, much of it approving. But his approval was not uncritical. He noted some contradictions, where Eck

30 D. Daniell, *William Tyndale, a Biography* (New Haven, CT and London, 1994), 110–49; D'Alton, 'Cuthbert Tunstal', 218–20.

31 Printed in Pollard, *Records*, 122–5.

32 Bristol Reference Library, 177/SR 62 (various works of Cyril 1524, trans. George of Trebizond), fols 78v, 155, 158v, 162, 188.

33 Oxford, Bodleian Library, Theta fol. 651(1) title page to Eck.

attributed texts to different popes.[34] He also noted scholarly problems. Eck prided himself on using originals but in one place he quoted from Gratian's *Decretum* (Dist 19 c.6) citing the passage as being from Augustine's *De doctrina Christiana.*[35] It seemed to say that papal decretals were to be venerated equally with scripture, thus arguing that Augustine subjected himself to the Apostolic See. Ridley's margin has 'this is *De doctrina Christiana* but the printed version is different.' Ridley, who owned Erasmus's Augustine, was right to query the argument.[36] Eck only quoted part of this, from Gratian, who paraphrased it by referring to writings accepted by Apostolic Sees and adding a sentence to make it refer to the papacy.

When reading Erasmus on Jerome, Ridley added to the index references to papal primacy and where early writers accepted it.[37] He likewise argued with Erasmus when Erasmus suggested that they had not done so or based arguments on what Ridley thought were historically dubious premises. Where Erasmus rejected as spurious a letter of Jerome to Pope Damasus, on the grounds that to address the pope as a monarch was anachronistic, Ridley disagreed and wrote: 'You lie evilly and craftily, apostate', citing a list of early writers who had thus addressed the pope.[38] Elsewhere he cited where he thought Jerome did so and in his margin wrote: 'O apostate Erasmus evil and blinded by hatred against the pontiff.'[39]

Ridley also very much objected to Erasmus's attitude to traditional hagiography, particularly its miraculous elements. Ridley had a liking for pious *exempla*, especially tales about Eucharistic miracles. This probably reflects his preaching. He owned William of Auvergne's works, printed in Paris in 1516 as an example of sound doctrine from the past (William was bishop of Paris 1228–49).[40] In notes about the Eucharist, Ridley included one to illustrate William's discussion about the presence of angels during the offering of mass: 'Jacques Faber (Lefèvre) tells

34 Ibid., Fol. Theta 651(1), Book 1, fols 8v, 30, a text attributed first to Nicholas and then to Hormisdas.

35 Ibid., Fol. Theta 651 (1), Book 1, fol. 33.

36 Augustine, *De Doctrina Christiana*, 2.25, ed. W. M. Green, CSEL 80 Sect. 6, part 6 (Vienna, 1963), 40 for the passage. *Corpus Iuris Canonici*, ed. A. Friedberg, 1 (Leipzig, 1879) at this canon quoted the variants and correct text in a note. DCL now lacks vol. 3 of the Augustine set, which has *De Doctrina*.

37 See additions to the index volume, DCL, D VII 5, fols 89, 216, 243, 321, 323.

38 DCL, D VII 1, part 2, fol. 197.

39 DCL, D VII 1, part 1, fol. 106v.

40 Cambridge, St John's College, O.3.19: *Operum Summa* (Francois Regnault, Paris, 1516).

a true story about this in the Epistle of Paul to Timothy.'[41] Sure enough, Lefèvre on 1 Timothy 4, writing in praise of the priesthood, described a man living a holy life who saw a *corona* over the priest's head during the consecration.[42] Ridley also noted a story from the *Penitentiale* of Thomas Chobham, about Maurice bishop of Paris, who when dying knew that he was offered an unconsecrated host.[43]

Erasmus notoriously would not tolerate this kind of story and his accounts of Jerome and Ambrose came shorn of much pious fiction.[44] In the 1527 edition of the works of Ambrose, Ridley noted: 'No Christian narrative, especially if it tells of miracles, can please Erasmus, but if Titus Livius or some pagan writer narrates such things they are fairly easily believed.' [45] Ridley also objected to what he he judged to be Erasmus's arrogance and innovation for its own sake. When editing *De viris illustribus* Erasmus suggested an emendation where his Latin and Greek versions did not agree. This annoyed Ridley who wrote:

> Let him who will see how foolishly and affectedly Erasmus innovates in everything. He says that the Latin of the New Testament should be corrected and returned to the Greek sources. But now he tries to criticise the Latin sources at the Greek streams.[46]

Erasmus was particularly critical of contemporary monasticism and this incensed Ridley, especially because Erasmus was an 'apostate.' When Erasmus wrote in his scholia to Jerome's letter to Rusticus that it would be better now if there were fewer monasteries because they were homes of superstition, Ridley's margin reads: 'this is evil rather than learned or pious . . . but Erasmus is always blind about the monastic life and the monastery,'[47] and elsewhere he repudiated Erasmus's account of early monastic history, writing: 'Here Erasmus slips filthily blinded by his inveterate hatred against his fellow monks.'[48] It is possible that

41 O. 3. 19, 2: fol. 22.

42 J. Lefèvre, *In Novum Testamentum*, 2 vols (Henry Stephanus, Paris, c.1515, at Durham University Library, Routh 7.c.9), 2: fol. 200.

43 DCL, P V 7: Denys the Carthusian, *Sermones de Sanctis* (Peter Quentel, Cologne, 1532) at foot of fol. ccxxvii; for Thomas's story, *Summa Confessorum*, ed. F. Broomfield, Analecta medievalia Namurcensia 25 (Louvain and Paris, 1968), 136–7.

44 E. F. Rice, *St Jerome and the Renaissance* (Baltimore, MD and London, 1985), ch. 5.

45 DCL, D VII 23, sig. AA5.

46 DCL, D VII 1, part 1, fol. 138.

47 DCL, D VII 1, part 1, fol. 20.

48 DCL, D VII 37, part 1, fol. 53.

Ridley here was particularly anxious that no reader would be misled; the book ended belonging to monks (and then ex-monks) of Durham.

Ultimately for Ridley matters like these were about English heresies in the 1520s and not questions which could be discussed at leisure by scholars in their studies pursuing the truth. When, in a throw-away remark, Erasmus said that baptismal vows were taken so young that people did not remember them, Ridley wrote in the margin: 'From this and from other very suspect sayings of Erasmus, has arisen the Anabaptist heresy in our age.'[49] He was not alone in blaming Erasmus for the Reformation. But one can see how galling it must have been to one who sympathized with much of the intellectual endeavour of the great scholar that it was not more overtly harnessed to the struggle against the Lutheran menace. To a conservative theologian in the 1520s and '30s Erasmus was an ambiguous ally.

Durham University

49 DCL, D VII 1, part 1, fol. 2v.

THE REINVENTION OF DEVOTION IN THE BRITISH REFORMATIONS*

by ALEC RYRIE

THE ideal Protestant life was built around two critical events: conversion and death. At the first, the believer received justification and the assurance of salvation; at the second, the promise once received came into its fullness. This pattern was implicit from the earliest days of the Reformation, and when the English Puritans of William Perkins' school mapped out a schematic for the Protestant life they made it explicit. Theologically, this pattern made a great deal of sense. However, it created a practical problem. Many believers had to endure a tediously long interval between these two high points. How was the good Protestant supposed to pass the time?

This was not a problem which troubled early modern Catholics. Their Church offered them endless religious activities: from the use of set prayers such as the rosary, through to attendance at Mass, pilgrimage and, *in extremis*, adopting a religious rule of life. But the Reformed Protestantism which became the established faith of England and Scotland in the sixteenth century condemned all of these practices (Lutheranism was a very different story). This was a faith which was wary of recommending any specific pious action, for fear of implying that such action might be taken to be meritorious and so detract from the all-sufficiency of Christ's atonement. Reformed Protestants received detailed instruction on what they were supposed to believe, but much less on how they were supposed positively to enact those beliefs from day to day. The New Testament scholar Edwin Freed has recently described the Reformation doctrines of justification by asking, 'Are baptized converts to sit drenched with righteousness, like ducks covered with oil, unable to move?'[1] This essay addresses the problem of how early modern English and Scottish Protestants lived out their faith. Their doctrines created a kind of pious vacuum; how did their piety fill it?

* Earlier versions of this paper were read at the University of Birmingham and the University of Durham, and I am grateful to colleagues there for their comments and suggestions.

1 Edwin D. Freed, *The Morality of Paul's Converts* (London and Oakville, CT, 2005), 40.

One traditional answer would run something like this. In the first generation or two of the Reformation, Protestantism was pure and uncorrupted by power and establishment. Its pieties were simple and holy. As time went on, however, carnal gospellers and backsliders contaminated that early purity by introducing crypto-popish rituals from which the weak could fashion their idols. The British Protestant worlds thus became split between those who wished to preserve the Gospel in its pristine condition, and who in England were labelled Puritans for their pains; and the conformists, compromisers and sell-outs who began by defending the dregs of popery in the Book of Common Prayer and ended up as Arminians and Laudians.

Partisan and tendentious as it is, this approach contains a kernel of truth. There was indeed a vision of a simple Protestant piety that was in place very early in the Reformation period, certainly by the reign of Edward VI (1547–53). This was an approach which saw the removal of false piety as a necessary precursor to building a true one; the question, therefore, was simply how far that process had to go, and how far the popish contamination had reached. However, at the same time that 'corrupted' pious traditions were being hurled out into the street, new ones were knocking at the door, often looking remarkably like the ones which had just been expelled. This was, obviously, a somewhat ticklish process, and those who were later called Puritans were particularly ready to accuse others of supping with the devil. Yet the Puritans were implicated too: Puritan piety also abhors a vacuum, and Puritans too had long years of pious living to fill. At the end of this essay we will return to this, and sketch the process by which one such new form of structured piety coalesced in Protestantism.

But first, we will examine that early vision of a simple Protestant piety: a vision which underpinned Protestant life for a century or more to follow, and of which you will still find traces today. There are many possible approaches to this early Protestant piety, but here we will consider it in four obvious, traditional and overlapping aspects: study, work, struggle and prayer.

I

Study, learning and doctrine were fundamental to Protestantism from the beginning. Good Protestants were expected to be interested in doctrine, to listen to sermons, and to read their Bibles and doctrinal treatises. If necessary, they should learn to read. They should attend and engage in debates and disputations on doctrinal questions. And these activities have to be taken seriously as ritual, pious activities, not just as intellectual ones.

The intellectualism of early Protestantism is hard to overestimate. One well-known and striking example of this comes from Foxe's *Actes and Monuments*. Foxe believed (probably wrongly)[2] that Hadleigh in Suffolk was an early centre of Protestant commitment, but his description of the village was very different in tone from the familiar tropes of eighteenth-century revival narratives. Foxe claimed that the people of Hadleigh

> became exceeding wel learned in the holye scriptures, as well women as men: so that a man might haue found among them many that had often read the whole Bible through, and that coulde haue sayd a great part of S. Paules epistles by hart, and very wel & readily haue geuen a godly learned sentence in any matter of controuersie. . . . The whole towne seemed rather an Uniuersitie of the learned, then a town of Cloth-making or labouring people.[3]

Protestantism was a movement born and bred in universities, and one of its ambitions was to turn the world into a giant university: a world in which Christians would spend their time in private study or in attending the lectures and seminars which they called sermons and prophesyings. Study and discussion were themselves pious activities for Protestants. When John Knox went on a missionary visit to the underground Protestant congregations in Scotland in the 1550s, he claimed that he spent his time engaged in 'doctrine', and in an open letter to those congregations suggesting how they should live their communal lives, he did not mention worship as such but urged that they spend their weekly meetings in discussing Scripture. Likewise, John Hooper's recommendation for Protestants in Marian England was that they assemble regularly 'to talk and renew among yourselves the truth of your religion', meetings which he hoped would include exposition of scripture. Indeed, James Hogg's famous satire of Scottish Protestantism, *The Private Memoirs and Confessions of a Justified Sinner*, suggested that

2 John Craig, 'Reformers, Conflict and Revisionism: the Reformation in Sixteenth-Century Hadleigh', *HistJ* 42 (1999), 1–23.

3 John Foxe, *Actes and Monuments of Matters Most Speciall in the Church* (London, 1583), 1518.

Protestants should abandon prayer altogether in favour of theological argument.[4]

This was a caricature, but the truth behind it was the Protestant conviction that salvation came not merely through faith, but through well-informed faith. No one disputed Luther's careful distinction between *assensus*, a mere belief which cannot save and which is indeed shared by the demons, and *fiducia*, a living, saving faith and personal trust in God; yet Protestants continued to insist on the primacy of knowledge. Hugh Latimer, the finest preacher of the first generation of English Protestants, relentlessly quoted Romans 10: 17 – 'faith comes by hearing' – and seems to have believed that he could, indeed, talk his hearers into God's Kingdom. The few early Protestant conversion narratives we have describe conversion as a process of education and of enlightenment – which is perhaps one reason why there are so few.[5] Godly learning was not merely valuable for a Christian, but essential. The Edwardian Book of Homilies opens with 'a fruitful exhortation to the reading and knowledge of Holy Scripture'. This points out that no-one can be called a lawyer, astronomer or physician who has not studied the law, astronomy or medicine. 'How can any man then say that he professeth Christ and his religion, if he will not apply himself . . . to read and hear, and so to know the books of Christ's gospel and doctrine!'[6] In 1549, John Hooper provided a prayer to be said before hearing the Bible read, which asked God 'to illuminate our minds, that we may understand the mysteries contained in thy holy law; and into the same self thing that we godly understand, we may be virtuously transformed': thus making understanding almost a part of the process of justification.[7] Archbishop Sandys insisted that 'where there is backwardness in knowledge, there must needs also be weakness of faith'.[8]

4 Alec Ryrie, 'Congregations, Conventicles and the Nature of Early Protestantism in Scotland', *P&P* 191 (2006), 45–76, at 53, 60–2; John Hooper, *The Later Writings of Bishop Hooper*, ed. Charles Nevinson (Cambridge, 1852), 590.

5 Alec Ryrie, *The Gospel and Henry VIII* (Cambridge, 2003), 157–8; Peter Marshall, 'Evangelical Conversion in the Reign of Henry VIII', in Peter Marshall and Alec Ryrie, eds, *The Beginnings of English Protestantism* (Cambridge, 2002), 14–37.

6 *Certain Sermons or Homilies Appointed to be Read in Churches in the Time of the Late Queen Elizabeth* (Oxford, 1844), 1, 5.

7 Hooper, *Later Writings*, 3.

8 Edwin Sandys, *The Sermons of Edwin Sandys, DD*, ed. John Ayre (Cambridge, 1841), 424.

Anthony Gilby asserted that 'the Lorde oure God is the God of knowledge'.[9]

Indeed, Protestants were reluctant to admit that there might be any other kind of spiritual nourishment. When expounding Psalm 23, Hooper insisted that the 'pleasant pastures' of the text refer to 'the pastures most pleasant and rich of his doctrine . . . and the sweet waters of the holy scriptures'.[10] Latimer, expounding St Paul's image of the armour of God in Ephesians 6, pointed out that the only offensive weapon mentioned in the text was the sword of the Word. Scripture, he deduced, is the Christian's only weapon. 'Only with God's word we shall avoid and chase the devil, and with nothing else.'[11] Sandys contrasted Catholic clergy who 'keep men occupied always in corporal and bodily exercise, which profiteth little' to their Protestant counterparts who 'train men up in the knowledge of Christ'.[12] Augustine famously described the Church as a mother; Calvin described it as a schoolmaster.

II

When not engaged in godly learning, Protestants were expected to live holy lives in the secular world, and to work at doing so. The good Protestant should live a generically holy life of self-sacrifice, simplicity and (especially) charity. The Protestant martyrologies, those sprawling books of exemplars which were a kind of replacement for Catholic hagiography, were full of humbling stories of such things. We read, for example, that when the Scottish preacher George Wishart was studying at Cambridge in the 1540s, he lived a life of rigorous self-denial, fasted regularly, slept on 'a pouffe of straw [and] coarse newe canuasse Sheetes', and bathed in cold water. He dressed simply and regularly gave his clothing to the poor.[13] Cambridge was used to extravagantly charitable Protestants: in the 1520s Latimer and his early mentor Thomas Bilney had been 'ever visiting prisoners and sick folk . . . moving them to patience and to acknowledge their faults'.[14] Protestant

9 Anthony Gilby, *An Answer to the Devillish Detection of S. Gardiner* (London?, 1548), fol. 2r.

10 Hooper, *Later Writings*, 197.

11 Hugh Latimer, *Sermons*, ed. George Elwes Corrie (Cambridge, 1844), 505.

12 Sandys, *Sermons*, 29.

13 Foxe, *Actes and Monuments*, 1268.

14 Latimer, *Sermons*, 335.

sermons are full of exhortations to charity and theatrical laments for the nation's cold-heartedness. However, simple charity as a core religious activity is unsatisfactory for two reasons. First, actually living this sort of life is remarkably difficult. Secondly, it is a poor marker of identity. Protestants clearly wanted it to be just that: the Elizabethan Homilies insisted that it is through charity that true Christians 'declare openly and manifestly unto the sight of men, that they are the sons of God, and elect of him unto salvation'.[15] Yet papists could be charitable too, and indeed, the lives of the mendicant orders and the clearer place of works in salvation meant that Catholicism managed to appropriate charity as distinctively its own in a way which Protestantism never did.

However, Protestantism claimed another kind of work much more successfully: gainful worldly labour. These are treacherous waters. Max Weber famously discerned a link between what the so-called 'Protestant ethic' and the so-called 'spirit of capitalism',[16] and for most of that century scholars who have tried to follow him into this subject have been holed below the water-line. Weber has a way of making Reformation historians slightly drunk, insofar as we are forced to admit that his evidence is selective, impressionistic and extremely unreliable, but that he nevertheless hit on a number of insights which we cannot quite shake off. It is, unavoidably, a subject which Reformation-era preachers addressed. Latimer returned again and again to the idea of vocation, insisting on the dignity of secular work. 'I am no more assured in my preaching that I serve God, than the servant is in . . . scouring the candlesticks.' One of Latimer's favourite sermon illustrations was the tale of how St Anthony, living as a hermit in the wilderness, was told by God that there was a cobbler in Alexandria whose life was more perfect than his own. The indignant saint hastened to find and interview this cobbler, who denied having any heroic virtue but described how he began each day with prayer, then spent the whole day 'in getting my living', all the while living honestly and instructing his family in godliness as best he could. And while Latimer certainly did not approve of acquisitiveness or greed, he added, 'if God sendeth . . . honours and riches . . . refuse them not.' He even preached a kind of

15 *Certain Sermons or Homilies*, 340, 347–8.

16 Max Weber, *The Protestant Ethic and the Spirit of Capitalism*, trans. Talcott Parsons (London, 1992; cf. first edition, 1930).

prosperity gospel, in which those who give generously to the poor will receive from God more than they have given.[17]

And these were common themes. The Elizabethan Homilies included a sermon on the subject, urging that 'every one ought, in his lawful vocation and calling, to give himself to labour . . . both for the getting of his own living honestly, and for to profit others'. This also warned, in very Weberian terms, that hired men who 'abuse their time in idleness' are thieves in God's eyes.[18] The English Primer of 1553, an authorized book of private prayers, included prayers for use by those in all stations of life: ministers and magistrates, of course, but also lawyers and even merchants, who are described as having a God-given ministry of bringing necessities across the sea and of building international unity in the process. Yet landlords are described in very negative terms. Perhaps Protestantism was already backing the monied interest against the landed interest?[19] And Protestant preachers of all stripes thundered relentlessly against idleness. For all this, however, their concept of vocation is (as Weber pointed out) a static one. Latimer insisted that 'God will that every man shall keep himself in his vocation, till he be further called of God' – which he made clear that God did not do very often. His concern for the subject seems to have been driven by two fears: first, that unauthorized lay people might take it on themselves to preach without (as he saw it) proper vocation; and second, that Protestants were open to the charge of antinomianism if he did not stress the need 'to apply ourselves to goodness, every one in his calling'.[20] So we cannot, of course, find the spirit of capitalism in the sixteenth century. What we can find are acknowledgements of the spiritual dignity of secular labour, of the legitimacy of earning an income for oneself and one's family, and fierce imprecations against idleness. And there is perhaps one point here that Weber missed. If Protestants indeed did place greater religious value on purposeful worldly labour, this was not simply because their theology permitted it, but because their phobia of ritual created a vacuum. Since Protestantism lacked pious acts with which time could be blamelessly and profitably filled, worldly work – which is at least time-consuming – might acquire that tincture.

17 Latimer, *Sermons*, 350, 392–3, 408–10, 513; idem, *Sermons and Remains*, ed. George Elwes Corrie (Cambridge, 1845), 94, 214.

18 *Certain Sermons or Homilies*, 459–60, 464–5.

19 Joseph Ketley, ed., *The Two Liturgies, AD 1549 and AD 1552, with Other Documents Set Forth by Authority in the Reign of King Edward VI* (Cambridge, 1844), 458–9.

20 Latimer, *Sermons*, 214; Latimer, *Sermons and Remains*, 26–39, 141, 151, 154.

III

Yet if work is a spiritual undertaking, that does not only or even chiefly mean worldly work. More important, perhaps, is the idea that the Christian life itself is a labour to be performed and, not least, to be monitored and assessed. The idea of the Christian life as a struggle is of course not distinctively Protestant, although it is to some extent distinctively early modern. The most influential devotional text of the whole century was Erasmus's *Handbook of a Christian Soldier*, which was built entirely on that metaphor. The idea flourished in Catholic piety too, most obviously amongst the Jesuits, and confessional strife only reinforced it. Yet Protestants gave a distinctive twist to this common inheritance, blending the emphasis on the Christian life as a struggle with Luther's so-called theology of the cross, his emphasis that true Christians are called to suffer. It was this blend of struggle and suffering which gave the Protestant life its particular and aggressive dynamic. Protestants expected a spiritual life which was linear, not cyclical: rather than moving through the rhythms of the old sacramental system, they expected to move on from conversion, through higher and greater knowledge and holiness, until death. Spiritual progress thus becomes essential, and backsliding (a very Protestant word) fatal. As Archbishop Sandys put it, 'Walk on, go forward. For if ye be in the way of life, not to go forward is to go backward. . . . Take heed, I say, of backsliding. . . . Go on from strength to strength, from virtue to virtue. . . . God grant that there be not a retiring from strength to weakness, from virtue to sinfulness!'[21]

It follows that this is a spirituality better suited to crisis and drama than to peace and tranquillity. That is partly because, from the very beginning, Protestants took persecution as a sign of God's favour, and came positively to relish it as a result. The threat of martyrdom, after all, gives the Christian life an unmistakable dynamic. However, most Protestants most of the time lived in more settled circumstances, where the great threat was not persecution but lukewarmness, being spat out of Christ's mouth, a condition of which Protestants were particularly frightened. Much Protestant piety, therefore, consisted of people living in settled times trying deliberately to unsettle themselves, and to create a sense of confrontation, crisis and progress. This is perhaps most

21 Sandys, *Sermons*, 233.

obvious in the perennial popularity of the martyr-stories, which allow readers vicariously to experience the trials of the martyrs and to daunt themselves a little by comparing themselves to their piety. John Foxe described his martyr-stories as a mirror in which readers might see themselves, and so be 'better prepared vnto like conflictes'.[22] Martyr-stories, like the fearful and urgently devoured news of horrors visited on good Protestants overseas, were also reminders that at any moment God's patience with Britain might be exhausted, persecution renewed, 'our houses razed, our lands extended [seized], our bodies imprisoned, our wives and children murdered before our eyes'.[23] Such fears were not unrealistic in the later sixteenth century, but they were also stoked by Protestantism's stubborn self-image as a remnant, a poor persecuted little flock in a sea of reprobation.[24]

We can see the same mindset at work in the Protestant unease with worldly good fortune: for those whom God loves, he disciplines. Another of Latimer's favourite sermon anecdotes was the tale of St Ambrose visiting a nobleman who had never known ill fortune of any kind; Ambrose concluded that God could not be present in such a house and swiftly left it, and not a moment too soon, because the earth promptly opened and swallowed it up.[25] Compare Martin Luther's spiritual agonies when he realised that he was not going to die a martyr's death, and he feared that God had not found him worthy of that honour.[26] And the Edwardian Book of Homilies preached that 'nothing should pierce our heart so sore, and put us in such horrible fear, as when we know in our conscience, that we have grievously offended God, and do so continue, and that yet he striketh not, but quietly suffereth us in the naughtiness that we have delight in.'[27] To live in peace was a sign of reprobation. As Hooper insisted, 'If we suffer not, all our religion is not worth a haw.'[28] John Bradford, facing his own martyrdom, compared suffering to a medicine: the worse it tastes, the better it is for you. 'Lustily, therefore, drink the cup; Christ giveth it.'[29]

22 Foxe, *Actes and Monuments*, xv.

23 Sandys, *Sermons*, 82.

24 Patrick Collinson, *The Religion of Protestants* (Oxford, 1982), 189–205.

25 Latimer, *Sermons*, 435–6, 483.

26 David Bagchi, 'Luther and the Problem of Martyrology', in Diana Wood, ed., *Martyrs and Martyrologies*, SCH 30 (Oxford, 1993), 209–20, at 212.

27 *Certain Sermons or Homilies*, 77.

28 Hooper, *Later Writings*, 283.

29 John Bradford, 'An Exhortacion to the Carienge of Chrystes Crosse', in Miles

And yet, corporal suffering for the faith was not usually available in Edwardian or Elizabethan England. Being mocked by one's neighbours or frightening oneself with far-off persecutions are poor substitutes for the real thing. In their search for a struggle, Protestants turned to more persistent and reliable enemies: the world, the flesh and the devil. One of Latimer's rhetorical tricks was to warn his audience that 'now in this hall, amongst this audience, there be many thousand devils. . . . If we could see them, we should perceive them to hop and dance upon our heads for gladness, because they have done unto us a mischief. . . . Therefore it is so ordained of God, that we should have war, yea, and nothing but war, a standing war.'[30] Thomas Becon agreed: 'The lyfe of manne vpon earthe is nothinge els then a warrefare and contynuall aflycte wyth her ghostly enemies. . . . Man in thys vale of miserye is neuer at quiet, nor hathe so much leasure as once to breathe.'[31] These are, of course, hardly original themes in Christianity, although put in extreme terms. More distinctive, perhaps, is the proposed method of fighting: an intensely reflexive life of self-examination and continual repentance. This was very early a matter not simply of keeping a constant watch over one's morals, but of observing one's own behaviour for the signs of election. Latimer was no hard-line predestinarian, rejecting the perseverance of the saints, but still preached that 'if you know your sin, and feel your own wretchedness and filthiness', and have faith and 'an earnest desire to amendment . . . you may be sure . . . that you are elect and predestinate to everlasting life.' By contrast, he had a warning for those who did not feel themselves locked in a constant spiritual struggle: 'the devil letteth them alone, because they be his already; he hath them in bondage, they be his slaves.' [32] The lay radical Thomas Broke wrote in 1548 that assurance of salvation lay in striving 'constantly against the deuel, ye world and the fleshe', and therefore urged his readers, 'consider well wyth thy selfe, whether thou be, a constant warryar agaynst synne'.[33] The Edwardian Book of Homilies urged Christians to 'try and examine our faith' not only

Coverdale, *Remains of Myles Coverdale*, ed. George Pearson (Cambridge, 1846), where wrongly ascribed to Coverdale: 227–78, at 247.

30 Latimer, *Sermons*, 438–9, 493.

31 Thomas Becon, *A fruitful treatise of fasting wherin is declared what ye Christen fast is* (London, 1551), sig. G1v.

32 Latimer, *Sermons and Remains*, 175–6; Latimer, *Sermons*, 441.

33 Thomas Broke, *Certeyn Meditations, and Thinges to be had in Remembraunce, and well Considered by Euery Christian* (London, 1548), sigs. B7r–8v.

through inner struggle, but through assessing one's own good works: 'Let us, by such virtues as ought to spring out of faith, shew our election to be sure and stable.'[34]

The pattern of piety thus recommended was an alarming mixture of subjectivity and objectivity: Christians were exhorted constantly to feel the gravity of their own sins, to struggle against temptation, and to bring forth repentance and its fruits, and at the same time to watch themselves doing so in order to find assurance of salvation. The anxieties which this kind of piety could produce are well known, but even for those who avoided that particular trap, one feature of this kind of piety is worth noting: its ability to become all-consuming, which might mean either exhausting or enthralling. The exhaustion is plain enough from some of the set prayers which some early Protestant authors offered to their readers for their use. They often provide a prayer which is to be prayed every day, prayers which typically include a dramatic denunciation of the whole of one's life up to that point as worthless and a plea for the grace totally to reorient oneself. Protestants were being asked to enter into radical acts of repentance every day, to treat every day as the first day of the rest of their lives.[35] Sustaining this kind of intensity for any length of time can never have been easy, and later Puritans came to spend much of their energy on doing so – as, too, did their Catholic contemporaries. But while Catholic self-examination could focus on the confessional, Puritans, lacking such structures, ended up creating that invaluable genre of documents, the spiritual journal. Spiritual journals, as well as being extremely time-consuming pious exercises, allowed Puritans to practice their introspection systematically, and to keep track of their spiritual progress – or, more commonly, lament and fret about their spiritual stasis. So we find the seventeenth-century preacher Oliver Heywood recording annual covenants with God in his journal, and each year cursing himself for his failure to keep them. His near-contemporary John Rastrick began another such covenant with a lament: 'Still the same sins, Lord!' As the recent work of Andrew Cambers has shown, these journals' authors repeatedly re-read them.[36] They were an ideal means not only to fight one's spiritual battles, but also anxiously to watch oneself doing so.

34 *Certain Sermons or Homilies*, 39.

35 For an official example, see Ketley, ed., *Two Liturgies*, 379–80.

36 Cited in Andrew Cambers, 'Reading, the Godly, and Self-Writing in England, c. 1580–1720', *Journal of British Studies* 46 (2007), 796–825. I am grateful to Dr Cambers for providing me with an advance copy of this valuable essay.

IV

This brings us to the final dimension of early Protestant piety: prayer, the heart of the question. Early Protestant prayer is a topic historians are only now trying to approach, the field having been led by literary scholars.[37] The historical study of prayer is of course formidably difficult, for it is an attempt to eavesdrop on people's relationships with God. It is doubly difficult when dealing with Protestantism, partly because we are dealing with a much narrower concept of prayer than in the Catholic tradition, and also because of the scrupulous reluctance of many Protestants to prescribe any practices of prayer at all.

This unease is most obvious in public prayer. It is one of the ironies of the English Reformation that its most enduring text, aside from the English Bible itself, is the Book of Common Prayer: and yet this came out of a religious culture that was very uneasy about public worship, which saw it as a minefield to be negotiated rather than an opportunity to be celebrated. As Catharine Davies has pointed out, very few Protestants in Edward VI's reign had anything positive to say in the defence of the Prayer Book service.[38] All agreed that public prayer was necessary; most accepted conformity to the Prayer Book for the sake of good order; but very few described worship or praise as worthwhile in themselves. Protestants' greatest concern about worship was fear that they might get it wrong and so offend God. This could result, again, in a stress on the laboriousness of worship. In 1604, Nicholas Bownd wrote, 'it is a very hard thing to serue God, as we should, and therefore in all parts of his worship wee must vse great diligence, that they may bee done in that manner, that he may fauourably accept them.'[39]

37 Amongst literary scholars' works, see Ramie Targoff, *Common Prayer: the Language of Public Devotion in Early Modern England* (Chicago, IL and London, 2001); Richard Rambuss, *Closet Devotions* (Durham, NC and London, 1998); and several essays by Kate Narveson, in particular 'Publishing the Sole-talk of the Soule: Genre in Early Stuart Piety', in Daniel W. Doersken and Christopher Hodgkins, eds, *Centered on the Word* (Newark, NJ, 2004), 110–26. The historical material is much thinner: see, for example, several essays by Virginia Reinburg, notably 'Hearing Lay People's Prayer', in Barbara Diefendorf and Carla Hesse, eds, *Culture and Identity in Early Modern Europe (1500–1800): Essays in Honor of Natalie Zemon Davis* (Ann Arbor, MI, 1993), 19–39; and John Craig, 'Psalms, Groans and Dogwhippers: the Soundscape of Worship in the English Parish Church, 1547–1642', in Will Coster and Andrew Spicer, eds, *Sacred Space in Early Modern Europe* (Cambridge, 2005), 104–23.

38 Catharine Davies, *A Religion of the Word: the Defence of the Reformation in the Reign of Edward VI* (Manchester, 2002), 118–22.

39 Nicholas Bownd, *Medicines for the Plague* (London, 1604), 134.

For most writers who addressed the subject, public worship had one overriding value: not its glorification of God, but its edification of the people – 'edification' meaning, of course, 'education'. The preface to the 1549 and 1552 Prayer Books is explicit as to the purpose of the daily Offices of morning and evening prayer: 'that the people (by daily hearing of holy scripture read in the Church) should continually profit more and more in the knowledge of God, and be the more inflamed with the love of his true religion.' The Offices as such were simply packaging for the Biblical material. The Prayer Book defines itself not as a liturgy for worship but as a teaching tool, indeed as a Scripture delivery mechanism. The famous essay on ceremonies in the Prayer Book likewise offers no positive defence of ceremonies aside from the claim that 'without some ceremonies it is not possible to keep any order or quiet discipline in the church'.[40] Those who were called on to defend the new liturgy were scarcely any warmer. Latimer told his hearers, 'it is a good and godly order, and God will have it so', but immediately admitted that he himself did not always attend the daily Offices. For, he said, if a parson is 'unable to teach the word of God...it were better for me to teach me family at home, than to go thither and spend my time in vain, and so lose my labour.'[41] Teaching was the yardstick.

However, edification was not limited to the preaching of the word and the ministry of the sacraments. Public worship also had a vital role in modelling good practices of prayer which the people might carry through to their private lives. Indeed, Ramie Targoff has persuasively argued that the Prayer Book service changed the ways in which English people prayed in private as well as in public.[42] Private prayer was, of course, something to which Protestant ministers endlessly exhorted their congregations. As the Elizabethan Homilies put it, 'there is nothing in all man's life . . . so needful to be spoken of, and daily to be called upon, as hearty, zealous, and devout prayer.'[43] Beyond such truisms, though, two points are worth noting. First, the definition of prayer is comparatively circumscribed: prayer is always verbal, even if not always spoken aloud, and consists essentially of repentance, thanksgiving and supplication. Second, it is here that we can see one of the sharper divisions between Puritan and 'hotter' Protestants on the

40 Ketley, ed., *Two Liturgies*, 17, 156.
41 Latimer, *Sermons and Remains*, 156–7.
42 Targoff, *Common Prayer*.
43 *Certain Sermons or Homilies*, 284.

one hand, and conformist or avant-garde Protestants on the other. Protestants of all stripes provided model prayers for their flocks to use in their private devotions, but (especially in Puritan hands) such 'prayers' were often a continuation of preaching by other means, substantial slabs of doctrine which authors placed in believers' mouths.[44] Like the Prayer Book itself, such prayers were teaching tools as much as devotional aids. But for conformists and those attracted by the ceremonial revival, they were or became more than that. In the early Reformation, we find moderate or eirenically-minded reformers producing prayers which echo medieval pious traditions: so we have formalized invocations of the Trinity or of Christ's wounds, or Queen Katherine Parr urging her readers to meditate inwardly on 'the book of the crucifix'.[45] A generation or two later, we find the rise of the genre which Kate Narveson calls the 'holy soliloquy', the published, stylized address of the soul to itself and to God. Such soliloquies drew on medieval patterning and, while they were unimpeachably Protestant in their theology, tended to avoid the anxiety and minute self-examination of Puritanism.[46]

The Puritan approach was subtly different. Although Puritans had no qualms about holy soliloquies as such, they increasingly disliked the use of written texts in prayer. If the words of Scripture themselves could be used as prayers, that was one thing, but Puritans would not put uninspired words into believers' mouths. This refusal again reflected the double bind which Protestant theology placed on devotion. For on the one hand, there is a stress on the importance of labour and persistence in prayer, on prayer as a part of one's struggle. Augustine Bernher cited Latimer as a model – 'oftentimes so long he continued kneeling, that he was not able for to rise without help'[47] – while Archbishop Sandys looked to the apostle James, who 'made his knees as hard as the hoof with continual praying'.[48] We are endlessly reminded that Christ sweated blood in the earnestness of his prayer in Gethsemane. And yet,

44 For example, see the form of prayer which Bishop Grindal prescribed for householders to use during the 1563 plague epidemic. This form opened with a long 'prayer' which rehearsed God's actions, the people's sins, and the Protestant interpretation of both, a thousand-word preamble to the briefest of actual requests. Edmund Grindal, *The Remains of Archbishop Grindal, DD*, ed. William Nicholson (Cambridge, 1843), 478–81.

45 Katherine Parr, *The Lamentacion of a Sinner* (London, 1547), sigs. B8v–D2v.

46 Narveson, 'Publishing the Sole-talk of the Soule'.

47 Latimer, *Sermons*, 144–5, 165–7, 322.

48 Sandys, *Sermons*, 38.

this labour was of an unusual kind, for believers could no more pray correctly by sheer effort than they could make themselves sweat blood. It was a commonplace that 'a few words spoken with faith is better than a long bibble-babble'; and that 'we ought alwaies to pray from our hearts, and neuer with the tongue onely.'[49] True prayer was by definition unfeigned, and could not be attained by human effort but by the work of the Holy Spirit. There were a range of ways in which authors and preachers tried to square this circle. John Hooper, awaiting execution, felt keenly the impossibility of the preacher's task: 'to bring myself and all men from knowledge and talk to feeling, consenting, and a full surrendering of ourselves', but to do so through the medium of 'knowledge and talk'. And yet in his evocative descriptions of such true prayer he seems to be trying to communicate God's Spirit to his readers by the raw force of his rhetoric.[50] Fifty years later, the Puritan divine Nicholas Bownd was more practical, urging his hearers to whip up zeal for prayer in themselves by sheer force of will: 'we must continually striue with our owne dulnesse in prayer . . . [and] must stirre vp the least desire that we haue, euen from the bottome of our hearts.' True fervency could be stirred up, he implied, as an act of the will, although he was careful to point out that 'the perfection of our obedience' lay not only in our labour towards perfection but also in our acknowledgement of our failure.[51]

However, what neither Hooper nor Bownd nor any other hot-gospeller would risk doing was teaching anyone how to feign true piety. That included a reluctance to put words in others' mouths. Perhaps the closest they would come is in the Pauline convention that believers would groan in prayer: pious groaning became an established feature of the ecclesiastical soundscape.[52] Yet as groaning was understood to be Spirit-led, so must believers' own experiences be: to offer words for them to use in prayer would be to make them parrots. Their encounter with God must be unmediated: they must taste and see that the Lord is good. This distrust for set forms eventually and logically spread to public as well as private worship. Long-standing unease with the Book of Common Prayer grew into open opposition when the Laudians used its vestigial ceremonial for their own purposes. As Milton put it in

49 Latimer, *Sermons and Remains*, 176; Bownd, *Medicines for the Plague*, 129.

50 Hooper, *Later Writings*, 219, 313–15.

51 Bownd, *Medicines for the Plague*, 130–2, 136–40.

52 Craig, 'Psalms, Groans and Dogwhippers'.

1649, set prayers 'imprison and confine by force, into a Pinfold of sett words, those two most unimprisonable things, our Prayers <and> that Divine Spirit of utterance that moves them'.[53] A godly minister would no more give you the words with which to pray than he would give you the words with which to speak to your own family. You had to do it yourself, or rather, the Spirit had to do it within you.

V

So there is a hole at the heart of Protestant piety, a hole which was left there quite deliberately. Indeed, the difference between Puritan Protestants and their more conformist brethren is largely that Puritans were more actively concerned to keep this hole open: to leave a God-shaped gap at the centre of their devotional life, which it was not right for human beings to try to fill. But this situation was, like Protestant piety itself, unstable. There were those who needed more to their struggle than simply study, work and unstructured prayer. And that meant, in practice, reinventing or importing aspects of Catholic devotional practice, while trying to cleanse them of their perceived errors or blasphemies. This is a large theme, which embraces much of the pious life of the sixteenth and seventeenth centuries. It includes the revival of sacramental piety within Protestantism; the rise of sabbatarianism; the new 'cult of saints' in Protestant martyrology; the emergence (very early) of formalized household prayers; or the place of music in the Protestant life, above all of course the singing of metrical psalms. Of course, it also includes the deliberate reintroduction of medieval and even contemporary Catholic devotional works into Protestantism, a practice so wide-spread as to constitute an admission that Protestant authors found it very difficult to produce detailed and nourishing devotional material within their own tradition. All of these examples of imported piety, significantly, were common both to Puritans and conformists.

Of all the devotional phenomena which developed on that basic structure of study, work, struggle and prayer, however, perhaps the most revealing example is that of fasting. In it we can trace a very neat arc from rejection to reinvention. Fasting is very much a ritual activity, and one which was deep-rooted in the Catholic tradition; but it also has strong Scriptural warrant. In the early years of the Reformation Protes-

53 John Milton, *Complete Prose Works of John Milton, vol. III: 1648–1649*, ed. Merritt Y. Hughes (New Haven, CT and London, 1962), 505.

tants across Europe deliberately broke prescribed fasts and denounced them as superstitious – most famously in Zurich in 1523,[54] when an ostentatious breach of the Good Friday fast was the trigger for a wider revolt. Protestants were rather slower to argue that fasting did have a place in the Christian life. England continued to prescribe Friday fasting after the Reformation, but the regime claimed that this was a purely secular measure whose purpose was to support the fishing fleet. The first English Protestant author seriously to defend fasting was Thomas Becon. In a tract on prayer in 1542 he argued that 'prayer is nothyng without fastyng, nor fastyng withoute prayer',[55] and he wrote a whole treatise on the right use of fasting in 1551. He was keen to emphasize that Protestant fasts were not like Catholic fasts. They were held either when an individual's conscience demanded it, or when a particular public emergency required a general fast, not according to a predetermined calendar. They were not meritorious works, but outward signs of inner repentance. As with prescribing set prayers, Protestants found themselves in tricky territory here, for Becon argued that a true fast only took place when the Christian is so overcome with sorrow for his own sins that 'the verye trouble of hys heart wyl not suffer him to eat or drynke'. Rather than a good work, fasting was a weapon to be used in the struggle against sin, and also a spur to prayer.[56] Yet in practice, not many early Protestants seem to have found that their hearts' sorrow stopped them from eating. Few Edwardian authors mentioned fasting. Latimer, in all his copious sermons, never touched on the subject, even in a sermon specifically against the sin of gluttony.[57] In around 1550 John Redman claimed that 'I cannot with [*sic*] great difficulty find one now in a whole cittie which fasteth one day,' because 'men be so afrayd of popish superstition'.[58] In 1565–6 John Knox claimed that in Scotland, preachers often addressed fasting, and that 'the godlie within this Realme have used the same as necessitie craved', but Knox had a weakness for sweeping generalizations of this kind and there is no particular reason to believe him. In 1563 the Catholic Ninian Winzet had felt confident in claiming that fasting had

54 Diarmaid MacCulloch, *Reformation: Europe's House Divided 1490–1700* (London, 2003), 139.

55 Thomas Becon, *A Newe Pathwaye unto Praier* (London, 1542), sigs. L8r–M1v.

56 Becon, *Fruitful Treatise of Fasting*, esp. sigs. C5v–6r.

57 Latimer, *Sermons and Remains*, 14–17.

58 John Redman, *The Complaint of Grace, Continued through all Ages of the World* (London, 1609), 77–8.

been entirely abandoned in Scotland.[59] Likewise, in England in 1563, Bishop Grindal worried 'that in no one thing the adversary hath more advantage against us, than in the matter of fast, which we utterly neglect'.[60]

It was Knox and Grindal who took the lead in bringing this anarchic state of affairs to an end. In the mid-1560s, both men prepared formal orders for fasting for their respective churches, orders which allowed for collective acts of penance in the face of public calamities. The theology behind these public fasts was very much Becon's: they were acts of collective public humiliation before God, marks of penance and spurs to prayer rather than righteous works.[61] The English Homily on fasting (probably Grindal's own work) followed Becon in seeing true fasting as arising from the troubled conscience of the individual.[62] However, in the end, both orders did lay out detailed prescriptions for how the fast ought to be kept: what was allowed to be eaten or drunk, when, by whom, and what sermons and public prayers ought to be attended during the period of the fast. From these small beginnings fasting became one of the great set-pieces of the Protestant life in Britain; regular fasts and the sermons which accompanied them were the sinews of the Parliamentarian war effort in the civil wars of the 1640s.[63]

It is easy enough to see why. In fasting, all the various dimensions of Protestant piety met. Fasting was above all an occasion for sermon-attendance and study. It was closely linked to charity: one of the key Biblical texts was Isaiah 58, which made that link explicit. One abstained from food in part so as to be able to give one's food to the poor. Protestant fasting was also not allowed to interfere too much with

59 John Knox, *The Works of John Knox*, ed. David Laing, 6 vols (Edinburgh, 1846–64), 6: 394; Ninian Winzet, *The Buke of Fourscoir-thre Questions* (Antwerp, 1563), sigs. G4v–G5r.

60 Grindal, *Remains*, 265; cf. Becon, *Fruitful Treatise of Fasting*, sig. I8v.

61 Grindal, *Remains*, 83–94; Knox, *Works*, 6: 393–417.

62 *Certain Sermons or Homilies*, 249.

63 The literature on Protestant fasting is surprisingly thin. See especially W. Ian P. Hazlett, 'Playing God's Card: Knox and Fasting, 1565–66', in Roger Mason, ed., *John Knox and the British Reformations* (Aldershot, 1998), 176–98; also Peter Iver Kaufman, 'Fasting in England in the 1560s: "A Thinge of Nought"?', *Archiv für Reformationsgeschichte* 94 (2003), 176–93; C. J. Kitching, ' "Prayers fit for the time": Fasting and Prayer in Response to National Crises in the Reign of Elizabeth I', in W. J. Shiels, ed., *Monks, Hermits and the Ascetic Tradition*, SCH 22 (Oxford, 1985), 241–50; and a classic essay by Hugh Trevor-Roper, 'The Fast Sermons of the Long Parliament', in Hugh Trevor-Roper, ed., *Essays in British History Presented to Sir Keith Feiling* (London and New York, 1964), 294–344.

secular vocations, as Protestants regularly warned against excessive zeal in fasting, so making oneself unable to serve either God or neighbour.[64] Fasting was also an occasion for inner labour, for wrestling with sin and with one's own flesh, mortifying and subduing it. And it was held both to arise out of the same appalled self-knowledge which good Protestants saw as the fount of prayer, and to make prayer that much more fervent and heart-felt. One could not, it was acknowledged, pray with proper fervency on a full stomach. 'The more the body is filled, the more the mind is dulled.'[65] Such fasting was self-consciously opposed to Catholic piety: it is typical that the Scottish order spent almost as much space denouncing the corruptions of Catholic fasting as laying out positively what good Protestants ought to do. And indeed, fasting could become a polemical, even an aggressive practice, especially when tied to public emergencies rather than to a regular calendar. This not only cultivated a duly Protestant sense of crisis, it also (if, as was often the case, the emergency was political or military) helped to focus attention on the deeds of the popish Antichrist. Best of all, fasting helped to fill the ritual vacuum in Protestant life while remaining de-ritualized: for after all, fasting is not an activity, but a deliberate abstention from activity, and so it remains accessible to a religious tradition which is so sceptical about pious action.

Fasting can serve as a symptom of the power and of the weakness of Protestant piety, an aggressively and obsessively self-aware religion which was concerned to stir up true fervour within the believer while remaining convinced that true fervour (like everything else of value) could only be stirred up by God himself. It is symptomatic of a restless, itchy piety, always struggling to edify God's temple and never pausing to dwell in it; an anorexic piety, deliberately starving itself of ritual resources, never independent of Catholic piety but never at ease with that dependence. Yet that very leanness and restlessness gives it its strength. It is only when we understand the peculiar quality of the Protestant experience of God that we can understand how it was that Protestantism could change the world.

Durham University

64 Becon, *Fruitful treatise of fasting*, sigs. B3v–4r, H1r; Grindal, *Remains*, 255.
65 Becon, *Fruitful Treatise of Fasting*, sigs. H7v, I3v.

REVIVAL AND RESURGENCE IN SIXTEENTH-CENTURY CATHOLICISM: THE CONTRIBUTION OF THE ITALIAN AND SPANISH DOMINICANS

by PATRICK A. PRESTON

THIS essay is intended as a contribution to the history of the revival and resurgence of Catholicism in the sixteenth century. The debates about this topic that have arisen since 1945 have mostly concerned either the nature and importance of Evangelism (where the most important views are those of Jedin, Simoncelli and Mayer), or the relative importance of the Inquisition and the Council of Trent in reforming the Church and responding to the Protestant threat (a debate which first pitted the views of Firpo against those of Jedin, and then, with particular reference to Cardinal Pole, those of Mayer against both of these).[1] Whereas the focus in the above debates has usually been on developments in religion and politics at the top of the Church, the intention in this essay is to concentrate instead on issues of reform as they were faced by perhaps the most influential mendicant order of the period. The sixteenth-century Dominicans did indeed have their impact on high politics as the argument below will show, but they were also very influential at local level and in the universities.

By the early decades of the sixteenth century, the Dominican Order had fallen into some disrepute. The main reason for this was the humanist critique of scholasticism, which exposed several problems. First there was the objection to faults of style in scholastic writing. Poor Latin, inelegant construction, and 'barbaric' vocabulary were taken as symptoms of mental confusion. Secondly, scholastic theology was thought of as misdirected. Since it was rationalistic and abstract and dealt with minute questions and subtle distinctions, it had no impact on the spiritual life of the committed Christian. Furthermore, scholastic theology was compromised by its reliance on the Vulgate translation of

1 See, for instance, the following: H. Jedin, *A History of the Council of Trent*, trans. E. Graf, 2 vols (London, 1957 and 1961); P. Simoncelli, *Evangelismo italiano: Questione religiosa e nicodemismo politico* (Rome, 1979); M. Firpo and D. Marcatto, eds, *Il Processo inquisitoriale del cardinal Giovanni Morone*, 6 vols in 7 (Rome, 1981–95); T. Mayer, *Reginald Pole: Prince and Prophet* (Cambridge, 2000).

the Bible, which the *ad fontes* approach of the humanists suggested was seriously inaccurate. No one did more to create and popularize this pejorative view of scholasticism than Erasmus. Since the greatest scholastic theologian was undoubtedly Aquinas, and since the doctrine of Aquinas was the foundation of all Dominican teaching and learning, the Dominican Order was probably the order most affected by the Erasmian critique.

There were, however, other reasons of a more local kind for the disrepute of the Dominicans at the *fin-de siècle*. In Germany, for instance, the reputation of the Order was adversely affected by the involvement of the Cologne Dominicans from 1510 onwards in the Reuchlin affair, when the 'Letters of Obscure men'[2] exposed them to ridicule in the eyes of the humanist elite. In Italy, on the other hand, the damage was done by the Observant Dominicans in Florence, who discredited themselves in the eyes of the papacy first by supporting the charismatic prophet Savonarola, and then, after his execution in 1498, by their obstinate behaviour in cultivating his memory, defending his prophecies and trying to implement his reform programme.[3]

The object of this essay is to show how, during the sixteenth century, the Dominican Order both disembarrassed itself of its unfortunate reputation at the *fin de siècle* and triumphantly responded to the challenges of the world of the Counter-Reformation. This story of revival and resurgence in the Catholic world tells of a balance that is restored between two aspects of early modern Catholicism which had been dangerously out of kelter. Equilibrium was achieved when some aspects of Erasmian humanism were rejected for example by Dominican theologians, or at the Council of Trent, while the rest were retained as part of the emerging ideology of the Counter-Reformation. Meanwhile, the vitality of the Dominican Order and the continued vigour and adaptability of Thomism were demonstrated by a series of developments on the one hand in Italy, and on the other, in Spain.

Developments in Italy

Despite the papacy's association with humanism from the time of Nicholas V, the Dominican Order in Italy had long doubted the

[2] First published at Hagenau in 1515 and 1516, and at Basel 1517.

[3] See L. Polizzotto, *The Elect Nation: the Savonarolan Movement in Florence 1494–1545* (Oxford, 1994), which considers all these matters in detail.

compatibility of Christianity with classical culture. The Blessed Giovanni Dominici had expressed this distrust at the beginning of the fifteenth century,[4] and Savonarola at the end of it.[5] It took the sixteenth-century Observant Dominican Catarino, ex-humanist and ex-piagnone, to reject classical humanism utterly, together with the Ciceronianism[6] and ecclesiastical art that went with it. His objections to the humanist emphasis on style undercut the humanist critique of scholastic modes of expression. Could the scholastics also be saved from the other charge, that their theology was a theology of the minute and the abstruse, and hence irrelevant to the spiritual life of the practising Christian? What seems to have happened is that the charge of irrelevance to the spiritual life was tacitly accepted, for Erasmian spiritualism was absorbed into the great tradition of sixteenth-century mysticism in Italy and in Spain.[7] The question then was whether scholastic theology shorn of its connection with spirituality had any remaining relevance. It obviously had, as the debates at Trent would in due course demonstrate: it was essential to the clarification and definition of the doctrines of the Church. Even in Erasmus's lifetime, it also provided the basis for the first theory of international law, though not in an Italian context.

While Catarino on the one hand and the Church on the other were thus neutralizing the humanist threat, other Dominicans were exerting themselves on their own behalf. One example is the effort made by the San Marco Dominicans to improve their standing by securing the recognition of Archbishop Antoninus of Florence, prior of San Marco 1436-46. By very skilful advocacy, they succeeded in 1523 in overcoming all objections to the canonization of the great Observant Dominican.[8] But, since the Dominicans of San Marco and the Minerva remained ardent admirers of Savonarola, their total rehabilitation was not fully secured until 1559 when, in the course of a *processo* against

4 In *Lucula Noctis* (1405). I have used the following edition: E. Hunt, ed., *Iohannis Dominici Lucula noctis* (Notre Dame, IN, 1940).

5 His attacks on the paganizing art of Florence in his day are a commonplace among historians of the period.

6 In the 'Claves Duae' 1543, Catarino condemned the humanist critique of the Scriptures on the grounds of style. See Ambrosius Catharinus Politus, *Claves Duae ad aperiendas Sacras Scripturas* (Lyons, 1543), 17–27.

7 From the 1564 Roman Index onwards, the Roman Indices condemned only those works of Erasmus that criticized fundamental features of the doctrine and practice of the Church. See *Index Librorum Prohibitorum* (Lyons, 1564), 23.

8 L. Polizzotto, 'The Making of a Saint: the Canonization of St Antonino, 1516–1523', *Journal of Medieval and Renaissance Studies* 22 (1992), 353–81.

Savonarola, they saved their hero from the condemnation on which Paul IV was intent by rejecting Savonarola's prophetic inspirations and the revolutionary potential of his message.[9] He remained thereafter what he had always essentially been, that is, a great spiritual master. In this form, the Savonarolan message was entirely acceptable to the Church of the Counter-Reformation, and Savonarolan spirituality henceforth entered the great stream of mysticism in both Italy and Spain.[10] It is significant that the Inquisitor who presided in this *processo* was the Dominican Cardinal Michele Ghislieri, Carafa's successor as Grand Inquisitor of the Roman Inquisition. It is no surprise to find that the Dominicans, their confidence restored, were active in the affairs of the Inquisition: the Order had never been attracted by the doctrines of the Protestant Reformers,[11] and the special vocation of the Order of Preachers had always been to teach and defend the truths of faith. This committed them inevitably to the struggle against heresy. So it was, then, that when the Roman Inquisition was reconstituted by the Bull *Licet ab initio* in 1542, Tommaso Badia, Master of the Sacred Palace, was one of its first six members. In like manner, Dominicans were active in the creation of the first Roman Index of Prohibited Books. At some time between 1547 and 1550, the Roman Inquisition called upon two Dominicans to compose an index. One was the Master of the Sacred Palace Egidio Foscarari, later Bishop of Modena; the other was Pietro Bertani, then Bishop of Fano.[12] Similarly the Dominican Order made a substantial contribution to the doctrinal and disciplinary legislation at the Council of Trent, particularly in the first phase of the Council, i.e. under Paul III from 1545 to 1547, when the great decree on Justification was promulgated. It should be observed that when it came to dealing with questions that Luther had raised, such as Justification, the humanists had and could have no answer, for these were theological problems and no humanist *qua* humanist was ever a theologian.[13] No

9 M. Firpo and P. Simoncelli, *I Processi Inquisitoriali contro Savonarola (1558) e Carnesecchi (1566–1567): una Proposta di Interpretazione*, Rivista di Storia e Letteratura Religiosa 18 (1982), 200–52.

10 St Philip Neri (1515–95), for instance, was strongly influenced by Savonarola.

11 Polizzotto, *Elect Nation,* 165–7. I know of no Italian example of a Dominican heretic, though of course in Germany Martin Bucer was a Dominican from 1506–21.

12 J. M. de Bujanda, *et al., Index de Rome, 1557, 1559, 1564: les premiers index romains et l'index du Concile de Trent*, Centre d'études de la Renaissance, Éditions de l'Université de Sherbrooke (Sherbrooke, Que., 1990), 29.

13 The Renaissance 'studia humanitatis' were grammar, rhetoric, literary studies, history and moral philosophy, but not theology.

wonder, then, that it 'was at Trent that St. Thomas Aquinas first really came into his own as the doctor communis among the theologians.'[14] The Dominican impact at Trent can be roughly indicated by the attendance figures: twenty-three Dominican bishops and twenty-eight Dominican theologians, including an impressive contingent from Spain, among them Bartolomé Carranza, Domingo de Soto and Melchor Cano. Not that the Dominicans necessarily agreed among themselves. A very lively debate at Trent arose first between Carranza and Catarino on whether the bishops' obligation to reside in their dioceses was by divine or by human law. Shortly afterwards Catarino was in conflict with de Soto on the question of the certainty of inherent grace. In both these disputes Catarino was fighting to defend the papal prerogative, which he regarded as the great imperative in the era of the Counter-Reformation. It was no doubt his support for the power and authority of the pope that made Catarino the trusted adviser of Cardinal Giovanni del Monte,[15] the principal papal Legate at the Council of Trent. Catarino's attempts to induce his Order to adjust to the new conditions of the sixteenth century in fact began well before Trent and continued until his death in 1553. He was the first Italian Dominican to advocate the doctrine of the Immaculate Conception of the Virgin,[16] and he was still advocating it in 1552, in spite of the fact that this advocacy isolated him from his Order: though the Immaculate Conception of the Virgin was a crucial doctrine in the development of Counter-Reformation spirituality, the Dominican Order long refused it chiefly because it was a doctrine that Aquinas did not teach.

But whatever differences there were among Dominicans in debating the great issues of the day, these differences did not weaken the Order. Evidence of the continuing vigour of the Italian Dominicans in the difficult times of the sixteenth century was the number of outstanding scholars and theologians who graced their ranks, especially Santi Pagnini (1470–1536), a biblical scholar and specialist in Oriental languages; Tommaso deVio Cajetan (1469–1534), the greatest Thomist of the sixteenth century; Tommaso Badia (1483–1547), Master of the

14 Philip Hughes, *The Church in Crisis: a History of the General Councils: 325–1870* (Garden City, NY, 1961), available at: http://mb-soft.com/believe/txs/trent.htm.

15 Julius III, 1550–5.

16 See P. Preston, 'Cardinal Cajetan and Fra Ambrosius Catharinus in the Controversy over the Immaculate Conception of the Virgin in Italy, 1515–51', in R. N. Swanson, ed., *The Church and Mary*, SCH 39 (Woodbridge, 2004), 181–90.

Sacred Palace, theological adviser to Contarini, disputant at Worms in 1540 and Regensburg in 1541, and Cardinal in 1542; Bartolomeo Spina (1475–1546), Master of the Sacred Palace in succession to Badia, and adviser to the Holy See and to the Fathers of the Council of Trent; Pietro Bertani, great theologian, papal Nuncio to Charles V 1548-50, Cardinal in 1551 and papabile in 1555; and Michele Ghislieri, Grand Inquisitor of the Roman Inquisition in succession to Gian Pietro Carafa, Pope 1566–72, and canonized in 1712.[17]

In view of the continued relevance of the Thomist doctrines and of the distinguished role of the Dominicans in the Counter-Reformation and the prosecution of heresy, it is entirely appropriate that at the Council of Trent the only book to be placed on the altar in addition to the Bible was St Thomas Aquinas's *Summa Theologiae*.[18] However damaging the humanist critique of scholasticism, plus the associated local fiascos, had been, then, there is no doubt that the Dominican Order in Italy was again in full vigour by the middle of the sixteenth century – a remarkable revival indeed.

Developments in Spain

As pointed out above, the Spanish Dominicans played an important part at the Council of Trent. Fittingly they also took a leading role in the prosecution of heresy. Juan Alvarez de Toledo, like Tommaso Badia, was one of the first 6 members of the Roman Inquisition when it was reconstituted by the Bull *Licet ab initio* in 1542. More particularly the Spanish Dominicans exercised their zeal for the faith in the tribunals of the Spanish Inquisition. It was in these tribunals that between 1520 and 1535, the Dominicans helped to silence the Spanish disciples of Erasmus, or at least those of them who endorsed the humanist critique of the Church, its doctrines and its Thomist ideology. But the spiritualist side of Erasmus – his emphasis on inward religion and interior illumination rather than an external faith expressed in public prayer, rituals and ceremonies – survived unscathed in Spain as in Italy to merge with the great current of Spanish mysticism, along with the spiritual teaching of Savonarola. Some of the most illustrious Spanish

[17] Another sixteenth-century Dominican saint was Caterina Ricci (1522–90), canonized in 1746.

[18] William Turner, 'Scholasticism', *Catholic Encyclopedia*, vol. 13 (New York, 1912), available at: http://www.newadvent.irg/cathen/13548a.htm

mystics of the sixteenth century were Dominicans, for example Melchor Cano (1509–60), Bartolome Carranza (1503–76) and Luis de Granada (1504–88).

Whatever esteem the Spanish Dominicans had lost in the late fifteenth and early sixteenth centuries had plainly been restored by 1535. But while this revival was both substantial and important, it is overshadowed by the remarkable developments of Thomism that were inspired at the University of Salamanca by the way in which the conquest, colonization and evangelization of the New World was proceeding. It is not the intention here to give a detailed account of the evolution of the Laws of the Indies, 1573, in which the Spanish Crown expressed its final opinion on the vexed questions of the rights of the Indians and the problem of the just war. It is enough to mention the crucial stages: the Laws of Burgos 1512–13; the Bull *Sublimis Deus*, 1537; the New Laws, 1542; and the Valladolid Juntas, 1550–1.

The Spanish absorption of the territories that they claimed in the Caribbean and the Americas was bedevilled by practical and theoretical questions. One that will not be examined here was the problem of imposing royal authority over the colonists. Much more serious was the question of the status of the Indians, whom it was initially difficult to associate with the Biblical story of the Creation. Were they animals who happened to look like human beings, or rational beings with souls to be saved? In the former case, it would be possible to exploit them at will. Even when the Bull *Sublimis Deus* declared in favour of the latter alternative, questions still remained. Were they capable of life in civilized society? And if they were, might they not perhaps be the 'natural slaves' described in Aristotle's 'Politics' Book I, as Sepulveda argued?

The question of the status of the Indians was being passionately argued on both sides well before 1512–13, when, in the Laws of Burgos, the Spanish Crown first tried to regularize the situation, but in the absence of any systematic legal theory to cover the case, the Crown was seriously impeded in its efforts to administer justice. But in so far as the settlers in the Indies were imposing their will by force of arms, and the Indians frequently resisted them, some guidance might be found in Aquinas, who deals with war in the *Summa Theologiae* (The Second of the Second, section 40).

What Aquinas says there is not sufficient, but it may well have been his knowledge of what Aquinas had said in section 40 that inspired the Dominican Francisco de Vitoria (1483–1546) of the University of Salamanca to produce in the *Relectiones de Indis* (written around 1532) and *De jure belli*[19] (both published for the first time in 1557) the kind of systematic legal theory that any attempt to provide a comprehensive solution to the dispute over the rights of the Indians and the settlers in the Americas required. This theory, normally regarded as the first treatise on international law, is another triumphant demonstration of the relevance of Thomism to the problems of Church and Society in the early modern era. The argument in a nutshell is as follows.[20] It begins with the Thomist distinctions between the natural and the supernatural order, and natural and supernatural law. These orders and laws are never at odds with each other. Neither can override the other. All forms of human life in the natural order are legitimate, since the natural order is the expression of the divine will. The legitimacy of the natural order and the accompanying natural law in which God established all human rights and duties cannot be compromised by later arrangements. Every human being is a citizen of the world by natural law. He neither loses nor acquires these rights by sin. Vitoria's achievement is in applying these principles to the situation created by the discovery of the New World, by the simple expedient of asking 'By what right?' The indigenous populations of the New World had a natural and therefore indefeasible right to the areas in which they lived and to govern themselves in those areas in the way they thought fit.[21] The upshot of this stipulation was first to reject the claim to possession based on discovery and conquest, and then to render irrelevant the Spanish claim to the New World by the Bulls of Alexander VI. The popes did indeed have authority, but it was spiritual authority only, and it could only be exercised over Christians. Even more remarkably, Vitoria argued that conquest intended as a necessary preliminary to conversion was likewise unjustified. It is true that there is an obligation on the Church to preach the Gospel throughout the world; and it is true also that the missionaries, as citizens of the world, have a right to preach in all parts of it without hindrance. But the faith cannot be imposed by force, for belief is an act of the will, i.e. an exercise of freedom. The faith cannot even be imposed on those who commit crimes against the natural order

19 Walter Schätzel, ed. and trans., *De indis recenter inventis et de iure belli Hispanorum in barbaros* (Tübingen, 1952).

20 See Venancio D. Carro, 'The Spanish Theological-Juridical Renaissance and the Ideology of Bartolomé de Las Casas', in J. Friede and B. Keen, eds, *Bartolomé de Las Casas in History: Toward an Understanding of the Man and His Works* (DeKalb, IL, 1971), 237–77.

21 Sociability and government were natural to man, but the mode of government was at the discretion of the people concerned.

for example by performing human sacrifices. Neither the pope nor any secular ruler has the right to punish the crimes of those who are not his subjects.

By what right then do the Spaniards intervene in the New World? They can interevene to defend their rights as citizens of the world to go wherever they please and to be treated humanely while there; they can defend their right to trade and settle, and to teach the truth, including religious truth, to those who wish to hear it, but only with the proviso that they respect the rights of the Indians. The intervention of the Spanish Crown might well be necessary in at least two circumstances: on the one hand to establish a system of jurisdiction by which the rights either of settlers or of the Indians might be protected; on the other hand to provide the official means of enforcing what the law requires.

Would the Spanish Crown be prepared to adopt this theological-juridical understanding of its own position? Both the Indian problem and Vitoria's solution to it were brought to the attention of the Spanish government by the Dominican Bishop of Chiapas, Bartolomé de Las Casas (1474–1566), who was tireless in his advocacy of the Indian cause from 1515 until his death fifty-one years later. Originally himself a Spanish colonist in the New World, he was ordained in 1512 and entered the Dominican Order in 1524. He was fifty at the time. Consequently he was too old ever fully to master the Thomist system of thought which was obligatory for all Dominicans, but in a sense this did not matter, for his importance in the Indian question was not the result of his grasp of theology but of his energy and determination as an advocate. By this advocacy he made many enemies particularly among the settlers in the New World. Inevitably these settlers found their advocate. He was the Spanish humanist Juan Gines de Sepulveda (1494–1573). Exact information about Sepulveda's early life is not easy to find. It seems that he became a priest and for a while he probably worked for Cardinal Cajetan when the latter was preparing his Commentaries on the New Testament. Sepulveda's knowledge of Greek would certainly have been useful to the cardinal, who was not an expert in that language. It does not, however, seem that Sepulveda was ever a Dominican as is sometimes claimed.[22] Perhaps that made it easier

22 See 'Juan Ginés de Sepúlveda, 1490–1573', available at: http://www.centrocisneros.uah.es/galpersons. asp?pag=personajes&id=103

for him to champion the colonists both in writing[23] and in person. He argued for the right of civilized peoples to subject 'savages' by force of arms. Consequently his advice was that the New Laws of 1542 should be revoked. In view of the differences of advice that the Spanish Crown received from Sepulveda and from Las Casas, Charles V decided to call for advice from the Royal Council (assisted by four learned theologians)[24] which was therefore summoned to meet at Valladolid in two series of juntas, one in 1550; and another in 1551. In these juntas, Sepulveda and Las Casas presented their cases in person.[25] As it turned out, the Royal Council produced no final resolution of the question and Sepulveda and Las Casas both considered themselves vindicated. Since, however, the Laws of the Indies 1573 seem to reflect the position that Las Casas had advocated, and since Las Casas continued to be well regarded by Charles V, it is usually thought that Las Casas had the better of it in their opinion.

However this may be, there can be no doubt of the significance of this Thomist doctrine of natural law developed so brilliantly by Vitoria and de Soto. It not only illustrates the continued importance of Thomism in the early modern universities: it is also a major contribution to the history of sixteenth-century Catholicism in the New World. Along with, for example, the refutation of the humanist critique of scholasticism, the abandonment of Savonarolan prophecy, and the role of the Dominicans in the prosecution of heresy (all discussed in the first half of this essay), it demonstrates the vitality of sixteenth-century Catholicism outside elite circles, as well as within them. This story of revival and resurgence in Southern Europe could easily have been extended by a study of the history of the Dominican Order in France, which certainly deserves investigation on the same lines.

University of Chichester

23 In 'Tratado sobre las justas causas de la guerra' where his main argument relies on Aristotle, 'Politics', Book I, which discusses 'natural slavery'.

24 One of them was Domingo de Soto, another Salamanca professor, who was in fact a disciple of Vitoria. De Soto had himself written various works on the Indian question, and was therefore well qualified to offer his opinion to the Royal Council.

25 For a discussion of the Valladolid Juntas 1550–1, see V. Beltran de Heredia, *Domingo de Soto: estudio biografico documentado* (Madrid, 1961), ch. 6.

THE REVIVAL OF PRACTICAL CHRISTIANITY: THE SOCIETY FOR PROMOTING CHRISTIAN KNOWLEDGE, SAMUEL WESLEY, AND THE CLERICAL SOCIETY MOVEMENT*

by GEORDAN HAMMOND

REFLECTING on the early endeavours of the Society for Promoting Christian Knowledge (SPCK) following its establishment in 1699, John Chamberlayne, the Society's secretary, confidently noted the 'greater spirit of zeal and better face of Religion already visible throughout the Nation'.[1] Although Chamberlayne clearly uses the language of revival, through the nineteenth century, many historians of the Evangelical Revival in Britain saw it as a 'new' movement arising in the 1730s with the advent of the evangelical preaching of the early Methodists, Welsh and English. Nineteenth-century historians often confidently propagated the belief that they lived in an age inherently superior to the unreformed eighteenth century.[2] The view that the Church of England from the Restoration to the Evangelical Revival was dominated by Latitudinarian moralism leading to dead and formal religion has recently been challenged but was a regular feature of Victorian scholarship that has persisted in some recent work.[3] The traditional tendency to highlight the perceived

* I would like to express my appreciation to David Wilson and John Walsh for their perceptive comments on an earlier draft of this essay.

1 Chamberlayne to Mr Deberinghen (3 December 1700), Cambridge University Library, MS SPCK Wanley E1/1, fol. 78. All SPCK manuscripts cited in this paper are housed in the Cambridge University Library.

2 B. W. Young, 'Knock-Kneed Giants: Victorian Representations of Eighteenth-Century Thought', in Jane Garnett and Colin Matthew, eds, *Revival and Religion since 1700: Essays for John Walsh* (London, 1993), 79–93. On the organization of the Church, Methodist historians Rupert Davies and E. Gordon Rupp conventionally stated that 'The very shape of the Church was antiquated'. See *A History of the Methodist Church in Great Britain*, vol. 1 (London, 1965), xxii.

3 For example, V. H. H. Green commented that Latitudinarians 'diluted the Christian faith to a ludicrous extent. It appeared no longer as a structure of dogma but a moral code'. See *John Wesley* (London, 1964), 4. See also Kenneth Hylson-Smith, *Evangelicals in the Church of England 1734–1984* (Edinburgh, 1988), 5–8. For a critique of the traditional view, see Jeffrey S. Chamberlain, 'Moralism, Justification, and the Controversy over Methodism', *JEH* 44 (1993), 652–78. John Spurr has questioned the commonly accepted etymology of the term

dichotomy between mainstream Anglicanism and the Revival has served to obscure areas of continuity such as the fact that Whitefield and the Wesleys intentionally addressed much of their early evangelistic preaching to like-minded brethren in pre-existing networks of Anglican religious societies and that Methodism thrived as a voluntary religious society.[4] Scores of historians have refuted the Victorian propensity to assert the Revival's independence from the Church of England.[5] The aim of this essay is to demonstrate that the late seventeenth- and early eighteenth-century revival of voluntary religion should be interpreted as evidence of the vitality and adaptability of the Church of England in the decades prior to the expansion of voluntary activity that increased alongside the Evangelical Revival.[6] A contribution is made to a growing body of scholarly work which argues that that 'the eighteenth-century Evangelical Revival had more to do with adaptations to structural changes in society, in particular, those

'Latitudinarian', arguing that it was coined to refer to clergy who peacefully carried out their duties during the Interregnum and rejected Calvinism, while William Spellman has contended that Latitudinarians differed little from their brethren on doctrine and pastoral care. See '"Latitudinarians" and the Restoration Church', *HistJ* 31 (1988), 61–82, at 82; idem, *The Latitudinarians and the Church of England, 1660–1695* (Athens, GA, 1993).

4 See Whitefield's *The Benefits of an Early Piety: a Sermon Preach'd at Bow-Church, London, before the Religious Societies . . .* (London, 1737); John S. Simon, *John Wesley and the Religious Societies* (London, 1921); John Walsh, 'Origins of the Evangelical Revival', in G. V. Bennett and J. D. Walsh, eds, *Essays in Modern English Church History* (London, 1966), 144–8 and 'Religious Societies: Methodist and Evangelical 1738–1800', in W. J. Sheils and Diana Wood, eds, *Voluntary Religion*, SCH 23 (Oxford, 1986), 279–302; Henry D. Rack, 'Religious Societies and the Origins of Methodism', *JEH* 38 (1987), 582–95; W. M. Jacob, *Lay People and Religion in the Early Eighteenth Century* (Cambridge, 1996), 77–92 and 'John Wesley and the Church of England, 1736–40', in Jeremy Gregory, ed., *John Wesley: Tercentenary Essays*, *BJRULM* 85: 2–3 (2003), 57–71; David Hempton, *Methodism: Empire of the Spirit* (New Haven, CT, 2005), 11–31.

5 Michael J. Crawford, *Seasons of Grace: Colonial New England's Revival Tradition in its British Context* (Oxford, 1991), John Walsh, '"Methodism" and the Origins of English-Speaking Evangelicalism', in Mark A. Noll, David W. Bebbington, and George A. Rawlyk, eds, *Evangelicalism: Comparative Studies of Popular Protestantism in North America, the British Isles and beyond, 1700–1990* (Oxford, 1994), 19–37, G. M. Ditchfield, *The Evangelical Revival* (London, 1998), and Mark A. Noll, *The Rise of Evangelicalism: the Age of Edwards, Whitefield and the Wesleys* (Downers Grove, IL, 2003) strike an appropriate balance between the Revival's debt to the past and its new emphases. W. R. Ward, *Early Evangelicalism: a Global Intellectual History, 1670–1789* (Cambridge, 2006) should help correct the imbalance caused by the traditional focus on placing the Revival's origins in the 1730s as his *Protestant Evangelical Awakening* (Cambridge, 1992) provided a corrective to the overemphasis of the Anglo-American origins of the Revival.

6 See Ford K. Brown's 'Ten Thousand Compassions and Charities', in idem, *Fathers of the Victorians: the Age of Wilberforce* (Cambridge, 1961), 317–60, where he provides lists of voluntary societies that proliferated alongside the growth of evangelicalism.

conductive to religious voluntarism, than with the death and rebirth of evangelical piety'.[7] This essay focuses on the clerical society movement as one wing of the SPCK's work, with particular reference to a Lincolnshire society and the light shed on it by the correspondence of Samuel Wesley (the father of John and Charles Wesley) with the SPCK.[8]

Voluntary societies arose in the Church as a diverse and loosely organized movement that transcended political boundaries and was dominated by pious High-Churchmen and devout young men.[9] The earliest manifestation of the movement began around the year 1678 with the organization of a London religious society under the direction of Anthony Horneck.[10] This was followed by associations aimed at moral and religious reform such as the Societies for the Reformation of Manners (SRM), active from around 1690, and charity schools, from around 1680, which in their early history were closely associated with the SPCK.[11] Thomas Bray proved to be an integral figure in the movement by establishing the SPCK in 1699 and the Society for the Propagation of the Gospel (SPG) in 1701. The effects of this revival were long lasting; some of the charity schools founded in this period have survived in modified form down to the present while the SPCK and SPG also continue their work to this day.

Although the voluntary movement was a diverse association of groups including religious societies and the SRM who diverged in

7 Crawford, *Seasons of Grace*, 14. In sociological terms, the origins of the Revival might be said to approximate the theory that what have often been thought 'to be . . . new beliefs and practices are in fact a sharply focussed reflection of the beliefs and practices of that part of society from which the movements draw their members'. Eileen Barker, 'From Sects to Society: a Methodological Programme', in idem, ed., *New Religious Movements: a Perspective for Understanding Society* (Lewiston, NY, 1982), 3–15, at 6.

8 While this essay focuses on the Lincolnshire clerical society, Wesley was also actively involved in establishing a religious society in Epworth. See Wesley, 'An Account of the Religious Society begun in Epworth, in the Isle of Axholm Lincolnshire Feb. 1 An: Dom: 1701/02' in MS Wanley, fols 186–94.

9 Craig Rose, 'The Origins and Ideals of the SPCK 1699–1716', in John Walsh, Colin Haydon, and Stephen Taylor, eds, *The Church of England c.1689–c.1833: from Toleration to Tractarianism* (Cambridge, 1993), 172–7. On voluntary societies in general, see Peter Clark, *British Clubs and Societies 1580–1800: the Origins of an Associational World* (Oxford, 2000).

10 Scott Thomas Kisker, *Foundation for Revival: Anthony Horneck, the Religious Societies, and the Construction of Anglican Pietism* (Lanham, MD, 2007).

11 On Anglican attitudes to the SRM, see Tina Isaacs, 'The Anglican Hierarchy and the Reformation of Manners 1688–1738', *JEH* 33 (1982), 391–411. On the charity school movement in London, see Craig Rose, 'Evangelical Philanthropy and Anglican Revival: the Charity Schools of Augustan London, 1698–1740', *London Journal* 16 (1991), 35–65.

terms of methods used to promote moral and spiritual reformation, the basic motivating ideals behind the movement are not difficult to pinpoint.[12] Leaders of this pietistic movement unanimously agreed that theirs was an age characterized by a blatantly obvious 'visible decay of Religion' where 'Deism, Prophaness, and Vice' were on the rise.[13]

During the first decade of their existence, the religious societies formed an alternative lifestyle to counter what many churchmen saw as a growing libertinism encouraged by Charles II and his court. Following the Toleration Act of 1689 and the expiry of the Licensing Act in 1695, it became evident to pious churchmen that they would have to combat the increased opportunity given to Dissenters and freethinkers to challenge the Church's established dominance of spiritual and intellectual life.[14] Leading clergymen such as Horneck and Bray agreed that a solution to the problem of religious 'declension' and new challenges to the Established Church was to propagate 'practical Christianity'. To bring unity of vision to the movement, a shared model of practical Christianity was needed and this was conveniently supplied by the primitive Church.[15] And the pristine practical Christianity of the primitive Church was seen to be nothing more than the imitation of Christ.[16] An

12 The SRM showed themselves to be somewhat distinct from the rest of the movement by accepting Dissenters into their rank and focusing their attention on providing intelligence to local magistrates to assist them in their work of enforcing the laws against immorality and profaneness.

13 'The First Circular Letter from the Honourable Society for Promoting Christian Knowledge to their Clergy Correspondents in the Several Counties of England and Wales' in MS Wanley, fol. 1. This view was held by the Archbishop of Canterbury, Thomas Tenison who detected 'a sensible growth of Vice and Prophaneness in the Nation'. See *His Grace the Lord Archbishop of Canterbury's Letter to the Right Reverend the Lords Bishops of his Province* (London, 1699), 1. Doreen Rosman is one of several scholars who has argued that this 'prevailing despondency ... helped to create an emotional climate conducive to religious revival'. See *The Evolution of the English Churches 1500–2000* (Cambridge, 2003), 148.

14 With the expiry of the Licensing Act, censorship of publications effectively ended allowing unprecedented freedom to criticize the Established Church.

15 For an overview on the ideal of primitive Christianity in the late seventeenth and early eighteenth century, see Eamon Duffy, 'Primitive Christianity Revived: Religious Renewal in Augustan England', in Derek Baker, ed., *Renaissance and Renewal in Christian History*, SCH 14 (Oxford, 1977), 287–300. Popular contemporary works included Horneck's, 'A letter to a person of quality concerning the lives of the primitive Christians', appended to the *The Happy Ascetick* (London, 1681), and Cave's, *Primitive Christianity* (London, 1673). The influence of these works extended well beyond the lifetime of the authors and became a source of inspiration for John Wesley.

16 J. Sears McGee has argued that exhortation to imitate Christ's behaviour was a distinctive and prominent Anglican teaching in the seventeenth century that was avoided by Puritans who tended to take a 'radical view of human depravity'. See *The Godly Man in Stuart*

anonymous biographer of Anthony Horneck aptly captured the movement's ideal of practical Christianity modelled on the primitive Church, stating that Horneck

> was for bringing the best of his Parishioners to a higher state of Christian Perfection, to more pure and Primitive Lives than they practiced. He had always in view, the Innocence and simplicity of the first Professor of our most Holy Religion, and burn[ed] with an ardent desire of bringing our Practice to their Standard, as his Predecessors had brought our Doctrine.[17]

In Samuel Wesley's elucidation of the voluntary religious society ideal, such societies, when 'reduced to the *Primitive Standard*', could perfect what was lacking in pre-Reformation monasticism by providing an avenue for the promotion of holy living open to those who had previously been excluded from such endeavours, namely, men of business and trade.[18]

By the time Samuel Wesley became a member of the SPCK the religious society movement within the Church of England had been growing for two decades under the able leadership of divines such as Horneck and William Beveridge.[19] In 1698, the cause of the societies was furthered by the publication of Josiah Woodward's *An Account of the Rise and Progress of Religious Societies in the City of London.* Before Wesley published his own endorsement in *A Letter Concerning the Religious Societies* as an appendix to the *Pious Communicant Rightly Prepar'd* (1700), he had read Woodward's inspirational *Account.* Wesley had been interested in the London religious societies for several years having preached a sermon in support of the SRM at St James's Church, Westminster, and before a religious society at St Brides in 1698.[20] Although by 1700 about forty societies had been founded in London, there had been few attempts to replicate them outside London; however, this was soon to change through the instrumental work of the SPCK. Wesley's

England: Anglicans, Puritans, and the Two Tables, 1620–1670 (New Haven, CT and London, 1976), 107–13, at 108.

17 *A Summary Account of the Life of the Truly Pious and Reverend Dr. Anth. Horneck, Minister of the Savoy* (London, 1697), 25–6.

18 Wesley, 'A Letter Concerning the Religious Societies', in *The Pious Communicant Rightly Prepar'd; or, A Discourse Concerning the Blessed Sacrament* (London, 1700), appendix.

19 Beveridge was a pivotal figure in promoting the primitive ideal through his devotional and scholarly work.

20 *A Sermon Concerning the Reformation of Manners* (London, 1698).

Letter lent support to the movement by advocating the formation of societies in rural parishes.

Wesley's *Letter* was endorsed by the SPCK who inserted it (along with Woodward's *Account*) into their packet of books drawn up in February 1700 for inclusion with the Society's second circular letter to clergymen who were corresponding members of the Society.[21] The support shown by the Society enabled the *Letter* to be available to a wider audience than would have otherwise been possible. In years to come, it continued to have a measure of influence as evidenced by a request made in 1709 by Robert Watts of St John's College, Oxford, that the *Letter* be reprinted in its entirety and included in the Society's catalogue of books.[22]

The evangelistic goals of the SPCK can be ascertained in their first few widely distributed circular letters to their clerical correspondents, scattered in parishes throughout England and Wales.[23] The first letter (approved in their minutes of 16 November 1699) describes their general view on the decline of religion and their vision for rectifying the deplorable situation that had arisen 'from the barbarous ignorance observable among the common people'.[24] This sad state of affairs came about as a result of 'want of due care in the education of the Youth', but 'if early instructed in the Principles of true Religion', in charity schools, these lost youth could yet be taught to fear God. The hope was expressed that the successful erection of such schools in London would serve as a model for their rural correspondents to emulate.[25]

It should be noted that although the SPCK took an overtly pessimistic view of the state of society, this was counterbalanced by their confident belief that the present state of affairs was not irreversible. In fact, the theological justification for the various voluntary societies lay

21 W. O. B. Allen and Edmund McClure, *Two Hundred Years: the History of the Society for Promoting Christian Knowledge, 1698–1898* (London, 1898), 167. Although the *Letter* was apparently published at this time as a SPCK pamphlet, the only copy of the *Letter* published apart from *The Pious Communicant* that I have been able to locate is a pamphlet dated 1724 with no reference to a publisher: Oxford, Bodleian Library, 141 k.515 (5).

22 Robert Watts to the SPCK (March 20, 1709), SPCK, D2/3, Abstract Letter 1588.

23 On the evangelical piety of the SPCK, see their 'The Form of Prayer Made Use of by the Honourable Society before they enter upon Business', in MS Wanley fols 10–12.

24 It should be noted that disparaging reports on the ignorance of the common people is insufficient evidence to prove that the Church was at a low ebb; evangelical clergy later displayed a similar predilection for pointing out the spiritual shortcomings of the lower orders.

25 MS Wanley, fols 1–3.

in their dual conviction that while vice and immorality were on the increase, they could, with divine assistance, further the unfinished business of the Reformation by co-operating with God to bring the nation to a sensible awareness of its sin and apostasy from God.[26] The Society concluded its letter by expressing its confidence that in partnership with evangelical clergymen they could 'retrieve the decays of Piety among us, and cause the power of the Gospel to appear to the unconverted'.[27]

The recommendation that clerical societies be established throughout the country was the focal point of the Society's second and third circular letters distributed in February and June 1700. Archbishop Thomas Tenison had recently sent out a circular letter to the bishops of his province urging clergy to meet together to discuss common problems faced in their respective cures with the aim of reforming 'Mens [sic] *Lives* and *Manners*'.[28] With its network of clergy correspondents, the SPCK was in an ideal position to further Tenison's proposal and duly stressed the benefit that might come from clerical associations. To avoid any appearance of subversiveness, the Society wisely requested that their correspondents seek the blessing of their diocesan before meeting together. In order to foster a common understanding, the SPCK asked its correspondents to forward copies to their bishops of the accounts they had distributed to them detailing the history of the voluntary societies that had recently been set up.[29] In the SPCK's view, the immediate reason for encouraging the gathering of local clergy was to give them an opportunity to inspire one another zealously to promote the rigorous performance of their ministerial duties and to provide an opportunity to discuss the formation of schools for the poor; however, the ultimate goal was promoting 'the salvation of the souls of men'.[30]

Despite the remoteness of Epworth from the centre of the voluntary movement in London, Samuel Wesley was well aware of the key role

26 Jeremy Gregory, 'The Eighteenth-Century Reformation: the Pastoral Task of Anglican Clergy after 1689', in Walsh, Haydon, and Taylor, eds, *Church of England c.1689–c.1833*, 67–85.

27 MS Wanley, fol. 3.

28 Tenison, *His Grace the Lord Archbishop of Canterbury's Letter*, 4.

29 See Allen and McClure, *Two Hundred Years*, 166–7 for a list of the books sent to corresponding members with the Society's second circular letter.

30 'The Second Circular Letter to the Clergy Correspondents, &c.' in MS Wanley, fol. 5, cf. fol. 7, and 'The Third Circular Letter to the Clergy Correspondents', fols 43–4.

the SPCK could play in promoting revival within the Church, and became a corresponding member of the Society a year after it was established.[31] In April 1700, a few weeks after he had become a member of the Society, Wesley attended two SPCK meetings in London. Fortunately, a key reason for Wesley's initial visit can be ascertained through an analysis of the Society's minute book, his subsequent letters to the Society, and 'An Account of a Society of some of the Clergy [and] others in Lincolnshire' found in the SPCK's Wanley manuscript.[32] The Society's minutes read, 'Mr. Adamson's of Burton Letter read with the Articles. Agreed on by a Society of Clergy in Lincolnshire, near Grantham'.[33] This was John Adamson, rector of Burton-Coggles, who would become a corresponding member of the society in the following month and a prebendary of Carlton Kyme in the diocese of Lincoln later in the year.[34] This clerical society had drawn up some 'Preliminary Articles' a week earlier which Wesley had evidently carried to the SPCK meeting.

The contents of the Lincolnshire society 'Articles' show that they were penned in response to the SPCK's second circular letter calling for the formation of clerical societies. Twenty-five clergy and four justices of the peace anonymously subscribed to the articles and agreed to meet once or twice a month between April and October of each year. The Society was designed to be a forum for the clergy to advise and assist one another regarding 'Cases of Difficulty' arising in their respective parishes.[35] While their primary aim was to encourage each other faithfully to carry out their clerical duties, the Society's secondary yet complementary goal was to promote a general reformation of manners in conjunction with sympathetic local magistrates. The entire design was intentionally modelled on the SPCK's advice.

After this initial contact with the SPCK, Samuel Wesley turned his attention towards the Society's request that clerical societies obtain the 'leave and direction' of their diocesan to carry forward their design. In a

31 Samuel Wesley was accepted as a member of the SPCK following the Society's receipt of his letter recorded under the date of 22 March 1700 with the note that he 'accepts the correspondence'. SPCK, D2/2, Abstract Letter 65.

32 The Wanley manuscript consists of transcriptions from original SPCK documents by Humphrey Wanley, Old English scholar and librarian who served successively as assistant secretary and secretary of the Society until June 1708.

33 SPCK Minutes, MS A1/1, 11 April 1700.

34 SPCK Minutes, 30 May 1700; John Le Neve, *Fasti Ecclesiae Anglicanae 1541–1857 IX Lincoln Diocese*, comp. Joyce M. Horn and David M. Smith (London, 1999), 49.

35 MS Wanley, fol. 146.

letter to the SPCK, dated 10 July 1700, he reported that he had followed the Society's directive to forward to his bishop copies of the accounts detailing the several societies set up for reformation. Fortunately, Wesley's diocesan, the Bishop of Lincoln, James Gardiner, had already declared himself in favour of more rigorous ecclesiastical administration through the renewal of the discontinued office of rural dean.[36] In his 1697 visitation *Advice to the Clergy of the Diocese of Lincoln*, Gardiner suggested that rural deans could assist him in his many duties by reporting 'The Ignorant, the Factious, the Scandalous, the Negligent, and the Dissenting' to the archdeacons, who could immediately correct and reform sinners. From reading Gardiner's *Advice*, Wesley would have been aware of his sympathy with the comprehensive kind of reform and renewal advocated by the SPCK in order to combat what he saw as an 'Age of Atheism, Infidelity, and Licentiousness'.[37] Wesley wisely built upon Gardiner's known interest in the restoration of rural deans by acquainting him with the Society's efforts to unite the clergy under rural deans so that they might associate with one another for the mutual promotion of religious piety among themselves and their respective parishioners through such means as the cultivation of religious societies, clerical societies, SRM, and charity schools. Wesley was pleased to report that Gardiner declared he would not 'discourage' those who formed themselves into clerical societies, at least not until he could implement his desire to unite his clergy under rural deans. As far as Wesley was concerned, gaining the approbation of Bishop Gardiner was only part of his overall strategy to promote the clerical society. In his letter, Wesley revealed that he was actively encouraging clergy to associate and suggested that Anthony Smith, the rector of Gainsborough, be written to on the subject of clerical societies.[38]

36 Bishop Edmund Gibson defined the office of the rural dean as 'the *Inspection* of the Lives and Manners of the Clergy and People, within their District, in order to be *reported* to the Bishop'. The difficulty with the office was that it 'hath always been of a Temporary Nature'. See *Codex juris ecclesiastici Anglicani: or, the statutes, constitutions, canons, rubricks and articles, of the Church of England, methodically digested under their proper heads. With a commentary, historical and juridical*, vol. 2 (London, 1713), 1011.

37 James Gardiner, *Advice to the Clergy of the Diocese of Lincoln* (London, 1697), 7, 26. Gardiner supported the movement for the reformation of manners and, as Wesley reported, did not oppose the formation of 'Societies' in his diocese. W. M. Jacob, 'Gardiner, James (1636/7–1705)', *ODNB*. On the widespread belief amongst churchmen that atheist clubs were on the rise, see Roger D. Lund, 'Guilt by Association: the Atheist Cabal and the Rise of the Public Sphere in Augustan England', *Albion* 34 (2002), 391–421.

38 SPCK, D2/2, Abstract Letter 135. It appears that Smith did not receive the initial

In July 1700, the Lincolnshire society began to draw up a detailed list of fourteen 'Articles of General Use and Conduct'. These 'Articles' followed the same pattern as their predecessor by focusing on the provision of holistic pastoral care while secondarily pointing out the need for the reform of manners. The 'Articles' encouraged parochial revival through a number of means including provision for daily services and monthly communion, the encouragement of family devotion and the supplying of devotional treatises for families, the catechism of children and the invitation of 'those of riper years' to the parsonage for further instruction, frequent parish visitation to take 'all oppertunities of testfying our Love by the obliging Carrage & Condecension even to the Meanest', and by forwarding the unifying vision of the voluntary society movement by emphasizing 'practical points' in their sermons.[39] Article thirteen provided guidance for future structuring of society meetings which were to be focused on the discussion of one or more of their particular clerical offices. This settled the agenda for the August and September meetings (the last two meetings we have records for) at which the clergymen selected the works of authors they were familiar with who dealt with 'Ministerial Duties', in order to collect abstracts out of them dealing with 'Methods and Directions as might be of use to us in the Discharge of our owne'.[40]

The Lincolnshire society was part of a wide-spread clerical society movement of which only fragmentary evidence has survived. From Samuel Wesley's correspondence with the SPCK, we know that the Lincolnshire society continued to meet in 1701 and together 'resolv'd to Catechise their Parishes all the somer-half-year'. Unfortunately, this letter is the last testimony regarding the society, most likely because of

letter from the Society, but eventually became a corresponding member of the SPCK following a second recommendation by Wesley. SPCK, D2/2, Abstract Letter 317; SPCK Minutes, MS A1/1, 12 and 15 August 1701.

39 MS Wanley, fols 149–51. The four tracts that were emphasized in the 'Articles' were: *A Pastoral Letter from a Minister to his Parishioners being an Earnest Exhortation to them to take care of their souls, and a preparative in order to render all his future methods of instruction more effectual to their edification* (London, 1699). [William Howell], *Prayers in the Closet, for the Use of all Devout Christians. Collected out of the Best Companion, by the Author of the same* (Oxford, 1692). John Williams, *A Brief Exposition of the Church-Catechism, With Proofs from Scripture* (11th edn, London, 1700). William Assheton, *A discourse against 1. drunkenness, 2. swearing & cursing published (pursuant to His Majesty's injunctions) to suppress debauchery and profaneness* (London, 1692). For more on books sent to Wesley via the Society, see Wesley to SPCK (10 June 1701), SPCK, D2/2, Abstract Letter 321.

40 MS Wanley, fol. 153.

the absence of SPCK letter books covering the period from 1702–7. Although the documentary evidence is limited, the SPCK abstract letter book covering the initial two years of the Society's existence clearly reveals the rapid growth of clerical societies. In this period, such societies were founded in twelve of the twenty-three dioceses in England and five in Wales, while in six other English dioceses there were favourable reports on the likelihood of societies being formed.[41] The abstract letter book indicates that the enthusiastic response to the SPCK's encouragement of clerical societies was one of the most significant achievements of their early years. Letters to the SPCK regarding clerical societies significantly outnumbered those devoted either to charity schools, SRM, or religious societies. Clerical societies were a development that rapidly spread to British dominions beyond the seas. One was soon set up in Jamaica under the direction of the bishop of London's commissary, Philip Bennet.[42] The larger vision of the SPCK was that clerical and lay societies would revive the Protestant interest throughout Europe.[43] Writing to a correspondent in Holland, John Chamberlayne expressed his belief that this revival had already begun visibly to lay hold of the nation stating,

> the Society think they cannot conclude this more to your satisfaction than by acquainting you that they have formed their Correspondencys in most of the Counties of this Kingdom, and have already found the happy effects by the Growth of Xtain Knowledge and ye Discouragement of Vice and Immorality in most places, so that there is a greater spirit of zeal and better face of Religion already visible throughout the Nation.[44]

The SPCK-inspired clerical society movement may be regarded as an under-appreciated aspect of a broader revival of voluntary religion that thrived in the Church of England in the half-century preceding the Evangelical Revival. This wide-spread movement provides evidence to demonstrate that the predominant Victorian characterization of the

41 An overview of the establishment of the various voluntary societies can be found by consulting 'An Index to ye Book of Abstracts to Number 276 inclusive' found pasted in Abstract Letter Book D2/2.

42 MS Wanley, fols 154–7. This society was founded in November 1700.

43 Daniel L. Brunner, *Halle Pietists in England: Anthony William Boehm and the Society for Promoting Christian Knowledge* (Göttingen, 1993); Sugiko Nishikawa, 'The SPCK in Defence of Protestant Minorities in Early Eighteenth-Century Europe', *JEH* 56 (2005), 730–48.

44 Chamberlayne to Mr Deberinghen (3 December 1700), Wanley MS, fol. 78.

eighteenth-century Church as stagnant and moralistic is erroneous. Recent evaluations of the eighteenth-century Church have lead to a greater appreciation for its dynamic nature and furthered our understanding of the ways in which the revivalists drew on currents of renewal already present in the Church.[45] Although in recent decades much progress has been made, further research is needed to assess the relationship between the late seventeenth- and early eighteenth-century Church and the rise of evangelicalism.[46] The interaction between Samuel Wesley, the SPCK, and the Lincolnshire clerical society provides an interesting case-study of one collaborative effort to revive the Church in the early eighteenth century. Methodologically and theologically, continuity between the voluntary movement and the Evangelical Revival is evident. On the methodological side, clerical efforts to promote godly zeal in one another and to spread the Gospel message to the poor through co-operative evangelism may be cited. On the theological side, we may cite the shared interest in practical over doctrinal matters, and the promotion of a 'practical Christianity' modelled on a shared ideal of imitating the practice of the primitive Church.

University of Manchester

[45] Although in its origins the revival was more of an Anglican than Dissenting movement, Old Dissent also made a contribution to the revival; see Michael Watts, *The Dissenters: from the Reformation to the French Revolution* (Oxford, 1978), 440 and Geoffrey Nuttall, 'Methodism and the older Dissent', *Journal of the United Reformed Church History Society* 2 (1981), 259–74.

[46] Hempton, *Methodism*, 18.

NARRATIVES OF CONVERSION IN ENGLISH CALVINISTIC METHODISM

by DAVID CERI JONES

IN May 1741, an anonymous Yorkshire Methodist sent George Whitefield a long letter in which he recorded the details of his nine-year-old daughter's evangelical conversion. Within a fortnight the letter was printed in *The Weekly History*, the magazine which had become the official mouthpiece of the Calvinistic wing of the Evangelical Revival by this point. Here is how Whitefield began his account:

> We have a little daughter about nine years old; one Lord's Day in the last winter, when she staid at home, she read one of your journals, and afterwards some sermons of yours we had got from London. It pleased God by his Holy Spirit so to impress her mind as is very remarkable. She desires me to tell Mr Whitefield (that sweet minister of Jesus Christ) what she has met with in reading his book, she says, such a change of Heart, that she can now pray to God, and converse with his people in such a manner as she could never do before that day. She is of a sprightly brisk temper, yet if she be never so much engaged in work or play, if she hears any body talk of you, or things relating to religion, she will come and hear, and put in her word about it.[1]

The author then went on to the case of his six-year-old son, who 'desires me to tell that good minister Mr Whitefield, that he loves him and his books, and believes when he can read them as well as his sister, he shall be like her.'[2] As if this were not sufficient, the author then proceeded with an account of the main contours of his own spiritual pilgrimage from nominal religion to evangelical faith, citing the influence of a godly mother who took him along to the local dissenting meeting-house. These three testimonies, compressed into a single narrative, were clearly designed to whet Whitefield's appetite, and concluded with the author's invitation to visit Yorkshire since, he

1 John Lewis, ed., *The Weekly History*, no. 12 (n.d.), 2.
2 Ibid.

wrote; 'we are much at a loss for some years past, few, comparatively, preaching the gospel of Christ, in any part of our neighbourhood'.[3]

The experience of conversion, or what evangelicals in the eighteenth century preferred to call the 'new birth', lies at the heart of any religious revival. If one accepts William G. McLoughlin's definition of revival as 'any series of spontaneous or organized meetings which produce religious conversions, whether they occur in one church, a dozen churches, or in hundreds under the leadership of a spectacular itinerant evangelists',[4] then people's accounts of their conversion become key to understanding the internal dynamics of religious revivals. However, narratives of conversion can be read on a number of levels. In the instance just quoted, what was essentially a private document, written primarily to George Whitefield, made the transition into the public sphere by its rapid publication in *The Weekly History*. In this transition it acquired a new function; it became a means of inducing similar experiences in those who read it, but it also became a didactic tool, helping new converts by providing them with a rudimentary theological discourse in which to situate their own experience. In his recent study of evangelical conversion narratives in early modern England, Bruce Hindmarsh has confessed to being unable to track down a significant body of Calvinistic Methodist autobiographical literature.[5] While there does not appear to be any evidence that either George Whitefield or Howel Harris assiduously collected conversion literature, in the systematic fashion of William McCulloch or Charles Wesley,[6] there is compelling evidence in the letters of Whitefield, and in the far more extensive correspondence of Harris,[7] that Calvinistic Methodists in both and England and Wales were accustomed to writing about their religious experiences.

Calvinistic Methodism, like the Evangelicalism of which it was a part, was an international movement, drawing together like-minded evangelicals from many parts of the Atlantic world. Its main concentra-

3 Ibid.

4 William G. McLoughlin, *Modern Revivalism: Charles Grandison Finney to Billy Graham* (New York, 1959), 7.

5 D. Bruce Hindmarsh, *The Evangelical Conversion Narrative: Spiritual Autobiography in Early Modern England* (Oxford, 2005), 193. See also the review of Hindmarsh's work by Henry D. Rack, *JEH* 57: 3 (2006), 619–21.

6 See Hindmarsh, *Evangelical Conversion Narrative*, chs 4 and 6.

7 See Boyd Stanley Schlenther and Eryn Mant White, *Calendar of the Trevecka Letters* (Aberystwyth, 2003).

tions were in London and the south-west of England, Wales and Scotland, and across the Atlantic from New England in the northern colonies, to Georgia in the south. Each of these places boasted an indigenous evangelical awakening; but they also shared proximity to the movement's premier revivalist, George Whitefield, and it was he who drew the disparate awakenings together, creating a Calvinistic renewal movement. He achieved this by the creation of a communications network which provided the sinews that linked the awakenings to one another.[8] At the heart of this network was a weekly magazine that kept its subscribers abreast of the progress of the gospel at home and abroad. *The Weekly History*, the title it bore during its most popular incarnation, was the brain-child of a London-Welsh printer, John Lewis.[9] It began life as *The Christian's Amusement* in 1740, but in April 1741 George Whitefield gave the publication his blessing. The magazine gave the Calvinistic revival much-needed cohesion,[10] at precisely the same time as it was coming under pressure from John Wesley's attempts to take over the whole English evangelical movement.

The main literary form adopted by those who provided material for these magazines was the familiar letter, most of which took the form of semi-journalistic accounts of the latest progress of the revival, but the magazine also became a repository for testimonies to the reality of the work of God in the life of the individual. Many of its issues contain autobiographical material in which individuals retold the story of their conversion or bore testimony to the ways in which God had been dealing with them subsequently. On one level these narratives were evidence of the reality of the Holy Spirit's activity, and therefore served as an authentication of their revivals. However, by urging readers to compare their experiences with the examples that appeared in print, the leaders of the revival hoped that their followers would examine them-

8 The network is explored in detail in Susan O'Brien, 'A Transatlantic Community of Saints: the Great Awakening and the First Evangelical Network, 1735–1755', *AHR* 91 (1986), 811–32; Frank Lambert, *'Pedlar in Divinity': George Whitefield and the Transatlantic Revivals* (Princeton, NJ, 1994).

9 For more on Lewis and his contribution to the Evangelical Revival, see David Ceri Jones, 'John Lewis and the Promotion of the International Evangelical Revival, 1735–1756', in E. Dyfed Roberts, ed., *Revival, Renewal and the Holy Spirit* (Carlisle, 2007 forthcoming).

10 It was joined by two closely-related publications, one Scottish and the other published in Boston; all three magazines borrowed and reprinted material from one another. For more on these, see Susan Durden, 'A Study of the First Evangelical Magazines, 1740–1748', *JEH* 27: 3 (1976), 255–75, at 257, 266–8; J. E. van de Wetering, 'The Christian History of the Great Awakening', *Journal of Presbyterian History* 44 (1966), 122–9.

selves against the stellar case-studies which they selected for print. The magazine, therefore, came to be used to regulate the spiritual experiences of Calvinistic Methodists, reinforcing Calvinistic norms of godly behaviour.

I have resisted referring to the autobiographical accounts that appeared in *The Weekly History* as conversion narratives, since that would imply that they consciously followed the stylistic conventions of that genre. In too many instances this appears not to have been the case. The writing of accounts of conversion within Calvinistic Methodism never seems to have been that formulaic. This is not to say that there are no examples of letters which adopted some, or indeed all, of the motifs of classical conversion narrative. Those who were prepared to record their experience of the new birth had, of course, plenty of models to follow in the journals of Whitefield and Wesley.[11] However, most of the accounts that appeared in *The Weekly History* tended to be shorter, more haphazard, and less fully developed. Some correspondents just summed up their experience in a short paragraph, often with few overtly personal references, preferring to express themselves by biblical proof-texting. Others began their letters with a brief summary of their conversion experience, almost by way of introduction, before they proceeded with the main substance of their correspondence. An employee at Whitefield's orphanage in Georgia, for example, began his letter;

> I am glad to have this opportunity to let you know what God has done for my soul: O how much reason have I to thank the Lord that he has been pleas'd to bring such a poor miserable sinner as I am out of darkness into his marvellous light![12]

Still others wove elements of their experience into letters which dealt with a wide array of other issues; in instances like this the actual conversion story has to be teased out of the surrounding extraneous detail.

Because of the variety of forms in which accounts of conversion appeared, it is difficult to give an accurate estimate of the number of

11 W. R. Ward, 'Introduction', in R. P. Heitzenrater, ed., *The Works of John Wesley, vol. 18: Journals and Diaries I* (1735–38) (Nashville, TN, 1988), 37–93; Lambert, *'Pedlar in Divinity'*, 75–84.

12 'From Mr J_ M_, to the Reverend Mr Whitefield', in John Lewis, ed., *The Christian History*, vol. 5, no. 1 (n.p., 1744), 56.

them that were printed in John Lewis's magazine. Their appearance was also not uniformly spread throughout its print-run, but correlates with the various highs and lows through which the Calvinistic revival passed. The early issues of *The Christian's Amusement* contain only a few brief narratives, but the amount of material increased markedly once Whitefield had taken over editorial control by mid-1741. From this point on there was a fairly regular supply of material from the inhabitants of his orphanage in Georgia, and a glut of material following Whitefield's two itineraries in Scotland at the end of the summer of 1741 and during 1742, when he travelled to Glasgow to fan the flames of the Cambuslang revival.[13] After this time the incidence of the narratives became much less frequent, probably due to the sharp drop-off in the enthusiasm surrounding the revival, and reflecting some of the difficulties facing the Calvinistic revival after 1743. There were, though, a few further peaks in the appearance of conversion material; notably during John Cennick's time as the leader of the Tabernacle Society in 1744, when Calvinistic Methodism made some significant inroads into Wiltshire,[14] and also following the beginning of Calvinistic Methodism in Plymouth after 1746.[15] The growth of Calvinistic Methodism in England was at best fitful, and the irregular appearance of conversion material in the pages of its official mouthpiece seems to reflect the problems the movement faced after its initial spurt of growth between 1739 and 1741, problems made all the more acute when its most passionate advocate, George Whitefield, chose to spend most of the mid- and later 1740s in the American colonies.

Those who wished to record their conversion experience were not without plenty of guidance on what was expected of them. In one of the first editions of *The Weekly History*, John Lewis printed a letter offering his readers advice on how to write 'an account of what they have experienced of the work of God upon their souls'. Those reticent about being identified publicly were assured that they could write anonymously, or just append their initials to the foot of their letters. But Lewis also offered guidelines on the spiritual content which should appear:

13 Arthur Fawcett, *The Cambuslang Revival: the Scottish Evangelical Revival of the Eighteenth Century* (London, 1971), 114–22.

14 Colin Podmore, *The Moravian Church in England, 1728–1760* (Oxford, 1998), 88–9.

15 C. E. Welch, 'Andrew Kinsman's Churches at Plymouth', *Report and Transactions of the Devonshire Association for the Advancement of Science, Literature and Art* 97 (1965), 212–16.

> The best way then is for every person simply to write what he once was in a state of nature, how and by what means he came to have the dawnings of light and grace upon his soul, and how it has been with him since that time.[16]

Narratives were to follow a trajectory from one's state by nature, through to the first stirrings of conviction of sin. The length of this period of conviction varied, but the narratives were to culminate with the actual release of the conversion moment itself, which was invariably followed by joy and peace. Closely following Calvinist notions of the Christian pilgrimage, converts were also requested to outline how God had been dealing with one's soul ever since, potentially the most important element of the narrative since assurance of salvation had become synonymous with one's ability to pinpoint the evidences of grace in one's life.[17]

Many of the accounts that were printed followed this pattern, either to the letter or in part, as different elements of the schema were foregrounded in different cases. In May 1742, Lewis published an issue of *The Weekly History* which was almost entirely made up of the testimonies of some of Whitefield's recent converts in England and Scotland. On 22 April, a correspondent, who identified himself only by the initials R. D., wrote in order to 'let you know what God hath done for my soul by those sermons I heard from you on Monday last'.[18] He had obviously been present when Whitefield preached at six in the morning at the fair held at Moorfields on Easter Monday,[19] and confessed that it was the day when he was 'brought to see the light'. The account begins with the author stating that he had intended spending the day at the fair, 'serving that Master of mine, the devil', but his attention was arrested 'when you was in prayer [which] had a deep effect upon my heart'. While listening to Whitefield preach, 'God was pleas'd to pour down the downings of the Spirit upon my soul'. He was convicted of his need of a Saviour, but it was only after a number of hours of intense conviction of sin, during which he felt 'my soul bowed down with my transgressions', that he emerged to testify that 'God did cloath me with

16 Lewis, ed., *The Weekly History*, no. 13 (n.d.), 2.

17 David W. Bebbington, *Evangelicalism in Modern Britain: a History from the 1730s to the 1990s* (London, 1989), 42–50.

18 Lewis, ed., *The Weekly History*, no. 13 (n.d.), 2.

19 Iain H. Murray, ed., *George Whitefield's Letters, 1734-1742* (London, 1976), 384–8.

his righteousness, surely I was cloathed with that scarlet coat dyed in the blood of Jesus'.[20]

In the same year, one of the housekeepers at Whitefield's orphanage in Georgia wrote a lengthy autobiographical account to a ministerial friend in Ireland, which was printed in the magazine. She wrote in order to testify to 'how the Lord has dealt with my soul since I saw you', and hoped to be able to 'speak freely of his Free Grace and Distinguishing Love to me a poor sinner'. She began with a detailed account of the protracted three years she had spent under intense conviction of sin, having discovered that God's Law was 'holy, just and pure, and I was unable to fulfil its demands'. Relief came only when her husband 'placed [her] under the droppings of the gospel', as she heard Whitefield preach his tried and tested sermon on the new birth at Charlestown. She wrote:

> He spoke with great power, and shew'd what a wretched estate man was in by nature, and what it was to be born again, and what it was not. – When he spoke of a professor without the Power of religion, I saw myself drawn out in large. When he spoke of the blessed estate of those who had a saving change wrought upon their souls – of this I found I was quite ignorant. When he spoke of Jesus Christ, and the benefits purchased by him, it was so sweetly, that I thought if I had a thousand worlds, I could part with them all to know my part in the dear Redeemers blood.

But it was not until shortly afterwards that the Lord 'appeared for me in an hour of distress', when she was able to respond to the invitations of the gospel and professed to having a heart 'so filled with love to the Lord Jesus, that it was the desire of my soul that sinners should have their eyes open to see their miserable state'.[21]

The redemptive-historical approach to be found in typical Calvinistic Methodist accounts such as these correlates closely with Bruce Hindmarsh's discovery that most evangelical narratives tended to be structured according to the biblical pattern of Creation, Fall, Redemption, and new Creation,[22] albeit with some elements given more promi-

20 Lewis, ed., *The Weekly History*, issue 58 (15 May 1742).

21 'From Mrs B_y, of the Orphan-house in Georgia, to the Reverend Mr G_t K_y, minister of the gospel in Ireland', in John Lewis, ed., *An Account of the Most Remarkable Particulars Relating to the Present Progress of the Gospel*, vol. 4, no. 3 (n.p., 1743), 61–78.

22 D. Bruce Hindmarsh, '"My chains fell off, my heart was free": Early Methodist Conversion Narrative in England', *Church History* 68: 4 (1999), 910–29, at 925.

nence than others depending on the personal circumstances of each writer. In this many of the narratives that appeared in *The Weekly History* are unremarkable, bearing obvious similarities to the material produced by Wesley's converts, the Moravians and others associated with the evangelical movement. However, this is not to say that the Calvinistic narratives which appeared in *The Weekly History* did not have a number of distinctive characteristics.

Many of them were overlain with Calvinist rhetoric. Letter writers characteristically laced their narratives with seemingly 'spontaneous' interjections such as: 'O Free Grace and rich mercy! O the wonderful, matchless, unparall'd love of God to my soul',[23] or 'O what wonders has God's Free Grace wrought in me! How has he delighted to love me!'[24] At the outset of their letters others professed their intention of 'speak[ing] freely of his Free Grace and distinguishing love to me a poor sinner'.[25] In the majority of cases there was very little discussion of the intricacies of the Calvinist order of salvation, an acceptance of its basic structure seems to have been largely taken for granted; the elements referred to most frequently being Election and God's distinguishing love, the extent and depth of human sinfulness and the imputed righteousness of Christ. Unlike the largely Presbyterian Cambuslang converts, many of whom had been schooled in the rigours of Reformed theology from a young age,[26] the Calvinistic Methodists who contributed to *The Weekly History* seem often to have acquired their theology during or shortly after their conversions. Only for a select few individuals did the pages of the magazine became a place in which they could explore the varying expressions of Calvinistic orthodoxy. In 1743, for example, one of Whitefield's female correspondents wrote to him 'rejoicing in God for his electing love'. Her letter, in which she fitted her experience into the structure of the Calvinistic *ordo salutis*, included an awareness of some of the distinctions between moderate and high or hyper Calvinism. Following Whitefield's lead, she steered clear of double predestination, adopting an infralapsarian position in which she

23 'From M_y L_y (a young girl in Merchant's Hospital, Edinburgh) to the Rev. Mr. Whitefield', in Lewis, ed., *The Weekly History*, no. 62 (12 June 1742), 3.

24 'The Copy of a letter to a friend in the country to Brother Howell Harris', in Lewis, ed., *Account of the Most Remarkable Particulars*, vol. 2, no. 1 (n.p., 1743), 62.

25 'From Mrs B_y, of the Orphan-house in Georgia, to the Reverend Mr G_t K_y, minister of the Gospel in Ireland', in Lewis, ibid., vol. 4, no. 3: 62.

26 T. C. Smout, 'Born again at Cambuslang: New Evidence on Popular Religion and Literacy in Eighteenth-Century Scotland', *P&P* 97 (1982), 114–27, at 123–7.

gave thanks for 'unmerited and Distinguishing Love: that he sho'd pass by so many, and look upon me, who am the chief of sinners'.[27]

The genre of conversion narrative, of course, had its origins in Puritanism, and had been definitively moulded by the Calvinism characteristic of most Puritans.[28] However, in the accounts in *The Weekly History*, Calvinism often appeared more as a partisan badge of identification than a coherently understood theological system. This should come as no real surprise. The majority of examples which I have quoted were written between 1740 and 1743, a period during which Whitefield's Calvinistic Methodists were under intense pressure from the Wesleyan revival. A formal split between Wesley and Whitefield over predestination had taken place in the summer of 1741,[29] following Whitefield's return to England from the American colonies. Finding that Wesley had ousted him as leader of the English movement, Whitefield was forced onto the defensive, and throughout 1741 and 1742 struggled to rebuild a viable Calvinistic revival in England.[30] It was undoubtedly these difficulties that led him to seek ever closer ties with the Welsh Methodists and to tie the Scottish Methodists and his colonial associates, with limited success, into a loosely interconnected Calvinistic renewal movement. *The Weekly History*, with its sister publications in Scotland and America, therefore, assumed even greater importance, becoming the public face of this international evangelical community. Since its Calvinism was its most bitterly contested feature, it is little wonder that many converts belligerently reiterated their beliefs in election and imputed righteousness, since these were the very doctrines that John Wesley found most objectionable.

Nearly all of the individuals who wrote accounts of their spiritual awakening, almost without exception, paid tribute to the decisive role played by Whitefield himself in their conversion. Whitefield was the 'Grand Itinerant', and none of the other revivalists could quite match

27 'From Mrs S_h B_r, to the Reverend Mr Whitefield', in Lewis, ed., *Account of the Most Remarkable Particulars*, vol. 4, no. 3: 59.

28 Patricia Caldwell, *The Puritan Conversion Narrative* (Cambridge, 1982); Ward, 'Introduction', in Heitzenrater, ed., *The Works of John Wesley, vol. 18*, 1–36; Hindmarsh, *Evangelical Conversion Narrative*, 33–52.

29 For contrasting perspectives on the Free Grace controversy, see Arnold A. Dallimore, *George Whitefield: the Life and Times of the Great Evangelist of the Eighteenth-Century Revival*, 2 vols (London, 1970 and Edinburgh, 1980), 2: chs 1–4; Herbert Boyd McGonigle, *Sufficient Saving Grace: John Wesley's Evangelical Arminianism* (Carlisle, 2001), chs 5–8.

30 David Ceri Jones, *'A Glorious Work in the World': Welsh Methodism and the International Evangelical Revival, 1735–1750* (Cardiff, 2004), 18–45.

either his enthusiasm for transatlantic travel, or the veneration with which he was held. The example of the nine-year-old girl who experienced the new birth after reading one of Whitefield's journals, with which this paper commenced, was by no means exceptional. In 1741 William McCulloch sent Whitefield an account of a typical young convert from Glasgow:

> When she heard tell of Whitefield she long'd to hear him; when she read his Journals she long'd much more to hear him: But when she read the account of God's dealings with him, she pray'd to hear him . . . but never felt her heart engaged in the work, till she heard Mr Whitefield's first sermon at Glasgow.[31]

In their letters to Whitefield, others testified that 'you have been a blessed instrument in the Lord's hand of bringing my poor soul, and many others, to the Lord Jesus Christ',[32] and 'I have just liv'd a heaven upon earth. O I have never experienced so much of his presence as I have found when I have been hearing you preach. Indeed I may call the park a Bethel; for surely God was in it many a time'.[33] The adulatory regard in which many held Whitefield often resulted in pangs of guilt for some correspondents who were worried that what they had actually experienced owed less to the activity of the Holy Spirit and more to the dynamism of Whitefield's oratory. A correspondent from Edinburgh in 1741 confessed:

> I can say I never found any thing so difficult all the days of my life, as to look beyond all means and instruments: for tho' I have been enabled in some measure to bless the Lord for the good I got by your ministry, yet I find there is always a hankering in my heart after the instrument.[34]

These narratives demonstrate that the evangelical writers were happy to cast their experience in terms of a decisive turning-point or crisis experience, through which they crossed from darkness into light.

[31] 'From the Rev Mr M__, in Scotland, to the Rev Mr Whitefield, in London', in Lewis, ed., *The Weekly History*, no. 51 (27 March 1742), 3.

[32] 'The copy of a letter to the Rev Mr Whitefield', in Lewis, ed., *The Weekly History*, no. 59 (22 May 1742), 1.

[33] 'From M. Finlyson, a young girl, to the Rev Mr Whitefield', in Lewis, ed., *The Weekly History*, no. 56 (1 May 1742), 3.

[34] 'From M__y L__y (a young girl in Merchant's Hospital, Edinburgh) to the Rev Mr Whitefield', in Lewis, ed., *The Weekly History*, no. 62 (12 June 1742), 2.

The Calvinistic narratives demonstrate the tension that existed between the more protracted method of conversion that had been characteristic of the Puritans and the more instantaneous experience which the Methodists, of all shades of opinion, tried to induce in their converts.[35] For Whitefield and his fellow Calvinistic Methodists the procedure associated with more protracted conversions was not necessarily jettisoned, but heavily truncated so that an individual might pass through the stages of conviction, conversion and joyful release into the full assurance of faith in the course of a single hour-long sermon.

Whitefield's prominence in many of these narratives also demonstrates his remarkable acumen as a self-publicist. The accounts demonstrate that he was, as Harry Stout has argued, the first 'religious celebrity',[36] whose fame had spread throughout the mid eighteenth-century British Atlantic world. His own autobiographical narrative and the handful of sermons that had found their way into print by the early 1740s had facilitated this, but the sheer volume of correspondence that bore witness to his decisive role, particularly after the split with Wesley in 1741, must have had a powerful psychological effect on the movement. The narratives that appeared in *The Weekly History* demonstrated to many of those Methodists, tempted perhaps to go off and join the Wesleyans, that Whitefield's ministry was still effective and that, despite appearances, the Calvinistic Methodist revival, of which he himself remained very much the focal point, was still being actively blessed by God.

The disparate nature of the conversion material which appears in the pages of the Calvinistic Methodist magazine makes statistical analysis problematic. What is clear, however, is that between 1741 and 1743 by far the largest number of narratives were those penned by children and young people. The magazine contains a substantial collection of narratives from the residents at the Orphan house, adjacent to the park in Edinburgh in which Whitefield preached in the open air for a fortnight during his first visit to Scotland during July 1741.[37] In many respects, these narratives have to be approached separately from many of the others which appeared in *The Weekly History*. Most of the children who

35 Bebbington, *Evangelicalism in Modern Britain*, 5–10; David Bebbington, 'Evangelical Conversion, c.1740–1850', *Scottish Bulletin of Evangelical Theology* 18: 2 (2000), 102–27.

36 Harry S. Stout, *The Divine Dramatist: George Whitefield and the Rise of Modern Evangelicalism* (Grand Rapids, MI, 1991), xiv.

37 Dallimore, *George Whitefield*, 2: 90–1.

wrote seem to have been pre-adolescents, but their letters were written in mature prose and demonstrated a knowledge and grasp of scriptural idioms which are in all likelihood beyond the ability of most ten-year-old children. It is possible that the narratives were a Sunday-school exercise, formed by the children themselves on a pattern offered by the teacher. In most cases, however, one suspects that the narratives are loosely based on interviews with the children, written up afterwards and given a more polished gloss. This raises questions about the extent to which these printed narratives reflect the authentic voice of their supposed authors. There is little doubt that many of them passed through an editorial process that saw their rough edges polished and their theological content refined, a fact that contributes to their lack of spontaneity and their slightly inauthentic appearance on first reading.

The juvenile narratives invariably contain very little personal detail, and the possibility that some of the language and expressions used were mimicked from what they had picked up in sermons, religious societies, or in the home cannot be discounted.[38] The case of a correspondent, identifiable only by her initials as A__ K__y, is typical. After bemoaning her unworthiness to be a subject of God's grace, she admitted to having been 'much under doubts and fear as to my interest in Christ'. Whitefield's arrival in Edinburgh, though, had made all the difference as the 'Lord has made you an instrument of both confirming, comforting and strengthening me in my interest in Him'. Since listening to Whitefield's sermon she confessed that she had;

> not had one hour of darkness. O the sweetness I felt in the time of your sermon! I cannot express with what pleasure I look'd and saw that God was my God; which makes me wonder how such a great King should come and dwell with such a vile sinner as I am.[39]

Despite the evangelical's strong belief in original sin, childhood, particularly its pre-adolescent phase, was still regarded as a state of comparative innocence. Most classical conversion narratives tended to begin with an account of early religious impressions, which were then lost once early adulthood was reached and ungodly patterns of life and thought had become engrained. By focusing on instances of precocious

38 Derec Llwyd Morgan, *The Great Awakening in Wales* (London, 1988), 49–50.

39 'From A__ K__ (another young girl in Merchant's Hospital, Edinburgh) to the Rev. Mr. Whitefield', in Lewis, ed., *The Weekly History*, no. 63 (19 June 1742), 3–4.

spirituality in the very young, the Calvinistic Methodists were creating an ideal of the pious life, wholly given over to the service of God from the youngest age; but they were also seeking to marshal still more compelling evidence about the authenticity of their revival, and of the special blessing of God which appeared to rest on the ministry of Whitefield.

The other group of narratives, written by children and adolescents, were penned by the residents of Whitefield's Georgia orphan house. Upon taking control of *The Weekly History*, Whitefield had quickly realized its potential as a vehicle for raising the profile of his orphan house and attracting funds for its upkeep. Aware that the orphan house was not without its critics, Whitefield used the magazine to disseminate positive propaganda about its activities. The greatest indicator of its success would be the conversion of its residents, since this would add the unquestionable seal of God's approval to the whole venture. From 1741 onwards the magazine included regular up-dates from the superintendent at Bethesda, James Habersham. However, these letters only occasionally contained news about practical matters; more often than not they consisted of accounts of the spiritual fortunes of the residents. Fever pitch was reached in the spring of 1741, when revival broke out at Bethesda, and the pages of *The Weekly History* duly reflected this new and exciting development, with three whole issues given over to short letters from residents testifying to the reality of their conversions.

Like the narratives from Scotland, these were also formulaic and in most instances almost devoid of personal references. The case of a ten-year-old girl who wrote to Whitefield to inform him that she had 'found great concern about my poor soul since your leaving us', was typical.[40] The narrative proceeded with pious hopes that her experience would not be transitory and that it would result in a genuine and solid conversion. On the whole, the narratives from the orphan house are slightly disappointing, devoid of the excitement and enthusiasm that we know from other sources had characterized this period in its life. Historians have tended to be very critical of the regime at Bethesda. Neil J. O'Connell has shown how the punishing schedule of daily devotions that the residents were expected to endure became fertile ground for the production of what he has called a 'group of juvenile religious

40 'Copies of several letters wrote by children at the Orphan house to the Reverend Mr Whitefield', in Lewis, ed., *The Weekly History*, no. 20 (22 August 1741), 4.

enthusiasts'.[41] From the evidence presented in *The Weekly History* it would be very difficult to judge the quality or reality of these children's religious experiences. Again the narratives were recorded by an intermediary, usually the Orphan-house chaplain, Jonathan Barber; any spontaneity there may have been is lost beneath the predictable stock of scriptural idioms. But for Whitefield these narratives were a further confirmation of divine approval of his 'house of mercy'[42] in the American colonies. Calvinistic Methodists in England, and especially in Wales it seems, lapped up their contents and they at least had the intended aim of making sympathetic readers reach into their pockets and part with what little spare cash they had in order to keep the venture afloat.[43]

In many respects the small selection of narratives examined in this paper are just the tip of an iceberg; they include only those published in *The Weekly History*, and none of them deal with the distinctive experience of the Welsh Methodists. They add further texture to the landscape depicted in Bruce Hindmarsh's *The Evangelical Conversion Narrative*, demonstrating the clear affinity between the Calvinist accounts and those produced by other groups within the early evangelical movement. But they also highlight a series of distinctive features. Perhaps the most obvious contrast is the way that many of these narratives straddled the private and public spheres. Many evangelicals wrote accounts of their conversion, but few published them as quickly, circulated them as widely or encouraged their regular reading to quite the same extent as the early Calvinistic Methodists.

Aberystwyth University

41 Neil J. O'Connell, 'George Whitefield and Bethesda Orphan-House', *Georgia Historical Quarterly* 54 (1970), 53–4.

42 'From Mrs B_y, of the Orphan-house in Georgia, to the Reverend Mr G_t K_y, minister of the Gospel in Ireland', in Lewis, ed., *Account of the Most Remarkable Particulars*, vol. 4, no. 3: 71.

43 See Jones, *'A Glorious Work in the World'*, 301–2.

THE PATTERN OF REVIVAL: JOHN WESLEY'S VISION OF 'INIQUITY' AND 'GODLINESS' IN CHURCH HISTORY

by DARREN SCHMIDT

On 24 August 1744, in a sermon at St Mary's, Oxford, John Wesley indicted what he perceived to be a poverty of 'Scriptural Christianity' within the University. Wesley began his homily by portraying an early declension of the Church; already in apostolic times, he maintained, the 'mystery of iniquity' had grown up alongside the 'mystery of godliness'. Wesley then painted a dramatic picture of enduring conflict between these two forces throughout church history, declaring, 'Here we tread a beaten path: the still increasing corruptions of the succeeding generations have been largely described from time to time, by those witnesses God raised up, to show that he had "built his church upon a rock, and the gates of hell should not" wholly "prevail against her".'[1]

Four decades and many miles later, in several sermons written in the 1780s, Wesley expanded this historical vision, identifying pivotal events and personalities on both sides of the conflict, and encompassing the history of the Methodist Revival itself. Moreover, in 1781, Wesley published *A Concise Ecclesiastical History, from the Birth of Christ, to the Beginning of the Present Century*, a four-volume abridgement supplemented with Wesley's own 'Short History of the People Called Methodists'.

At first glance, one might find Wesley's historical attention, in the midst of his tireless work as preacher, evangelist and organizer, curious or surprising. Indeed, Wesley's view of church history does not often feature in scholarship. The exceptions tend to rely either on his sermons or his larger publications, rather than this work as an integrated whole, and do not consider in depth the broader implications of

[1] John Wesley, Sermon 4, 'Scriptural Christianity', in *Sermons I–IV*, ed. Albert C. Outler, vols 1–4 of *The Bicentennial Edition of the Works of John Wesley*, ed. Frank Baker and Richard Heitzenrater (Nashville, TN, 1976–) [hereafter: *WJW*], 1: 161–9, sections I–II, quote at 169, II.9, with reference to Matt. 16: 18. For background on this sermon, see 1: 109, 113–16.

his historical interpretation.[2] We find, however, through examining his rendering in sermons and in his *Concise Ecclesiastical History*, that church history was hardly a passing interest for Wesley. As shall be demonstrated, a pattern emerges in his thought, a storyline of spreading iniquity or declension interrupted by divine action and revived Christian godliness. This pattern Wesley articulated as early as 1744; but in the 1780s he developed it considerably, and, most significantly, extended it to encompass the movement of which he was at the helm. His historical vision, then, not only sheds light on our understanding of Wesley himself, but also raises the issue of history's role in relation to how Wesley, alongside other evangelical leaders, perceived the Revival.

I

We begin with a summary of Wesley's historical sketches, drawn from three sermons written and published between 1783 and 1787, in which he sought to represent 'iniquity' and 'godliness' in the full sweep of church history.[3] Wesley described Christianity in apostolic times as more simple and pure, but he saw this period as short lived. He called Pentecost (Acts 2) a dawning of genuine Christianity, yet found ample New Testament evidence that 'the mystery of iniquity' was at work nearly from the Church's inception. Wesley exclaimed, 'We have been apt to imagine that the primitive church was all excellence and perfection! ... But how soon did the fine gold become dim!'[4] During the ensuing centuries, Wesley traced spreading spiritual decay, interrupted by persecutions resulting in 'longer or shorter seasons wherein true

[2] Significantly more attention has been given to the broader subject of Wesley's engagement with Christian tradition(s). Articles dealing with Wesley's historical interpretation are referenced below.

[3] Sermon 61, 'The Mystery of Iniquity' (1783), *WJW* 2: 452–70, Sermon 68, 'The Wisdom of God's Counsels' (1784), 2: 552–66, and Sermon 102, 'Of Former Times' (1787), 3: 442–53. Sermon 104, 'On Attending the Church Service' (1787), 3: 469–70, §§13–16, contains a shorter, but characteristic, summary. These sermons appeared first in Wesley's *Arminian Magazine* and then in his four-volume continuation (vols five through eight) to *Sermons on Several Occasions* (London, 1788).

[4] 'Mystery of Iniquity', *WJW* 2: 455–61, §§11–23, quotes at 460–1, §§21, 23; see also 'Former Times', 3: 451, §18. Whilst Wesley's interest in 'primitive' Christianity is evident in the source material, his statement here reminds that his primitivism can be overstated. Compare Luke L. Keefer, Jr, 'John Wesley: Disciple of Early Christianity', *Wesleyan Theological Journal* 19: 1 (1984), 23–32, at 28, 30, who acknowledges Wesley's perception of the 'mystery of iniquity' early in church history, but maintains that his primitivism is 'a hermeneutical key to his life'.

Christianity revived', and by occasional godly examples. Tertullian and Montanus, in his estimation, lived holy lives 'against the general corruption of Christians' and suffered as a result.[5] Wesley likewise sharply contrasted the characters of the fifth-century heretic Pelagius, whom he speculated should be ranked among the holiest of his day, and his opponent Augustine, whom he sarcastically called 'a wonderful saint!', and described as 'full of pride, passion, bitterness, censoriousness, and . . . foul-mouthed to all that contradicted him'.[6] Wesley reserved his harshest condemnation for the Emperor Constantine, castigating his alleged conversion as 'the grand blow' which had done more damage to the Church than persecution. From this point in history, 'the Christians did not gradually sink, but rushed headlong into all manner of vices. Then the mystery of iniquity was no more hid, but stalked abroad in the face of the sun.'[7] Wesley proceeded to paint with a broad, bleak stroke the Church spanning from ancient times to the Reformation: 'for fourteen hundred years, it was corrupted more and more, as all history shows, till scarce any either of the power or form of religion was left'.[8]

Wesley depicted the same pattern of declension, with occasional moments of renewal, in the period between the Reformation and his own day. Henry Rack aligns Wesley's interpretation with those of his contemporary Anglican Evangelicals Joseph Milner and Thomas Haweis, who 'picked out scattered sparks of light in the dark ages of popery which preserved the truth until the Reformation dawned'.[9] But whilst they may have shared a similar (and traditionally Protestant) view of medieval Roman Catholicism, Wesley construed the Reformation as a transient renewal rather than a dramatic resurgence of vital Christianity. He did praise Luther's opposition to Rome as an occasion

[5] Ibid., 461–2, §§24–6, quote at 462, §26; see also 'Wisdom of God's Counsels', 2: 555, §9. Wesley defended Montanus in a separate essay, distinguishing him from other 'heretics' espousing more suspect theology, and, whilst acknowledging varied opinions, concluding that 'Montanus was not only a truly good man, but one of the best men then upon earth'. Wesley, 'The Real Character of Montanus', in *The Works of John Wesley*, vol. 11 (3rd edn, Grand Rapids, MI, 1979), 485–6.

[6] 'Wisdom of God's Counsels', *WJW* 2: 555–6, §9.

[7] 'Mystery of Iniquity', *WJW* 2: 462–3, §27; other examples of Wesley's scorn for Constantine include Sermon 66, 'The Signs of the Times', 2: 529, §7, and 'Former Times', 3: 449–50, §§15–16.

[8] 'Wisdom of God's Counsels', *WJW* 2: 555, §8, with allusion to II Tim. 3: 5; see also 'Attending the Church Service', 3: 470, §14.

[9] Henry D. Rack, *Reasonable Enthusiast: John Wesley and the Rise of Methodism* (2nd edn, London, 1992), 349.

of divine providence; 'Yet', he bemoaned, 'even before Luther was called home the love of many was waxed cold.'[10] Ultimately, the Reformation was 'exquisitely trifling' in that it had brought change externally, but not in 'tempers or lives'.[11] Similarly, in Britain 'real witnesses of true scriptural Christianity' had arisen, whose testimony eventually faded with the end of persecution and the increase of affluence. This latter trend culminated, in Wesley's view, with the Restoration, which ushered in widespread 'infidelity' and 'immorality' lasting into his own time.[12]

In these sermons, Wesley always sought to link the distant past with contemporary experience. On the negative side, in 'The Mystery of Iniquity' (1783) Wesley pondered whether the 'general apostasy' evident in history made a future 'general reformation' imperative. Moreover, he warned his audience against nominal Christianity, and especially the love of riches, which he believed had 'in all ages been the bane of genuine Christianity', the chief cause of its corruption. Finally, he exhorted sincere Christians to be watchful in the face of 'the wickedness which overflows the earth', and thankful for their preservation.[13]

In 'The Wisdom of God's Counsels' (1784), Wesley focused positively on 'providential' interspersions which acted against the spreading tide of corruption, and made direct application to Methodists. Wesley sought to place the Methodist Revival within the panorama of redemption history, especially God's 'wisdom' as demonstrated through the growth of the Church. The Revival, though, was pre-eminent:

> We may in some measure trace this manifold wisdom from the beginning of the world: from Adam to Noah, from Noah to Moses, and from Moses to Christ. But I would now consider it (after just touching on the history of the church in past ages) only with regard to what he has wrought in the present age, during the last half century; yea, and in this little corner of the world, the British islands only.[14]

10 'Wisdom of God's Counsels', *WJW* 2: 556–7, §10, quote at 556.

11 'Mystery of Iniquity', *WJW* 2: 465, §29; see also 'Former Times', 3: 449, §14, and 'Attending the Church Service', 3: 470, §15. In the latter, Wesley tempered this judgement, saying that the Reformation *had* brought internal transformation and reintroduced '[m]ore of the ancient, scriptural Christianity' throughout Europe; but its results were not lasting.

12 'Wisdom of God's Counsels', *WJW* 2: 557–8, §§11–12; also 'Former Times', 3: 449, §§13–14.

13 'Mystery of Iniquity', *WJW* 2: 466–70, §§31–6.

14 'Wisdom of God's Counsels', *WJW* 2: 554, §6.

Wesley then connected seemingly inconspicuous individuals, through whom (he believed) God had renewed the Church through the centuries: alleged 'heretics' Montanus and Pelagius, the 'poor monk' Luther, the early Puritans, and William Law with his publication in the 1720s of the *Practical Treatise on Christian Perfection* and the *Serious Call to a Devout and Holy Life*. Wesley linked Law's books directly with the rise of the Methodist societies: 'Here the seed was sown which soon grew up, and spread to Oxford, London, Bristol, Leeds, York, and within a few years to the greatest part of England, Scotland, Ireland.' A downturn, however, followed each historical instance of revival. Wesley did not exempt Methodists: he perceived that some already had lost their religious vitality, and he made an extensive appeal to his audience, to beware the pitfalls of waning zeal or material indulgence.[15] He concluded more hopefully, observing that God continually 'raised up' new leaders possessing the ardour of their Methodist forebears, and adding that falterers were not beyond God's mercy.[16]

'Of Former Times' (1787) illuminates further Wesley's conception of the Methodist Revival situated within broader history. Wesley aimed to counter the apparently prevalent notion that society had declined from a distant golden age. After offering a bleak portrayal of civilization and Christianity from the early eighteenth century backward to apostolic times, he asserted: 'So early did the "mystery of iniquity" begin to work in the Christian church! So little reason have we to appeal to the former days, as though they were "better than these"!'[17] In juxtaposition to the historical picture, Wesley praised signs of progress in his own day, such as an increase of religious tolerance and charitable works, both of these to an unprecedented degree.[18] But once again, chief in his mind was the Revival in Britain:

> I cannot forbear mentioning one instance more of the goodness of God to us in the present age.... He caused near fifty years ago as it were a grain of mustard seed to be sown near London, and it has

15 Ibid., 554–65, §§7–21, quote at 558, §12; see also Sermon 63, 'The General Spread of the Gospel' (1783), *WJW* 2: 490–2, §§13–15. Outler sets Wesley's thoughts here within the context of his journey from London to Edinburgh, during which he recorded his 'mixed feelings about the uneven progress of the Revival, his alarm over various signs of weakened discipline within the Methodist ranks' (551).

16 Ibid., 565–6, §§22–4, quote at 565, §22.

17 'Former Times', *WJW* 3: 448–51, §§11–18, quote at 451, §18.

18 Ibid., 449, 451–2, §§13, 19, 21.

> now grown and put forth branches, reaching from sea to sea. Two or three poor people met together in order to help each other to be real Christians. They increased to hundreds, to thousands, to myriads, still pursuing their one point, real religion, the love of God and man ruling all their tempers, and words, and actions. Now I will be bold to say such an event as this, considered in all its circumstances, has not been seen upon earth before, since the time that St. John went to Abraham's bosom.[19]

He concluded with a ringing eschatological note, calling the present 'the day of [God's] power, a day of glorious salvation, wherein he is hastening to renew the whole race of mankind in righteousness and true holiness'.[20]

II

Wesley's vision of revival, expressed in sermons, is reflected by his *Concise Ecclesiastical History* (1781). Wesley derived this publication from German Lutheran scholar Johann Lorenz von Mosheim's *Institutionum historiae ecclesiasticae antiquae et recentioris* (1755), a multi-volume work seen as a pioneering and influential Enlightenment church history,[21] and from its popular English translation (with additional notes) by Presbyterian minister Archibald Maclaine (first published in 1765).[22] An extensive comparison of Wesley's work with those of Mosheim and Maclaine is beyond the scope of this study; nonetheless, a brief analysis makes several important contributions.

In the first place, Wesley's prefatory remarks reflected the themes on which he elaborated in sermons. His stated intent was to draw out the

[19] Ibid., 452–3, §§20, 22. See Sermon 112, 'On Laying the Foundation of the New Chapel' (1777), *WJW* 3: 577–92, esp. 587–9, II. 6–13, for a parallel description of the Revival as unprecedented in English, possibly broader, church history.

[20] 'Former Times', 3: 453, §23.

[21] Euan Cameron, *Interpreting Christian History: the Challenge of the Churches' Past* (Oxford, 2005), 149–52.

[22] Maclaine's work, entitled *An Ecclesiastical History, Antient and Modern, from the Birth of Christ, to the Beginning of the Present Century:* . . ., was reissued in 1767, with four subsequent editions within Wesley's lifetime (1768, 1774, 1782, 1790). References to Maclaine's editions are from *Eighteenth Century Collections Online*, Gale Group, available at: http://galenet.galegroup.com/servlet/ECCO. Wesley did not elucidate his precise sources; in his Preface, he spoke loosely of Mosheim's work 'published thirty or forty years ago', and Maclaine's translation published 'a few years since'. Wesley, *A Concise Ecclesiastical History, from the Birth of Christ, to the Beginning of the present Century*, 4 vols (London, 1781), 1: iii–iv.

internal vitality of the Church, marked by 'righteousness, and peace, and joy in the Holy Ghost'. This was a corrective to Mosheim, who (Wesley speculated) was not 'much acquainted with Inward Religion', since he equated the Church's 'internal state' only with its learning, government, doctrine, rites and ceremonies.[23] Wesley emphatically warned his readers that saints were few in number 'in every age'. Using language which echoed 'Scriptural Christianity' (1744) and became a familiar refrain in later sermons, he asserted: 'As *the mystery of iniquity* began to *work* even in the days of the Apostles, so not long after they were removed from the earth, it brought forth a plentiful harvest. It overspread the face of the earth.'[24]

Secondly, whilst Wesley's sermons were sparse on details, the historical examples he gave were not erratic pickings, but rather gleanings from his abridgement of Mosheim's monumental history. Wesley's inserted commentary in the *Concise Ecclesiastical History* closely corresponded with the content of his later sermons: here he defended Montanus and Pelagius as seemingly holy men, expressed doubts that Constantine ever truly converted, and described Constantine's day as detrimental to 'real Christianity'.[25] Wesley's plot of spreading corruption interrupted by providence and his cast of godly characters drawn from the Church's fringes featured in Mosheim's original account. Wesley's stamp seems to have been a revival leader's flair: more dramatic language in negatives and positives, more eagerness to identify evil or degradation on the one hand, divine action or godly example on the other.

Wesley's *History* also mirrors his attempt in sermons to place Methodism within the sweep of church history. His very inclusion (with little introduction) of his 112-page 'A Short History of the People Called Methodists' in the final volume reveals this perspective.[26] Wesley's effort was also a rebuff to Archibald Maclaine, who in his translation of Mosheim had added a table listing Wesley with George

23 Wesley, *Concise Ecclesiastical History*, 1: v–vi.

24 Ibid., vii–viii (emphasis in original).

25 Ibid., 113–14, §§10–11, esp. §11 (Montanus), 151–3, §§7–8, esp. final paragraph of §7 (Constantine), 245–8, §§17–19, esp. 248 n. 'a' (Pelagius), compared with Mosheim, *Ecclesiastical History*, trans. Archibald Maclaine, 5 vols (new edn, London, 1774), 1: 192–4, §§23–4, 261–5, §§7–9, 421–4, §§23–4. On Montanus and Pelagius, Wesley fulfilled his purpose, stated in his Preface, to redeem 'the Character of truly good men' to whom Mosheim and Maclaine had 'not done justice' (1: vii).

26 Ibid., 4: 169–281.

Whitefield and the Moravian Brethren as eighteenth-century 'Heretics or Enemies of Revelation'.[27] But beyond this personal grievance, Wesley had grander designs: in Rupert Davies' words, he 'clearly believed that Methodism was an important phenomenon in the history of the church, likely to become permanent and deserving a chapter in an *Ecclesiastical History*'.[28] In the narrative, based on his journals, Wesley highlighted instances of hostility towards himself and other Methodists (but also of providential escape from injury),[29] and drew an historical parallel between the negative reception of his last Oxford sermon, 24 August 1744, and the expulsion on the same day in 1662 of nearly two thousand ministers from the Church of England.[30] He also framed his account with references to Maclaine's accusation of 'heresy', and concluded with biblical allusions to suffering for Jesus's sake.[31] Finally, he emphasized the inconspicuous growth of the Revival, implicitly linking Methodists with earlier Christian examples of tiny 'seeds' which had reinvigorated the Church. For instance, of progress in Newcastle upon Tyne in late 1742, he wrote:

> I never saw a work of God in any other place so evenly and gradually carried on. It continually rose step by step. Not so much seemed to be done at any one time as had frequently been at Bristol or London, but something at every time. It was the same with particular souls. I saw few in that ecstatic joy which had been common at other places. But many went on calm and steady, increasing more and more in the knowledge of God.[32]

27 Ibid., 4: 169, §1. Rupert E. Davies terms the 'Short History' a 'corrective' to Maclaine. He refers to Maclaine's 1768 edition, but the table appears already in 1765: Mosheim, *Ecclesiastical History*, trans. Maclaine, 2 vols (London, 1765), 2: 624. For Davies' comments, see *The Methodist Societies: History, Nature and Design*, ed. Davies, vol. 9 of *WJW*, 425, and 426 n. 3, also 426–503 for his critical edition of the 'Short History'.

28 *WJW* 9: 425, echoed by Ken MacMillan, 'John Wesley and the Enlightened Historians', *Methodist History* 38: 2 (2000), 121–32, at 127.

29 Wesley, *Concise Ecclesiastical History*, 4: 176–7, §13; 178, §16; 181–3, §§23–5; 185, §28; 194–5, §34; 200–1, §40; 207–8, §47 as examples.

30 Ibid., 187, §30.

31 Ibid., 169, §1; 280–1, §82. Biblical allusions (indexed in *WJW* 9, ed. Davies) are to Matt. 5: 11 and Acts 20: 24; these also appear at 176–7, §13.

32 Ibid., 180, §21.

III

From consideration of Wesley's sermons and *Concise Ecclesiastical History*, several points emerge as facets of an overarching pattern of revival in history. Firstly, Wesley tended to find his examples of 'vital' Christianity among the relatively obscure, downtrodden, or marginalized. This aspect encompasses his portrayal of a corrupting Church, his identification of the love of wealth as a primary precipitator of decay, his attempts to redeem perceptions of several 'heretics', and his view of persecution by authorities as an instrument of renewal. Wesley's descriptions of Methodism's humble beginnings, Methodist experiences of scorn and open hostility, and the failings or reversals of particular leaders, also fit within this overall impression. As John Walsh observes, Wesley developed 'the historical theory that all great religious revivals began on the edges of society among the poor and insignificant, rather than at the center, where power and prestige were located'.[33]

Secondly, Wesley's vision of revival was focused by two key theological elements: providence and eschatological progression. Wesley believed that God's providence ensured Christianity's survival and intermittent flourishing through the ages. Thus Wesley saw widespread corruption as an immediate precursor to revival, a sign that God would soon intervene.[34] The Church would never sink into complete apostasy; God would always preserve 'true' Christianity, through persecution or some other means.[35] Wesley's eschatological belief demonstrates, moreover, that the pattern of 'iniquity' and 'godliness' was not so much a cycle as a spiral, with an upward trajectory. This is evident in his sermon, 'Of Former Times', in which he called the Methodist Revival the dawn of God's 'day' of power and salvation. History was moving towards a goal, culminating in a time when holiness would prevail.[36]

33 Walsh, '"Methodism" and the Origins of English-Speaking Evangelicalism', in Mark A. Noll, David W. Bebbington, and George A. Rawlyk, eds, *Evangelicalism: Comparative Studies of Popular Protestantism in North America, the British Isles, and Beyond, 1700–1990*, Religion in America series, ed. Harry S. Stout (Oxford, 1994), 19–37, at 32.

34 For examples, 'Mystery of Iniquity', *WJW* 2: 453, §7; 'Wisdom of God's Counsels', 2: 556, §10, and 558, §12; and 'General Spread', 2: 485–8, §§1–8.

35 'Mystery of Iniquity', *WJW* 2: 457, §15, and 462, §26. Compare 'Scriptural Christianity', 1: 167–9, II. 5–8, for an early articulation of this belief.

36 'Former Times', *WJW* 3: 453, §23. This counters Outler's pessimistic rendering of Wesley's conception as 'a tragic drama of fallings away and partial restorations from each of which, in its turn, there then followed yet another falling away' (Introduction to 'Mystery of

A glimpse at Wesley's sermon entitled 'The General Spread of the Gospel' serves to encapsulate his perception of a pattern. With striking simplicity, Wesley provided his rationale: 'As God is one, so the work of God is uniform in all ages. May we not then conceive how he *will* work on the souls of men in times to come by considering how he *does* work *now?* And how he *has* wrought in times past?'[37] He then looked to the story of the Revival. Echoing his description of its progress in his 'Short History', he posited that God occasionally might bring an initial 'torrent of grace', but more typically would work in gentle, subtle ways; God's kingdom would 'silently increase wherever it is set up, and spread from heart to heart, from house to house, from town to town, from one kingdom to another'.[38] Finally, he cast a glance to the future, expressing his belief that God would continue to work 'in the same manner', but also that the end of the pattern was approaching: '. . . I cannot induce myself to think that God has wrought so glorious a work to let it sink and die away in a few years. No; I trust this is only the beginning of a far greater work – the dawn of "the latter day glory".'[39]

IV

What is the significance of this pattern for our understanding of Wesley, and of the Revival? First of all, his fusion of a universal historical scope and language of progress together with his providential outlook supports the conclusions of scholars who see Wesley as a mediator of Enlightenment intellectual currents and evangelical religion.[40] Here was a Revival leader who appropriated modern ideas and resources – including Mosheim's well-respected *Ecclesiastical History* – in service of Christian renewal. Secondly, Wesley's thinking emerges as

Iniquity', *WJW* 2: 451). I am grateful to Reginald Ward for emphasizing to me the importance of Wesley's eschatological outlook for his historical interpretation.

37 'Former Times', *WJW* 3: 489, §10 (emphasis in original); also 'Signs of the Times', 2: 526, §3; 530, §8.

38 'General Spread', *WJW* 2: 490–3, §§13–17, quotes at 493, §17. Walsh, '"Methodism" and the Origins of English-Speaking Evangelicalism', 33, observes Wesley's contrast, in letters, between more dramatic but short-lived revivals in Scotland and America, and the steadier, longer-lasting progression of the Methodist Revival.

39 'General Spread', *WJW* 2: 492–3, §16.

40 On Wesley and Enlightenment historiography, see Ted A. Campbell, 'John Wesley and Conyers Middleton on Divine Intervention in History', *Church History* 55 (1986), 39–49, and MacMillan, 'John Wesley'; also Rack, *Reasonable Enthusiast*, 32–3, 167–8, 383-8, for general descriptions of Wesley's engagement with Enlightenment thinking.

remarkably consistent through his career, from his vision of 'iniquity' and 'godliness' articulated at Oxford in 1744, almost at the outset of the Revival, to its fuller expression in the 1780s, encompassing the events of the intervening decades. This inclusion of Methodism demonstrates, thirdly, that church history for Wesley was not peripheral, but was in fact fundamental to his understanding of his own career and the broader Revival. According to Ted Campbell, Wesley turned to former ages for 'a precedent or example for the renewal of Scriptural Christianity in his own generation'.[41] Finally, Wesley's historical interest and identification of a revival pattern raises a question for consideration in a wider context. That Wesley's providential approach to history was replicated among early nineteenth-century Methodists has been argued previously.[42] But Wesley's vision also brings to mind similar interests among other eighteenth-century Revival figures – one thinks of Jonathan Edwards's *History of the Work of Redemption*, and the production of church histories by Anglican Evangelicals John Newton, Thomas Haweis, and Joseph and Isaac Milner. To what extent, then, might Wesley's view fall within a broader, distinctly evangelical interpretation of history through which leaders sought to contextualize, perhaps validate, their experience of revival?[43]

One final observation is necessary. In his sermons, and undergirded by his *Concise Ecclesiastical History*, Wesley discerned a pattern in church history, a picture of the spreading tide of corruption, pushed back by God's action in preserving or prospering 'genuine' Christianity, bringing seasons of hope and renewal. But his theological convictions reminded him that the pattern was dynamic, and not completely predictable or comprehensible to human eyes – Wesley did speak, after all, in terms of 'mysteries'.[44] As he expressed in 'The Wisdom of God's

41 Ted A. Campbell, 'Christian Tradition, John Wesley, and Evangelicalism', *Anglican Theological Review* 74: 1 (1992), 54–67, at 65–6.

42 Russell E. Richey, 'Methodism and Providence: a Study in Secularization', in Keith Robbins, ed., *Protestant Evangelicalism: Britain, Ireland, Germany, and America, c. 1750–c. 1950: Essays in Honour of W. R. Ward*, SCH.S 7 (Oxford, 1990), 51–77, at 55.

43 Michael J. Crawford, in *Seasons of Grace: Colonial New England's Revival Tradition in Its British Context*, Religion in America series, ed. Harry S. Stout (New York and Oxford, 1991), 127, suggests briefly, with Edwards's *History* in view, that eighteenth-century British and American evangelicals shared a unique historical interpretation which focused on revivals.

44 Joseph W. Seaborn, Jr, in 'Wesley's Views on the Uses of History', *Wesleyan Theological Journal* 21 (1986), 129–36, at 130, observes Wesley's critique of David Brainerd, who in his journal (extracted by Jonathan Edwards) appeared to 'usurp God's prerogative in prescribing the pattern for revival in the New World'.

Counsels', God had planted the Church like a tiny mustard seed and nourished it until, marvellously, 'it grew into a great tree, notwithstanding the uninterrupted opposition of all the powers of darkness'.[45] Divine prerogative was also at work in the Methodist Revival. Wesley, after setting Methodism within the much more expansive history of the Church, concluded his sermon with a rousing statement reflecting not only his vision of revival, but also a sense of awe surpassing any scrutiny:

> You see here, brethren, a short and general sketch of the manner wherein God works upon earth in repairing his work of grace wherever it is decayed through the subtlety of Satan, and the unfaithfulness of men, giving way to the fraud and malice of the devil. Thus he is now carrying on his own work, and thus he will do to the end of time. And how wonderfully plain and simple is his way of working . . . of repairing whatsoever is decayed. But as to innumerable particulars we must still cry out, 'O the depth! How unfathomable are his counsels! And his paths past tracing out!'[46]

St Mary's College, University of St Andrews

45 'Wisdom of God's Counsels', *WJW* 2: 553, §5.
46 Ibid., 566, §25.

'I WILL ONCE MORE SHAKE THE HEAVENS': THE 1762 REVIVAL IN WALES

by ERYN M. WHITE

THE Evangelical Revival in eighteenth-century Wales actually consisted of a number of separate 'great collective spiritual outpourings', as John Walsh described them,[1] which seem to have been completely spontaneous and unplanned. By the nineteenth century, periodic revivals had become accepted as a characteristic of Welsh Nonconformity, but were perhaps increasingly less spontaneous. Historians have suggested that arranged revivals became more common in a Welsh context as a result of the influence of the ideas of Charles Finney in the 1830s and 1840s.[2] Daniel Rowland's first biographer, John Owen, condemned this as a 'forcing system' which he thought was 'calculated only to increase the number of unsound professors'.[3] In contrast, Owen emphasized the genuine unplanned nature of the eighteenth-century revivals. This paper examines the origins and influence of one of those unplanned revivals which occurred between 1762 and 1764, the first general renewal of Calvinistic Methodism in Wales after its initial beginning in the 1730s and the model for the future revivalist tradition.

The roots of the Evangelical Revival in Wales are usually traced back to 1735, the year in which its two leading figures, Daniel Rowland and Howel Harris, went through their individual conversion experiences. Rowland was the curate of the Cardiganshire parishes of Llangeitho and Nancwnlle; Harris was a layman who became the general superintendent of the Methodist societies. The two men first met in 1737, and

[1] John Walsh, '"Methodism" and the Origins of English-Speaking Evangelicalism', in M. A. Noll, D. W. Bebbington, and G. A. Rawlyk, eds, *Evangelicalism: Comparative Studies of Popular Protestantism in North America, the British Isles, and Beyond, 1700–1900* (Oxford, 1994), 19–37, at 33.

[2] Richard Carwardine, 'The Welsh Evangelical Community and "Finney's Revival"', *JEH*, 29: 4 (1978), 463–80; D. W. Bebbington, *Evangelicalism in Modern Britain: a History from the 1730s to the 1980s* (London, 1989), 116–17. See also Christopher B. Turner, 'Revivalism and Welsh Society in the Nineteenth Century', in J. Obelkevich, ed., *Disciplines of Faith: Studies in Religion, Politics and Patriarchy* (London, 1987), 311–23; J. Holmes, *Religious Revivals in Britain and Ireland 1859–1905* (Dublin, 2000), 51–98.

[3] John Owen, *Memoir of Daniel Rowlands* (London, 1848), 127.

agreed on a collaboration which marked the birth of the Calvinistic Methodist movement in Wales. Among the early converts to the cause was William Williams of Pantycelyn, Carmarthenshire, acknowledged as the third in the trio of early leaders. A period of growth followed until the mid-1740s, after which progress slowed somewhat. Disagreements between Harris and his colleagues led to his expulsion in 1750 and his retreat to his home in Trefeca in Breconshire to establish a religious community and to serve as an officer in the Breconshire militia. However, a fresh revival broke out in 1762 and Harris, newly released from his commission, rejoined the movement in 1763. By 1750 over 400 societies had been established, mainly in south Wales. With an average of twenty to twenty-five members to each society, the membership would have been somewhere in the region of 10,000, a very small minority of the population. Whole societies and individual members were lost in the aftermath of the 1750 division and it was the 1762 revival which really ensured the survival and success of Methodism as a movement which would transform the religious geography of Wales.[4]

Despite its significance, among historians and the public at large, within Wales and beyond its borders, the 1762 revival receives scant attention. One of the few modern accounts was R. Geraint Gruffydd's article in 1969, which focused on William Williams's role in the revival.[5] The main reason for this neglect is the lack of sources. We are indebted to Howel Harris for preserving a wealth of documents for the period prior to 1750, sources which now form the Trevecka Manuscripts of the Calvinistic Methodist Archive in the National Library of Wales. His subsequent absence, however, removed the movement's main archivist, which means that records thereafter are scarce. The earliest mention in the Calvinistic Methodist Archive comes in January 1763 in a letter from Thomas William of Glamorgan, who describes substantial numbers being converted in Neath, where the Abbey was used to conduct meetings attended by 'poor colliers'. He wonders that Harris is not part of this work:

> How is it that poor Wales has lost so many prayers, admonitions,

4 For accounts of Welsh Methodism see Gomer M. Roberts, *Hanes Methodistiaeth Galfinaidd Cymru: Y Deffroad Mawr* (Caernarfon, 1973); Derec Llwyd Morgan, *The Great Awakening in Wales* (London, 1988).

5 R. Geraint Gruffydd, 'Diwygiad 1762 a William Williams o Bantycelyn', *Journal of the Historical Society of the Presbyterian Church of Wales* 54: 3 (1969), 68–75; 55: 1 (1970), 4–13.

> warnings, wooings &c? Where is the poor pilgrim that suffered hunger & cold gone? Where's the tender loving, laborious carefull Father gone? Where's humble self denying groaning fruitfull broken sympathizing Harris gone? Where's the painfull, laborious mournfull diligent pride trampler world despiser Harris gone?[6]

Harris's diary provides some useful information recorded after his return to the Methodist cause in 1763, otherwise we are dependent on more disparate snippets of information from contemporary diaries and letters, along with printed accounts from the nineteenth century.

None of the available sources explain when, how and why the revival commenced, although it is apparent that it began in Daniel Rowland's own parish of Llangeitho and it is frequently referred to as the Llangeitho Revival. The natural assumption is that it began as the result of Rowland's preaching, since he is acknowledged to have been one of the most effective Welsh preachers of his age. One of the first histories of the early Methodist movement, written by John Hughes in the 1850s, claimed that the revival first broke out in Llangeitho when Rowland read a phrase from the Litany, 'by thine agony and bloody sweat'.[7] There can be little doubt that Rowland's ministry played a key role in this renewal of enthusiasm, since he had long attracted scores of Methodist pilgrims. Evidence of his activities throughout the 1750s can be found in the diary of John Thomas, from south Cardiganshire, which reveals how often Rowland preached in the area. On Easter Sunday 1759, Thomas had travelled to Llangeitho to hear Rowland and recorded:

> How strange it is to see the godly people who congregate in Llangeitho – the look on their cheerful faces without shows that they have hearts boiling with joy within – I do not regret making this journey as there is no price to be placed on Mr D. Rowlands preaching.[8]

If that was the situation described in Easter 1759, it seems hardly surprising that revival erupted by 1762.

Harris initially believed Rowland to have been solely responsible for

[6] Aberystwyth, National Library of Wales, Calvinistic Methodist Archive [hereafter: NLW and CMA], Trevecka MS 2838b, 25 January 1763.
[7] John Hughes, *Methodistiaeth Cymru*, 3 vols (Wrexham, 1851–6), 2: 249.
[8] Aberystwyth, NLW, MS 20515C, 15 April 1759.

the awakening. However, he later recorded in his diary William Williams's account of the origins of the revival: 'that this was not by any man but by the Lord Himself, or by some of the meanest of all the exhorters . . .'[9] It is another conversation relayed in Harris's diary which brings us closest to a first-hand account of the outbreak of revival. This took place with William Richard of Cardiganshire, a lay preacher who had the charge of the societies along the southern stretch of the Cardigan Bay coastline, from St David's in Pembrokeshire to Llwyndafydd, near New Quay, in Cardiganshire. From William Richard Harris '. . . heard of the beginning of this last Revival in Cardiganshire, and how that word went through him when the first cried out at Llangeitho, "I will once more shake the heavens" '.[10] The implication is that William Richard was present on the occasion when the first signs of renewal became evident, when 'the first cried out'. Beyond this brief statement, there are no details regarding the numbers affected or the nature of the occasion: whether church service, sermon, prayer meeting or society meeting. Some have taken William Richard's words here as evidence that he was one of those 'meanest of all the exhorters' mentioned by William Williams.[11] I very much doubt, however, that Williams would have categorized him thus, since William Richard had been a prominent member of the Association since 1743. He was eminent enough to be one of the six signatories to the letter in May 1762 which is regarded as Harris's official invitation to return to the Methodist fold.[12] He was respected enough for William Williams to write an elegy in his memory after his death from consumption in 1770, recalling his former colleague's ability to touch the hearts of his audience.[13] It is quite likely that William Richard played a part in the 1762 revival, but unlikely that Williams's reference to 'the meanest of exhorters' starting the work included him. It may very well be, therefore, that there were a number of early revival meetings in the Llangeitho area, which involved not only Daniel Rowland and William Richard, but probably several other less well-known local exhorters. Neither Methodist history nor its usually rich folklore record their

9 Aberystwyth, NLW, CMA, Diaries of Howel Harris, no. 241, 3 August 1763.

10 Ibid., 29 November 1763. Reference to Heb. 12: 26.

11 For example, Eifion Evans, *Daniel Rowland and the Great Evangelical Awakening in Wales* (Edinburgh, 1985), 309.

12 Aberystwyth, NLW, CMA, Trevecka MS 2472, 19 May 1762.

13 N. Cynhafal Jones, ed., *Gweithiau Williams Pant-y-celyn*, 2 vols (Holywell, 1887–91), 1: 478–82.

names, but one could speculate that among them were some of the exhorters that developed in the area under Rowland's ministry, including William Richard Lloyd, Griffith Lewis Siôn, Evan Dafydd Jenkin and Dafydd Lewis.[14] As these had all been fostered by Rowland, their contribution may well have been attributed to the benefits of Rowland's ministry in general.

In addition to Rowland's ministry, and to the effects of preaching in general, most sources concur that the other major factor behind the 1762 revival was the publication of a volume of hymns by William Williams, *Caniadau y Rhai sydd ar y Môr o Wydr* ['The Songs of those who are on a Sea of Glass']. The first history of Welsh Methodism, by Robert Jones in 1820, states that the revival broke out on the day that Williams brought this book to Llangeitho.[15] Harris, as he rejoined the movement in 1763, initially described the revival as a 'spirit of singing', although when he came to participate in the meetings himself he was more inclined to call it an awakening or revival.[16] There seems little doubt that singing was a vital element and that Williams's hymns were central to the excitement which characterized Methodist meetings between 1762 and 1764.

I have so far looked at internal factors when seeking the roots of the revival, yet external factors have often been examined as possible explanations of periodic religious resurgence. Death, dearth and disease are frequently associated with outbreaks of intense religiosity. Certainly in the 1830s and 1840s revivals coincided with cholera epidemics which concentrated people's minds on the last things.[17] However, the period around 1762 was by no means one of the worst experienced in Wales. If economic hardship were to inspire a revival in the third quarter of the eighteenth century, then 1756–8 was a much more likely period, as years which witnessed food shortages and riots.[18] There seems to be no

14 Hughes, *Methodistiaeth Cymru*, 2: 12–13; Gomer M. Roberts, *Y Deffroad Mawr*, 256–62.

15 Robert Jones, *Drych yr Amseroedd*, ed. G. M. Ashton (Cardiff, 1958), 85–6.

16 For example, Aberystwyth, NLW, CMA, Diaries of Howel Harris, no. 240, 15 February 1763; 16 February 1763; 29 March 1763; 6 April 1763; 12 May 1763; 3 August 1763.

17 Turner, 'Revivalism and Welsh Society', 314–15; Kenneth S. Jeffrey, *When the Lord Walked the Land: the 1858–62 Revival in the North East of Scotland* (Milton Keynes, 2002), 33–4; Russell Davies, *Hope and Heartbreak: a Social History of Wales and the Welsh, 1776–1871* (Cardiff, 2005), 333.

18 Geraint H. Jenkins, *The Foundations of Modern Wales: Wales 1642–1780* (Cardiff, 1987), 260–1; Melvin Humphreys, *The Crisis of Community: Montgomeryshire 1660–1815* (Cardiff, 1996), 63–8; David W. Howell, *The Rural Poor in Eighteenth-Century Wales* (Cardiff, 2000), 178–88.

obvious correlation between this revival and social, economic or political factors, which, in this instance at least, leads one to agree with David Hempton's suggestion that: 'It is hard to resist the conclusion that religious attraction or repulsion is a transaction that is neither straightforwardly economic nor political'.[19]

If one were to look for root causes of the revival outside the existing Methodist movement, it is hard to overlook the growth of literacy as a contributory factor. Mark Noll has, after all, pointed to the importance of the social and cultural context as a background to revival[20] and it has long been accepted in the historiography of the first Methodist revival in Wales that the work of the eighteenth-century educational initiatives played a vital role. The increase in literacy in Wales was chiefly the result of the circulating school system pioneered by Griffith Jones, rector of Llanddowror, Carmarthenshire, from the 1730s onwards. Jones died in 1761, but would doubtless have disapproved intensely of what he would consider to be the revival's excesses, despite the fact that as a young clergyman he had been summoned to answer to his bishop for his own itinerant habit before enthusiastic congregations. He was nonetheless revered by all the Methodist leaders, who had benefited from his advice and who were well aware of the contribution of his schools in spreading knowledge of the Bible. By the time of Jones's demise in 1761, some 3,325 schools had been established and at least 200,000 pupils taught to read. To place that in context, the estimated population of Wales in the mid-eighteenth century was around 489,000. By the 1760s, the schools had spread widely throughout the country, creating a more literate population, increasingly ripe for the Methodist gospel.[21]

Despite the uncertainty which obscures the roots of the revival, some of its major characteristics are quite plain and would be repeated in subsequent awakenings. The centrality of communal singing was established, with Williams providing hymns to serve as an outlet for the spiritual fervour of those awakened. As in the 1730s, preaching was of

19 David Hempton, 'Evangelicalism in English and Irish Society, 1780–1840', in Noll, Bebbington, and Rawlyk, eds, *Evangelicalism*, 156–76, at 158.

20 Mark A. Noll, *The Rise of Evangelicalism: the Age of Edwards, Whitefield and the Wesleys* (Leicester, 2004), 15–16.

21 See Geraint H. Jenkins, '"An Old and Much Honoured Soldier": Griffith Jones, Llanddowror', *Welsh History Review* 11: 4 (1983), 449–68, at 455–7; E. M. White, 'Popular Schooling and the Welsh Language c. 1660–1811', in Geraint H. Jenkins, ed., *The Welsh Language Before the Industrial Revolution* (Cardiff, 1997), 317–41.

vital importance, not just for travellers to Llangeitho but throughout Wales, as increasingly enthusiastic preaching by local exhorters was augmented by periodic visits from leaders of the movement whose reputation inevitably drew large crowds.[22] The fervent response was also a major characteristic of this revival and a matter of some controversy. John Wesley reported in his journal in 1763 that the agitations were obviously on the part of 'honest, upright men', who had 'little experience, either of the ways of God or the devices of Satan. So he serves himself of their simplicity in order to wear them out, and to bring discredit on the work of God.'[23] Other commentators were even more blunt. David Lloyd, the Arian minister of Llwynrhydowen, Cardiganshire, wrote in 1764 that:

> The Methodists after having kept quiet for several years have of late been very active. Their Number increases, and their wild Pranks are beyond Description. The worship of the day being over, they have kept together in ye Place whole Nights, singing, capering, bawling, fainting, thumping and a variety of other Excercises.[24]

This criticism led to a defence of the more physical manifestations of revival spirit from the leaders of the movement. Daniel Rowland claimed, 'You English blame us, the Welsh, and speak against us and say, "Jumpers, jumpers". But we, the Welsh have something also to allege against you, and we most justly say of you, "Sleepers, sleepers".'[25] More immediately, Williams took up his pen once more, this time to produce his first works of prose, *Llythyr Martha Philopur* (1762) and *Ateb Philo-Evangelius* (1763). In the first book, Martha writes to her religious mentor, Philo-Evangelius, drawing on verses from the Bible to justify the dancing, crying and jumping that characterized the converts. The choice of a female character suggests that this revival, as did the revivals of the 1730s and 1740s, gave women an enhanced opportunity to express their spirituality. The second book provides Philo-Evangelius's response, in which Williams takes the opportunity to express his view

22 For examples in Glamorgan, see *The Diary of William Thomas of Michaelston-Super-Ely, near St Fagan Glamorgan 1762–1795*, ed. R. T. W. Denning (Cardiff, 1995), 119; Gomer M. Roberts, 'Calvinistic Methodism in Glamorgan, 1737–1773', in Glanmor Williams, ed., *Glamorgan County History, vol. 4: Early Modern Glamorgan* (Cardiff, 1974), 499–533, at 526–8.

23 Quoted in Gruffydd, 'Diwygiad 1762', 72.

24 G. Eyre Evans, ed., *Lloyd Letters (1754–1791)* (Aberystwyth, 1908), 52.

25 Owen, *Memoir*, 85–6.

of Christian history as a continuous cycle of renewal and apathy, culminating in his exclamation on the latest awakening, 'O summer's day, it came, it came!'[26] The pattern Williams suggests here was played out over the years to come with periodic outbreaks of renewal, just as he had outlined. The leadership were not wholly at ease with the agitation apparent in such revivals and Williams insisted that converts went through the usual rigorous process of examination before being accepted as full members, a procedure which seems not to have been followed in the 1904–5 revival, which may partly explain the subsequent falling off in membership.

Many of these characteristics, which would manifest themselves in later revivals, appeared to be completely natural and spontaneous. If there is any evidence of forethought behind this revival it may be found in the attempts to achieve a reconciliation between Harris and his former colleagues. Much of the impetus behind this came from William Williams, who later admitted to Harris that '. . . till the Lord did come with these late showers of Revival, all was gone to nothing'.[27] Williams's concern regarding the decline during the years of division is apparent when he says of the pre-revival period: 'The desire of many ministers was to see the hour; there were a thousand sighs for the sun to rise. At last it came; "our grief turned to dancing".'[28] His desire for renewal may have led him to regard reconciliation with Harris as the means of revitalizing the movement. The first attempts at reconciliation in 1759 failed,[29] but on 19 May 1762 Harris was invited to return. An undated letter from Williams to Harris was very probably written at that time, since in it Williams explained that he had persuaded his colleagues to issue the 'invitation' and had countered the fears of some exhorters that Harris would adopt an autocratic attitude if restored to his old status. Harris was called to return to labour in fields which were ripe for harvesting, needing only 'faithfull Labourers'.[30] It was not until 15 February 1763 that a successful reunion took place. If the revival broke out when Williams's hymnbook reached Llangeitho, there are

26 G. H. Hughes, ed., *Gweithiau William Williams, Pantycelyn, Cyfrol II: Rhyddiaith* (Cardiff, 1967), 16.

27 Aberystwyth, NLW, CMA, Diaries of Howel Harris, no. 241, 3 August 1763.

28 Hughes, *Gweithiau William Williams*, 16.

29 Roberts, *Deffroad Mawr*, 395–6.

30 Aberystwyth, NLW, CMA, Bala Group, 624; Hugh H. Hughes, *Life of Howell Harris* (London and Newport, 1892), 359; B. S. Schlenther and E. M. White, *Calendar of the Trevecka Letters* (Aberystwyth, 2003), 411.

indications that the volume actually emerged from the printers at the end of 1761,[31] so that the first signs of revival could have been seen as the new year dawned in 1762. Therefore, although it is impossible to be certain about the timing of the start of the revival, it had quite obviously begun well before Harris returned. Harris soon found himself called upon to itinerate as before: 'I hear of much awakening in the country', he noted, 'and I am asked to go to all the old places again'.[32] In Williams's efforts to ensure his return, we may see an awareness that the movement was in dire need of renewal, whether or not it was envisaged that Harris's return would be the catalyst for an explosion of enthusiasm.

Knowing Williams's concern regarding the state of Welsh Methodism, is it possible that his collection of hymns in 1762 was intended to have the effect they did? It certainly appeared that in the 1904–5 revival hymns and religious songs were deliberately chosen in order to evoke an emotional response.[33] Could there be a similar intent in 1762? *Môr o Wydr* is generally regarded as one of the finest volumes of Williams's work as a mature hymn writer.[34] Williams had received complaints that his previous hymns displayed such assurance of faith that they were not suited to weaker Christians, but seemed to have taken this into account with *Môr o Wydr* since he claimed in the foreword that even the weakest should feel free to sing these new works.[35] They called to those who needed strength and guidance because they dwelt in darkness or were lost in the wilderness, an image which appeared in one particular hymn, 'Arglwydd, arwain drwy'r anialwch'. The English version appeared later in 1772, with the same imagery in the opening lines: 'Guide me, O thou great Jehovah/Pilgrim thro' this barren land'. Although these hymns had an obvious appeal to those affected by revival, Williams invariably tailored his writing to the needs of his audience and there is little reason to suppose that he specifically intended this collection to inspire an awakening.

31 Gomer M. Roberts, *Y Pêr Ganiedydd*, 2 vols (Llandysul, 1949/58), 2: 250.

32 Aberystwyth, NLW, CMA, Diaries of Harris, no. 240, 6 April 1763.

33 For the 1904 revival, see Eifion Evans, *The Welsh Revival of 1904* (Bridgend, 1969); R. Tudur Jones, *Faith and the Crisis of a Nation: Wales 1890–1914* (Cardiff, 2004); Noel Gibbard, *Fire on the Altar: a History and Evaluation of the 1904–05 Revival in Wales* (Bridgend, 2005).

34 See Derec Llwyd Morgan, *William Williams Pantycelyn* (Caernarfon, 1983), 17–19, 54–65; G. T. Hughes, *Williams Pantycelyn* (Cardiff, 1983), 75–124.

35 Cynhafal Jones, *Gweithiau*, 2: 128–30; Roberts, *Y Pêr Ganiedydd*, 49–66; G. T. Hughes, *Williams Pantycelyn* (Cardiff, 1983), 79.

To sum up, it was the 1762 revival that really established not only Methodism's survival after a difficult period but its enhanced status as a truly national movement, since, after 1762, it was increasingly able to recruit throughout the country. The mention of colliers in Neath serves as a reminder that Wales at this time was on the brink of the industrial take-off which was to transform its demography. Methodism prospered as a result of these developments, as its greater flexibility enabled it to adapt to the needs of the new communities in a way which the Established Church found hard to emulate. The emotions of the 1762 revival may also have been the cause of Bishop Squire of St David's decision to expel Daniel Rowland from his curacies in 1763,[36] a sign that the future relationship with the Church might be tense. One further significance of the revival was that it also established William Williams's status as the major literary figure of Welsh Methodism, both in poetry and prose.

Although the lack of sources makes further detailed research on the 1762 revival difficult, its significance is such that it deserves to be included more often in discussions of revival in Wales and beyond. In addition to its importance within a Welsh context, it also has relevance to wider discussions of the nature and characteristics of revivalism, especially in terms of the contribution of hymn singing in producing outbreaks of revival. It was this revival which demonstrated conclusively that the early enthusiasm of the Evangelical Revival in Wales could be reignited, in order to reinvigorate existing congregations and to attract new members. Many of its central themes would be repeated time after time in the nineteenth century, whose culture of revivalism to a large extent grew out of the experiences of 1762–4. If Welsh revivals became more contrived in their nature, it was the spontaneity of 1762 that they were aiming to reproduce.

Aberystwyth University

36 Eifion Evans, *Daniel Rowland*, 323–6; Raymond L. Brown, 'The Expulsion of Daniel Rowland from his Curacies: an Oral Tradition?', *Journal of the Historical Society of the Presbyterian Church of Wales* 20 (1996), 31–5.

REFORMATION, REVIVAL, AND REBIRTH IN ANGLICAN EVANGELICAL THOUGHT, c.1780–c.1830

by GARETH ATKINS

FOR Anglican Evangelicals, terms like 'awakening' and 'revival' pointed rather to reinvigoration and the recovery of old glories than to some new and disturbing disjunction.[1] Those seeking change, remarked Rowland Hill, would do well to follow the example of the reformers, who 'did not *innovate*, but *renovate*, they did not *institute*, they only *reformed*.'[2] Nevertheless, this still left many – like Hill – balancing their urge to reform on the one hand with the importance of Anglican 'regularity' on the other. Several initiatives bore the mark of this tension. For example, the foundation of the Church Missionary Society (CMS) in 1799 owed much to frustration with the inactivity of the Society for Promoting Christian Knowledge (SPCK) and the Society for the Propagation of the Gospel (SPG). The new society was 'founded upon the *Church-principle*, not the *High* Church principle', remarked John Venn, who stressed that it was possible to express Gospel zeal within a solidly Anglican framework.[3] As the *Missionary Magazine* commented perceptively, 'a set of people will no doubt contribute to this whose predilection for the Church and dislike to Methodists and Dissenters, would have effectively kept them from aiding the [London Missionary Society]'.[4] The *Christian Observer,* founded in 1802 to be the periodical mouthpiece of 'moderate' Evangelicalism, evinced the same concerns in its first number, when it promised 'to correct the false sentiments of the religious world, and *to explain the principles of the Church*'.[5] As the leading Evangelical 'regulars' maintained, only this uneasy balancing act could bring far-reaching change. 'Be more than ever circumspect, maintain a perfect consistency of character, show yourselves the true friends of the Church by avoiding everything which

1 It is worth pointing out that 'evangelical' is used here as a general term, referring to adherents of all denominations, whereas the capitalized 'Evangelical' denotes members of the Church of England holding similar theological doctrine.

2 Edwin Sidney, *The Life of the Rev. Rowland Hill* (London, 1834), 398.

3 Charles Hole, *The Early History of the Church Missionary Society* (London, 1896), 31.

4 *Missionary Magazine*, 20 May 1799.

5 J. and J. P. Pratt, *Memoir of the Rev. Josiah Pratt* (London, 1849), 11.

might weaken her interests, and then abide all consequences', advised Robinson in 1802.[6] Rowland Hill – hardly notable for his regularity – echoed the opinions of many when he commented, 'Surely a *reformation* of that which is wrong may be effected without a *demolition* of that which is right'.[7]

As the Evangelical place in the Church became more assured, regularity and adherence to 'Church-principles' became more pronounced. Nineteenth-century biographers were ever eager to demonstrate the advances of the previous generation, emphasizing 'the low and lukewarm state of religion in our Church, in the latter part of the last century', as against its 'vastly improved and flourishing condition', through the rekindling of living faith.[8] But this did not lead Evangelicals to excuse the apparent excesses of their forebears. 'To do *now* as he [Berridge] did *then* would do much harm', remarked Simeon.[9] John Venn was eager to downplay his father's earlier indiscretions as a field preacher.[10] Ardour was to be applauded, but imprudence – especially from the vantage point of the 1810s and '20s – was decidedly to be frowned upon. 'Instead of bringing into vigorous action the practiced wisdom of our reformers, they adopted sudden plans of their own, which were often ill-suited to the then agitated elements around them,' wrote Edwin Sidney.[11] Yet desperate times had clearly called for desperate measures, and so we find Sidney commenting wryly that: 'a flame had just been enkindled by the fire and zeal of certain energetic individuals, who possessed *much more of the fervour, than of the wisdom of Christianity*'.[12] Perhaps in *awakening* a sleeping nation, such energy was to be applauded, but with the conformity and the churchmanship of later times came a need for greater subtlety.

This paper aims to re-examine the Evangelical place in the Church of England, suggesting that their engagement with the establishment shaped a peculiar perspective on the national past. While vital believers saw their encounter with the Almighty in terms of Ruin, Redemption

6 Hole, *Early History*, 54.

7 Sidney, *Rowland Hill*, 382.

8 James Jerram, ed., *The Memoirs & a Selection from the Letters of the late Rev. Charles Jerram, M.A.* (London, 1855), 336.

9 Charles Smyth, *Simeon and Church Order* (Cambridge, 1940), 249, 256.

10 Michael M. Hennell, *John Venn and the Clapham Sect* (London, 1958), 268–73.

11 Edwin Sidney, *The Life, Ministry, & Selections from the Remains, of the Rev. Samuel Walker* (London 1835), 280.

12 Ibid., 279.

and Regeneration, Anglicans from the 1780s onward were increasingly apt to interpret English history itself along the lines of a similar *ordo salutis*, one of Reformation, Revival and Rebirth.

I

The closing decades of the eighteenth century witnessed a rapid change in Britain's moral climate. This move has long fascinated commentators, who have pointed out that the period was one of structural instability (the rise of the middle classes),[13] changing social morality (prompted by the moral panic attending the loss of the American colonies)[14] and economic or demographic change (industrialization). For writers such as Ford K. Brown, Boyd Hilton, and perhaps most famously, G. M. Young, the period from about 1780 to 1830 was one in which evangelical theology, tenets and mores came to permeate the middle classes, and indeed to shape the concept of 'respectability'.[15] Indeed, it might be suggested that the period bounded at one end by the American Revolution and at the other by the Great Reform Act – roughly speaking – delineates a 'second phase' of the Revival, during which evangelicals came to believe in the possibility of widespread social change, not just individual conversion.[16] As Wilberforce reminded readers of his *Practical View*, 'Religion is the business of everyone . . . its advancement or decline in any country is so intimately connected with the temporal interests of society, as to render it the peculiar concern of a political man.'[17]

Yet despite growing influence in both Church and politics, the

13 Muriel Jaeger, *Before Victoria: Changing Standards and Behaviour, 1787–1837* (2nd edn, London, 1967); Harold Perkin, *The Origins of Modern English Society, 1780–1880* (London, 1969).

14 Dror Wahrman, 'Percy's Prologue: from Gender Play to Gender Panic in Eighteenth-Century England', *P&P* 159 (1998), 113–60; Joanna Innes, 'Politics and Morals: the Reformation of Manners Movement in Later Eighteenth-Century England', in Eckhardt Hellmuth, ed., *The Transformation of Political Culture: England and Germany in the late Eighteenth Century* (Oxford, 1990), 57–118.

15 Ford K. Brown, *Fathers of the Victorians* (Cambridge, 1961); Boyd Hilton, *The Age of Atonement: the Influence of Evangelicalism on Social and Economic Thought, 1785–1865* (Oxford, 1988); G. M. Young, *Victorian England: Portrait of an Age* (London, 1936).

16 See esp. Brown, *Fathers of the Victorians*, for an exhaustive and often caustic commentary on the evangelical reforming urge.

17 William Wilberforce, *A Practical View of the Prevailing Religious System of Professed Christians, in the Higher and Middle Classes in this Country, Contrasted with Real Christianity* (London, 1797), viii.

Evangelical position was not without ambiguities. The central importance of personal salvation did not always sit easily with the idea of an established Church which embraced all within its bounds; moreover, critics found 'the religion of the heart' theologically divisive, and its practitioners somewhat distasteful. Nevertheless, it is possible to discern a move towards greater 'regularity' and a more self-avowed attachment to the Anglican Church from the closing years of the eighteenth century. Scenting the possibility of more far-reaching change, the generation of clerical leaders which came to maturity in the 1780s and '90s – Charles Simeon, Thomas Robinson, John Venn and a host of others – increasingly regarded conformity to Anglican forms as a *sine qua non*. 'Consistent and sincere churchman' was no longer a suggestion of potential lukewarmness, but an accolade; thoroughgoing change could only be brought about by those within the clerical ranks. By the early nineteenth century this feeling was almost universal among Evangelical clergymen, and had moved beyond mere pragmatism. 'The conscientious churchman, to be consistent to himself, must maintain that the existing restraints are essential to the existence of our establishment', wrote E. T. Vaughan in 1816, adding that 'this establishment is essential to the existence, or at least to the well being, of true religion.'[18]

This shift is by no means new to historians of the Revival.[19] Indeed, by the late nineteenth century the place of Evangelicals in the established Church was already a subject which interested writers like Overton, Hole and Stock.[20] In *Charles Simeon and Church Order* (1940), Canon Smyth again raised the question of attitudes to Anglican conventions, drawing out contrasts between the behaviour of earlier 'irregulars' (such as John Berridge) and the aims of 'regulars' (namely Charles Simeon at Cambridge).[21] Geoffrey Best focused on similar

18 E. T. Vaughan, *Some Account of the Life, Ministry, Character, & Writings of the late Rev. T. Robinson, M.A.* (London, 1815), 131.

19 John D. Walsh, 'The Yorkshire Evangelicals in the Eighteenth Century, with Especial Reference to Methodism', unpublished Ph.D. thesis, University of Cambridge, 1956, 214–32; J. C. D. Clark, *English Society, 1660–1832* (Cambridge, 2000), 296–300; Grayson Carter, *Anglican Evangelicals: Protestant Secessions from the Via Media, c.1800–1850* (Oxford, 2001).

20 John H. Overton, *The English Church in the Nineteenth Century* (London, 1894), 51–109; Hole, *Early History*; Eugene Stock, *The History of the Church Missionary Society*, 4 vols (London, 1899–1916).

21 Smyth, *Simeon and Church Order*. See also idem, 'The Evangelical Movement in Perspective', *Cambridge Historical Journal* 7 (1941–3), 160–74, which poses a succession of pertinent questions about the place of Evangelicals in the Church of England, several of which remain unanswered.

issues in 1959, concluding correctly, but cautiously, that most Evangelicals 'conceived of the Church of England as potentially their ideal of a visible church'.[22] More recently, Grayson Carter has addressed the question from the other side of the fence, pointing out that for some individuals the problems raised by the concept of establishment were serious indeed, underlined by the departure of over a hundred clergymen from the Church of England between 1800 and 1850.[23] Still, for most 'mainstream' Evangelicals the idea of an established Church as the lynchpin of national spirituality was increasingly persuasive. Historians have tended to assume that the Evangelical move towards 'regularity' stemmed simply from pragmatism, based on an appreciation of the social influence and pastoral reach of the established Church. Certainly this played a part, but it is apparent that by about 1800, Evangelicals were more and more prepared to discuss ideas of nation and polity, and to use such concepts as tools in their apologetic armoury. In particular, the development of a set of historical arguments provided vital believers with the basis for a convincing critique of the contemporary Church and establishment.[24]

II

Joseph Milner's *History of the Church of Christ*, published in six volumes in the late 1790s, stands as the pre-eminent Evangelical work of history, both in range and in impact upon its readership. Sir James Stephen was to remark in the 1840s that: 'The Church History of Joseph Milner is one of those books which may perish with some revolution of the moral and religious character of the English race, but hardly otherwise',[25] and for Charles Jerram, another mid-century writer, it was not Milner's pastoral and educational labours but his celebrated history along a 'new' line which had been his lasting legacy.[26] The premise of

22 G. F. A. Best, 'The Evangelicals and the Established Church in the Early Nineteenth Century', *Journal of Theological Studies*, ns 10 (1959), 63–78, at 71.

23 Until the publication of John Wolffe, *The Expansion of Evangelicalism, 1790–1840* (forthcoming), Carter, *Anglican Evangelicals*, provides the most pertinent and up-to-date bibliography.

24 The only existing work focusing on Evangelicals and history writing – a neglected aspect of the 'serious' worldview, considering their predilection for history as a genre – is John D. Walsh, 'Joseph Milner's Evangelical Church History', *JEH* 10 (1959), 174–87.

25 James Stephen, *Essays in Ecclesiastical Biography*, 2 vols (London, 1849), 2: 58.

26 Jerram, *Memoirs*, 296.

the work was simple. Ecclesiastical history had hitherto concentrated overly on schisms, heretics and religious debates, giving undue ammunition to detractors of Christianity.[27] In his 'Ecclesiastical History on a new Plan' Milner aimed to celebrate genuine piety wherever he could find it, tracing the history of the true – for which read evangelical – Church throughout the ages by examining 'men who have been REAL, not merely NOMINAL Christians'. Conventional preoccupations with doctrines, ceremonies or visible expressions were irrelevant.[28] Instead, luminaries such as Ambrose, Jerome, Gregory the Great and others were measured according to Milner's evangelical yardstick, which emphasized New Testament-centred doctrine and the essential importance of justification by faith. Although Milner made only passing mention of the establishment principle, his *History* provided a convincing apologetic foundation, underlining that Evangelical orthodoxy was no mere novelty. '[Evangelicals] had always been confident in their appeal to Scripture', comments John Walsh: 'Milner helped to strengthen their appeal to history'.[29]

Perhaps the greatest opposition to Evangelicalism in the 1790s came from High Church divines like George Tomline and Charles Daubeny, who characterized the creed as extremist, anti-establishment and fundamentally non-Anglican. 'If Mrs More be really of Mr Wilberforce's school, her faith, like his, is Calvinism in disguise, and *her attachment to the Church of England*, of a very questionable kind', charged Daubeny in the *Antijacobin Review*.[30] 'Mr Wilberforce' was also condemned for 'railing against the clergy of the establishment', and in the *Guide to the Church* (1798) was censured by Daubeny, who warned portentously that 'there should be no Schism in the body'. Against a background of revolutionary threat, and possible invasion, the most potent accusation was of disloyalty to Church and State, not in action but – more subversively – in words and doctrines. Writers from all sides waded into the fray. Sir Richard Hill, the notoriously outspoken MP, jumped to Wilberforce's defence with *An Apology for Brotherly Love*

27 Interestingly, Milner had already tried to counter the claims of Gibbon and Hume concerning Christianity and the past. See Joseph Milner, *Gibbon's account of Christianity considered: together with some strictures on Hume's dialogues concerning natural religion* (London and York, 1781).

28 Joseph Milner, *The History of the Church of Christ*, 6 vols (2nd edn, Cambridge, 1800), ix–x.

29 Walsh, 'Milner's Church History', 186.

30 John Overton, *The True Churchman Ascertained* (2nd edn, York, 1802), 14.

(1798), to which Daubeny riposted in the same year with *An Appendix to the Guide to the Church*. Hill managed two more publications, *Reformation-truth Restored* and *Daubenism Confuted* (both 1800), before Daubeny hit back with the weighty *Vindiciae Ecclesiae Anglicanae* (1803). Another writer, Thomas Ludlam, played on atavistic fears by labelling Scott, Newton, Milner, Venn and Robinson as 'Puritans'; George Croft of Oxford and the liberal churchman Robert Fellowes produced similarly scorching anti-Evangelical tracts.[31]

Arguably the most considered response came from John Overton, a Yorkshire clergyman, who argued in *The True Churchman Ascertained* (1801) that conversion, not conformity, was the key to salvation. The theology of the Church of England, he asserted, was much closer to Evangelical moderate Calvinism than the anti-Jacobin Reviewers would admit. 'Either . . . the Church of England considers *all* persons real Christians who are comprehended within her external pale', he reasoned, 'or she considers only *some* of her visible members entitled to this character, and the rest mere nominal and professed Christians'.[32] The most significant result of Overton's work was to ground the Evangelical defence firmly on adherence to the received texts and traditions of the Anglican Church. Similar arguments were adopted by James Bean in *Zeal Without Innovation* (1808), where he maintained that Anglican formularies were essentially sound, but had been choked through cold, orthodoxy and heartless formality.[33] Questions about loyalty were thus neatly dealt with, for few High Churchmen disputed that the Liturgy, Homilies and Articles were to be treated as normative, laid down for all time at the Reformation.

Simultaneously, this stance provided the basis for a powerful critique of prevailing ideas and practices. As one writer remarked, only Dissenters like Watts, Doddridge and Guise in the eighteenth century had preached what the Church of England subscribed to, whereas her own divines had neglected to teach or believe her own truths.[34] If his readers found Evangelical doctrines problematic, Bean proposed, 'let them try the clergyman in whose character they have any interest, by

[31] Edwin Sidney, *The Life of Sir Richard Hill* (London, 1839), 448; Brown, *Fathers of the Victorians*, 172; see ibid. ch. 5 for a more detailed account of the controversy between the Anti-Jacobin Reviewers and the Evangelicals.

[32] Overton, *True Churchman*, 103–4, 106.

[33] James Bean, *Zeal Without Innovation* (London, 1808).

[34] Sidney, *Samuel Walker*, 380.

what they hear from his own lips, and see in his own actions, compared with the Bible and the common Prayer Book'.[35] In an especially revealing exchange, Bishop Tomline's *Refutation of Calvinism* (1811) was comprehensively crushed by the celebrated theologian and preacher Thomas Scott, who pointed out that his opponent had mistakenly chosen phrases from the Book of Homilies to brand as Evangelical cant. As Milner's *History* had suggested that vital tenets were no innovation, so the writings of Overton, Bean and Scott aimed to give evangelicalism a more Anglican pedigree.

III

Reverence for Anglican forms was by no means unique to Evangelicals. Wilberforce, for example, had called upon broadly favourable associations when he reminded his fashionable readership that serious Christianity was 'the Religion of the most eminent Reformers.'[36] Yet the Evangelical attachment went much deeper. The keynote doctrines of Original Sin, New Birth and Justification by Faith found ample support in the writings of Cranmer and the founders of the Church. Indeed, Simeon went as far as to claim that 'no other human work [was] as free from faults' as the Book of Common Prayer.[37] Yet equally, some puzzled over what they found therein. How was it possible to reconcile the undoubted need for individual salvation with statements such as that of the Nineteenth Article, that 'the visible Church of Christ is a congregation of faithful men'?

Such comments were particularly problematical for Evangelical incumbents. As Thomas Robinson found at Leicester, 'Religion was a feeble and sickly plant' which 'consisted for the most part in names and forms, and a sort of pharisaical attendance upon one service on the Sunday'. A small religious society, 'people cordially attached to the doctrines and disciplines of the Church of England' waited for redemption and deliverance.[38] Numerous clergy would have echoed Richard Cecil's anguish on encountering an unawakened congregation, 'Can

35 Bean, *Zeal Without Innovation*, x–xi.

36 Wilberforce, *Practical View*, 273.

37 Abner William Brown, *Recollections of the Conversation Parties of the Rev. Charles Simeon* (London, 1868), 62. Simeon, Cecil and other regulars were wont to exult in 'the excellencies of our truly evangelical liturgy'. See also Smyth, *Simeon and Church Order*, 291, 9.

38 Vaughan, *Some Account*, 57–8.

these dry bones live?'[39] In a series of missionary sermons, Legh Richmond made the problem explicit. 'Nominal Christianity', he claimed, 'was, after all, little better than Heathen ignorance; while it involved greater guilt, and a more tremendous responsibility'.[40] Here was the worst of both worlds, for the nominalist had the outward appearance of saintliness, but manifested none of the godly fruits.

In discussing Evangelical attitudes to the Church, Carter has emphasized that 'the ancient Jewish state was, *pari passu*, always a paradigm for the modern Christian state', and it is clear that Old Testament precedents carried strong resonances for those who mobilized the language of national salvation or apostasy.[41] On the other hand, drawing on New Testament references, the polity could convincingly be likened to a household (Eph. 2: 19–22), a Church (Rev. 3: 14–22) or even a body with interdependent limbs and members (1 Cor. 12: 12–31). 'As families grew into nations, the same practical ideas prevailed', wrote Milner, highlighting that such metaphors overlapped and could be interchangeable.[42] Nevertheless, the idea of a national 'conversion' seems to have been especially persuasive. Indeed, it was apologetically extremely useful, for advance or decline could be plotted according to the celebration or neglect of Reformation principles.

As we saw earlier, the Reformation 'moment' had set the bounds of Anglican spirituality for good, in Evangelical eyes at least. Yet if this conversion 'moment' had marked the rebirth of the national Church, Evangelical experience in the parishes seemed to confirm that the nation had strayed towards mere observance, despite enjoying all the advantages of scriptural forms. The ideas of rebirth, subsequent decline and later revival provided a potent metaphor for those seeking the recovery of true national belief. We should bear in mind that the notion of a uniting event, potentially relevant and literally vital to all, was already stamped upon every believer's *psyche* through personal conversion and the redemptive power of the Cross. The process of sanctification which followed, especially within the moderate Calvinist framework beloved of many Evangelicals, was not one of constant triumph, but was marked by constant, bitter struggle against indwelling

39 Josiah Pratt, *The Works of the Rev. Richard Cecil*, 3 vols (2nd edn, London, 1816), vol. ?: 38.

40 T. S. Grimshawe, *Memoir of Legh Richmond* (London, 1827), 252.

41 Carter, *Anglican Evangelicals*, 29.

42 Joseph Milner, *Reflections on Ecclesiastical Establishments* (London, 1835), 8.

sin and worldly temptation. *Simul justus et peccator,* the Christian would remain imperfect until the day he died. In practice, this also enabled Evangelicals to reconcile their historical ideal with the present malaise: the national 'body' was not unregenerate, but over time had lapsed into heartless formality. This impression was further confirmed when Evangelicals considered a nation in which the problem was not atheism, but a widespread and deep-rooted nominalism. While in preaching to their congregations Evangelicals were to call for repentance, conversion and faith, in addressing the polity they were to reaffirm Paul's exhortation to 'walk worthy of the vocation wherewith ye are called', rather than clamouring for social or institutional revolution.[43]

IV

While this can be little more than a preliminary essay on such a broad subject, it is possible to draw a number of conclusions. First, it would be crass to argue that the Evangelicals abandoned individual belief for some communal brand of salvation. Like other contemporaries, they were apt to draw unlikely or unexpected links between Old Testament theocracy, Pauline exhortation, parables, psalms and prophecy. Nevertheless, this essay claims that the visible Church took on greater importance, and that the trope of national salvation, in a collective sense as well as more individually, had come to underpin Evangelical thought by the first decade of the nineteenth century. Secondly, it must be acknowledged that the trope of Britain as a 'new Israel' was not a new one, and that it gained particular momentum in the 1820s and '30s through prophetic speculation and missionary fervour. However, it should be emphasized that mainstream Evangelical thought found its roots more in appeal to the past than in prophetic conjecture regarding the future.

Such ideas point to fertile veins of further research. The increasingly close relationship between Church-minded Evangelicals and old-fashioned High Churchmen has never been fully investigated.[44] Ventures such as the Parker Society – founded in order to republish the writings of the Reformers – illustrated a set of shared theological and historical presumptions which have not yet been fully explored. Ideas

43 Eph. 4: 1.

44 The subject finds some mention in Peter Toon, *Evangelical Theology 1833–1856: a Response to Tractarianism* (London, 1979), 43.

of history and shared narrative might also enrich our view of parties, politics and intellectual ideas in the wider Church, especially in response to the uncertainties of the 1830s. 'Before 1833', Burns makes clear, 'the Reformation was not a contentious issue among English churchmen', highlighting that the Tractarian project manifested not only new theological distinctions, but a teleology directly opposed to the well-rehearsed narrative of Reformation and revival.[45] Indeed, it might be argued that ecclesiastical politics in the 1830s and '40s could be considered as a clash of narratives, between traditional static interpretations of Anglican history on the one hand, and more progressive (Liberal) or backward-looking (Tractarian) ideas on the other.

Yet in spite of such fundamental challenges, many still watched and waited for the eventual consummation of the Revival, the restoration of true Anglican principles. In the postscript to a work of 1835, Sidney invoked the glories of the anticipated apotheosis:

> Now then is the time for the Church of England to arise in all her strength, to enlarge her field of action, to open wide the doors of her fold, to shew the spirituality of her doctrines, the excellence of her discipline, the beauty of her ordinances – and she will soon recall the scattered affections of those who have wandered from her communion, and be made a blessing to a people recovered from their dissensions by the uniting spirit of the gospel of Christ.[46]

Magdalene College, University of Cambridge

[45] Arthur Burns, 'English "Church Reform" Revisited, 1780–1840', in Arthur Burns and Joanna Innes, eds, *Rethinking the Age of Reform* (Cambridge, 2003), 136–62, at 154–7.
[46] Sidney, *Samuel Walker*, 282–3.

WILLIAM WILBERFORCE'S *PRACTICAL VIEW* (1797) AND ITS RECEPTION

by JOHN WOLFFE

> Never, perhaps, did any volume by a layman, on a religious subject, produce a deeper or more sudden effect.

THIS in 1826 was the judgement of Daniel Wilson, vicar of Islington and later bishop of Calcutta, looking back on the publication on 12 April 1797 of William Wilberforce's *Practical View of the Prevailing Religious System of Professed Christians in the Higher and Middle Classes of this Country Contrasted with Real Christianity*. Wilson went on to argue that the book 'contributed in no small measure, to the progress of that general revival of religion which had already been begun'.[1] It subsequently became a historiographical commonplace that the book was 'the handbook of the Evangelicals';[2] but its impact on British religion also had other important dimensions that need to be explored.

The 1790s were indeed a decade of revival, both in the specific classic meaning of the word, and the wider sense of resurgence and renewal. Notable local and regional movements of revival included those at Bala in North Wales in 1791, a striking Methodist upsurge in Wilberforce's own Yorkshire constituency from 1792 to 1796 and outbreaks in Cornwall in 1794 and 1798–9. Meanwhile there was less dramatic but still significant spiritual resurgence evident in the impact of effective evangelical ministries in the established Churches, such as those of John Newton in London, Charles Simeon in Cambridge and Sir Henry Wellwood Moncrieff in Edinburgh.[3] It was to this latter more moderate socially elite aspect of the movement that Wilberforce's book primarily contributed. It should also be seen in the political context of war with France and radical unrest at home, pressures that

1 William Wilberforce, *Practical View . . . with an Introductory Essay by the Rev. Daniel Wilson* (Glasgow, 1826) [hereafter: *Practical View* 1826], xvii, xxxvii.

2 Ian Bradley, *The Call to Seriousness: the Evangelical Impact on the Victorians* (1976), 19.

3 See John Wolffe, *The Expansion of Evangelicalism: the Age of Wilberforce, More, Chalmers and Finney* (Nottingham, 2006), 35, 45–53.

seemed to come dramatically together on 17 April 1797, just five days after the publication of the *Practical View*, when the fleet at Spithead mutinied, soon to be followed by that at the Nore.

In 1797 Wilberforce was already a weighty political figure as a representative of Yorkshire and a close, but not uncritical, friend of the prime minister, William Pitt. During the previous eight years his name had become particularly associated with the campaign against the slave trade, but the *Practical View* fits into a pattern of parallel concern for moral and spiritual regeneration at home, which dated back to his conversion in 1785, and his establishment of the Proclamation Society in 1787. By 1797 there was a growing body of other literature on the reformation of manners, including books by two of Wilberforce's 'Clapham Sect' friends, Hannah More's *Thoughts on the Importance of the Manners of the Great to General Society* (1788) and Thomas Gisborne's *An Enquiry into the Duties of Men in the Higher and Middle Classes of Society in Great Britain* (1794). The *Practical View*, however, was more explicitly spiritual in its emphasis than either More's or Gisborne's books, and it also served by way of somewhat belated public apologia for Wilberforce's evangelical conversion a decade before, a step that had itself appeared a radical, implicit challenge to prevailing religious and social mores.

Wilberforce was highly intelligent, but he was not a systematic thinker. He wrote as he spoke, and it is indeed probable that he dictated the draft to a secretary. Thus the style is discursive and repetitive, redeemed by passages of great feeling and persuasive eloquence. He was not well versed in contemporary theological literature, sat loosely to distinctions between Arminianism and Calvinism, and disarmingly admitted that despite his pivotal emphasis on original sin, he had never read Jonathan Edwards's authoritative work on the subject. Rather Wilberforce's approach was based on his own direct exegesis of Scripture: he urged his readers to test his statements against 'the language of the sacred writings' and affirmed that 'from the decision of the word of God' there can be no appeal. His objective was to offer a practical prescription for Christian living rather than an exposition of abstract 'speculative' doctrine.[4]

Wilberforce began by charging professed Christians with an igno-

[4] BL, Arthur Young Papers, Add. MS 35,127, fols 442–9, Wilberforce to Young, 8 September 1797; William Wilberforce, *Practical View* (1st edn, London, 1797) [hereafter: *Practical View* 1797], 4–5.

rance of the real teachings of Christianity, because they failed to study the Bible in any depth.[5] He then juxtaposed the 'professed Christian' view of human nature as 'naturally pure and inclined to all virtue', with the 'real Christian' view that it was fundamentally corrupt, evil and depraved.[6] He discussed issues of personal conduct such as Sunday observance and duelling, but argued that the 'grand radical defect in the practical system of these nominal Christians' was a spiritual one, 'forgetfulness of all the peculiar doctrines of the Religion which they profess – the corruption of human nature – the atonement of the Saviour – and the sanctifying influence of the Holy Spirit.'[7] In a pivotal passage, which he drew particularly to Pitt's attention, he then urged those striving for holiness to 'lay afresh the whole foundation of their Religion', not through fruitless efforts in their own strength to reform their manner of life, but rather by responding to the call

> gratefully to adore that undeserved goodness which has awakened them from the sleep of death; to prostrate themselves before the Cross of Christ with humble penitence and deep self-abhorrence, solemnly resolving to forsake all their sins, but relying on the Grace of God alone for power to keep their resolution.[8]

True holiness was therefore a consequence not a cause of reconciliation with God.

In a subsequent chapter Wilberforce turned to analysis of the 'present State of Christianity in this Country', maintaining that religion was so 'intimately connected with the temporal interests of society' that it should be a particular concern of politicians. Religion indeed was essential for good order. He judged though that material prosperity had dulled religious sensibilities, was distressed at the unbelief and spiritual lukewarmness of leading writers such as David Hume and Adam Smith, and alarmed at the venomous moral malignity that he believed was growing in France as a consequence of the revolutionary renunciation of Christianity. For the nation as for individuals, the solution lay in a turning to real Christianity, a matter not of radical innovation, but of recovering 'the good old principles of the Church of England', as they

5 Ibid., 7–23.

6 Ibid., 26–7.

7 Ibid., 193–9, 219–21, 320.

8 Ibid., 325; Robert Isaac Wilberforce and Samuel Wilberforce, *The Life of William Wilberforce* [hereafter: *Life of Wilberforce*], 5 vols (London, 1838), 2: 202.

had been established at the Reformation. Wilberforce equated the 'real Christianity' he described with 'the Religion of the most eminent Reformers' of the sixteenth century. Moreover, despite his perception of the current pastoral ineffectiveness of the Church of England, he was a firm believer in the potential of the established Church as a basis for rechristianization. Spiritual regeneration was quite as essential for national security in this world as for individual salvation in the next.[9]

The book was a substantial publishing success. Wilberforce himself helped to stimulate interest by presenting copies to his well-connected friends.[10] It went through five editions during the course of 1797.[11] A first American edition appeared in Philadelphia in 1798, with a list of influential subscribers, including Elias Boudinot, director of the United States mint, Benjamin Rush, the distinguished physician and social reformer, and William White, the Episcopalian bishop. Matthew Carey, a prominent Roman Catholic bookseller, ordered twenty-four copies.[12] Boston editions followed in 1799 and 1803. Meanwhile in Britain, the book reached its eighth edition in 1805, its twelfth in 1817 and its fourteenth in 1820.[13] At the time of Wilberforce's death in 1833 it was regarded as 'a stock book', which publishers always kept in print because they knew there was a steady ongoing demand for it.[14] Wilberforce himself never revised or added to the work but in 1826 it was republished as part of a series of 'Select Christian Authors' with a substantial introductory essay by Daniel Wilson.[15] Wilson's version itself reached a fourth edition in 1833, and it was reprinted again in 1835, 1838, 1846, 1854 and 1871.[16] The American Tract Society published a revised edition in New York around 1830, and in Britain the Religious Tract Society published a twenty-four page abridgement.[17] A Dutch translation appeared in 1817, a French one in 1820, and a Spanish one, including Wilson's introduction, in 1827.[18] The

9 Ibid., 364–422.

10 *Practical View* 1826, xviii.

11 British Library catalogue.

12 Philadelphia: John Ormrod, 1798, 'Subscribers' Names'. This appears as an unpaginated list of subscribers bound into the end of the book.

13 British Library catalogue.

14 John Scott, *The Character, Principles and Public Service of the Late William Wilberforce* (London, 1833), 21.

15 *Practical View* 1826.

16 British Library catalogue; COPAC.

17 Library of Congress Catalogue; Religious Tract Society, First series, Vol. 15, No. 567.

18 *Het ware Christendom vergeleken met de heerschende denkwijze van deszelfs belijders bijzonder*

book continued to be republished in the late nineteenth and twentieth centuries, and the most recent edition, published in Massachusetts in 1996 with an introduction by Charles Colson, indicates its appeal to the contemporary American religious Right.[19]

The *Practical View* was regarded by Wilberforce's own evangelical constituency as having a highly strategic role in the progress of religious revival. On its publication John Newton, the clerical patriarch of Anglican evangelicalism, observed that it 'will be read by Persons in the higher Circles, who are quite inaccessible to us little folks'.[20] The *Evangelical Magazine* considered it 'a valuable publication' and in order to avoid any risk of lessening its impact forbore from 'pointing out blemishes accidental to all human publications'.[21] Beilby Porteus, the bishop of London, who was sympathetic to the evangelicals, thought that the work, and other similar ones, made a considerable impact and was indicative of '*some* degree of returning seriousness'.[22] Thirty years later, Daniel Wilson was in no doubt at to its importance. He saw the *Practical View* as shifting the balance of opinion on religion among the British elite, and making evangelicalism seem a credible option to those with serious spiritual thoughts. Wilson emphasized particularly its influence on the younger generation of Anglican clergy, the stimulus that it gave to other writers, the encouragement that it gave to the faithful, and its importance in preparing the political ground for greater state support for the religion in the form of the church-building grants of the 1810s and 1820s.[23] While numerous other factors contributed to the revival, in Wilson's view

> this particular book occupied a post nobly and singularly: it was a mighty instrument in carrying forward the great work, and advancing it in its progress – an opportune and powerful agent, in

in de hoogere en middelstanden (n.p., 1817); M. Frossard, trans., *Le Christianisme des Gens de Monde, Mis en Opposition avec le Véritable Christianisme*, 2 vols (Montauban, 1821); José Muñoz de Sotomayor, trans., *Perspectiva Real del Cristianismo Practico, ó Sistema del Christianismo de los Mondanos, en las Clases Alta y Mediana de Este Pais Parangonado y Contrapuesto al Verdadero Cristianismo* (London, 1827). Wilberforce's sons (*Life of Wilberforce*, 2: 205) stated that there were also German and Italian translations, but no copies of these are listed in the respective national online catalogues.

19 Kevin Charles Belmonte, ed., *A Practical View of Christianity* (Peabody, 1996), xix, xxvi.

20 Oxford, Bodleian Library, MS Wilberforce c.49, Newton to W, 18 April 1797.

21 *Evangelical Magazine* 6 (1798), 39–40.

22 *A Charge Delivered to the Clergy of the Diocese of London in the Years 1798 and 1799 by the Right Reverend Beilby, Lord Bishop of that Diocese* (London, 1799), 32–7.

23 *Practical View* 1826, xxxviii–xliv.

> concurrence indeed with, and in succession to, and in advance of others, but still a powerful agent, through the mercy of God.[24]

Some individuals were profoundly influenced by the *Practical View*. Legh Richmond, an Anglican evangelical clergyman and later an influential author, read the work while a curate and became impressed with 'the corruption of the human heart, and the way of salvation by Jesus Christ.' Wilberforce prompted him to closer study both of the Bible and of the Reformers.[25] Probably the most significant of the personal conversions in which the *Practical View* was instrumental was that of Thomas Chalmers, the later leader of the Evangelical party in the Church of Scotland, then an academically able but spiritually unfocused young parish minister in Fife. Chalmers commenced reading the book on Christmas Eve 1810 after his elder sister Lucy had died of consumption the previous day. His sense of loss and awareness of mortality combined with an acute consciousness of sinfulness arising from his impatience with other difficult family circumstances, particularly his father's incipient senility. Since his thirtieth birthday the previous March he had been seeking to rectify a sense of 'estrangement' from matters of eternity through keeping a journal and engaging in a course of serious spiritual reading. On Christmas Day he recorded that 'I'm delighted with Wilberforce and hope for much edification from his performance'. On 29 December, he commented that 'Wilberforce's observations on the subject of temper highly applicable to my case.' The following day he became 'more impressed with the humility of the peculiar doctrines'. The arrival of the New Year as he completed the book helped to reinforce Chalmers's sense of spiritual new beginnings. The process continued in the early months of 1811: on 29 January he felt 'more cordially than ever that my sufficiency is of Christ' and on 23 February he noted that 'I feel myself on the eve of some decisive transformation in point of religious sentiment'.[26]

Later in his life, Chalmers attributed his transition to evangelical convictions primarily to his reading of Wilberforce, who convinced him of 'the depravity of our nature, of our need of an atonement, of the

24 Ibid., xlv.

25 T. S. Grimshawe, *A Memoir of the Rev. Legh Richmond* (2nd edn, London, 1828), 26–7.

26 Edinburgh, New College Library, Chalmers Papers, CHA 6.1.3, 17 March 1810, CHA 6.1.4, 24, 25, 26, 29, 30, 31 December 1810, 1, 7, 29 January, 23 February, 17 March 1811, CHA 3.4.51, Chalmers to James Chalmers 24 December 1810; William Hanna, *Memoirs of the Life and Writings of Thomas Chalmers DD, LLD*, 4 vols (Edinburgh, 1849), 1: 182–9.

great doctrine of acceptance through that atonement, [and] of the sanctifying influences of the Spirit'. Above all, he came to see the core of Christianity as 'Believe in the Lord Jesus Christ, and thou shalt be saved.' Human beings, Chalmers now believed, were impotent to work out their own righteousness, but righteousness put on by faith 'secures our acceptance with God'. He was now 'very much in the habit of recommending' the *Practical View* to others.[27] In 1829 he looked back on it as 'next to the Bible', a qualification Wilberforce himself would have heartily endorsed, the book 'most instrumental in affecting a great change in my views of Scriptural and Divine truth.'[28]

Hindsight though tends to simplify complex processes. Just as a reading of Chalmers's diary for late 1810 and 1811 indicates that a range of other influences, literary and personal, were contributing to his process of fresh spiritual discovery, immediate reactions to the publication of the *Practical View* were more diverse than Wilson acknowledged. The comments of reviewers were mixed and some lively pamphlet controversy ensued. In general Anglican evangelicals and orthodox Protestant dissenters were enthusiastic about the book, although *The Protestant Dissenters's Magazine* did perceive an inconsistency in Wilberforce's condemnation of duelling while he continued to support the war with France.[29] The review in the High Church *British Critic* was also predominantly positive in tone, describing the book as 'one of the most impressive . . . on the subject of religion, that have appeared within our memory', although it did detect an anti-clerical and pro-methodist bias.[30]

There was more substantive critique on two fronts. First, from a High Church perspective, Charles Daubeny, later archdeacon of Salisbury, was provoked to address his *Guide to the Church* to Wilberforce. Daubeny professed respect for Wilberforce and his book, but considered that it offered an inadequate doctrine of the Church, which Daubeny held was 'a spiritual society under the regular establishment of its Divine Founder'.[31] Second, and more far reaching, was an attack from rational Christians, particularly Unitarians, who argued that

27 Chalmers to Alexander Chalmers, 14 Feb. 1820, 9 June 1825, quoted in Hanna, *Chalmers*, 185–7.

28 Oxford, Bodleian Library, MS Wilberforce c. 3, fol. 251, Chalmers to Sir John Sinclair, 9 February 1829.

29 *Protestant Dissenters' Magazine* 4 (1797), 196–8.

30 *British Critic* 10 (1797), 294–303.

31 Charles Daubeny, *A Guide to the Church in Several Discourses* (London, 1798), vii.

Wilberforce's doctrines, above all his emphasis on universal human depravity, were in fact at odds with the Scripture he claimed as his authority. The *Monthly Review* acknowledged the popular appeal of Methodism, representing teachings analogous to Wilberforce's, but thought that 'success is in no case a proof of truth'; it affirmed that Christianity was primarily a matter of conduct rather than belief, and argued that its authority must be grounded in an appeal to reason.[32] John Evans, a General Baptist minister, published a work by his recently-deceased colleague Charles Bulkley which he presented as a riposte to Wilberforce's 'reasonings on the corruption of human nature'.[33] A Unitarian critic, Gilbert Wakefield, argued that Wilberforce's principles were incompatible with Christ's own conduct and teaching, which he summed up as 'he went about, doing good.' He saw Wilberforce as inconsistent in supporting the war and the Pitt government.[34] The most extended polemic against Wilberforce was by Thomas Belsham, minister of the Gravel Pit Unitarian Chapel in Hackney. Belsham argued that Wilberforce demeaned the character of God by suggesting human beings were created morally corrupt. He also claimed that his scriptural exegesis was flawed, for example in ascribing divine authority to the words of one of Job's comforters, when it was clear from the context that they were not mouthpieces for the Almighty.[35]

Wilberforce himself did not reply to these attacks, but other writers appointed themselves his defenders. Thus Daubeny drew responses from the eccentric evangelical MP Sir Richard Hill and from an anonymous 'minister of the Church of England'.[36] Both Belsham and Wakefield were answered by other pamphleteers, and there was also a specific defence of Wilberforce's advocacy of Sunday observance.[37]

32 *Monthly Review*, enlarged series, 23 (1797), 241–8.

33 Charles Bulkley, *An Apology for Human Nature* (London, 1797), 2.

34 Gilbert Wakefield, *A Letter to William Wilberforce, Esq, on the Subject of his late Publication* (London, 1797).

35 Thomas Belsham, *A review of Mr Wilberforce's Treatise entitled "A Practical View of the Prevailing Religious Systems of Professed Christians" etc. in Letters to a Lady* (London, 1798), 31–45.

36 Richard Hill, *An Apology for Brotherly Love and for the Doctrines of the Church of England* (London, 1798); idem, *A Letter to the Rev. Charles Daubeny, LLB, on some passages contained to in his Guide to the Church and his Letter to Mrs Hannah More, by a Minister of the Church of England* (Bath, 1799).

37 Thomas Williams, *A Vindication of the Calvinistic Doctrines of Human Depravity, the Atonement, Divine Influence, &c. in a series of Letters to The Rev. T. Belsham* (London, 1799); George Hutton, *An Appeal to the Nation on the Subject of Mr Gilbert Wakefield's Letter to William Wilberforce* (Nottingham, 1798); Samuel Palmer, *An Apology for the Christian Sabbath* (London, 1799).

Such enthusiastic but obscure friends, however, may have served Wilberforce rather less well than the weighty critiques from Belsham and Daubeny, which drew attention to the *Practical View*, and implicitly recognized it as an important contribution to religious discourse. Thomas Williams's reply to Belsham appeared to cast Wilberforce in a unduly narrow Calvinist guise, while an attack on Wakefield by the literary hack John Watkins was criticized by the *Evangelical Magazine* for its 'temper and spirit' and for wandering into political matters.[38]

It was also apparent that even those who were positively impressed by the book, were more or less selective in their assimilation of its ideas. Wilberforce's close friend Henry Thornton wrote that 'Many of his gay and political friends admire and approve of it; though some do but dip into it.'[39] The agriculturalist Arthur Young, currently distressed by the terminal illness and death of a much-loved daughter, read the book closely and felt it brought him 'to a better sense of my dangerous state'. He did, however, find it difficult to understand and wrote to Wilberforce to raise several questions.[40] In part these related to matters not covered in the book, stirred particularly by Young's recent bereavement. Wilberforce comforted him with his belief that the dead would know those they had loved on earth in the hereafter. Young though was evidently uneasy with the core of the argument, sharing the discomfort of some of Wilberforce's published critics with his conviction of human depravity. Wilberforce responded that he considered this a matter of 'the first importance', albeit in a 'practical' rather than speculative way. 'I am perfectly persuaded', he told Young, 'that it is our entertaining too low conceptions of our own natural corruption and weakness, which renders us so slow in pursuing Holiness, so cold in our acknowledgement for that strength from above which is so freely offered to us.' On the other hand someone with 'a strong practical sense of this great truth' would be rendered humble, watchful, and constant in prayer for the guidance and strength of the Holy Spirit.[41] Wilberforce sent Young a further lengthy letter on this point in July 1799, maintaining that, contrary to Unitarian arguments, when Jesus said

38 *Evangelical Magazine* 6 (1798), 41; 7 (1799), 464.

39 Quoted in *Life of Wilberforce*, 2: 200.

40 M. Betham-Edwards, *The Autobiography of Arthur Young with Selections from his Correspondence* (London, 1898), 287–8, 297; BL, Young Papers, Add. MS 35,127, fols 438–9, Wilberforce to Young, 15 August 1797.

41 Ibid., fols 442–9, Wilberforce to Young, 8 September 1797.

'suffer little children to come unto me' he was affirming their helplessness rather than their innocence.[42]

In the meantime, Young was inspired to write a pamphlet of his own, in which he sought to extend the influence of the *Practical View* to the lower classes.[43] During his recent tours of the country Young had observed much popular irreligion and radicalism, and he now advocated a programme of church-building as the best response. The argument came over as more social and political than religious: Young appeared imprecise in his reference to Wilberforce's account of the 'doctrines of the gospel', and was criticized by the *Evangelical Magazine* for his emphasis on church-building rather than preaching.[44]

A rounded understanding of the reception of the *Practical View* thus needs to balance an acknowledgement of its importance in promoting evangelicalism with an awareness that Wilberforce's understanding of 'real Christianity' was by no means uncontested. Indeed the significance of the *Practical View* may lie as much in the extent to which it stirred debate on this matter, as in the straightforward dissemination of Wilberforce's own interpretation. It stimulated the High Church arguments of Daubeny, recognized as important antecedents of the Oxford Movement,[45] encouraged statements of liberal and rational Christianity, and provided a basis for the appropriation of some evangelical causes even by those who struggled with the core spiritual teachings of the movement. It certainly contributed powerfully to revival, but in understanding the nature of that revival it is important to avoid the distortions of hindsight and partisan interpretation.

The Open University

42 Ibid., 35, 128, fols 127–8, Wilberforce to Young, 20 July 1799.

43 Arthur Young, *An Enquiry into the State of the Public Mind Amongst the Lower Classes; and on the Means of Turning it to the Welfare of the State, in a Letter to William Wilberforce, Esq. MP* (Dublin, 1798). Wilberforce commented on a draft (BL, Young Papers, Add MS 35,128, fol. 12, 4 March 1798).

44 Young, *Enquiry*, 23; *Evangelical Magazine* 6 (1798), 305–6.

45 See Peter Nockles, *The Oxford Movement in Context: Anglican High Churchmanship, 1760–1857* (Cambridge, 1994).

NAPOLEON AND THE REVIVAL OF FEMALE RELIGIOUS COMMUNITIES IN PARIS, 1800–14

by GEMMA BETROS

IN December 1807, representatives from thirty-five French female religious communities wrote to Napoleon, reminding him that their associations were 'essentially religious'. They stated that any attempt to secularize them would bring about their death and they announced their wish to remain subject to the authority of the Church in all that concerned their spiritual lives and interior regimes.[1] These women, whom Napoleon had called to Paris especially, thereby warned the Emperor that although he may have been responsible for the official revival of their communities, he could not assume control over every aspect of their existence.

This essay examines an often-neglected episode in the history of the revival of the Church in France. The extraordinary growth of female religious communities in the nineteenth century is well known, yet there has been little investigation into the origins of this growth or the conditions that shaped it.[2] By looking at the process of re-establishment, this essay shows that the revival of female religious communities was neither preordained, nor easy. Those communities that attempted to re-form following the destruction of the French Revolution faced numerous challenges, especially in their relationship with the state, while the Napoleonic administration found itself forced to make concessions when dealing with the religious communities whose help it could not do without and whose continued presence seemed non-negotiable. The result was a revival that, although initially dictated from above, came to rest on a process of compromise and negotiation on both sides, the terms of which would characterize the

[1] Paris, Archives nationales (hereafter: AN), F/19/6247, *Adresse à Sa Majesté l'Empereur des députées au Chapitre général des Sœurs de la Charité* (2 December 1807).

[2] The one historian to have examined the subject in detail is Léon Deries, *Les congrégations religieuses au temps de Napoléon* (Paris, 1929). The second half of the book addresses female congregations. See also Victor Bindel, *Histoire religieuse de Napoléon*, 2 vols (Paris, 1940), 2: 47–55. More recent contributions are found in Claude Langlois, *Le catholicisme au féminin* (Paris, 1984), 67–151 and Jacques-Olivier Boudon, *Napoléon et les cultes* (Paris, 2002), 157–63.

growth of female religious communities throughout the nineteenth century.

The question of Napoleon and the revival of female communities has on occasion been presented as a battle between Napoleon and the nuns, from which the nuns emerged victorious.[3] This interpretation rests upon a narrative of female constancy and virtue of the type that could survive any adversary, even Bonaparte.[4] Yet, while female piety certainly played an important role in the revival of these communities, the advantages involved for the state must also be considered. Later historians have therefore considered the extent of Napoleon's role in their revival and ensuing growth.[5] Although this is an important line of inquiry, it necessarily focuses on authorized communities and thereby overlooks the reunion of former monastic communities, which usually remained unauthorized.[6] This essay attempts to adjust the parameters of the debate by examining the revival of both monastic religious orders, whose members took solemn vows and lived under the rules of enclosure, and secular communities, whose members took 'simple' vows and were permitted to undertake certain activities in society such as teaching, nursing, and serving the poor.[7] It asks how this revival came about, why it developed the way it did, and what it meant for the women involved. The case-study of Paris, where reunited communities were under constant observation, offers essential insight into this process.

The French Revolution had officially suppressed all religious communities, yet the uneven application of its legislation meant that this destruction was neither complete nor permanent. The decree of 13 February 1790 had suppressed all communities whose members took solemn vows, offering them a pension upon their return to society.[8]

[3] Deries, for example, writes that Napoleon was 'defeated by the nuns'. Deries, *Congrégations religieuses*, 221.

[4] See, for example, Bindel, *Histoire religieuse*, 2: 203 and Jean Boussoulade, *Moniales et hospitalières dans la tourmente révolutionnaire: les communautés de religieuses de l'ancien diocèse de Paris de 1789 à 1801* (Paris, 1962), 10.

[5] Langlois, *Catholicisme au féminin*, 111; and Boudon, *Napoléon*, 157–63.

[6] Historians are often too quick to equate the anti-monastic laws of the Revolution with the end of monasticism, a point noted by Langlois himself. Langlois, *Catholicisme au féminin*, 67.

[7] For a discussion of the differences between regular and secular communities, see Derek Beales, *Prosperity and Plunder: European Catholic Monasteries in the Age of Revolution, 1650–1815* (Cambridge, 2003), 17–22.

[8] *Archives parlementaires de 1787 à 1860: recueil complet des débats législatifs et politiques des Chambres françaises, Première série*, XI (13 February 1790), 591.

While the majority of male religious took up this offer, most women, much to the consternation of the National Assembly, either hesitated or refused to leave altogether.[9] Many remained in their convents for as long as possible. Although the communities that staffed France's schools, hospitals and prisons were initially conserved, they too were suppressed on 18 August 1792.[10] Yet police records reveal that at least several hundred women quickly regrouped in Paris.[11] Members of the community of Saint Thomas de Villeneuve were even able to stay in their main house throughout the revolutionary decade.[12] As was often the case with revolutionary policy, a gap had opened between principle and practice, a gap which Napoleon found himself forced to address.

Napoleon believed from a young age that the Church was a danger to the unity of the state.[13] Although he later came to appreciate the value of religion, particularly in terms of its influence over the populace, these early views clearly influenced his approach to reinstating religious communities. When he came to power as First Consul in 1799, Napoleon inherited a society divided in its attitude towards religion. A persistent Jacobin element was ready to interpret any sign of leniency towards the Church as evidence that revolutionary achievements were being compromised.[14] Yet, on the other hand, public opinion had for several years been calling for the return of religion in society.[15] This was at least partly influenced by the fact that, after a decade of disruption, primary education was almost non-existent and hospitals were in a state of ruin. Revolutionary experiments in hiring lay people to fill the roles of nursing and teaching sisters had been largely unsuccessful, and departmental assemblies were soon discussing the return of female communities to staff the nation's hospitals.[16] The

9 Beales, *Prosperity and Plunder*, 258.

10 *Archives parlementaires*, XLVIII (18 August 1792), 350–6.

11 Paris, AN, F/7/2514, 55–708. These records, dating from 28 June to 5 December 1793, provide the names of at least 252 former nuns living in the Section de l'Observatoire in Paris. Their addresses show that many of them were living together in small groups.

12 Gaëtan Bernoville, *Les religieuses de Saint-Thomas-de-Villeneuve (1661–1953)* (Paris, 1953), 182–3.

13 Frédéric Masson and Guido Biagi, eds, *Napoléon inconnu: papiers inédits (1786–1793)*, 2 vols (3rd edn, Paris, 1895), 1: 148–50.

14 Paul Dudon, 'Le Concordat et les congrégations', *Etudes* 86 (Jan–Mars 1901), 623–44, at 629 and Bindel, *Histoire religieuse*, 2: 120.

15 See, for example, *Le Grondeur ou Le Tableau des Mœurs publiques* 3 (30 November 1796), 2.

16 Deries, *Congrégations religieuses*, 210–11.

solution, formulated at a time when negotiations for Napoleon's concordat with Rome had only just begun, was to re-establish religious communities under the auspices of the state.[17]

Their revival began with the re-establishment of the Filles de la Charité, or Sisters of Charity. In 1791, the congregation had staffed 421 institutions throughout France, forty of which were in Paris.[18] The Sisters of Charity were both experienced and, at least until 1791, popular.[19] Perhaps more to Napoleon's liking was their centralized structure, which saw all novices trained in Paris before being sent where needed in France.

The Minister of the Interior, Jean-Antoine Chaptal, authorized the re-establishment of the community in Paris by a decree of 1 nivôse year IX (22 December 1800).[20] He instructed the superior of the congregation, Antoinette Deleau, to summon her former companions to train young women to work in hospitals. To ensure the success of the enterprise, the government provided significant financial and material aid. As the Sisters' former mother house, seized in 1793, was being used for military storage, the administration donated the unsold house of another order.[21] Chaptal also arranged the donation of an annual sum of 12,000 francs, to come from the general expense budget for hospices, and an annual pension of 300 francs to fund the training of girls from poor families. These measures ensured a steady supply of personnel but also tied the future of the community to the state.

A project to re-establish the very institutions banished with so much bile and effort in the preceding decade had to be handled delicately.[22] Chaptal forestalled potential criticism in three ways. First, he presented

17 The Concordat made no mention of religious communities, although the Organic Articles (1802) suppressed all ecclesiastical establishments except chapters and seminaries and banned religious titles. 'Articles Organiques de la Convention du 26 Messidor an IX', reprinted in Jean-Etienne-Marie Portalis, *Discours, rapports et travaux inédits sur le Concordat de 1801* (Paris, 1845), 67.

18 Paris, AN, F/19/470, 'Tableau des établissements que les Sœurs de la Charité occupent dans le Royaume' (Paris, [May 1791]) and L//1054, dossier 2, pièce 52, 'Sœurs de la Charité, Liste alphabétique de leurs établissements tant en France qu'à Paris' ([n.d.]).

19 In April 1791 a series of attacks had been launched against the sisters in Paris and throughout France. See Paris, AN, F/19/470 'Note des maisons où les sœurs ont été le plus maltraitées' [n.d.].

20 The decree is reprinted in Deries, *Congrégations religieuses*, 212–13.

21 Article 2 granted them the house of the Orphélines in the rue du Vieux Colombier.

22 Chaptal later wrote that 'the re-establishment of a religious corporation contrasted with all the ideas of the time.' Jean-Antoine Claude Chaptal, *Mes souvenirs sur Napoléon* (Paris, 1893), 71.

the revival of religious communities as the restoration of revolutionary law, which had initially permitted the women of 'establishments of charity' to continue their work. Second, he portrayed the Sisters of Charity as the only individuals who could fulfil the required tasks. The revolutionary decade had, he declared, shown that care for the sick could 'only be assiduously administered by those persons vowed by their state to the service of hospices and directed by the enthusiasm of charity'. Finally, throughout the text of the decree, he carefully avoided any terminology that could suggest that the Sisters of Charity was a religious organization. Sister Deleau became 'citizen Dulau [sic]', the congregation was now a 'corporation' and its future novices were called 'students'. The state may have revived a religious community, but Chaptal's wording suggests that this had little to do with religion. In meeting urgent social requirements, the administration here trod a careful line between appeasing one sector of the population and attempting to avoid the ire of another.

The upheaval of the Revolution ensured that restoration was no less difficult for the communities themselves. An 1802 circular sent by Antoinette Deleau drew attention to 'the infractions' that had crept into the observance of vows in the past decade. In some houses, the regular routine of prayer and work had been lost. Certain sisters had even used the banning of the religious habit as 'a pretext for following the spirit and maxims of the world', socializing openly with outsiders, making purchases at will, and even inviting visitors back to the convent.[23] One year later, Deleau again condemned the abuses brought by the 'sinister liberty' of the Revolution, noting, among other problems, excessive attention to hair and clothes and a lack of deference amongst the sisters of some houses.[24] While revival was being imposed from above, the superiors of re-established communities could find themselves attempting restoration of a different kind from below.

Not all communities could be authorized. In April 1801, the Minister of Police, Joseph Fouché, had ordered an inquiry into all houses in Paris where former nuns had reunited to live as a community.[25] Although incomplete, it identified 460 nuns living in seventy-

23 Paris, Archives des Filles de la Charité, Dossier: Sœur Antoinette Deleau. Antoinette Deleau, *Circulaire* (Paris, 2 February 1802). The religious habit had been banned on 6 April 1792.

24 Ibid. (Paris, 1 February 1803).

25 Paris, AN, F/7/6291, pièce 70 (Paris, 27 germinal, year IX [17 April 1801]).

seven different houses.[26] Some of these were informal reunions, perhaps driven by financial need. Others were remnants of former Parisian communities or even more formal re-establishments. The Carmelites of the rue de Vaugirard, for example, had gathered in 1797 when Camille de Soyecourt, a Parisian Carmelite, used her inheritance to purchase a new residence in which to re-establish the order.[27] Authorization of such well-known monastic orders, however, posed too great a risk. The problem grew as new communities, often founded in the provinces, began to establish branches in Paris where they felt their presence was most needed. One such community, the Dames des Sacrés Cœurs de Jésus et Marie, arrived in 1804. Although they would later take on a small amount of teaching, their chief purpose was to atone for the Revolution through the Perpetual Adoration of the Blessed Sacrament, a purpose that would seem to preclude official approval.[28]

Napoleon attempted to resolve the situation with the decree of 3 messidor, year XII (22 June 1804).[29] The decree was principally aimed at the male community of the Pères de la Foi, present in Paris since 1800 and suspected of hiding Jesuits.[30] Yet it also stated that all authorized and unauthorized communities had to submit their statutes and rules to the Conseil d'Etat for approval or be dissolved. It thereby sent a powerful message to all reunited religious communities in France that the price of revival was to be constant surveillance.

Yet there seems to have been little attempt to clamp down on unauthorized communities and section authorities were confused about how to proceed.[31] Jean-Etienne Portalis, the minister for ecclesiastical affairs (the 'Ministre des Cultes'), meanwhile granted numerous provisional authorizations.[32] Teaching orders were particularly favoured, both for the purposes of education and because of their perceived

26 Ibid. 'Maisons où sont réunies les ex-religieuses pour y vivre en communauté' (1801).

27 Henriette de Vismes, *Camille de Soyecourt, Carmélite au grand Cœur, 1757–1845* (Paris, 1938), 102–4.

28 [Anon.], *Notice sur Madame Henriette Aymer de la Chevalière: fondatrice des Dames des Sacrés Cœurs de Jésus et de Marie, et de l'Adoration perpétuelle du Très Saint-Sacrement de l'Autel* (Paris, 1835), 16–17.

29 Paris, AN, F/19/6256, 'Projet de décret sur les Associations religieuses' (3 messidor, year XII [22 June 1804]).

30 The Jesuits had been dissolved in France in 1764. See Beales, *Prosperity and Plunder*, 153–6.

31 See, for example, Paris, AN, F/7/3001, 'Opinion' (2 complémentaire, year XII [18 September 1804]).

32 Langlois, *Catholicisme au féminin*, 114–15.

ability to influence the poor.[33] The Ursulines, the Visitandines, and the Dames de Saint Maur were all authorized in the spring of 1806.

Their statutes demonstrate the state's efforts to impose a standardized organization upon female communities.[34] Authorized communities were to be placed under the jurisdiction of the ordinary, or local ecclesiastical authority, with the aim of limiting influence from Rome and maintaining state control. Articles concerning the possession and disposal of property ensured that nuns, rather than being dead to the state, were now subject to its rules like any other citizen. Even the internal regime of a community was now an official matter.[35] These attempts to reshape the character of female religious communities represented perhaps the greatest impact on their revival.

Yet unauthorized monastic communities continued to escape official interference. In 1807, the author of one ministerial report seemed resigned to the fact that 'as long as there were Catholics in France' there would be individuals who would deliver themselves to this 'genre of life'.[36] The state therefore pursued a policy of tacit toleration, deciding that cloister was acceptable as long as it was 'purely voluntary', that the wimple and the veil were 'objects of little importance, and a costume like any other', and that as long as the state did not exempt female religious communities from Episcopal surveillance, or recognize the civil death imposed by solemn vows, the 'renaissance' of monastic communities could not be proven.[37] It was hoped that if these communities were tolerated, disruption would be avoided, and that if they remained unauthorized, they might eventually die out. Like the institution of the monarchy, monasticism had become another *ancien régime* institution restored in all but name.

Napoleon was meanwhile planning the centralization of authorized female communities, a project that began with the 1805 appointment

33 See, for example, the discussion of the importance of religious education in Paris, AN, F/19/6247, 'Rapport général sur toutes les associations de dames charitables existantes actuellement dans l'Empire' (30 October 1807).

34 See, for example, Paris, AN, F/19/6256, 'Statuts des Sœurs de la Visitation' (1 May 1806).

35 See, for example, a complaint from Cardinal Fesch about investigations into the 'interior regimes' of female communities. Paris, AN, F/19/6247 (Fontainebleau, 11 November 1807).

36 Ibid., 'Rapport général sur toutes les associations de dames charitables existantes actuellement dans l'Empire' (30 October 1807).

37 Ibid.

of his mother, known as Madame Mère, as the official protector of the Sisters of Charity and other nursing sisters. Napoleon had long been concerned by the number and variety of female religious communities and disliked the fact that they were involved in such similar activities.[38] He now envisaged their unification under the Sisters of Charity, imagining a type of army of nuns to staff the nation's hospitals and charitable institutions.[39] Portalis senior warned against this proposal, stressing the unique history and identity of each community.[40] Above all, he believed that 'where a religious institution is concerned, it would kill the institution to separate it from what makes its soul.'[41] Despite this advice, the plan continued to circulate and became one of the main points of discussion at the meeting Napoleon called in Paris in 1807 for all authorized communities.

The General Chapter opened on 27 November 1807 in the hôtel of Madame Mère and closed on 2 December, the anniversary of Napoleon's coronation. The occasion was in many ways a publicity stunt, but for the sisters present it offered the opportunity to voice the concerns raised by their state-managed revival. Among these was the proposed unification to which, as Portalis had predicted, they strongly objected. Citing their differences in history, character and routines, they argued that 'fusion' would destroy the 'happy rivalry' between them that came from doing the 'same good by diverse means'.[42] The very point that irritated Napoleon was thereby presented by female religious communities as advantageous. The deputies also protested against being granted only provisional authorization, arguing that it made them feel merely 'tolerated and suffered'. This temporary status, they argued, discouraged potential members, put off donors, and damaged the 'zeal' of the faithful.[43] The sisters also used the meeting to request greater

38 Deries, *Congrégations religieuses*, 220.

39 Napoleon to Portalis, Letter No. 8749 (17 May 1805) in *Correspondance de Napoléon Ier* (Paris, 1958–70), 10: 519.

40 'Rapport à l'empereur sur les congrégations religieuses de femmes s'occupant du soin des maladies et des pauvres, 13 Prairial, An XIII' [2 June 1805] in Portalis, *Discours*, 480–94, at 488–91.

41 'Rapport à l'Empereur sur la nécessité de ne laisser établir dans l'état d'association religieuse qu'avec l'autorisation du gouvernement et après avoir pris connaissance de ses statuts [...] (24 fructidor an XIII)' [11 September 1805], in Portalis, *Discours*, 532–3.

42 Paris, AN, F/19/6247, 'Adresse à Sa Majesté l'Empereur des députés au Chapitre général des Sœurs de la Charité' (2 December 1807).

43 Ibid.

financial aid and to ask that the state put an end to the interference of hospital administrators in their professional and religious activities.

These concerns, championed in a report by Madame Mère, did not go unheeded.[44] A decree of 3 February 1808 granted numerous allowances and donations to all authorized communities and a circular sent by the Minister of the Interior attempted to clarify the role of hospital administrators.[45] Plans to unify different hospital congregations were temporarily discarded. The state thereby confirmed its commitment to the revival of these particular female communities while showing that it could be persuaded to do so on their terms.

It continued, however, to pursue centralization in other areas. Yet several projects to give the Ursulines sole responsibility for female education in France remained unrealized.[46] A project to unify those communities responsible for female imprisonment under the Refuge de Saint Michel similarly failed as the order's houses fought to keep their autonomy.[47] Again, the administration found itself forced to rescind its plans for centralization as female communities asserted their individual identities.

The problem came to a head with a schism amongst the Sisters of Charity after they finally received definitive authorization on 8 November 1809. This required that, like all authorized communities, they be placed under the spiritual direction of the local ecclesiastical authority. But the congregation had traditionally been directed by a male superior from the Lazarist congregation and when the current superior, abbé Hanon, protested, he was imprisoned. The Ministry's subsequent efforts to impose its policy produced a rupture in the congregation which lasted for two years, led to the departure of over fifty sisters, and was resolved only with the expulsion of 165 others. The new minister for ecclesiastical affairs, Félix-Julien Bigot de Préameneu, was forced to realize that he had misjudged the situation.[48] The episode again displays how the Napoleonic regime, in orchestrating the revival

44 Paris, AN, F/19/6247, 'Rapport de Madame sur le Chapitre général des Sœurs de la Charité' (27 November 1807).

45 Langlois, *Catholicisme au féminin*, 122 and 129.

46 See for example the project of February 1814, a draft of which remains in Paris, AN, F/19/6247.

47 Deries, *Congrégations religieuses*, 223.

48 Langlois, *Catholicisme au féminin*, 132–5. The documents concerning the affair are held in Paris, AN, F/19/6344.

of female religious communities, had underestimated the importance of tradition.

Increasingly unable to dictate the exact terms of the revival, Napoleon resorted to monitoring it with greater ferocity. This was partly achieved through the creation of the Petit Conseil in October 1807, charged with finding out everything there was to know about France's religious communities. In 1808, a major census was organized.[49] As relations with Rome deteriorated, police surveillance was increased to assess the loyalty of female communities. An 1811 report on thirty-nine known reunions in Paris claimed, for example, that the Carmelites were 'dangerous papists', while the Sisters of Charity were 'reasonably papist' but 'precious for humanity'.[50]

Although both authorized and unauthorized female communities would continue to be closely monitored and officially subject to the law, many were by now gathering enough momentum to take charge of their own growth. Authorizations increased after 1810 and already authorized communities continued to expand with state support. In 1810, the congregation of the Mère de Dieu, for example, requested and was granted a new building to accommodate its expanding noviciate.[51] By 1815, approximately 400 women were joining the religious life each year.[52]

In 1805, Portalis had warned Napoleon he would 'kill' religious institutions if he attempted to separate them from their souls.[53] The minister had, as usual, identified the crux of the issue, a fact witnessed two years later when the nuns that Napoleon called to Paris warned that state interference in religious matters would mean the death of their associations. As it happened, there were no brutal deaths for female communities, although some did fade away. Rather, a process of conciliation and tolerance unfolded on both sides which rested on the Napoleonic administration recognizing and permitting the diversity of female communities, albeit under strict surveillance.

49 Paris, AN, F/7/8071 and F/19/6293, 'État général des congrégations religieuses de femmes' (1808). The results are discussed in Boudon, *Napoléon*, 161–2.

50 Paris, AN, F/19/470, 'Etat des maisons ou réunions religieuses existantes dans Paris' (5 March 1811).

51 Paris, AN, F/19/471 [Letter to the Minister of the Interior] (27 July 1810).

52 Boudon, *Napoléon*, 162.

53 'Rapport à l'Empereur sur la nécessité de ne laisser établir dans l'état d'association religieuse qu'avec l'autorisation du gouvernement et après avoir pris connaissance de ses statuts [...] (24 fructidor an XIII)' [11 September 1805], in Portalis, *Discours*, 532–3.

The revival of female religious communities demonstrates the paradox created by a state that wanted to retain and secularize the services of religious communities but which wanted to bring these communities, like the Church, under its own control. Examining this revival reveals how both Napoleon and female religious communities were forced to address the unsolved problems of the Revolution, problems which raised questions of liberty of religious belief and practice, and of who, in a modern state, should be responsible for education, nursing, charity, and for shaping a moral society.

Peterhouse, University of Cambridge

THE RESURGENCE OF COLONIAL ANGLICANISM: THE COLONIAL BISHOPRICS FUND, 1840–1

by ROWAN STRONG

REVIVAL and resurgence is not simply something that happens to individuals or groups of persons; it is a phenomenon that takes place within organized communities, institutions, and societies. The Church has existed in history as an organized society of believers, and this institutional dimension of Christianity has frequently shaped Christian history and the influence of Christianity on wider society for better and worse. Indeed, it could be argued that this is the dimension of Christianity which has been most influential historically. However, in the case of the Church of England in the British Empire its organized influence as a Church was seriously curtailed by its restricted and partial institutional existence throughout the eighteenth century in the North American colonies. There it existed without a bishop to provide local leadership and an effective counterweight to local lay elites. When that situation reversed and the British state began to support colonial bishoprics after the loss of the thirteen colonies in the new United States of America, the Church of England remained largely at the mercy of fluctuating political agendas to supply colonial bishops with sufficient legality and infrastructure.[1] However, in the early 1840s the Church of England underwent a resurgence in the British Empire as a consequence of developing a new response to its metropolitan political situation, which initiated a revival in its colonial engagement.

In 1840 Charles Blomfield, Bishop of London, wrote a public letter to the archbishop of Canterbury, proposing the establishment of a fund to endow colonial bishoprics. It was time, he believed, that the Church of England undertook its own extension to the colonies of the empire and no longer left this to individuals. Blomfield maintained that it was still ostensibly the duty of a Christian government to attend to the spiritual needs of its colonies, but this duty, unfortunately, had not been effectively carried out. Sections of Parliament, he said, were now

1 See Rowan Strong, *Anglicanism and the British Empire c.1700–1850* (Oxford, 2007).

questioning the maintenance and extension of the Church of England as a state obligation and 'there does not appear to be much hope of our obtaining, at the present moment, in the actual state of the public revenue, any considerable aid from the national resources, for the purpose of planting and maintaining the Church of this country in its colonies'.[2] For Blomfield, planting the colonial Church of England had come to have a necessary episcopal character.

> [I]f we desire the good to be complete, permanent, and growing with the Church's growth, we must plant the Church amongst them in all its integrity. Each colony must have, not only its parochial, or district pastors, but its chief pastor, to watch over, and guide, and direct the whole. An episcopal Church, without a bishop, is a contradiction in terms.[3]

He envisaged a colonial pattern of settlement that was integrally Anglican, complete with a bishop from the first. 'Let every band of settlers, which goes forth from Christian England, with authority to occupy a distinct territory, and to form a separate community, take with it not only its civil rulers and functionaries, but its bishop and clergy.'[4] Blomfield remained convinced that although it was a requirement of the government of a Christian state both to maintain and extend Christianity in all its dominions that, nevertheless, the British government was now most unlikely to do so.[5] In the colonies themselves there was either a dearth of sufficient resources to provide for Anglican expansion, or a colonial indifference arising, in part, he believed, from that very situation of previous Anglican insufficiency on the ground. So, if the government shirked its duty then the Church had to take this up.[6] His proposed fund would be established specifically for the moderate endowment of bishops in British colonies by the purchasing of land there; it would be administered by the bishops of the Church of England; and it would be complementary to money raised in the colonies themselves.[7] It was now time for the Church of England to grasp the nettle of its own colonial future. Blomfield, by this time, was

2 Charles Blomfield, *A letter to His Grace the Lord Archbishop of Canterbury, upon the formation of a fund for endowing additional bishoprics in the colonies* (London, 1840), 4.
3 Ibid., 5.
4 Ibid., 7–8.
5 Ibid., 9–10.
6 Ibid., 11.
7 Ibid., 12–13.

already committed to church extension as a means of addressing the spiritual and material destitution of the urban masses of his vast diocese, with parishes becoming centres for Christian philanthropy.[8] As bishop of London the needs of the colonial Church inevitably came before him also because his see had traditional responsibility for colonial churches in the empire. No sooner did Blomfield see a need than he felt compelled to find a solution. He found his colonial solution in empowering the Church of England to act solely from its own resources to promote Anglicanism in the empire.

The letter resulted in a meeting of male Anglican lay and clerical worthies at Willis's Rooms in London on 27 April 1841 to commence the proposed fund. This public occasion was a platform for notable metropolitan Anglicans to publish their views on Anglicanism and empire. The chorus of voices was led off by the archbishop of Canterbury, William Howley, who drew attention to factors that militated against the development of colonial Anglicanism, chief of which was the absence of bishops in these territories for episcopal rites, discipline, and superintendence. 'A Church without a Bishop can hardly deserve the name of episcopal', Howley affirmed. He blamed current colonial lack of institutional Anglican provision on a number of factors, including the previous history of British inattentiveness to religion in the establishment of their colonies as compared with the French. As a consequence the Church of England declined while Dissent had grown in the American colonies. After the loss of these colonies 'the mistake was perceived', said Howley, so that the British government began to inaugurate colonial bishops in Canada, Nova Scotia, and the West Indies.[9] But now the Church would have to go it alone in imperial church extension. This was gentle criticism of government dereliction of its duty towards the national Church from a mild and conciliatory archbishop. But Howley, despite his almost innate conservatism, was also a realist who had come to understand the changed circumstances of the 1830s, perhaps through working with Blomfield.[10]

Blomfield followed Howley with a much more direct speech stating

8 Peter C. Hammond, *The Parson and the Victorian Parish* (London, 1977), 33; Stewart J. Brown, *The National Churches of England Ireland and Scotland 1801–46* (Oxford, 2001), 83.

9 *Proceedings at a meeting of the clergy and laity officially called by His Grace, The Lord Archbishop of Canterbury, and held at Willis's Rooms, 27th April, 1841, for the purpose of raising a fund towards the endowment of additional colonial bishoprics* (London, 1841) [hereafter: *Proceedings*], 3–4.

10 Edward Carpenter, *Cantuar: the Archbishops and their Office* (London, 1971), 290–9.

that this plan for colonial bishops was a virtual confession of past neglect by the partnership of Church and state, albeit this had been reversed in the past twenty-five years.

> But I know, also, that the results which have followed from what has already been done, are such as will increase our condemnation if we do no more. The neglect . . . of a century and a half lost us our American provinces. The pious and charitable efforts of the last few years have enabled us to confer with safety the invaluable boon of liberty upon the slave population of our colonies; for I believe, in my conscience, that if Episcopacy had not been established in the West Indies, it would have been, I will not say impracticable, but far more dangerous than happily it has been found to be, to discharge that vast debt of justice and mercy.[11]

Blomfield proposed the first resolution for the meeting, 'That the Church of England, in endeavouring to discharge her unquestionable duty of providing for the religious wants of her members in foreign lands, is bound to proceed upon her own principles of Apostolical order and discipline'. Asking who it was should discharge that duty, he upheld the traditional Anglican view that this was undoubtedly the responsibility of a Christian state.

> Let us leave the State to consider its duty; let *us* be diligent and faithful in performing ours. That it is, indeed, the duty of the State, of every Christian State, as administering one province of God's universal empire, to provide that all its subjects should have the full enjoyment of their Christian privileges and means of performing their Christian duties, – and in order thereto, to send out from time to time an adequate supply of labourers into the Lord's harvest, – I shall ever be forward to contend. We have only to look at the fruits which have been gathered from that harvest-field, where it has been duly cultivated, and at the briars and noxious weeds which overspread its surface where it has been neglected, to convince us, that, if the full and complete discharge of this duty on the part of the State would have drawn largely upon the country's resources, the non-performance of that duty has occasioned it an expenditure of tenfold the amount.[12]

11 *Proceedings*, 6.
12 Ibid., 7.

As episcopacy was 'essential to the perfectness of the Church' it was therefore culpable that Britain had not extended this principle to her overseas churches compared with the missions of the Roman Catholic Church. The state had repeatedly refused this request of the Church over the past century and a half. But now there were requests coming not just from the Church in England but also from the colonial churches themselves. It demonstrated that this want of bishops was global because British dominions now extended over all the earth. The obligation for such a worldwide episcopal provision was especially accentuated for the Church of an imperial nation.

> It is impossible for any one, who has considered the nature of the case, not to perceive that the Church of this country, the reformed Church of a country entrusted by Divine Providence with an empire of unprecedented magnitude, whose commerce is extended to the utmost parts of the globe, whose language now begins to be spoken in the remotest regions of the earth, a Church whose members are wafted over seas unknown to our forefathers: – that such a Church must be in the highest sense of the term a Missionary Church.[13]

This colonial extension of the episcopal Church of England was not principally a missionary obligation discharged by missionary societies, but rather was the responsibility of the Church itself regardless of what the state did, or did not do, about it.

Henry Thomas Pelham, third earl of Chichester, in seconding Blomfield's resolution, also saw it as a means to rectify the neglect of Anglican extension in British history which had resulted in 'the moral and religious destitution of the British Colonies'. Pelham was a Whig and an Evangelical who was one of the Ecclesiastical Commissioners until 1878 and President of the Church Mission Society (CMS) for half a century.[14] The continued dereliction of religion resulted in 'a state of things most adverse to the mere civil prosperity of the Colonies, and to the stability of their connexion with his country'. 'Some imperial bond greater than mere commerce was required; some connecting moral principle, stronger than has yet existed, to attach the inhabitants of our

13 Ibid., 12.

14 G. Le G. Norgate, rev. H. C. G. Matthew, 'Pelham, Henry Thomas, 1804–1866', ODNB, 15: 692–3.

vast and growing Colonies to their Mother Country'. For the earl this imperial unifying principle was the 'preservation of our common faith' and the establishment of its religious institutions, to whit, the national Church. Bishops were necessary if the faith and Church of the colonies was to be similar to that of Britain. The Church, in this instance, should be ready to lead the state, though it was the duty of both to provide for the religious needs of its people at home or abroad.[15]

The resolution having been passed unanimously, Justice Sir John Taylor Coleridge proposed a second one. 'That the want of Episcopal superintendence is a great and acknowledged want in the religious provisions hitherto made for many of the colonies and dependencies of the British Crown.'[16] The bishop of Winchester, the Evangelical Charles Sumner, seconded this resolution, asserting that as a nation Britain had not made the Christianizing of its colonies a priority, having done 'little or nothing' about it. 'We have sent, – I speak in a national sense, – we have sent out our ships, but we have not sent our religion. We have sent out our commerce, but we have not sent our religion . . . We have sent out our very crimes, but not our religion.' The nation had done little in the way of extending the Church of England to the empire and now that prospect looked as unlikely as ever. 'It is well known that it is the policy of the present day . . . to look upon all religious persuasions in our Colonial Dependencies with the same degree of favour'.[17]

John Labouchere[18] moved a third resolution which was agreed to unanimously, 'That the acquisition of new Colonies, and the formation of British communities in various parts of the world, render it necessary that an immediate effort should be made to impart to them the full benefit of the Church, in all the completeness of her ministry, ordinances, and government'. He wished he could give the government as much credit for promoting the spiritual welfare of the colonies as for their temporal, or for upholding the interests of the Church of England, but it had been very remiss in this respect. In doing so the government had overlooked 'one of the most efficient means of

15 *Proceedings*, 13–14.

16 Ibid., 15, 17.

17 Ibid., 18.

18 John was the brother of the more prominent Henry Labouchere who, until September 1841, was President of the Board of Trade in Lord Melbourne's cabinet.

ensuring the allegiance and attachment of the inhabitants of those colonies'.[19]

Britain had 'guardianship' over one-eighth of the world's population and one-eighteenth of the surface of the globe, Archdeacon Henry Manning reminded the assembly, and the providence of God had entrusted to Britain the responsibility of evangelizing these colonial populations. Britain held her empire on this evangelistic condition. Britain was falling into 'moral arrear' in its continued neglect of spiritual provisions for these populations. This ethical indebtedness could well result in what happened in the United States – the revolt of the colonies and the despoiling of the Church of England in revolution.[20] Manning also pointed to Australia. Penitential colonies were established there without any attention to the spiritual means of recovering the convicts.[21] He repeated the theme of imperial unity grounded in a common Anglicanism throughout the empire, but gave it a new twist of ensuring imperial longevity. An empire required unity with itself, but this would only come if the Church of England was enabled to export both its doctrine and its discipline so as to organize genuinely functioning colonial churches. If that were done then Britain would have a share in the perpetuity promised by Christ to his Church, with an empire founded upon a common religion as the glue of its unity.

> had we bound them [the former colonies of the United States] to us by sending forth amongst them the polity of the Church . . . though we might not yet have stood in the dominant relation of Mother Country to that great Colony, we might have knit that mighty land to us in such a bond of peace as would have defied all that interest could do to render us asunder, and to bring us in collision.[22]

Still prepared at this time in his life, before his conversion to Roman Catholicism in 1851, to be publicly and aggressively confident of the divine and apostolic commission of the Church of England, Manning called for the Church of England to be spread across the globe because it had been given by God for the 'pure restoration of the one Catholic faith, which . . . holds forth the brightest light in Christendom'.[23]

19 *Proceedings*, 20–2.
20 Ibid., 24.
21 Ibid.
22 Ibid., 25.
23 Ibid.

William Gladstone submitted the next resolution. At the time he was the young Tory MP for Newark in the ultra-Tory Duke of Newcastle's interest and had just that month finished revising the fourth edition of his *The State in its Relations with the Church* which expressed his support for the Anglican confessional state.[24] The work was an exposition of the Church-state partnership paradigm that had operated in Anglican ecclesiastical, political, and imperial circles since at least the early eighteenth century. Originally written in 1838 Gladstone's book was, as H. C. G. Mathew has pointed out, 'probably the last point at which a general defence of Anglican hegemonic nationalism could be attempted'.[25] Gladstone affirmed that the state was a moral entity that had a duty to uphold religious truth and therefore to require conformity to that truth which was enshrined in the divinely instituted Church of England. David Bebbington has drawn attention to Gladstone's Notebooks for 1835 where the young politician encapsulated this argument as a series a propositions which later would be enshrined in his book.

> That government is not an optional but a natural institution.
> That governments are human agencies: rational: collective: and of functions sufficiently influential for good or evil to render them responsible to God.
> If they have a moral being, they must also have a religious profession.
> That where there is unity of government, there must be unity of this religious profession.
> That this unity need not rigorously apply to circumstantials, even of importance, but of substance.
> That it would be absolutely broken were the same government of the same kingdom to maintain & profess in one part of it a form of Christianity which anathematised that which it maintains in another.[26]

24 H. C. G. Mathew, *Gladstone 1809–1874* (Oxford, 1988), 40–3. Gladstone had already established himself as having a public interest in the colonies, and was, briefly, during the government in Sir Robert Peel, Under-Secretary of State at the Colonial Office for two months in 1835. In subsequent years, as an opposition MP, he spoke regularly in the Commons on colonial affairs, an interest probably stimulated by his father's West Indian estates. In 1845 Peel would appoint him Colonial Secretary. David W. Bebbington, *William Ewart Gladstone: Faith and Politics in Victorian Britain* (Grand Rapids, MI, 1993), 105.

25 Mathew, *Gladstone*, 41.

26 Bebbington, *The Mind of Gladstone: Religion, Homer, and Politics* (Oxford, 2004), 55–6.

For Jonathan Clark, Gladstone's book was the 'obituary notice' of the old regime.[27] Indeed, Gladstone's political leader, Sir Robert Peel, was horrified at the impractical politics it now represented.[28]

So the Gladstone of 1841 was still an ultra-Tory and a High Churchman who was only just beginning a transition through that decade toward a more moderate conservatism, and from a (now) old-fashioned High Church establishmentarianism towards Tractarianism. Consequently, in 1841, he continued to uphold that the exclusive contract between the Church of England and the state held true abroad where, aside from the equally established Church of Scotland, no assistance should be given by the British government to other churches or faiths.[29] Gladstone, on the verge of a decade of intellectual and theological change, maintained the Church of England was essentially an autonomous, true, and divine community, and therefore was the only proper partner for the state in England which, as a moral entity, was to be concerned with the upholding of truth. Accordingly, Gladstone affirmed at the 1841 public meeting that the temporal connections between colonies and metropolis could be augmented by 'ties of spiritual brotherhood'.[30] He considered it was not an obligation primarily for the colonists themselves because it took some time before colonial prosperity, either as individuals or as a colony, was sufficient for the purpose. The majority of colonists were from the labouring classes, without capital, and almost completely caught up in a battle with the land for subsistence.[31] If the Church was to wait until colonists' prosperity had risen sufficiently for them to invest in religion they may already have fallen into a habit of religious neglect. The Church needed to bridge this gap between colonial disability and ability if the habits of religion were to be kept alive in the colonial context. Gladstone also posited that if the time should come when colonies became independent then former colonies would only maintain their connections with Britain if previous imperial foundations 'were deeply laid in the recognition and maintenance of a common faith'.[32] Gladstone encapsulated the feeling of the Anglicans at the meeting about the demise of

27 J. C. D. Clark, *English Society 1660–1832: Religion, Ideology and Politics during the ancien regime* (2nd edn, Cambridge, 2000), 561.

28 Donald Read, *Peel and the Victorians* (Oxford, 1987), 134.

29 Bebbington, *Mind of Gladstone*, 56.

30 *Proceedings*, 26.

31 Ibid., 27.

32 Ibid., 28.

the previous relationship in the empire between the British state and the Church of England.

> And therefore much as has been said of the duty of the State with regard to this matter, – a duty up to this moment so partially fulfilled, and ardently as I long to see the day when that duty shall be more adequately recognised, yet I do not scruple to utter a sentiment in which I am sure I shall carry with me universal concurrence, that we should lament to see the State in such sort charging itself with the fulfilment of these sacred obligations, as to make the provision for the religious wants of the Colonies altogether a mechanical, or altogether a legal matter, and thus depriving the members of the Church amongst us of the opportunity of bringing their free-will offerings into the treasury of God.[33]

The same year, 1841, not only saw the launch of the Colonial Bishoprics Fund, but also a declaration by the bishops of the United Church of England and Ireland on colonial bishops as a consequence of that fund; and also the passing of the Colonial Bishops Act. The declaration was largely the bishops' public acceptance of responsibility for administering the fund established just the previous month. However, it also contained a statement about the Church of England and the colonies generally; that 'insufficient provision' had been made for her members overseas which now required the Church of England's assistance in the form of colonial bishoprics to be established in thirteen parts of the empire, beginning with New Zealand, but also including South Australia, Port Philip, and Western Australia. The bishops thought it unwise to proceed 'without the concurrence of her majesty's Government' and so appointed a Standing Committee of their number with powers to confer with ministers.[34] As a consequence, later that same year Parliament passed the Colonial Bishoprics Act (5 Vict., c. 6) which gave legislative authority to the Church of England to create bishops for the colonies in keeping with the purpose and intent of the fund and the declaration, although legislating bishops for British subjects rather than missionary purposes strictly speaking.[35] Also in 1841, the bench of bishops of the Church of England became vice-presidents of the CMS,

33 Ibid., 29.

34 R. P. Flindall, *The Church of England, 1815–1948: a Documentary History* (London, 1972), 94–7.

35 Ibid., 98–100.

so bringing together the Church and the most active and extensive Anglican missionary society; that society having already agreed that the hierarchy of the Church of England should be the final arbiter in any dispute between itself and colonial bishops.[36]

Therefore, in the early 1840s leading national Anglican figures in Church, politics, the judiciary, and among the aristocracy were publicly advocating the Church of England initiate its own programme of colonial church extension, quite apart from the state. In doing so they were publicly critical of the state for not maintaining what they understood to be its proper concern to support the national Church in the colonies. Although they were mindful of such support in recent decades, it was apparent to them by this time that this period of a renewed state-Church alliance in the empire was not going to be sustained. This acceptance of the finitude of state assistance for the Church of England, and the consequent resolutions to act autonomously in promoting a colonial Anglicanism, were new aspects of the Anglican discourse on empire in the early years of the 1840s.

These public statements in the early 1840s constituted rare and direct criticism of the state offered by Anglican pillars of the establishment, although it was couched in less than fiery terms. Speaker after speaker at the 1841 meeting had something to say about how the state had deserted its religious obligations to the Church of England, despite the reinvigoration of that alliance in the past few decades. Blomfield in his public letter of 1840 had stated that there did not seem much hope of Parliament supporting any longer the colonial planting of the Church of England, although he remained convinced that it was a duty of Britain as a Christian state to do so. Archbishop Howley pointed out that the British government had provided for an Anglican establishment in its Canadian colonies as a consequence of the rebellion and loss of its remaining North American ones. The implication from this cautious High Churchman that this lesson should continue to be learned was there for all to draw. Other speakers were more explicit. The Earl of Chichester urged the Church to lead the state in this regard, though it was undoubtedly the duty of both to provide for domestic as well as colonial religious needs. For Bishop Sumner the prospect that the state would again privilege the Church of England in the colonies

36 C. Peter Williams, *The Ideal of the Self-Governing Church: a Study in Victorian Missionary Strategy* (Leiden, 1990), 14.

rather than all denominations looked dismally unlikely to change, leaving the Church to do her duty unaided. Labouchere also regarded the government as having been inattentive in this colonial duty, thereby risking the future allegiance of its colonies; while for Manning that dereliction placed Britain in moral indebtedness to the colonies. Gladstone, still a Tory, was unambiguous in stating that the maintenance and extension of colonial religion was a duty of the whole nation and not just the Church, which the state until then had only 'partially fulfilled' but which should be 'more adequately recognised'.[37] So all the principal speakers at the launch of this new colonial initiative by the Church of England were united in lamenting the demise of the state's involvement in the transplantation of their Church in British possessions overseas. All were equally sure that the present situation was unlikely to change. As a consequence, they supported this move by the Church of England to assume greater responsibility for its own colonial development without the support of the state.

P. J. Welch in the 1960s believed that the co-operation between the state and the Church of England continued to be strong into the 1840s, despite some disagreements over practical politics in this decade, based on his assessment of the close working relationship between the Prime Minister, Sir Robert Peel, and Bishop Blomfield. However, even Welch's own evidence demonstrated that the disagreements between Church and state were substantive, including the failure to retain the separate bishoprics of Bangor and St Asaph notwithstanding the overwhelming support of the bench of bishops; and the lack of political support for the maintenance of parliamentary grants for church extension.[38] Rather than the old co-operation, the criticism of the state expressed publicly at the launch of the Colonial Bishoprics Fund and the assumption of greater colonial activism by the Church of England represented a watershed response to the situation the Church found itself in by the 1840s. This was a realistic acknowledgement of developments of the 1820s and '30s, a period which has been called a 'constitutional revolution' by Geoffrey Best,[39] and the 'end of the Protestant Constitution' and the old order by Jonathan Clark.[40]

37 *Proceedings*, 29.

38 P. J. Welch, 'Blomfield and Peel: a Study in Co-operation between Church and State, 1841–1846', *JEH* 12 (1961), 71–84.

39 Geoffrey Best, 'The Constitutional Revolution 1828–1832, and its Consequences for the Established Church', *Theology* 52 (1959), 226–34.

40 Clark, *English Society*, ch. 6.

Between 1828 and 1832 the Church of England lost its hegemonic status in England as a result of the passing of the repeal of the Test and Corporation Acts in 1828 legally disbarring Dissenters from public office, the Catholic Emancipation Act in 1829, and the Reform Act enfranchising a portion of the middle classes, the level of society where Dissent was strongest. These were elemental changes to what was encapsulated in the concept of the 'Protestant Constitution' by which Anglicanism, monarchy, and an aristocratic social order provided the prevailing set of ideas that constituted the ideological framework of English political, cultural, and social life throughout the long eighteenth century. Of these ingredients, Clark argues, Anglicanism constituted the most significant and influential; so much so that he believes England constituted a confessional state during this period in that, while other religious bodies existed and were agreed to exist legally, they were only tolerated and never formally permitted to enter the political institutions and offices of the state. It was this hegemonic relationship which can be clearly seen in the colonial policy of the British government since the loss of the North American colonies whereby the Church of England was actively introduced into colonies and supported by endowment in India, as also in Canada and the West Indies. This colonial endowment was an imperial mirror image of the same official support for the established churches domestically, as in the parliamentary grants in 1818 and 1824 for church extension in England and Scotland.[41] After 1815, according to Clark, with social unrest increasing the Church of England became even more important as the guarantor of social and constitutional order and concurrently came under attack from those excluded from that system.[42] To upholders of the status quo the Church alone appeared to be able to provide the requisite theoretical and ideological counter to the theorists of Dissent and revolution. Old Dissent was associated with pro-revolutionary positions and this, and its individualism, made its nationalism and patriotism very conditional. New Dissent was conservative but placed the nation and nationalism very much after a converted Christianity and conscience that knew no national boundaries in its fellowship of the converted. But the old Anglican theology provided a basis for civil society that qualified individualism by the greater impor-

41 Stewart J. Brown, *The National Churches of England, Ireland, and Scotland* (Oxford, 2001), 68–72.

42 Clark, *English Society*, 421–8.

tance of communal Christianity and church allegiance.[43] So the Anglican theorist John Bowles, a High Church layman, could comment even in 1815 that the constitutional order of the country was 'composed of two distinct establishments, the one civil, the other ecclesiastical, which are so closely interwoven together, that the destruction of either must prove fatal to both'.[44]

Bishop Blomfield, who initiated this drive for greater colonial autonomy by the Church of England, had himself previously been a proponent of the old regime. Born in 1786, he rose to the episcopal bench as bishop of Chester in 1824. During that episcopate he was an opponent of Catholic emancipation on the basis that as heretics they had no place in the Protestant Constitution of England. He did, though, favour the repeal of the Test and Corporation Acts, but not from any large sympathy for Dissenters but on the basis that using the Sacrament of Holy Communion as a political test was a profanation which the Church of England clergy could well do without.[45]

It was the union with Ireland in 1801 and the incorporation of 100 Irish MPs into Westminster that eventually led in 1829 to Catholic emancipation as the catalyst for the end of this old order, and brought an end to the Anglican hegemony within it. In its place came a storm of anti-clericalism and anti-church militancy as a consequence of the Church of England's belated and unhappy opposition to political reform.

But while there was Anglican lamenting in the late 1820s and early 1830s at the passing of the old ways,[46] the ultimate response of the Church of England to this fundamental alteration in its place in English society and its alliance with its rulers was to assert its own independence now that the state had deserted its responsibilities towards the Church. As evidence of this Clark points to the Tractarian Movement of the 1830s and '40s, and to a growing ecclesiastical assertiveness among the younger generation of High Churchmen, such as Walter

43 William Stafford, 'Religion and the Doctrine of Nationalism in England at the Time of the French Revolution and the Napoleonic Wars', in Stuart Mews, ed., *Religion and National Identity*, SCH 18 (Oxford, 1982), 382–95.

44 Clark, *English Society*, 433.

45 Malcolm Johnson, *Bustling Intermeddler? The Life and Work of Charles James Blomfield* (Leominster, 2001), 27–9.

46 For example, the annual anniversary sermon to the Society for the Propagation of the Gospel in Foreign parts by George Murray, Bishop of Rochester, *A Sermon* (London, 1832), 12–13.

Hook, Vicar of Leeds.[47] But evidence for a new Anglican assertiveness can also be found in the episcopal preachers of the Society for the Propagation of the Gospel in Foreign Parts during the 1830s. In 1835 Richard Bagot, bishop of Oxford, while deploring that the government of a Christian nation should have withdrawn its support for the Society, called on his hearers to fill the gap left by the government. It was, he said, 'our duty as Christians to increase our private and individual exertions, proportionally to such a loss, in every practicable way', and he proposed parish committees to encourage lay involvement with the Society and the increase of 'smaller donations'.[48] The next year, the bishop of Gloucester and Bristol drew attention to the fact that 'at the very moment' when North American emigration increased, annual grants of public money for the Church of England in those colonies was withdrawn. Ultimately, he foretold, this would have a deleterious effect on imperial unity for 'no bond of union is so strong between distant nations as that of a common faith and a common worship'. The remedy he also called for was greater support for the Society among churchmen at home.[49] The feisty Henry Phillpot of Exeter as preacher in 1838 managed to make his point in a backhanded way by disclaiming any intention to 'charge our rulers with neglecting their first duty' because this was not such an occasion. The government was ready, he professed, to perform this duty but it was 'deterred by the unrighteous, the unchristian clamour against every expenditure which has religion for its object, especially if it be in that form which the laws of the land recognize as true'. If the government would but realize that they too would face the judgement of God he was sanguine they would recall their duty and unite in reversing the present policy of putting 'National Piety on a short allowance'.[50]

The drive for imperial self-sufficiency by the Church of England in the early 1840s must be placed alongside these statements of the 1830s, and its more recognized domestic responses as part of this watershed in the development of Anglicanism in response to the demise of the old order. The 1840s were, as Hans Cnattingius identified in 1952, the turning point of change for Anglicanism whereby it evolved into 'a World Church'. It was change that had already been foreshadowed

47 Clark, *English Society*, 359–60.
48 Richard Bagot, Bishop of Oxford, *A Sermon* (London, 1835), 9–10.
49 James Monk, Bishop of Gloucester and Bristol, *A Sermon* (London, 1836), 12–13.
50 Henry Phillpot, Bishop of Exeter, *A Sermon* (London, 1838), 13–14.

outside Britain and the empire in the 1830s with the idea mooted in 1835 by Bishop George Washington Doane of New Jersey for missionary bishops to lead, rather than follow, missionary outreach. These ideas were picked up by Bishop Samuel Wilberforce and Bishop Blomfield in the late 1830s.[51] The catalyst for this greater initiative by the Church of England towards missionary expansion has been ascribed by Cnattingius to a demand within that Church stimulated by the Oxford Movement, and to the *rapprochement* between the CMS and the bishops. But this is to ascribe too much to the Church, and not enough to the fundamental paradigm shift that dethroned Anglicanism from its hegemonic position in the years 1828 to 1832. Change was forced upon the Church which took a decade to embrace it. It also attributes too much to the Oxford Movement which, as a consequence of increasing Roman Catholic sympathies and Newman's *Tract XC* was, in the early 1840s, a more marginalized movement within Anglican circles of power, looked at by Evangelicals and High Churchmen with suspicion and hostility.[52]

The episcopal foundation for colonial Anglicanism was not agreed to by all metropolitan Anglicans; the CMS and its innovative secretary, Henry Venn, being the major exceptions. Venn strongly believed that bishops were for the consolidation of a missionary church once it was established, rather than being part of the initial evangelistic thrust. The conflict between these two ideals came to a head in the 1850s in India.[53] However, this distinction should not be exaggerated, as Venn was not anti-episcopal. He agreed to the alteration in the CMS structure which made the bishops the final arbiters in its disputes, and that missionary Anglican Churches should be episcopal, even to being at the forefront of agitating for a native, rather than European, episcopate. It was more an argument about precisely when that episcopal structure was to be in place, at the very commencement of a mission or subsequently, rather than any dispute over episcopacy as such. Both Anglican sides affirmed an episcopal church; their dispute was over just when that episcopacy should be instituted in new churches.

In the early 1840s a new imperial paradigm for the Church of

51 Hans Cnattingius, *Bishops and Societies: a Study of Anglican Colonial and Missionary Expansion, 1698–1850* (London, 1952), 200–6.

52 Frank Turner, *John Henry Newman: the Challenge to Evangelical Religion* (New Haven, CT, 2002), chs 7 and 8.

53 Williams, *Ideal of the Self-Governing Church*, 9–21.

England was created from within the central power structures of the Church itself. It was a new way of being Anglican imperially that evidently caught the imagination of some very significant Anglicans in England. The fabulously wealthy Angela Burdett Coutts, heiress to the Coutts banking fortune, gave £35,000 in 1845 to endow the new dioceses of South Australia and Cape Town, and £50,000 in 1858 to endow a bishopric in British Columbia when that became a crown colony.[54] The new imperial paradigm was the initiative of the bishop of London who was probably the most powerful and active bishop at the time, notwithstanding the two archbishops. It had the support of other principal Anglicans, both lay and clerical, and from the rising generation in Church and state such as Gladstone and Manning. A new Anglican imperial paradigm arose at this time because these influential and mainstream Anglicans understood only too well that the old one was defunct and most unlikely to rise again from its political grave. Blomfield's initiative with regard to the Colonial Bishoprics Fund provided these Anglicans with the requisite practical direction in a paradigm shift for Anglicanism to adapt to the new domestic and imperial reality which now left it without its former hegemonic status in the British metropolitan and colonial world. It was one in which episcopacy was now to be the basis for a global Anglicanism. Bishops would now be indispensable to colonial Anglicanism, their presence guaranteed and resourced by the Colonial Bishoprics Fund; and not just for British colonies but wherever significant numbers of Anglicans were to be found. Consequently, the fund also proposed to endow a bishopric for Anglicans in Europe,[55] and the bishop in Jerusalem, that Newman so opposed because it was a combined project with Lutherans, was to ensure the genuinely episcopal character of a future Anglican Church in the Holy Land.[56] Now that the Church of England was conscious of its need to act autonomously, it was no longer prepared to subjugate or suppress its episcopal character as it had done in the North American colonies for most of the eighteenth century. The new paradigm was for a deliberately and consciously episcopal Anglican Church as a given for colonial Anglicanism. The Church of England had bowed to the inevi-

54 Diana Orton, *Made of Gold: a Biography of Angela Burdett Coutts* (London, 1980), 105, 185.

55 'Declaration of a meeting of archbishops and bishops, held at Lambeth, on Tuesday in Whitsun week 1841', in Flindall, *Church of England*, 95.

56 Turner, *John Henry Newman*, 395–7.

table that the British Empire was now no longer likely to be an Anglican one, but was determined that, by its own actions, a revived Anglicanism would be more consciously engaged with the empire than ever before.

Murdoch University

THE OXFORD MOVEMENT AS RELIGIOUS REVIVAL AND RESURGENCE

by PETER B. NOCKLES

IT was 'one of the most wonderful revivals in church history', to be compared to the religious revival in the 'days of Josiah towards the close of the Jewish monarchy'.[1] This extravagant comment referred not to the Evangelical Revival of the eighteenth century, that paradigm of all religious revivals, but to something which the author, writing in 1912, characterized as 'the Catholic Revival'.

The idea of a revival or resurgence in either the individual soul or the life of the Church as a whole is as old as Christian history. Yet in the vast recent explosion of scholarship on the subject of religious revival, the term itself and whole framework of discussion continues to be applied primarily to Protestant Evangelicalism. While religious resurgence has not been tied to a specific theological or denominational tradition, religious revival (which is often classified in terms of a hierarchy of significance from 'Awakenings' downwards) and especially 'revivalism' (a term used to describe religious movements of enthusiasm) has tended to become synonymous with Evangelicalism.

A sophisticated series of tests or criteria for revival or revivalism has been developed and refined by historians of Evangelicalism working at the 'coalface' of eighteenth- and nineteenth-century (and sometimes) later sources. However, I hope that there is still room to view and discuss religious revival within a different religious tradition which never surrendered its right to claim the term and concept as its own. In their introduction to a stimulating edition of essays *On Revival: a Critical Examination* (2003), Andrew Walker and Kristin Aune suggest that it is time to reconfigure the term 'revival' to include the regeneration of all religions and religious traditions.[2] In this spirit, I hope to recover and reapply the term 'religious revival' to a well-known religious movement emanating from within the nineteenth-century Church of England (though with ramifications far beyond that

[1] H. P. Denison, *The Catholic Revival: a Retrospect and a Warning* (Bath, 1912), 11.

[2] A. Walker and K. Aune, eds, *On Revival: a Critical Examination* (London, 2003), introduction, xxiii.

communion), which is commonly viewed as standing for everything which Evangelicals and Evangelical 'revivalists' detested as a 'revival of Popery' – the Oxford Movement. A brief study of the Oxford Movement in the context of the theme of the present volume will reveal the extent to which 'revival' and 'revivalism' remained contested terms and by no means the monopoly of one religious tradition.

The commencement of the Oxford Movement is historically dated from 1833 with its classic phase extending only to 1845, the year of Newman's conversion to Roman Catholicism. Some date its *terminus ante quem* to what many regarded as that cataclysmic event or, in Dean Church's words, 'the catastrophe'.[3] However, among second or third generation Tractarians the idea of a 'Catholic' or 'Church Revival' encompassing a broader time span and involving something wider than the twelve years of the Oxford or academic phase of the Movement had taken root by the 1860s. That this movement initially represented and saw itself as a resurgence of a particular theological tradition within Anglicanism, that of High Churchmanship, is not contentious. However, to present it as a religious revival might be regarded as problematic. Yet the number of histories of the Oxford Movement published between that decade and the 1930s, with the phrase 'revival' in their title is indeed striking. This usage, in fact, can be dated to as early as 1840 when Samuel Francis Wood, one of the relatively minor figures in the Tractarian firmament, drew up a document (now in the Borthwick Institute, York) entitled *The Revival of Primitive Doctrine*.[4] Wood's use of the term 'revival' in this context is significant, as is the evidence for his original title of 'high church revival', crossed out on the Borthwick manuscript copy.

In what senses then did the leaders of the Oxford Movement regard what they were doing as instigating a religious revival? The early Tractarians certainly claimed to be reviving the principles, teaching,

3 R. W. Church, *The Oxford Movement: Twelve Years, 1833–1845* (London, 1892), ch. 19.

4 Fr James Pereiro discovered and identified this document in the papers of the Borthwick Institute and it has been included in an appendix to a recent publication by him. I owe this reference to him. See York, Borthwick Institute, Halifax Papers, Box A2 42.3, S.F. Wood, *The Revival of Primitive Doctrine* [1840]. Samuel Francis Wood (1809–43), matriculated from Oriel College in February 1827 and was one of the last fruits of Newman's tutorial methods before they were ended by Provost Hawkins. He was the second son of Sir Francis Lindley Wood, Bart. His elder brother, Charles, became the first Viscount Halifax. For Fr Pereiro's edition of Wood's manuscript, see J. Pereiro, *'Ethos' and the Oxford Movement: At the Heart of Tractarianism* (Oxford, 2007), 252–65. See also 40–2, and esp. 65–71, for further discussion of the Oxford Movement as a religious revival to which the author is indebted.

and practices of the early Church and of the seventeenth-century Anglican or Caroline divines, principals on which they argued the Church of England was grounded, after a long period of decay and neglect in the 'desert' of the eighteenth century: a period when, according to Tractarian propagandists, only a 'faithful remnant' of orthodox clergy and laity had remained.[5] The Tractarians insisted that they were not introducing any new principles nor were they in any sense innovators. A distinction has been drawn between 'revival' and 'renewal', and the Tractarian programme might better be encapsulated by the latter term. The label that many Tractarians might have been happiest with (and which was famously applied to one of their supporters, Hugh James Rose) was that of 'restorers of the old paths',[6] but there was a dynamic principle also at work within Tractarianism and one which carried many of its followers far from the Movement's original moorings. Revival meant a recovery or restoration of tradition which involved sacramental, spiritual, and ultimately also liturgical and architectural dimensions, but in the context of the 1830s and 1840s this could seem like counter-revolution, and still more so at a later date with the restoration of sisterhoods and even monastic communities within the Church of England. It was widely recognized also that whereas at Oxford the Revival was essentially doctrinal, at Cambridge it was ecclesiological or architectural.

Before any revival of particular neglected doctrines such as Apostolical Succession and Tradition as a co-ordinate Rule of Faith or neglected practices such as fasting and almsgiving was attempted and propagated by the *Tracts for the Times*, Newman and Keble were convinced that the ground had been prepared by a poetical, spiritual, and intellectual revival. They had in mind the influence of the historical novels of Sir Walter Scott, the verse of the 'Lake Poets' Wordsworth, Southey, and Coleridge, and Coleridge's philosophy, along with the intellectual revival represented by the so-called Oriel *Noetics* such as Edward Copleston, Richard Whately, John Davison, and others. As Newman put it in an influential article in the *British Critic* in April 1839, their writings were 'a growing tendency to that character of mind and feeling of which Catholic doctrines are just the expression', and

5 See P. B. Nockles, *The Oxford Movement in Context: Anglican High Churchmanship, 1760–1857* (Cambridge, 1994), 3–6.

6 See J. W. Burgon, 'Hugh James Rose: Restorer of the Old Paths', *Lives of Twelve Good Men*, 2 vols (4th edn, London, 1889), 1: 116–295.

were evidence of a resurgence of the religious mind of the Church towards 'something deeper and truer than had been provided in the last [i.e. eighteenth] century'[7]. In short, intellectual, philosophical, and poetical resurgence and revival provided the seed-bed on which the theological resurgence and revival represented by Tractarianism could take root.

The growth in the terminology of 'Catholic Revival' and (from the 1890s onwards) of 'Anglican' or 'Church Revival', or even 'Anglo-Catholic Revival' owed something to an increasing 'Anglo-Catholic' wish to believe that the revival which originated in the Oxford of the 1830s represented something broader within the Church of England than the Oxford Movement itself. The attraction of this viewpoint was that the course and progress of the 'Catholic Revival' could be more readily presented as unaffected by the loss of Newman in 1845 and subsequent conversions to Rome. Therefore, its usage carried something of an 'agenda' of stressing the Anglican loyalty and continuity of the Oxford Movement at the expense of those from rival extremes who were arguing that its natural trajectory was always towards the Church of Rome.[8] As one writer from this standpoint, put it: far from signalling the end of the Movement, Newman's 'secession, tested as nothing else could have done, the soundness of the principles at the base of the Catholic Revival'.[9] In short, to privilege the term 'Catholic Revival' over that of the 'Oxford Movement' had the advantage of sidelining or downplaying the role of the wayward genius of John Henry Newman.

However, the application of the term 'Catholic Revival' to the contemporaneous revival in the English Roman Catholic Church, in itself enriched, if not inspired, by the Tractarian conversions to Rome, meant that the Anglo-Catholic appropriation of the term did not go unchallenged from English Roman Catholics. The term 'Anglican Revival', as used by the church historian J. H. Overton and later, by the Swedish commentator, Yngve Brilioth,[10] and that of the 'Anglo-

[7] J. H. Newman, 'Prospects of the Anglican Church', *Essays Critical and Historical*, 2 vols (London, 1871), 1: 268 (originally published as 'The State of Religious Parties', *British Critic* [April, 1839]).

[8] The convert Newman himself argued this line persuasively in his *Lectures on Certain Difficulties Felt by Anglicans in Submitting to the Catholic Church* (London, 1850).

[9] 'What Might Have Been', 'Cardinal Newman', Oxford, Magdalen College, Bloxam Papers, Ms. 306, 152.

[10] J. H. Overton, *The Anglican Revival* (London, 1897); Y. Brilioth, *The Anglican Revival: Studies in the Oxford Movement* (London, 1925).

Catholic Revival' and the 'Orthodox Revival' employed by Canon S. L. Ollard and C. B. Moss,[11] was a perhaps unconscious recognition of the contested nature of the term 'Catholic Revival' and the fact that it was so readily claimed by English Roman Catholic writers. Nonetheless, the terminology of 'Catholic Revival' also had its attraction for Anglo-Catholics as presenting a counterpoise to, or even completion or 'fulfilment' of, the Evangelical Revival of the preceding century. Nonetheless, the tendency of Evangelicals to monopolize the term and concept was not easily to be dislodged. What was at stake here was not simply radically differing concepts of what constituted a religious revival and above all, 'revivalism' (the very idea of which came under scrutiny from those within the 'Catholic' tradition), but the truth or falsehood of the religious doctrine on which the spiritual experience of revival was or ought to be based.

Religious revivals according to the Evangelical model tended to be particularly pronounced in regional localities (such as Cornwall, and parts of Wales and Scotland), and the main focus was on its effects on the soul of individuals. The emphasis has tended to be on 'revivalism' as much as revival, with revival viewed as a short-term phenomenon. In fact, the growing interest in and emphasis on religious revivals in this sense among Evangelicals may be a mark of failure rather than long-term success. Nonetheless, institutional aspects of revival have not been neglected in the Evangelical model.

One of the classic Evangelical definitions of religious revival and revivalism was set forth by Daniel Wilson, the younger, in 1851. One of his definitions was, 'a return of spiritual life to a languid church after a period of neglect or decline'.[12] An important element for Wilson was that of the Church as a whole being recalled to a sense of its spiritual mission. It cannot be denied that the institutional Church of England as a whole was spiritually awakened by the great Evangelical Revival of the eighteenth and early nineteenth centuries, even if much of the evangelical revivalist energy also fed into Methodism and the nonconformist churches. Moreover, sympathetic historians of the Oxford Movement might claim that Wilson's definition just noted manifestly applied to the revival which followed the rise of Tractarianism in 1833

[11] S. L. Ollard, *The Anglo-Catholic Revival* (London, 1925); C. B. Moss, *The Orthodox Revival, 1833–1933* (London, 1933).

[12] D. Wilson, jnr, *The Revival of Spiritual Religion the Only Effectual Remedy for the Dangers which now Threaten the Church of England* (London, 1851), 4.

and that it represented as much a reaction against the supposed spiritual aridity of the eighteenth century as did Evangelicalism. After all, one of Wilson's criteria for a true religious revival was that of the raising up of individuals as agents of revival endowed with special gifts.[13] The special gifts of Newman, Keble, Froude, and Pusey, as leaders of the Oxford Movement could be regarded as supplying this criteria. There would seem then to be much common ground here. However, High Churchmen and Tractarians, or at least their 'Anglo-Catholic' descendants, articulated a distinctive understanding of religious revival different from that of the classic Evangelical model as expounded by Daniel Wilson and by modern historians of Evangelicalism such as Mark Noll.[14] At the heart of the difference was the altogether greater emphasis on the corporate idea and life of the Church contained in the 'Catholic' model. It was a difference which was well articulated in many of the publications celebrating the centennial of the Oxford Movement in 1933.

For all the growth in 'regularity' and greater attention to Church order characteristic of the second or third generation of Anglican Evangelicals, a trend that has been well documented, High-Church critics insisted that the original Evangelical Revival itself was individualistic rather than institutional in its main focus. Such critics maintained that the primary attention of Evangelical revivalists was lavished on the soul of the individual rather than on his or her incorporation into the Divine community represented by the Church in its corporate capacity. For Anglo-Catholic writers celebrating the 'Catholic Revival', the Evangelical Revival had been flawed because 'so long as an individual was converted, the Evangelical appeared indifferent about the particular communion to which he might enlist'. In this respect, the Evangelical Movement of the eighteenth century was deemed to have lost 'the institutional idea' which 'the Puritanism of the sixteenth and seventeenth centuries' had retained and promoted.[15]

Those who pushed the idea of a 'Catholic Revival' in the nineteenth-century Church of England that encompassed but was by no means merely co-terminus with the Oxford Movement, viewed it in the

13 Ibid., 5.

14 See, for example, M. A. Noll, *The Rise of Evangelicalism: the Age of Edwards, Whitefield and the Wesleys* (Leicester, 2004).

15 W. J. Sparrow Simpson, *The History of the Anglo-Catholic Revival from 1845* (London, 1932), 10.

words of a leading Anglo-Catholic author writing at the time of the centenary of the Movement, as

> but one of a series of movements in which the Institutional and Sacramental and Ministerial aspects of Religion were set forth in the forefront of religious thinking.

Such movements were strictly defined as a series of endeavours, temporarily checked by 'a succession of reactions', 'to restore certain elements in the Church's faith and practice which had for the time become obscured'. This broad definition allowed for continuity with a Catholic Revival at the end of Queen Elizabeth's reign and more especially 'in the time of Bishop Andrewes and Archbishop Laud', discontinuity with a 'violent Protestant Reaction in Cromwell's time', and then renewed continuity with 'a Catholic Revival at the Restoration', followed by a further 'reaction' after the deprivation of the Nonjurors leaving the Church's 'future in the power' of latitudinarians.[16] However, this model (with its self-conscious definition of revival in terms of the 'institutional' and the 'sacramental') appeared to leave little or no room for any accommodation with the eighteenth-century Evangelical Revival. The same Anglo-Catholic author concluded that

> Protestantism in the early nineteenth century had largely lost belief in the Church as a supernatural institution transmitted from one century to another. It fixed attention on the first century as described in Scripture, and regarded the following centuries down to the sixteenth more or less as deviations from the Gospel. The History of the Church was constantly represented as departures from the mind of Christ.[17]

The 'Catholic Revival' then, according to the Anglo-Catholic model, as it had evolved by the end of the nineteenth century, was essentially regarded as a 'Church Revival' in direct antagonism to the individualist Protestant spirit of Evangelicalism.

Anglican Evangelical opponents of the Oxford Movement such as Daniel Wilson and Francis Close presented a diametrically counter model of religious revivalism based on a particular definition of doctrinal truth that no less sought to exclude the 'Catholic Revival' or 'Church Revival' model as a genuine religious revival. In his *Revival of*

16 Ibid., 9.

17 Ibid., 1–11.

Spiritual Religion (1851), Wilson was anxious to delineate the 'special marks' which he claimed would 'serve to distinguish' a 'genuine revival of religion' 'from spurious ones'. He clearly had the contemporary challenging phenomena of Tractarianism very much in mind. He was even ready to acknowledge the plausibility of current claims that it be recognized as a movement of genuine religious revival:

> The recent Romanising movement in our own Church has been designated by some as a religious revival, and in a certain sense it has been so. The subject of religion has attracted public attention. Its external duties have been more sedulously performed than formerly. There has been more activity among the clergy. Many acts of liberality and self-denial have been exhibited. Much earnestness and zeal for the interests of the church have been shown.[18]

However, Wilson insisted, these were, 'not necessarily the marks of a revived state of religious feeling. The Word of God gives us very different evidences by which to judge of it'.[19]

The grounds of Wilson's rejection of the claims of the 'Catholic Revival' or Oxford Movement were, unsurprisingly, doctrinal. Wilson's insistence that a 'deep sense of sin committed against God and lowliness and prostration of soul in the Church' as 'one of the first and hopeful marks of a genuine revival of religion',[20] might not seem to rule out Tractarianism and certainly not the characteristic preaching of Dr Pusey with its emphasis on the enormity of post-baptismal sin. However, Wilson was adamant that it did, because the Tractarians were 'dark' in their views of the Atonement and Justification by Faith alone. In short, a genuine religious revival was incompatible with the propagation of 'false doctrine'. Ironically, given the well-known Tractarian reaction against the rational 'evidence theology' form of religious apologetic associated with latitudinarian divines such as William Paley,

18 Wilson, *Revival of Spiritual Religion*, 5–6. Francis Close, Dean of Carlisle, and a prominent Evangelical, in spite of his virulent anti-Tractarian strictures, was also ready to concede the spiritual 'revival' dimension of Tractarianism and that Evangelicals needed to be unremitting in pursuit of holiness. See F. Close, *The "Catholic Revival"; or Ritualism and Romanism in the Church of England, illustrated from "The Church and the World": a paper read at the annual meeting of "The Evangelical Union of the Dioceses of Carlisle", printed and published at their request* (London, 1866).

19 Ibid., 6.

20 Ibid.

Daniel Wilson condemned Tractarianism as an obstacle, rather than agent, of religious revival because of its 'intellectualism'. Wilson regarded the emphasis on learning and what he called 'the idolatry of intellect' promoted by Tractarians as well as Broad-Churchmen as inimical to the simplicity of the Gospel and to a truly evangelical understanding of religious revival.[21] As Wilson put it,

> The Tractarian heresy, did not, I conceive, take its rise in a taste for forms and ceremonies as much as in a reverence for antiquity, a desire to exercise the reasoning powers, and indulge the habit of study by a research into fathers, and councils, and learned divines. This first gave the taste for medieval principles and practices.[22]

However, it is possible to get behind the hardened polemical positions outlined above, and find much in common between the Evangelical Revival and Oxford Movement. In many ways the Oxford Movement, like the Evangelical revival, was more a movement of the heart than of the head. As Owen Chadwick has concluded, it was 'primarily concerned with the law of prayer, and only secondarily with the law of belief'.[23] Above all, the corporate religious revival represented by Tractarianism depended upon or was at least indebted to the preceding revival of the religious lives of individuals represented by Evangelicalism. As is well known, many of the future Tractarians (such as the Wilberforce brothers) had been reared in Evangelical households. They, and others such as Mark Pattison and Walter Kerr Hamilton, feeling the doctrinal limitations of contemporary Evangelicalism and the spiritual limitations of contemporary 'high and dry' churchmanship, were actually drawn into Tractarianism by what Pattison called 'the inner force of an inherited pietism of an evangelical type'.[24] In this way, a form of Evangelical religious revivalism fed and transmuted into Tractarian spirituality. Moreover, many of those (such as Henry Edward Manning) who were not from Evangelical families came to embrace 'living religion' through contact with Evangelicals even while they at the same time took up High-Church doctrinal positions. In Manning's case, as James Pereiro has shown,

21 Ibid., 14.

22 Ibid., 14–15.

23 O. Chadwick, 'The Mind of the Oxford Movement', idem, *The Spirit of the Oxford Movement: Tractarian Essays* (Cambridge, 1990), 1.

24 See Brilioth, *Anglican Revival*, 167–8.

there was a conscious harnessing of a more 'subjective' Evangelical devotional fervour to his inherited 'objective' High-Church doctrinal position.[25]

In conclusion, the spiritual character and strength of the Oxford Movement owed much to the earlier Evangelical Revival. Indeed, a case has been made that Tractarianism was only one of several religious revival or resurgence movements of the late 1820s and 1830s. Timothy Stunt, David Bebbington and others have argued that many of the Oxford Evangelical seceders from the Church of England of this period, such as John Nelson Darby and Benjamin Wills Newton who helped establish the Plymouth Brethren, shared certain attitudes with the early Tractarians.[26] Bebbington goes further, arguing that the radical Evangelicals of the 1820s were 'not just similar to the Tractarians but were actually an earlier phase of the same movement that in the 1830s proliferated into many strands – including the Brethren and the Catholic Apostolic Church as well as Tractarianism'.[27]

Robert Wilberforce, who himself made the transition from Evangelical to Tractarian (and ultimately to Rome), Gladstone and several others, regarded both movements as essentially complementary or even 'companions', the one flowing out from and fulfilling the other.[28] Evangelicals themselves may have resented having their own revival viewed as a mere transition or staging post to a 'Catholic revival' which they regarded at best with suspicion, at worst as 'heresy'. Nonetheless, the Evangelical Revival had produced that essential preliminary resurgence of the spiritual life of the Church of England without which the Tractarian message might have fallen on stony ground and captured few hearts. In that strict spiritual sense, the one revival did indeed depend on the other. For even the most party-minded Tractarian apologists insisted that the 'Catholic revival' encompassed a revival of 'practical', 'inward' or 'personal religion' as well as a restoration of externals and structures and the economy of worship.[29]

[25] J. Pereiro, *Henry Edward Manning: an Intellectual Biography* (Oxford, 1998), 12–13, 16–17.

[26] T. Stunt, *From Awakening to Secession: Radical Evangelicals in Switzerland and Britain 1815–35* (Edinburgh, 2000), ch. 8, esp. 214–15; D. Bebbington, *Evangelicalism in Modern Britain: a History from the 1730s to the 1980s* (London, 1989), 94–6.

[27] Bebbington, *Evangelicalism in Modern Britain*, 96.

[28] R. I. Wilberforce, *The Evangelical and Tractarian Movements: a Charge Delivered to the Clergy of the Archdeaconry of the East Riding* (London, 1851), 10–11.

[29] J. H. Blunt, *What have thirty years of Church Revival done? Reprinted with additions and corrections, from "The Ecclesiastic", April 1861* (London, 1861), 13–15.

In the last resort, the Oxford Movement does not fall into the same category as that of the classic understanding of revival in the Evangelical tradition, whether large-scale or local. Yet in its effects and impact, it can be claimed as comparable to the Evangelical Great Awakenings of the eighteenth and early nineteenth centuries in its impact not only on the Church but to some extent on society at large. It represented a recapturing of the temper and *ethos* (a key Tractarian 'buzz' word) of a lost age of faith (the primitive and also medieval Church), a restoration to general use (in terms of doctrine, devotion, liturgy and worship) of beliefs and practices that had become rare. The Church in its corporate capacity and energy (diocesan structures and organizations) was strengthened and renewed, but at the cost of doctrinal disunity and party spirit. The elements of discontinuity and continuity represented by the Oxford Movement can be related to the distinction sometimes drawn between 'renewal' and 'revival' in recent studies on the subject. In his essay on ' "Revival" in the New Testament' in Walker and Aune's study *On Revival*, Max Turner has distinguished 'renewal' which, he argues, connotes 'continuity' and a 'strengthening of what gone before', from 'revival' which, he contends, tended to stress 'discontinuity' by connoting 'some dead (or exceedingly weak) existence brought back to vigorous life and health'.[30] The Oxford Movement arguably fulfilled both descriptions, with a dynamic tension between the two. However, the revival and resurgence of a distinctive religious tradition represented by the Oxford Movement has certainly left a contentious and divisive legacy.

John Rylands Library, University of Manchester

[30] M. Turner, ' "Revival" in the New Testament?', in Walker and Aune, eds, *On Revival*, 3–21, at 7.

CULTURE AND PIETY IN THE FAR WEST: REVIVAL IN PENZANCE, NEWLYN, AND MOUSEHOLE IN 1849

by D. W. BEBBINGTON

A brief but classic account of a Cornish revival is to be found in Salome Hocking's book *Some Old Cornish Folk*, published in 1903. Writing semi-fictionally but also semi-ethnographically about a number of years before, the author, herself sprung from Cornish Methodism, described the thronging penitents, the exuberant singing and the 'thrill of excitement' that went through the village. Crucially she commented on the circumstances. The revival, she explained, had arisen 'at a time when no one was thinking about it, and no special services were being held. It seemed to have nothing to do with the preacher either ...'[1] The event, she was suggesting, was entirely spontaneous. Although it was triggered by a young girl going forward to kneel as a convert below the pulpit, the subsequent stir was not the result of any earlier contrivance. The awakening was unexpected, not planned. Much of the writing about revivals – periodic episodes of religious enthusiasm attended by mass conversions in evangelical Protestantism – revolves around this distinction. Nineteenth-century advocates of revivals, in America as well as in the British Isles, contrasted the older pattern in which 'Christians waited for them as men are wont to wait for showers of rain' with the later way in which the episodes were promoted by 'systematic efforts'.[2] Subsequently historians have taken up the theme. John Kent, the leading commentator on English revivals of the Victorian era, while recognizing the existence of planning among some early nineteenth-century Methodists, places the dividing line between the prevalence of contagious spontaneity, and the use of devices to achieve conversions, after 1860. The

[1] Salome Hocking, *Some Old Cornish Folk* (1903; St Austell, 2002), 155, 154. On the book and its context, see Alan M. Kent, *Pulp Methodism: the Lives and Literature of Silas, Joseph and Salome Hocking, Three Cornish Novelists* (St Austell, 2002).

[2] Calvin Colton, *The History and Character of American Revivals of Religion* (London, 1832), 5, quoted by John Kent, *Holding the Fort: Studies in Victorian Revivalism* (London, 1978), 18.

mass urban evangelism of Dwight L. Moody and Ira D. Sankey in the 1870s was clearly of a different kind, pointing towards the methods of Billy Graham in the twentieth century, from the artless techniques of John Wesley's early preachers.[3] There was a shift over time from ingenuous unsophistication to deliberate professionalism.

The nature of the transition, however, is much less clearly illuminated in the secondary literature than might be hoped. What actually happened in revivals has been very little studied. All too often accounts of revivalism have tended towards the general. There has been a natural concern among those sympathetic to the practice of revival to stress the widespread extent of the phenomenon, often leading them to assemble a great deal of disparate material and not to make distinctions between different patterns of awakening.[4] Historians have usually been most interested in the causes of revival, often wanting to engage with the theories of E. P. Thompson about the relation of religious excitement to radical mobilization or the common view that awakenings have been symptoms of community dislocation or economic recession. In establishing (as it has been fairly firmly established) that no constant correlations exist between such political, social or economic factors and the emergence of revivals, commentators have necessarily looked for the common features of a large number of awakenings, whether at different times or in different places. Their work has aimed to generalize rather than to particularize. Yet it is only accounts of specific revivals that enable us to understand their ethos, and especially the balance between the unplanned and the contrived. The potential of a particularizing method is illustrated in a recent study by Ken Jeffrey of the revival of 1858 to 1862 in the north-east of Scotland, which shows that different styles with contrasting degrees of planning were proceeding in parallel in city, countryside and coastal settlements.[5] It is true that the question of typicality arises for any local study, but it is only the multiplication of careful dissections of individual revivals that will resolve the issue of how representative any given episode may be.

[3] Kent, *Holding the Fort*, 30–1.

[4] J. E. Orr, *The Second Evangelical Awakening in Britain* (London, 1949), suffers from this weakness.

[5] K. S. Jeffrey, *When the Lord Walked the Land: the 1858–62 Revival in the North-East of Scotland* (Carlisle, 2002). The book contains a valuable survey of the various historical interpretations of revival at 27–37.

Far more work of a detailed kind on specific places needs to be done. We need to move from the general to the particular.

That step entails a thorough study of the internal dynamic and the external setting of the churches concerned in revival. On the one hand, the state of devotional life, all too often ignored in general accounts, calls for examination. It was the religiosity of the people that, when quickened, gave rise to revival. On the other, the whole surrounding ambience of the churches requires scrutiny. The place of those active in revival, whether as promoters or as converts, has to be understood in all the circumstantial detail of its communal context. We certainly need to know about the preconditions of revival that earlier accounts have usually taken as their central topic, but particular attention also ought to be paid to spirituality and to the total way of life of the area. That is what is attempted here. If older work took 'religion and society' as its rubric, this case-study takes 'piety and culture' as its major themes. It explores a Cornish Methodist subject. In England Methodists formed the most revivalist denominational grouping, and they were at their strongest in Cornwall. David Luker has already written a doctoral thesis on Methodism in Cornwall and has published an article on revival there. His conclusion is that we need to discover far more about internal developments and adherents' aims than has previously been customary.[6] This paper seeks to achieve that goal. By drawing on the copious Methodist circuit records as well as the census, the Cornish press and other local sources, it aims to present a picture of revival in the far west that gives due weight to the whole cultural setting and the piety at the heart of the movement.[7]

We need to begin by setting the scene. In the mid-nineteenth century Cornwall, a county extending far into the Atlantic, retained a certain seclusion. The Tamar bridge connecting the Cornish railways with the national system was not to be opened until 1859, and even then Penzance, the westernmost town in England only eight miles short

[6] David Luker, 'Revivalism in Theory and Practice: the Case of Cornish Methodism', *JEH* 37 (1986), 603–19, at 619. See D. H. Luker, 'Cornish Methodism, Revivalism and Popular Belief, c. 1780–1870', unpublished D. Phil. thesis, University of Oxford, 1987, specifically ch. 7.

[7] I am pleased to acknowledge a British Academy grant that enabled me to conduct the bulk of the research for this paper. I am also extremely grateful for the help of John Probert, Cedric Appleby and other specialists in Cornish Methodist history, and for the guidance of the staff at the Cornwall Centre, the Cornwall County Record Office, the Courtney Library of the Royal Institution of Cornwall, Truro, and the Morrab Library, Penzance.

of Land's End, was fully 325 miles away from London. In 1849 the normal route to the capital was by coach to the north coast of the county, by boat up the Bristol Channel and by coach again from Bristol to London. The area round Penzance contained some good arable land, but far more significant was the mining of copper and tin in its hinterland. Copper extraction had boomed during the early nineteenth century and was to reach its peak in the 1850s; tin, which had long been a staple Cornish product, was to outlast copper. Miners lived near Penzance, though few had homes in it, and a good deal of the metal was exported through its harbour. Shipping, which increased by 30–40% over the decade down to 1848, was the foundation of the town's wealth.[8] Penzance was also taking the first steps towards exploiting its mild climate to attract tourists for their health. Following a much publicized visit in 1846 by Victoria and Albert to St Michael's Mount in the bay, the town advertised itself as 'the Montpellier of England'.[9] So Penzance was a commercial rather than an industrial centre, and, notwithstanding its undoubted remoteness, even added a touch of the urbane to the urban. By the time of the revival it contained a population of some 9,200.[10]

The other two foci of revival, Newlyn and Mousehole, also gained their living from the sea, but more directly, by fishing. Newlyn, lying a mile south of Penzance, was the chief fishing station on Mount's Bay. Possessing a population of about 2,100, less than a quarter the size of Penzance, it consisted of two settlements, accessible to each other only when the tide was right. The inhabitants of Newlyn Town were nearly all fisherfolk; the people of Street-an-Nowan, where the Wesleyan Methodist chapel stood, and the adjacent Tolcarne were more varied, for there was a large brewery, together with several shops and workshops, and the urban influences of Penzance were closer by. Nevertheless the roughly three hundred boats were the mainstay of the place, taking more pilchards and mackerel than anywhere else in Cornwall.[11] The scarlet-coated fishwives were a local sight, and by the 1880s the artists of the Newlyn school were to delight in depicting the rude

8 *Penzance Journal*, 22 November 1848, 4.

9 W. Penaluna, comp., *An Historical Survey of the County of Cornwall*, 2 vols (new edn, Helston, 1848), 2: 46.

10 The standard histories of Cornwall and Penzance are Philip Payton, *Cornwall: a History* (2nd edn, Fowey, 2004), and P. A. S. Pool, *The History of the Town and Borough of Penzance* (Penzance, 1974).

11 Penaluna, *County of Cornwall*, 2: 151–2.

simplicity of their menfolk. The artists used to complain, however, that their subjects insisted on whiling away the long sittings by singing tuneless hymns.[12] Mousehole, three miles south of Penzance and round a projection in the cliffs from Newlyn, was even more single-mindedly devoted to fishing. Once a market town, it had never fully recovered from a burning by the Spaniards in 1595 in retaliation for the defeat of the Armada. It seemed a repository of the region's past, being the home of the reputed last speaker of the Cornish language, Dolly Pentreath, who had died in 1777. Older people at the time of the revival had known Methodists who had once been smugglers.[13] Mousehole was roughly half the size of Newlyn, with about 1,100 people and eighty boats.[14] Maritime experience formed the outlook of the inhabitants, so that the leading Mousehole class leader in the revival could remark on his deathbed in 1870 that, despite acute physical pain, he was 'quiet on a calm sea'.[15]

The ecclesiastical balance in Penzance differed sharply from that in the fishing villages. The Church of England was reasonably strong in the town, which fell within the historic parish of Madron. The parish church was a mile and a half away, so that Penzance itself was served by a chapel of ease, St Mary's, which was rebuilt on a commodious scale in 1832–5. An additional Anglican place of worship, St Paul's, was opened in 1843. The relative resources of church and chapel can be illustrated from donations for the support of the town's day schools in 1849: whereas £14 was raised for the Wesleyan institution, £44 was collected for the National School of the Church of England.[16] In terms of worshippers, the honours were more even. At the 1851 religious census, when the Wesleyans obtained 29% of the attendances in the town, the Church of England secured 43%.[17] In Newlyn and Mouse-

12 Pat A. Waller and Glyn Richards, 'Non-conformity in Newlyn', in Veronica Chesher, ed., *Newlyn Life, 1870–1914: the Village that Inspired the Artists* (Penzance, 2003), 101–8, at 103. On Newlyn, see Margaret E. Perry, *Newlyn: a Brief History* (Newlyn, 1999).

13 Richard Treffry, *Memoirs of Mr. Richard Trewavas, Sen., of Mousehole, Cornwall* (London, 1839), 53.

14 On Mousehole, see Nettie M. Pender, *A Short History of Mousehole with Personal Recollections* (Mousehole, 1970), and Margaret E. Perry, *Mousehole: a Brief History* (Newlyn, 1998).

15 *Wesleyan Methodist Magazine*, December 1870, 575.

16 *Penzance Journal*, 7 February 1849, 4. *Penzance Gazette*, 7 March 1849 [4].

17 J. C. C. Probert, ed., *1851 Religious Census: West Cornwall and the Isles of Scilly* (n.p., n.d.). The percentages are proportionate shares of total attendances. Other percentages are taken from this source. The remainder of the Penzance churchgoers were split between several other chapels including two of different Methodist persuasions.

hole, by contrast, it was Methodism that dominated. In both places, the second best attended place of worship was a type of Methodist chapel, Primitive in Newlyn and Teetotal in Mousehole, while the Church of England still suffered from memories of the fish tithe imposed until as recently as the 1830s.[18] The parish church that in theory served the two villages was up the hill behind Mousehole at Paul, a hamlet named after the church's dedication, and few of the fishing population darkened its doors except for funerals. At the 1851 census, perhaps prudently, it made no return of attendances. The Wesleyans claimed as many as 60% of worshippers in Mousehole. In Newlyn in February 1849, while the revival was flaming, a renovated ex-Methodist chapel was opened as the first Anglican place of worship in the village.[19] At the religious census, however, when the Wesleyans attracted 40% of the worshippers, it drew a mere 13%. Penzance was still a place where the established Church enjoyed cachet, but in the fishing villages it had been practically disestablished by popular choice.

It will be useful to set out the events of the awakening before proceeding to analyse them. The first happenings were in Penzance. Around Christmas 1848 one or two young people professed conversion, and very rapidly a movement developed among the youth of the Wesleyan chapel.[20] Whereas normally only five or so new members were admitted on trial each quarter, in the three months down to the end of the year as many as forty-six were received.[21] In Mousehole there was a conversion at the late evening watchnight service on New Year's Eve, and at a Sunday school teachers' meeting the following day two people revealed themselves to be 'penitents', that is convinced of their sinful state and active in seeking salvation. During a short period of about ten days many others in the village joined them in their earnest quest. At that point the fishing boats departed for the mackerel fishery off Plymouth, but the revival continued among the inhabitants who were left behind. Meanwhile the first signs of an awakening were seen at Newlyn on Sunday 14 January, when the boats were already setting

18 *Cornish Telegraph*, 5 December 1860 [4].

19 *Penzance Gazette*, 28 February 1849 [4].

20 Robert Young, 'Revival of Religion in the Penzance Circuit', *Wesleyan Methodist Magazine*, January 1850, 35. This is the source for otherwise unattributed information in this paragraph.

21 Truro, Cornwall County Record Office, Circuit Schedule Book for Penzance Circuit [hereafter: Penzance Circuit], 1843–9, MR/PZ/31. The other statistics in this paragraph are from this source.

off, and gradually built up to an even greater intensity than in Mousehole. Before the end of March the fishermen were back and participated fully in the stirring times. During the first quarter of the year there were 187 admissions of new members on trial at Penzance, 240 at Mousehole and as many as 266 at Newlyn. On a single day, Easter Monday, 9 April, at a series of special services in Newlyn, about one hundred people professed conversion. In March and again in June there was a torrent of public testimony to changed lives at the love-feasts observed in Penzance and at similar gatherings held in the fishing villages. Fresh admissions on trial in the quarter ending in June were sixty-four for Penzance, forty-eight for Mousehole and 105 for Newlyn. Then, however, the boats set off for the Irish fishing grounds and the revival tailed off, with thirty-five, fifteen and thirty-three new admissions in the third quarter and normal figures in the last quarter. Overall the total membership of the Penzance circuit rose in twelve months by no less than 70%. It was a transformative experience for the district.

Preceding events undoubtedly had a bearing on the awakening and it is worth considering, in the first place, how far economic circumstances impinged on its genesis. The 1848 fishing season had been poor. In August 1848 it was noted disconsolately that the pilchards had disobligingly swum off into deep water or else to the vicinity of Land's End.[22] Unless 'some peculiar good fortune' should transpire, reported the *Penzance Gazette* in December that year, 'we shall have to record one of the most discouraging seasons which has been experienced in this bay.'[23] The fishing population depended exclusively on their catches, and so the prospect of a hard winter may have contributed to rousing minds to eternal things. Yet the start of the 1849 fisheries was much more satisfactory. By February the Penzance fish market was being abundantly supplied with turbot, brill, salmon, eel, cod, ling and sole. Newlyn boats were taking large quantities of mackerel off Plymouth and finding good prices for their catches.[24] Although the summer expedition to Irish waters was 'very unsuccessful' that year and local landings much below average, so that by the autumn there was 'abject poverty' in Newlyn and Penzance,[25] at the height of the revival

22 *Penzance Journal*, 30 August 1848, 4.
23 *Penzance Gazette*, 13 December 1848 [4].
24 *Penzance Journal*, 21 February 1849, 4.
25 Young, 'Revival of Religion', 39.

the chief source of income of the fishing villages had been flourishing. It is just possible that gratitude to the Almighty for renewed prosperity after a meagre season encouraged religious enthusiasm, but direct evidence is lacking. In any case, it is implausible in this instance to connect the awakening with poor economic circumstances.

A definite link, however, can be made with a very different factor, alarm about cholera. In 1832, when the last outbreak had taken place in Britain, the Methodist superintendent in Penzance had attributed a revival of that year in part to 'pestilential diseases'.[26] The knowledge that life might suddenly be cut short had turned thoughts towards seeking salvation. The town of Penzance had experienced the epidemic, especially in the confined courts near the quay, with sixty-four deaths in a period of three months, and Newlyn had suffered even worse, with perhaps as many as a hundred fatalities.[27] From August 1848 there were fears of a recurrence. Diarrhoea and dysentery, often the precursors of cholera, increased in Penzance.[28] The people of the town read anxiously in their newspapers of the inexorable westward advance of the scourge over Europe: from St Petersburg to Berlin, to other towns in Germany and eventually to a Prussian vessel in the port of Hull.[29] By mid-October there were fatal cases elsewhere on the east coast, and in the following month a Penzance sailor died of cholera on board one of the port's own schooners quarantined at Ramsgate.[30] It was reported that 'the public are anxiously enquiring "What is to be done?"'.[31] The Penzance health committee passed resolutions and the council resolved to initiate steps for the creation of a local board of health.[32] The process reached a peak of activity in January, the very month when the revival took off. The Board of Guardians decreed fresh sanitary measures; a government inspector held a two-day hearing on 10 and 11 January to establish the need for a board of health; and the press, in urging 'every proper precaution', deprecated the 'foolish apprehensions' that were abroad.[33] The popular worries were undoubtedly related to questions of

26 John Hobson, 'Revival of Religion in the Penzance Circuit', *Wesleyan Methodist Magazine*, May 1832, 365.

27 Pool, *Penzance*, 121–2. *Penzance Gazette*, 15 November 1848 [3].

28 *Penzance Journal*, 16 August 1848, 3.

29 Ibid.; 23 August 1848, 3; 20 September 1848, 3; 4 October 1848, 3.

30 *Penzance Gazette*, 18 October 1848 [4]; 29 November 1848 [4].

31 *Penzance Journal*, 25 October 1848, 4.

32 Ibid., 20 September 1848, 3; 27 September 1848, 4.

33 *Penzance Gazette*, 3 January 1849 [3]. *West Briton*, 19 January 1849 [3]. *Penzance Gazette*, 17 January 1849 [3].

faith. Even the *Penzance Gazette* hoped that the planning would, 'under Providence', avert an outbreak.[34] The expectation around the beginning of 1849, though, was that the epidemic would soon strike the area. Twelve months later the senior Wesleyan minister was able to voice the relief of his people at having 'entirely escaped the ravages of pestilence'.[35] For a while, however, fear of death encouraged fear of the Lord.

Another type of awareness of mortality was often a powerful influence in places so dependent on the sea. There were deep-seated anxieties about the ever-present risk of death in the frail vessels. At night fishermen of the west of England avoided parts of the shore where there might have been wrecks in the past. Many of them claimed to have heard the voices of dead sailors calling to them.[36] Most of the coastal folk had lost relatives or friends by shipwreck. In October 1848 a young Newlyn fisherman was lost at sea, but, because such events were so frequent, it does not seem to have had much impact.[37] In December, however, the weather turned stormy and a succession of gales battered the area.[38] On Thursday 14 December, a schooner in distress was seen in the natural amphitheatre of Mount's Bay. Crowds came out to watch as, in a strong wind and a heavy sea, the boat, the *James Whearne* of St Ives, tried to make towards Penzance, but then, on the opposite side of the bay, it suddenly capsized. The six men and a boy in the crew were all lost.[39] The harrowing melodrama, an unusually public spectacle of death, took place shortly before the first stirrings of awakening in Penzance and must surely have played a part in turning thoughts to questions of eternity. On Saturday 23 December, with destructive gales still blowing, Welsh colliers and other vessels crowded into Penzance harbour, causing collisions and rumours of more serious disasters, and on Christmas Day itself two schooners left the port only to run ashore not far away, one losing a boy.[40] The people of Penzance, who showed 'intense fear and sympathy' on such occasions, thronged to the harbour to witness the scene on Christmas Eve, and the events were

34 *Penzance Gazette*, 18 October 1848 [4].
35 Young, 'Revival of Religion', 39.
36 Robert Hunt, *Popular Romances of the West of England*, 2nd series (London, 1865), 146.
37 *Penzance Gazette*, 11 October 1848 [4].
38 *Penzance Journal*, 20 December 1848, 4.
39 Ibid.; *Penzance Gazette*, 20 December 1848 [4].
40 *Penzance Gazette*, 27 December 1848 [4].

sufficiently worrying to prompt the council to resolve to shoulder a heavy debt by extending the town pier.[41] The terrifying weather and the loss of life will have reinforced the preoccupation with death arising from the progress of the cholera.

If the community at large was moved to anxiety by these circumstances, the Methodists had their own internal reasons for looking for a religious awakening. It has come to be appreciated that in the nineteenth century there was often a rhythm of revival. Churches that had experienced an awakening would expect another to take place after a few years. The only consistent factor preceding revivals, according to Richard Carwardine, was a belief that they were desirable and must be repeated.[42] Accordingly churches engaged in intense bouts of prayer for a fresh visitation by the Holy Spirit and confidently expected their prayers to be answered. The Methodists of south-west Cornwall had particular cause to follow this pattern. In 1814 their part of the county, together with the mining heartland, had been enflamed by the 'Great Revival'. It was described by a contemporary as a 'glorious work'; there were scenes of agony, with people 'on their knees for six, twelve, or twenty hours, without intermission, crying aloud for mercy'; and over 5,000 new members crowded into the movement.[43] Another general awakening in the south-west of the county took place in 1831–2, and there were lesser episodes at Mousehole in 1818 and 1828, in all three places in 1838–9, in Penzance in 1841–2 and in Mousehole and Newlyn in 1844.[44] There can be no doubt that supplication for revival became a deeply rooted feature of Methodist spirituality in the area. In Penzance, it was said after the 1831–2 revival, 'our friends unite in ardent and unceasing prayer for the continued prosperity of Zion'.[45] Memories of the Great Revival in particular lingered as a paradigm for what Methodism should ideally be about. Robert Young, the superintendent minister during the 1849 awakening, had published a book on Wesleyan revivals, chiefly in England but also in other parts of the

41 J. H. Rigg, *Wesleyan Methodist Reminiscences: Sixty Years Ago* (London, 1904), 72. Pool, *Penzance*, 139.

42 Richard Carwardine, *Transatlantic Revivalism: Popular Evangelicalism in Britain and America, 1790–1865* (Westport, CT, 1978), 56.

43 John Riles, *An Account of the Revival of the Work of God in the County of Cornwall* (Penryn, 1814), 8, 20. M. S. Edwards, 'Cornish Methodism: a Study in Division, 1814–1857', unpublished MA thesis, University of Birmingham, 1962, 23.

44 Hobson, 'Revival of Religion', 361–5. Penzance Circuit, 1837–43, MR/PZ/30; 1843–9.

45 Hobson, 'Revival of Religion', 362.

world, before he came to Cornwall. By far the longest account was of the revival in the county during 1814.[46] For pastor and for people recollections of the Great Revival served as a spur to seek another similar event. The expectation was so powerful as to verge on being self-fulfilling.

Another dimension of Methodist piety was a sublime confidence in the future. It was not just that members felt assured of going to heaven, for they also believed that the cause of Christ was destined, according to the promises of scripture, to triumph all over the earth. The whole world, declared Robert Young in a missionary sermon of 1846, 'shall become one vast and holy temple of spiritual worshippers'.[47] Contemporary events seemed to vindicate that standpoint, technically labelled postmillennialism. The European revolutions of 1848, Cornish Methodists were told by William Arthur, a connexional missionary secretary, in the following year, had ushered in a 'glorious dawning of the spread of liberty of conscience' which would lead to the triumph of the pure gospel on the continent. Accordingly they threw themselves into the enterprise of world missions, certain that they were participating in the purposes of the Almighty. The Cornish district missionary meetings shortly before Easter were for Methodists the high point of the church year, far surpassing Easter itself in significance. Every year the greatest luminaries of the Wesleyan pulpit were despatched to the county for a preaching jamboree. The main public meeting of 1849 in Penzance, where Arthur spoke, was 'densely crowded' and the immense sum of £171 was raised over the anniversary weekend.[48] Partly in consequence, the Wesleyan Methodist Missionary Society enjoyed enormous support in the area. A missionary auxiliary had existed at Mousehole from 1820, commissioning eighteen 'young females' to engage in competitive collecting for the global cause.[49] Forty copies of the monthly *Juvenile Missionary Offering* circulated in the village in 1846, outdoing Newlyn's ten by a large margin.[50] Joseph Carne, a rich banker of Penzance, had a seat on the missionary society committee in London from 1836 to 1849, and Robert Young had actually served as a missionary between

46 Robert Young, *Showers of Blessing; or, Sketches of Revivals of Religion in the Wesleyan Methodist Connexion: With Observations Thereon* (London, 1844), 229–49.

47 Robert Young, 'A Missionary Sermon', *Cornish Banner* (1846–7), 14.

48 *Penzance Gazette*, 4 April 1849 [4].

49 Treffry, *Memoirs of Mr. Richard Trewavas*, 158–62.

50 Penzance Circuit, 1843–9, 27.

1820 and 1826.[51] Penzance itself had sent Samuel Symons to the Gambia in 1842, though he had succumbed to yellow fever within two years.[52] The Methodism of the area was a hotbed of missionary enthusiasm.

The spiritual confidence associated with the missionary project had its repercussions for revival. Conversion was at the centre of both. If the world was rapidly turning Christian, the chapel attenders of Cornwall were inspired to feel that they must follow. Symons had sent back a leather collecting bag made by the people of the Gambia to Jane Dennis, a missionary zealot in Penzance. Jane was an invalid, confined to her bed by a spinal problem, but held regular prayer meetings in her room during which, according to a later memory, she would 'often be in an ecstasy'. Each year the visiting dignitaries for the missionary anniversary filed into her room so that they could receive the contents of her collecting bag. The room was also the place where many conversions took place under Jane's tutelage.[53] Jane Dennis symbolized what contemporaries called the 'reflex action' of missions. Those who supported evangelistic effort overseas were constantly reminded of the duty to sacrifice ease and of the imperative to pray for conversions. This formula prepared the way for revivals in the locality. The chairman at a meeting of the Penzance Juvenile Wesleyan Missionary Society in November 1848 was Edward Rowe, a printer and bookseller, several of whose own children were to be converted in the revival that began the following month.[54] The missionary atmosphere of the household must have affected its young people. Again, the revival in Mousehole actually started immediately after missionary speakers had addressed a meeting there.[55] Following the revival, some of the young women who had professed faith for the first time discarded the artificial flowers that, as their minister severely remarked, had 'done questionable service in days of folly', and turned them into decorations for a work basket in which they placed articles for sale in support of overseas missions. Young converts of both sexes gave £10 as a thank-offering to the missionary

51 *The Report of the Wesleyan-Methodist Missionary Society* (London, n.d.), xv, for successive years.

52 Elaine Horner, *Samuel Symons: Missionary to the Gambia, 1842–44* (n.p., n.d.).

53 *Cornish Telegraph*, 17 June 1903, 2.

54 *Penzance Journal*, 6 December 1848, 4. Young, 'Revival of Religion', 35, where one of the society stewards was Rowe, probably the one with three children converted.

55 *Wesley Banner*, April 1849, 56.

cause.[56] Even more strikingly, three of the young Mousehole converts volunteered in the following year to act as boatmen on a quixotic missionary venture to the southern tip of Patagonia. All the party perished, but the publicity given to these 'martyrs of the south' led to some of the first sustained efforts to plant Protestantism in South America.[57] The revival was to contribute to the missionary cause, but the converse was also true. Devotion to the missionary enterprise had helped prepare the churches for revival.

These various antecedent factors meant that, even if the awakening of 1849 showed certain characteristics of spontaneity, there were influences at work among the Methodists of the Penzance district that predisposed them to revival. Furthermore, there are reasons for seeing the events of that year as the result of conscious planning. The ministers in the circuit had been appointed to produce organized revivals. The attitude of the pre-eminent figure in Wesleyan Methodism in these years, Jabez Bunting, has sometimes been misinterpreted as involving hostility to revival for the sake of orderly control, but in reality he believed in encouraging awakenings so long as they did not disrupt regular circuit life. 'We may excel in getting revivals', he told the 1837 Conference, 'but we have yet to learn how to manage them.'[58] His ideal, then, was managed awakenings. Leading laymen in Cornwall, sharing his opinion, were troubled that Methodism in the county, though full of vitality, needed better organization, not least to ensure connexional loyalty.[59] George Smith of Camborne urged the authorities to appoint gifted ministers to the Cornwall district. 'It is not rant, nor senseless declamation, nor a profusion of terrific epithets, which is likely to produce a revival', he wrote a few years later, '. . . but plain earnest, forceful utterance of sterling Gospel truth'.[60] Accordingly in 1846 two ministers were selected for the task of blending more discipline into the enthusiastic ways of the Cornish.[61] Stationed at Truro for three years, in

56 Young, 'Revival of Religion', 38.

57 G. P. Despard, *Hope Deferred, not Lost: a Narrative of Missionary Effort in South America in connection with the Patagonian Missionary Society* (London, [1852]), 136. Phyllis Thompson, *An Unquenchable Flame* (London, 1983).

58 Benjamin Gregory, *Side Lights on the Conflicts of Methodism* (London, 1899), 246.

59 William Dale to Jabez Bunting, 12 July 1839 and 15 July 1842, in W. R. Ward, ed., *Early Victorian Methodism: the Correspondence of Jabez Bunting, 1830–1859* (Oxford, 1976), 225–9, 273–6.

60 George Smith, *History of Wesleyan Methodism*, 2 vols (London, 1858), 2: 604.

61 Rigg, *Wesleyan Methodist Reminiscences*, 54–5.

1848 they moved to Penzance and so presided over the revival in the circuit there. The junior minister was John H. James, one of the first products of the Theological Institution that Bunting had established in 1836 to train able exponents of denominational principles. James had married the daughter of William Dale, the most prominent Truro layman, and already by 1839 had been seconding his father-in-law's calls for efficient ministerial leadership in Cornwall.[62] He fulfilled his early promise, going on to become secretary (1870) and president (1871) of Conference, and was celebrated on his death for having combined 'culture and the revivalistic *forte*'.[63] James was placed in Cornwall to be an exponent of directed revivals.

So was his superintendent minister, who also acted as chairman of the whole Cornwall district, Robert Young. Possessing rich missionary experience from Jamaica and Nova Scotia, at the time of the revival Young was in his early fifties and still a man of great energy. He showed a certain sternness, condemning ministers who excited 'the spirit of levity by pitiful witticisms or ludicrous anecdotes'.[64] Yet he was himself a ready raconteur, enjoyed playing with his children and attracted deep affection as well as great respect from his flock.[65] He was strongly in favour of revivals, composing in 1844 the standard Wesleyan handbook on the subject, *Showers of Blessing*. He approved of the Cornish style of intense revivalism, exhibiting the Penzance circuit as a good example of a place where awakenings had generated solid church growth. Nevertheless he upheld the official Wesleyan view, as codified in the minutes of the Liverpool Conference of 1820, that revival was best pursued by regular church work rather than by artificial stimuli.[66] His zeal, according to his official obituarist, was tempered by 'sound judgment and unusual self-control'.[67] The Wesleyan authorities twice entrusted him with responsibility for delicate negotiations in other parts of the world: in 1843–4 he travelled round the West Indies to resolve differ-

62 Ward, ed., *Early Victorian Methodism*, 229. *West Briton*, 1 October 1891, 3. London, National Archives, Returns for the 1851 Census for Cornwall, HO 107/1918 [hereafter: 1851 Census], fol. 693.

63 *West Briton*, 8 October 1891, supplement, 2.

64 Robert Young, *Suggestions for the Conversion of the World, respectfully submitted to the Christian Church* (London, 1841), 49.

65 Rigg, *Wesleyan Methodist Reminiscences*, 68. Robert Young, *The Serious Inquirer after Salvation affectionately addressed* (2nd edn, London, 1838), 8. *Cornish Telegraph*, 29 August 1851 [2].

66 Young, *Showers of Blessing*, 456, 273–4.

67 *Wesleyan Methodist Magazine*, September 1866, 847.

ences of opinion that had arisen among the missionaries; and in 1852–4 he was despatched to Australia to tell the Wesleyans that they must become independent and self-supporting, so that they would have to pay for the South Seas missions themselves.[68] Young possessed the supreme diplomatic skill of presenting unwelcome news in a favourable light, and it is not surprising that on his successful return from Australia he was rewarded with the presidency of Conference in 1856. Similarly in the Penzance circuit Young headed off the Wesleyan reform movement that elsewhere, even in Cornwall, caused immense disruption during 1850–1.[69] Robert Young was therefore particularly gifted to turn Cornish revivalism into more disciplined channels.

Young had a penchant for projects. His most ambitious, published in 1841, was a plan for nothing less than the conversion of the whole world. This goal could be achieved, he argued, if each converted person brought one soul to God every year. He calculated that, if the scheme were adopted by only 3,000 people at the start, within twenty years the entire population of the globe would be Evangelical Christians. To help the enterprise along, it would be useful to raise £5 millions for the support of 20,000 missionaries, which could easily be achieved if, in order to contribute to the cause, only a quarter of real Christians gave up half a pint of malt liquor per day.[70] It is not surprising that, immediately after arriving as superintendent minister in Penzance in August 1848, he launched several schemes. The Sunday school staff were gathered for tea and, under Young's guidance, passed resolutions designed to increase their efficiency.[71] The superintendent had the local preachers' meeting arrange to reopen St Clare Street Chapel, where there had previously been fitful efforts to start a second Wesleyan cause in the town. A committee under the leadership of a retired minister in the congregation, John Reynolds, was entrusted with visiting the neighbourhood to drum in new attenders.[72] And at the September quarterly meeting, Young summoned the lay leaders in the circuit, as he later put

[68] London, University of London, School of Oriental and African Studies, Wesleyan Methodist Missionary Society Home and General Minutes, FBN 7, 22 November 1843, 27 March 1844. Robert Young, *The Southern World: Journal of a Deputation from the Wesleyan Conference to Australia and Polynesia* (London, 1854).

[69] *Cornish Telegraph*, 11 July 1851 [2].

[70] Young, *Suggestions for the Conversion of the World*, 71–3, 92, 98.

[71] *Penzance Journal*, 20 September 1848, 4.

[72] Truro, Cornwall County Record Office, Penzance Wesleyan Methodist Local Preachers' Minute Book, 1845–63, MR/PZ/12, 26 September 1848, 32.

it, 'to anticipate and labour for a revival of religion'.[73] The scene was deliberately set for the awakening that duly followed.

During its course, Young controlled events with a firm hand. There is no detailed account of his procedure at Penzance, but he had described his customary approach in *Showers of Blessing* and, since we know that he followed its prescriptions in a revival at Truro in 1847, he will also have followed the same pattern two years later. One regular bane of revival services was the arrival of young men bent on organizing practical jokes. Accordingly Young stationed stewards at the doors to check what he called 'the ungodly and profane'.[74] A problem arising from undue ardour was a willingness to carry on until late hours that aroused criticism among outsiders. In the awakening of 1832 Penzance had kept a meeting going until eleven o'clock and Mousehole had continued until nearly midnight for a whole week.[75] At Truro in 1847, by contrast, Young insisted on closing by ten o'clock. There was resistance among those wedded to traditional ways, but the superintendent overbore them.[76] Young's key policy, however, was what he called the separation of penitents. Those anxious for salvation were invited forward to the communion rail to receive spiritual advice. This method, professedly pragmatic in motivation, was designed to allow those concerned about their sins to take a decisive action. It also meant that busy-bodies no longer had an excuse for wandering about the chapel to intrude their advice on the most exciting cases, so that often two or three were 'shouting into the ears of a poor sinner in distress, and expressing themselves in different language, and with much incoherency'.[77] Instead advice was given only by designated counsellors who would be able to adapt their guidance to each individual's circumstances. Young attempted the separation of penitents at Truro in 1846, but the congregation, unaccustomed to the new procedure, simply ignored him. By 1847, however, the strategy worked.[78] It was part of what Young termed the proper 'management' of revivals.[79]

At Penzance such methods successfully imposed a particular char-

73 Young, 'Revival of Religion', 34.

74 Robert Young, 'Recent Revival of Religion at Truro', *Wesleyan Methodist Magazine*, June 1847, 610.

75 Hobson, 'Revival of Religion', 362, 365.

76 Young, 'Religion at Truro', 611.

77 Young, *Showers of Blessing*, 423–8, 451.

78 Young, 'Religion at Truro', 610.

79 Young, *Showers of Blessing*, 447, 458.

acter on the awakening. On his arrival in the town, Young was dismayed to discover that the children of what he called 'old and respectable' Wesleyan families were 'addicted to levities', so giving signs of being unconverted. He and his colleague took pains to speak in public of the requirement of commitment and in private of the need for repentance. When the revival came, it was overwhelmingly among those between fourteen and twenty-five years of age.[80] There is no record, in fact, of any convert over the age of twenty-five other than the thirty-year-old daughter of a former minister.[81] Previous revivals, such as one at Mousehole in 1818, had also harvested chiefly the young,[82] but in Penzance in 1849 the converts had further characteristics. The managed tone of the revival made it acceptable to 'intelligent and educated' young people.[83] Both sexes were drawn in, so that fresh weekly classes were begun for boys as well as girls – though the change was most apparent among the girls, who 'discarded superfluous ornaments, and adopted a quiet and godly attire'.[84] Brothers and sisters were converted together or in rapid succession, so that solitary recruits from a family were a rarity. There was a pattern of household conversion. The early closing of the meetings was explicitly aimed to avoid disrupting family life and part of the purpose of the ban on strolling counsellors was to eliminate those who were 'little acquainted with the rules of polite society'.[85] It is evident that the revival was deliberately moulded so as to cater for the prosperous families of the town with whom Young closely identified. His own older daughter, Elizabeth, afterwards married the eldest son of W. D. Matthews, a wealthy ship-owner, the proprietor of the town's only dry dock and later three time mayor, the son almost certainly being a convert during the revival.[86] Conversion was being treated as a natural step for junior members of prospering Wesleyan households, a rite of passage rather like confirma-

80 Young, 'Revival of Religion', 34–5, 36–7, at 34.

81 *Wesleyan Methodist Magazine*, November 1849, 1213 (Maria Akerman).

82 B[enjamin] Carvosso, ed., *The Efficacy of Faith in the Atonement of Christ: exemplified in a Memoir of Mr. William Carvosso, Sixty Years a Class-Leader in the Wesleyan-Methodist Connexion* (London, n. d.), 92.

83 Young, 'Revival of Religion', 37.

84 Ibid., 38.

85 Young, 'Religion at Truro', 611; idem, *Showers of Blessing*, 450–1.

86 G. C. Boase, *Collectanea Cornubiensia* (Truro, 1890), col. 543. Young, 'Revival of Religion', 35, noting that five children of a circuit steward were converted. Matthews was the circuit steward with five children between the ages of fourteen and twenty-three. 1851 Census, fol. 741.

tion. Recruitment was no longer expected to be from the unchurched community, but from names already associated with Methodism. Growth was becoming an internal phenomenon.

This diagnosis is confirmed by the arrangements made during the revival for the care of converts. Methodism allocated newcomers to classes, each meeting weekly under a leader, and the sources allow us to discover something of their character. Of the twenty-seven class leaders operating in Penzance at the peak of the revival in the first quarter of 1849, only four received a lion's share of the recruits, altogether well over half those who professed conversion. Their classes admitted between nineteen and forty members on trial, whereas the next largest intake was only nine and several classes received no fresh members at all.[87] All four of the big recruiters possessed special reasons for an interest in the young. One, the already mentioned W. D. Matthews, was a chapel steward with responsibility for the future welfare of the cause and was in addition the father of a family that was particularly affected by the awakening, almost certainly with five children converted. Matthews took as many as thirty-three into a single class, which must have made for lively meetings. The second class leader, Richard Barnes, was the proprietor of Regent House Academy, a private school in the town much patronized by Wesleyans, and so had a professional concern for children.[88] The third, Richard George, received a high proportion of the first wave of converts around Christmas, and he remained a key figure in similar phases of religious excitement right down to 1863, regularly welcoming large numbers of new members into his class. George, who was married but childless at the age of forty-three, did business as a confectioner in the town centre. His shop was known for its excellent macaroons, and so must have been popular with the young people of the town.[89] The last class leader attracting a significant number of new admissions was Richard Hosking, a master mason, then only twenty-seven himself and so having an immediate affinity with the young people. He soon became a local preacher and continued to

[87] Penzance Circuit, 1843–9.

[88] G. C. Boase, *Reminiscences of Penzance*, ed. P. A. S. Pool (Penzance, 1976), 24–7. *Wesleyan Methodist Magazine*, December 1849, 1318. During the revival Barnes's nineteen-year-old assistant at Regent House, Caleb Shipman, started a boys' class of converts, and shortly afterwards George Bettany, the master at the Wesleyan day school in the town, joined him as a class leader.

[89] Penzance Circuit, 1849–64, MR/PZ/32. 1851 Census, fol. 525. Boase, *Reminiscences of Penzance*, 28.

gather large numbers of new members into class in subsequent years right down to a revival in 1872.[90] While the classes led by others maintained a more even-paced pastoral role, the groups led by these few men were the cutting edge of Wesleyan mission. Evangelism was becoming the care of experts who took a particular interest in young people. George and Hosking in particular were men who concentrated on enlisting new recruits. A distinct category of soul-winners was emerging.

In the more polished setting of Penzance, therefore, the restrained and orderly style of revival promoted by Robert Young was associated with internal growth, youthful converts and evangelistic specialists. The fishing villages of Mousehole and Newlyn, however, were very different places. The dwellings were small, cramped and crowded in a restricted area, throwing people together. The fishermen generally operated their boats on a system of shares, so that the boat-owner, the captain and the crewmen all took a proportion of the proceeds of the catch.[91] The result was an egalitarian atmosphere and a strong sense of community. Nicknames were common, and at funerals all the inhabitants would turn out, taking turns to carry the corpse up the hill to the churchyard.[92] In such settings traditional ways survived tenaciously. The fishermen were noted for their superstition. No pasties, saffron cakes or looking glasses were tolerated on board ship; women, rabbits and preachers must not be seen just before a voyage.[93] Fairy folk were supposed to dwell in holes in the cliff, and offerings of fish for a deity named 'Bucca', perhaps a regional variant on 'Puck', were still being left on the beach within a decade or so of the revival. The people of Mousehole seem to have abandoned this custom earlier and so to have derided Newlyn folk as 'Buccas'.[94] This measure of detachment from inherited practice in Mousehole may have been a result of a thirst for education connected with the greater strength of Methodism in the village. In 1818 Mousehole Wesleyans had begun a book club, circulating volumes bound in black oil-cloth and selling them off after a

90 Penzance Circuit, 1849–64; 1864–77, MR/PZ/33. 1851 Census, fol. 736.

91 John Corin, *Fishermen's Conflict: the Story of a Cornish Fishing Port* (Newton Abbot, 1988), 27.

92 *Cornish Telegraph*, 28 November 1860 [4].

93 Charles Thomas, *The Taboo in Cornwall* (n.p., 1951), 25. Pender, *Short History of Mousehole*, 38.

94 William Bottrell, *Traditions and Hearthside Stories of West Cornwall*, 2nd series (Penzance, 1873), 245, 246; 3rd series (Penzance, 1880), 156.

year.[95] A Methodist day school was opened in Mousehole in the year before the revival, whereas Newlyn had to wait until 1859 for its equivalent.[96] Yet superstition and Methodism were undoubtedly compatible in both villages. Belief in invisible wandering spirits, according to an unfriendly Anglican commentator, was actually encouraged by Methodist local preachers.[97] It is known that after evening chapel, a Mousehole villager might resort to an old man's house for a charm to cure toothache.[98] Traditional patterns of behaviour were more likely to endure in the small and tight-knit communities.

There was also a feature of Methodist belief that was stronger outside Penzance than within the town. That was the conviction that after the moment of conversion there was a further decisive crisis in the spiritual life, the entry on entire sanctification. A believer, John Wesley had taught, might progress to the point of receiving perfect love, a condition in which the desire to do wrong was eradicated from the soul. It was an experience often associated with intense spiritual awareness and a species of boisterous revivalism. All Methodists formally acknowledged the doctrine, but as the nineteenth century advanced fewer expected the experience.[99] That was particularly true in more sophisticated environments such as Penzance. We know that in 1817 three entered perfect love in the town and many members of the circuit, some of whom may have been people of Penzance, were said to have obtained it in the aftermath of the revival of 1832.[100] Thereafter, however, there is no evidence for the experience in the town. Young, as a loyal Wesleyan, taught entire sanctification, but was acutely aware that some hypocrites claimed it though showing 'unholy tempers' and did not dwell on the subject.[101] While there is no indication of the doctrine at Newlyn, however, it was clearly widely credited at Mousehole. Richard Trewavas, a patriarch of the society there, and

95 Percy Harvey, 'Mousehole alias Porthennis: the Chronicle of a Seafaring Community' (typescript, 1994), 110.

96 Harvey, 'Mousehole', 145. *Wesleyan Education Committee Report* 20 (1859), 42.

97 William Bottrell, *Traditions and Hearthside Stories of West Cornwall* (Penzance, 1870), 179.

98 Pender, *Short History of Mousehole*, 38.

99 D. W. Bebbington, 'Holiness in Nineteenth-Century British Methodism', in W. M. Jacob and Nigel Yates, eds, *Crown and Mitre: Religion and Society in Northern Europe since the Reformation* (Woodbridge, 1993), 161–74.

100 Carvosso, ed., *Efficacy of Faith*, 84. John Hobson, 'New Chapels Opened in the Penzance Circuit', *Wesleyan Methodist Magazine*, July 1833, 523.

101 Young, *Suggestions for the Conversion of the World*, 79, 51.

William Carvosso, a travelling evangelist based in the village, were its exponents in the first third of the century.[102] Benedict Carvosso, William's brother and a Mousehole class leader, upheld perfect love down to his death in 1823.[103] Benedict, in turn, was a profound influence over the formative years of Joseph Wright, a class leader and local preacher who in 1849 was the leading figure among Mousehole Wesleyans.[104] When several fishermen, converted during the revival, visited Young some time afterwards to thank him for his efforts among them, they 'bore testimony to the efficacy of His blood to cleanse from all sin'.[105] In Mousehole the doctrine of entire sanctification evidently played its part in fostering a more intense form of revivalism than appeared in Penzance.

In both the fishing villages there are signs that there was a great deal of the raw excitement that was traditional in Cornish revivals. A Newlyn clergyman diagnosed them a little later as 'a "survival" of Druidism ... a return to that ecstatic worship of the heathen Celt which only ecclesiastical authority restrained during the past ages'.[106] Although Young's account of the revival, the only one available, did not go into detail about its emotional content, it is clear from stray phrases in his description that the events were passionately felt. Some individuals were suddenly awakened in the open air, fell on their knees and 'cried aloud for mercy'; fishermen at sea could be 'in solitary agony all the night'; and, coming ashore, they would be embraced by 'tearful but joyful' wives.[107] Sturdy seafarers 'sobbed aloud and tears streamed down their cheeks' as they recounted their conversions.[108] Young was quite prepared to tolerate such emotional display. Having grown used to similar happenings in the West Indies, he was convinced that forms of expression varied according to temperament.[109] He recognized that Cornish revivals had usually been noisy, exuberant affairs, and objected

102 Treffry, *Trewavas*, 68. Carvosso, ed., *Efficacy of Faith*, 15–16, 286.

103 *Wesleyan Methodist Magazine*, June 1824, 425.

104 Ibid., December 1870, 575.

105 A[delaide] W. Young, 'Reminiscences: a Fisher of Men', *Cornish Methodist Church Record*, March 1893, cutting in Truro, The Royal Institution of Cornwall, The Courtney Library, Thomas Shaw Collection, Mousehole section.

106 W. S. Lach-Szyrma, *A Short History of Penzance, S. Michael's Mount, S. Ives, and the Land's End District* (Truro, 1878), 185.

107 Young, 'Revival of Religion', 37, 35.

108 A. W. Young, 'Reminiscences: a Fisher of Men'.

109 Young, *Showers of Blessing*, 441, 435.

only to allowing singing and praying at the same time.[110] He was too skilful a diplomat to attempt to impose the same order on the fishing villages that he demanded at Penzance. So intense did the Mousehole revival become that it led to a painful episode. Mary Wright, a widow of around sixty living in the village, attended a Wesleyan prayer meeting on Christmas Eve 1848, before the awakening had begun, and was terrified when her nephew, who was giving out a hymn, fell down as if dead.[111] As the revival emerged, her thoughts turned to religion, she became alarmed about her spiritual state, and, instead of reaching a sense of forgiveness, she lapsed into 'a morbid state of the feelings'. One Saturday morning she rose early, went downstairs and calmly cut her own throat. The coroner's inquest brought in a verdict of temporary insanity.[112] Perhaps surprisingly, the suicide was not seized on by opponents to condemn the revival. The consternation it created in the village may even have advanced the awakening. The episode is an extreme instance of the way in which events in the fishing villages broke through the restraints successfully introduced in the town.

The character of the awakening in the fishing villages was therefore very different. There was no special harvest among the young, for every age group was affected. Whereas at Penzance converts were rarely over twenty-five, and so usually unmarried, here there were plenty of younger men over twenty-one, married as well as single. There were also men of sixty-five and over, even into their eighties.[113] Instead of age limiting the conversions, there was a remarkable division by gender. In Mousehole, and perhaps in Newlyn too, it was the custom for men and women to sit on opposite sides of the chapel.[114] The separation at worship no doubt reflected patterns of sociability deriving from the specialization of labour within a fishing economy, with men going to sea and women responsible for fish curing. The same social arrangement recurred in the revival. At Newlyn, where the Wesleyans were preponderantly female before the awakening, there was a gendered division between some of its settings. Women had a prominent place in

110 Delta [Robert Young], 'Revivals of Religion – No. II', *Cornish Banner* (1846–7), 219. Most of the account of revivals published in this periodical that Young edited while at Truro is extracted from *Showers of Blessing*, but there are occasional alterations, of which this is one.

111 *Penzance Journal*, 31 January 1849, 4. This source gives the victim's age as 59; the source in the next note gives it as about 63.

112 *Penzance Gazette*, 31 January 1849 [4].

113 Young, 'Revival of Religion', 37.

114 J. J. Beckerlegge, *Two Hundred Years of Methodism in Mousehole* (Mousehole, 1954), 24.

cottage prayer meetings, but men held their own meetings for prayer in boats at sea.[115] Young remarked on the frequency of men among the converts in both villages. There was a gathering in Newlyn where three or four elderly men wept together in distress; and on Easter Monday, the hundred converts in the village were chiefly men. At Mousehole there were alternate phases when the awakening was predominantly male or female. At first the men took the lead, but soon they had to go to sea and so there was a time when wives, daughters and sisters were the subjects of the revival. Then, when the boats returned, the men took over once more.[116] In the aftermath of revival the two sexes paid separate and very gender-specific tributes to their minister: some of the men named one of the fishing boats the *Robert Young* while the women gave him a silver-plated teapot.[117] By contrast with Penzance, where the revival reaffirmed the solidarity of the family, in the fishing villages it followed the traditional gender divisions of the settlements. Outreach was not just gathering the young of the congregation but was penetrating the area as a whole. In Mousehole and Newlyn revival was a community affair.

There was, however, a significant difference between Mousehole and Newlyn. Whereas in Mousehole the awakening soon faded away, in Newlyn it was more protracted. Although the number of new members was roughly equal in the two places during the first quarter of 1849, there were more than twice as many in Newlyn as in Mousehole during the second and third quarters.[118] The contrasting patterns of recruitment are explicable in terms of the role of the class leaders. In Mousehole many of the classes were naturally led by fishermen. One of the four leading recruiters at the peak of the revival, William Beadon, was a ship's captain.[119] His new admissions fell from thirty-one in the first quarter to two and one in the next two periods. Likewise three other class leaders who can be identified as involved in fishing had only a single new recruit between them in the second and third quarters.[120]

115 Young, 'Revival of Religion', 37. The prominence of women in cottage prayer meetings is brought out by Deborah Valenze, *Prophetic Sons and Daughters: Female Preaching and Popular Religion in Industrial England* (Princeton, NJ, 1985).

116 Young, 'Revival of Religion', 35–7.

117 1851 Census, fol. 199. A. W. Young, 'Reminiscences: a Fisher of Men'.

118 Penzance Circuit, 1843–9; 1849–64. Information about new admissions in this paragraph is taken from these volumes.

119 1851 Census, fol. 223.

120 John Ash, William Harry and Thomas Matthews: 1851 Census, fols 225, 224.

Only one of the class leaders who was a fisherman, Joseph Wright, managed to keep up his work of adding new converts, and he was exceptional in being the leading figure in the Methodist society. It seems clear that the community was incapable of sustaining revival for more than a few weeks when its keenest advocates were absent at sea. In Newlyn, by contrast, the nine class leaders were more varied in occupation: two had private means, three were grocers, one was an artisan, two cannot be firmly identified and only one was definitely a fisherman.[121] These people were generally available to be called from their work to assist those seeking salvation.[122] The one class leader who proved a relatively weak recruiter, with only four members on trial in the first quarter and only two in the next two quarters together, was a fisherman. The exception confirms the overall case: it was hard for a place like Mousehole, where community leaders were seafarers, to keep up a long revival, but it was much easier in Newlyn, where occupations were far more varied. The dynamic of the Wesleyan classes therefore reflected the specific circumstances of the two villages. It is clear that there was no planned or imposed uniformity. The revivals of Mousehole and Newlyn were faithful reproductions of the distinctive environment of each place.

In any overall view of the events of 1849, however, the more marked contrast was between Penzance on the one hand and Mousehole and Newlyn on the other. The cultural difference is well illustrated by the circulation of the fairly weighty *Wesleyan Methodist Magazine* in the three places. Four years before the revival, when Penzance had eighteen subscribers, Mousehole had only four and Newlyn only a single one.[123] Penzance, with its more sophisticated readers, was a natural scene for an organized, orderly revival run by selected specialists. The event drew in young people from the congregation, but few outsiders, so inaugurating an era when Methodism in the town recruited largely from its own ranks.[124] Mousehole and Newlyn, with a less inhibited piety, experienced a more emotional awakening. Growth was still commonly from

121 Respectively Abraham Chirgwin, Susan Tonkin; Nicholas Berriman (though his shop was in Penzance), Benjamin Dale, George Richards; William Wallis; ? Hosking, ? Smith (both unidentifiable in census); and Richard Richards. 1851 Census, fols 309, 267; 624, 306, 236; 283; 277.

122 Young, 'Revival of Religion', 36.

123 Penzance Circuit, 1843–9, 26.

124 The process was national. Robert Currie *et al.*, *Churches and Churchgoers: Patterns of Church Growth in the British Isles since 1700* (Oxford, 1977), 71.

the outside, with the whole community stirred and a large number of older converts of both sexes. It was not long afterwards, however, before the changes already apparent in Penzance began to affect the fishing villages. In 1860, when revival again visited the villages, the chief class leaders taking in the converts were the Wesleyan day-school teachers of the two places.[125] Additions to the church were now expected to come from the children and were left to the professionals. By the 1890s Newlyn was holding a pre-planned mission with a paid district evangelist and Mousehole was conducting a revival, again organized in advance, complete with enquiry room and described as 'less loud and sensational than those of former times'.[126] Even in these haunts of old-fashioned ways the transformation of the revival tradition was in the longer term irresistible.

The awakening of 1849 was therefore at a point along a continuum that extended from the spontaneous to the contrived. It turns out not to have been the result of some unpredictable religious impulse such as Salome Hocking envisaged. The fear of death, whether from cholera or drowning, was clearly at work, as were hopes of a revival and the example of foreign missions, preventing the event from being entirely unprompted even before any deliberate encouragement. The ministers, however, set out both to foster the revival spirit and to turn it into acceptable channels. They succeeded in generating a revival at Penzance that was suffused with respectability. In the fishing villages, however, they bowed to the exuberant manners of the more traditional communities. In what was apparently a single happening, there were strikingly different styles of revival proceeding simultaneously, with even Newlyn and Mousehole revealing some contrasts. The microcosm of these places in south-west Cornwall reveals something of what was really happening in awakenings as culture and piety interwove. The microcosm, furthermore, sheds light on the macrocosm of the chronology of revival. There was evidently a shift over time from an earlier freedom of expression to a later imposition of decorum, from the spirit of the eighteenth-century Evangelical Revival to the institutions of twentieth-century mass evangelism. In the middle of the nineteenth

125 Levi Woolley of Mousehole and John Champion of Newlyn. Penzance Circuit, 1849–64.

126 *Cornish Methodist Church Record*, April 1893; and 1895, Truro, The Royal Institution of Cornwall, The Courtney Library, Thomas Shaw Collection, Mousehole section.

century Mousehole and Newlyn stood a little before the midway point of the process while Penzance was located some way after it. The fishing villages were closer to John Wesley and the town to Billy Graham.

University of Stirling

REVIVALISM, HISTORIANS, AND LIVED RELIGION IN THE EASTERN CANADA–UNITED STATES BORDERLANDS

by HANNAH LANE

HISTORIANS of evangelicalism in Canada and the United States have long debated the timing and nature of changes in revivalism in the northeast during the nineteenth century and the vocabulary that best describes these changes. Calvinist and Arminian theologies provided two approaches to this history: revivalism and 'declension' as widespread but cyclical, and wholly dependent on God; or revivalism as a dispersed but continual force, sustained also by human effort. The former framework has informed studies of Baptists and Congregationalists, and the latter, studies of Methodists, whose history did not fit common periodizations of the Second Great Awakening.[1]

Early studies of evangelicalism in nineteenth-century British North America portrayed Methodist revivalism in the Atlantic colonies as less enthusiastic and declining earlier than either Methodist revivalism in Upper Canada or Baptist revivalism in the Maritimes and northern New England. Baptist revivalism also weakened over the century, especially in churches most removed from 'New Light' origins.[2] This portrait relied on instructions given to Methodist missionaries by their English sponsors and on the assumption that greater enthusiasm reflected North American influences. Such interpretations overlooked not only the enthusiasm still within English Wesleyan Methodism, but also the diversity within evangelicalism in the northeast as a whole. Moreover, revisionists argue that traditional and transformed reviv-

[1] Kathryn Long, *The Revival of 1857–58: Interpreting an American Religious Awakening* (New York and Oxford, 1998); Richard Carwardine, *Trans-Atlantic Revivalism: Popular Evangelicalism in Britain and America 1790–1865* (Westport, CT, 1978); David Hempton, *Methodism: Empire of the Spirit* (London and New Haven, CT, 2005).

[2] Goldwin French, *Parsons and Politics: the Role of the Wesleyan Methodists in Upper Canada and the Maritimes* (Toronto, Ont., 1962); Neil Semple, *The Lord's Dominion: the History of Canadian Methodism* (Montreal, Que. and Kingston, Ont., 1996); George Rawlyk, *The Canada Fire: Radical Evangelicalism in British North America 1775–1812* (Montreal, Que. and Kingston, Ont., 1994).

alism persisted within older denominations until the early twentieth century.[3] Thus, the history of revivalism is part of ongoing debate on the nature and timing of modernization and secularization.[4]

The concept of 'lived religion', in which local institutional and popular religion are understood as interwoven rather than oppositional,[5] provides an innovative approach to the study of revivalism in communities shaped by British and American influences. The parish of St Stephen, New Brunswick and the neighbouring districts of Calais and Baring, Maine are located at the head of the tide on an international boundary river. In this cluster of small towns and settlements, revivalism from the 1830s to the early 1880s was a recurring phenomenon, but neither continuous nor in decline.[6] Yet though earlier revivalism coincided with the last significant immigration of British Protestants to these places, economic and demographic forces offset the impact of later revivalism on church growth.

The focus of this essay will be on the earliest organized group with the richest sources – the Wesleyan Methodists (1785) – with some discussion of Baptists and Congregationalists. By the 1820s, Methodist congregations in St Stephen were connected to English Wesleyans, Methodists in Calais to the Methodist Episcopal Church, and Congregationalists had organized locally. During the 1830s, Regular (Calvinist)

3 G. A. Rawlyk, ed., *Aspects of the Canadian Evangelical Experience* (Montreal, Que. and Kingston, Ont., 1997); Eric R. Crouse, *Revival in the City: the Impact of American Evangelists in Canada* (Montreal, Que. and Kingston, Ont., 2005); Nancy Christie and Michael Gauvreau, *A Full-Orbed Christianity: the Protestant Churches and Social Welfare in Canada 1900–1940* (Montreal, Que. and Kingston, Ont., 1996).

4 David Marshall, *Secularizing the Faith: Canadian Protestant Clergy and the Crisis of Belief, 1850–1940* (Toronto, Ont., 1992); Janice Holmes, *Religious Revivals in Britain and Ireland 1859–1905* (Dublin, 2000).

5 David D. Hall, ed., *Lived Religion in America: toward a History of Practice* (Princeton, NJ, 1997). The few Canadian studies to take this approach include Lynne Marks, *Revivals and Roller Rinks: Religion, Leisure, and Identity in Late-Nineteenth-Century Small-town Ontario* (Toronto, Ont., 1996), and Marguerite Van Die, '"The Marks of a Genuine Revival": Religion, Social Change, Gender, and Community in Mid-Victorian Brantford, Ontario', *Canadian Historical Review* 79 (1998), 524–63.

6 This is documented more fully in Lane, 'Tribalism, Proselytism, and Pluralism: Protestants, Family, and Denominational Identity in Mid-Nineteenth Century St Stephen, New Brunswick', in Nancy Christie, ed., *Households of Faith: Family, Gender, and Community in Canada 1760–1969* (Montreal, Que. and Kingston, Ont., 2002), 103–37; Lane, 'Methodist Church Members, Lay Leaders and Socio-economic Position in Mid-Nineteenth Century St Stephen, New Brunswick', unpublished PhD thesis, University of New Brunswick, Fredericton, 2004 and eadem, 'Re-Numbering Souls: Lay Methodism and Church Growth in St Stephen, New Brunswick, 1861–1881', unpublished MA thesis, University of New Brunswick, Fredericton 1993.

Baptists built churches and Methodism expanded, but a subsequent Methodist schism led to the formation of a second Congregationalist church. After mid-century, Presbyterians, non-Calvinist Baptists and Adventists organized churches, which, like those of the Congregationalists and Regular Baptists, served both sides of the river.[7]

In the 1861 census of St Stephen, Wesleyan Methodists were the single largest religious group, at 26% of a population of 5,160. Only a minority of local Congregationalists and Baptists lived on the New Brunswick side of the river, constituting 5% and 7% of this total. These figures for nominal religious adherence[8] have no equivalent in censuses for Calais and Baring, whose combined population was enumerated at 6,030 in 1860. According to this census, Baptist and Congregationalist meeting houses in Calais could seat at least 500, but Episcopal Methodist meetinghouses were smaller.[9] These denominations all held Sunday services, week-night prayer meetings, and occasional revival meetings.

This paper's sources are denominational records and newspapers, especially representations of religious experience and practice. As forms of cultural construction, these are a mixture of portrait and prescription. The texts followed stylized literary forms: jeremiad, exhortation, 'spiritual report' or 'revival intelligence', and the spiritual history or religious obituary. Their language was drawn from historic Christian and nineteenth-century discourse, including the evangelical vernacular.[10] The focus will be on references to revivalism as the term is used in the vocabulary of the time, rather than on revivalism defined more broadly and theologically.

The most systematic records survive for the Wesleyan Methodists in St Stephen and the Regular Baptists on both sides of the river. In at least

[7] I. C. Knowlton, *Annals of Calais, Maine, and St Stephen, New Brunswick* (Calais, 1875; rpt. St Stephen, NB, 1875), 10–14; Rev. Joshua Millet, *History of the Baptists in Maine* (Portland, ME, 1845), 369–70; T. W. Acheson, 'Methodism and the Problem of Methodist Identity in Nineteenth-Century New Brunswick', in Charles H. H. Scobie and John Webster Grant, eds, *The Contribution of Methodism to Atlantic Canada* (Montreal, Que. and Kingston, Ont., 1992), 107–23.

[8] *Census of the Province of New Brunswick* (Saint John, NB, 1861); 'adherence' and 'adherents' follow nineteenth-century usage, referring to what was recorded on Canadian census returns.

[9] 'Social Statistics', Censuses of Calais and Baring, 1850 and 1860, available on microfilm at Maine State Archives, Augusta, Maine, USA.

[10] Ann Taves, *Fits, Trances, and Visions: Experiencing Religion and Explaining Experience from Wesley to James* (Princeton, NJ, 1999).

twenty-nine years between 1830 and 1881, ministers, lay leaders, or a local newspaper reported a revival in one or more of five Wesleyan Methodist congregations.[11] Baptists tended to reserve the term 'revival' for numerical success; the three largest Baptist congregations reported revivals in at least eighteen years between 1834 and 1881.[12] Although the rural Baptist church in St Stephen remained weak, a new village church formed after a revival in the late 1860s.[13] Maine Congregationalists looked for signs of revival within their regular worship, and rarely used special services. According to one minister, the older church experienced its first revival in the winter of 1836–7 and 6 or 7 revivals' during the writer's two pastorates between 1839 and 1867; the other church had 'enjoyed 4 revivals' between its organization in 1846 and the late 1870s.[14]

From seasonal work habits, the long evenings, and perhaps the psychological effects of shorter and colder days, winter in the northeast was 'by long-established custom' the revival season.[15] A few revivals began in the January union week of prayer meetings observed by local Methodists and one or more other denominations from the late 1850s on. 'Protracted meetings' could last several hours, and some revivals lasted several months. Evangelicals also held longer services connected with official gatherings and meetings held over several days to which people might travel from various distances, by the 1850s also called 'camp meetings'. Some Wesleyan Methodists, Baptists, and Congregationalists were leery of interdenominational overnight meetings as an 'old west' religious form, despite their resemblance to earlier models, but this view was not typical of these denominations as a whole.[16] A few

[11] See the annual 'Spiritual Reports' and letters sent to the Committee of the Wesleyan Missionary Society, available on microfilm at Provincial Archives of New Brunswick, Fredericton, New Brunswick, Canada; after 1855, the best sources are *The Provincial Wesleyan* and local newspapers.

[12] *Minutes*, Washington Baptist Association, Maine, 1843–62; *Minutes*, Maine Baptist Convention, 1834–81; H. V. Dexter, 'Farewell Sermon', *St Croix Courier*, 22 April 1869.

[13] *Minutes*, New Brunswick Association of Baptists, 1834–44; *Minutes*, Western New Brunswick Association of Baptists, 1845–81.

[14] Michael D. Carter, *Converting the Wasteplaces of Zion: the Maine Missionary Society 1807–1862* (Wolfeboro, NH, 1990); Seth H. Keeler, *The Apostolic Method of Church Extension* (Augusta, ME, 1853), and idem, *A Semi-centennial Discourse, delivered at Calais, Me., June 3, 1879. Minutes*, Washington Baptist Association, Maine, 1843–62; Maine Baptist Convention, 1834–81; H. V. Dexter, 'Farewell Sermon', *St Croix Courier*, 22 April 1869.

[15] *Provincial Wesleyan*, 22 November 1851; 10 November 1869; 31 January 1872.

[16] Lane, 'Re-Numbering Souls', 77–9, 83–4; W. Ralph Richardson, 'Methodist Revivalism and the Baptists of Eastern British America in 1858', in David T. Priestly, ed., *A Fragile*

open-air services, but no camp meetings, were held in St Stephen and Calais, although some evangelicals were camp meeting leaders elsewhere. A minister in St Stephen had participated in a New Brunswick meeting with reportedly four thousand in attendance and traditional Methodist 'shouting'.[17]

Literary conventions and divergent accounts of the same revival make it difficult to distinguish consciously figurative language from more literal descriptions. Moreover, ministers tried simultaneously and sometimes contradictorily to portray both order and sincere emotional display. The concern for order is evident in an 1836 representation of 'protracted meetings . . . during which no unnecessary noise or confusion intruded upon the deep and lasting solemnities of the scene.'[18] In one revival account, 'a most solemn feeling seems to rest upon the whole assembly;' in another of the same revival, 'Old and young were seen mingling their prayers and tears at the Altar Crying God to be merciful to me a sinner.' A much later writer praised 'the absence of excitement or the exercise of the loud mouthed protestations, so often seen at religious meetings', including those previously held in this church. Instead, 'earnest men and women wrestle in prayer, pleading for forgiveness for themselves and others.'[19]

Other emotions were also key to local revivals: one minister wrote in 1858 that 'the friends are saying with tears in their eyes, these are good days – happy times.'[20] For a few Methodists, a revival might lead to what was described in the vocabulary of entire sanctification, Christian perfection, or holiness. Originally referring to the achievement of perfect love of God and neighbour, sanctification was increasingly associated with an ambiguous post-conversion experience, reached gradually or climactically.[21] The physicality of local revivals consisted mainly of movement from bench or pew to the front of the church, and the

Stability: Definition and Redefinition of Maritime Baptist Identity (Hantsport, NS, 1994), 21–34; Joseph Ricker, *Personal Recollections* (Augusta, ME, 1894), 102–3.

17 *Provincial Wesleyan*, 2 October 1856; 5 October 1871; 29 August 1860.

18 'Spiritual Report', St Stephen Circuit, 1836, available on microfilm at Maritime Conference Archives, United Church of Canada, Sackville, New Brunswick, Canada; see also Carter, *Converting the Wasteplaces of Zion*, 53.

19 Enoch Wood, Committee of the Wesleyan Missionary Society, 16 February 1844 and 'Spiritual Report', St Stephen Circuit, 1844, available on microfilm at Maritime Conference Archives, see n. 18 above; *St Croix Courier*, 29 November 1867.

20 *Provincial Wesleyan*, 20 May 1858; see also 23 March 1864.

21 See Lane, 'Re-Numbering Souls', 66–71.

altar call was also part of regular Methodist worship.[22] Being overcome by emotion to the point of falling to the ground was uncommon locally in this period, but not unheard of.[23] An 1860 revival in a nearby parish in which St Stephen Methodists participated may have reflected widely disseminated accounts of the Ulster revival of 1859: during a regular Sunday service 'a young woman lately arrived from Ireland was struck with deep conviction . . . and . . . at our Friday evening prayer-meeting, she suddenly sank down upon the floor, and after remaining there a short time began audibly to whisper.'[24]

Some Wesleyan Methodist ministers in the Maritime colonies portrayed their revivalism as more respectable than that of other denominations. But they did so because it had remained enthusiastic enough still to require defending. In a controversy over the annual legislative grant to the Wesleyan Academy in Sackville, New Brunswick, a Church of England member described a revival there as 'a species of Fanatiscism' [sic] and two other members of the council deplored the 'religious excitement'. In 1859, an account of a 'powerful and glorious revival' among Methodists from St Stephen and neighbouring communities included a response to local critics.[25]

Writers on revivals perceived them as having occurred or not occurred for various reasons, from the spiritual state of the congregation to more specific factors. Individuals concerned about their own spiritual state inspired ministers or lay leaders to make extra efforts. Obvious hindrances to revivals were local conflicts or preoccupation with rebuilding chapels after fires or storms. Both past commentators and present scholars have found the influence of social context inconsistent in explaining either revival efforts or their relative success. Ministers generally found political questions a negative influence, with the exception of the temperance movement, which some perceived as part of an authentic revival, and others as a distraction. While urban revivals in the northeast in 1857 and 1873 partially reflected trade depressions, news of these revivals was more influential in St Stephen

22 *Provincial Wesleyan*, 10 September 1862; 4 May 1874.

23 T. Watson Smith, *History of Methodism in Eastern British North America*, 2 vols (Halifax, NS, 1877), 2: 251–2; Robert Cooney, *Autobiography of a Wesleyan Methodist Missionary* (Montreal, Que., 1856), 212–14.

24 *Provincial Wesleyan*, 6 June 1860.

25 Cited in John G. Reid, *Mount Allison University: a History, vol. 1: 1843–1914* (Toronto, Ont., 1984), 38–41; *Provincial Wesleyan*, 7 April 1859.

and Calais and predated local economic downturns.[26] Revivals spread because churches were inspired by the example or success of others. For example, personal networks of 'revival intelligence' connected local evangelicals to the Moody revivals in Boston.[27] A novelty in 1878 was the co-operation between local ministers and less prominent professional itinerants in a three month revival.[28]

Ideally for churches, the most tangible effects of revivals were larger congregations and especially new members. Wesleyan Methodists, Congregationalists and Baptists shared similar but not identical criteria for church membership. Their official theological understandings of the language and psychology of conversion varied; and religious obituaries suggest that these also varied among individuals and those who memorialized them. Some Methodist members were remembered as having been spiritually awakened during revivals, but converting later; others, even early in the century, experienced conversion as 'a gradual and uniform process'.[29] For membership, all three denominations required expression of religious experience to clergy and lay leaders or other members. Whereas Methodist members also included those awakened but still seeking conversion, Congregationalists[30] and Baptists[31] needed to show that they were fully and genuinely converted. These denominations also varied in their acceptance of members from other denominations, and in their criteria for continued membership, which for the Wesleyan Methodists was still based on attendance at class meetings.

Most but not all of the members of evangelical churches had joined at some point during a revival year, though whether during or because of a specific revival service is impossible to say except for a few whose

[26] Lane, 'Re-Numbering Souls', 76–7, 178–80, 185–7; Michael J. McClymond, 'Issues and Explanations in the Study of North American Revivalism', idem, ed., *Embodying the Spirit: New Perspectives on North American Revivalism* (Baltimore, MD, and London, 2004), 1–46.

[27] *Provincial Wesleyan*, 31 March 1877.

[28] *St Croix Courier*, 10 January – 21 February 1878, *Provincial Wesleyan*, 2 March 1878; Records, St Stephen Circuit, 1878.

[29] *Provincial Wesleyan*, 19 April 1855; see also Christie, 'Re-Numbering Souls', chs 4 and 5.

[30] *Historical Sketch of the First Congregational Church, Calais, Maine, with Confession of Faith, Covenant, Rules and Catalogue of Members to May, 1877* (Boston, MA, 1877); Records of the Congregational Church, Calais, Maine, 1825–81 (xerox, Maine Historical Society, Portland) and of the First Orthodox Congregational Church, Milltown, 1845–81 (Provincial Archives of New Brunswick), *Manual of Congregationalism* (Portland, ME, 1859).

[31] See Ricker, *Personal Recollections* and note 13 above.

obituaries included this information. Yet despite recurring revivals, overall church involvement was lower than that implied in some nostalgic assumptions about the past. The best available information on attendance suggests that roughly half of Wesleyan Methodist families enumerated in 1871 in St Stephen were regular attenders. With regard to the smaller group of actual church members, in the 1861 census, just over one fourth of individuals over the age of fourteen and enumerated as Methodist adherents were members between 1860 and 1862, and another fifth were former or future members in other years between 1840 and 1881. With more complete records and less demanding requirements for continued membership, 40% of the small number of Congregationalists in St Stephen were current members, but almost all had been members some time between 1825 and 1881.

Further analysis of these records shows that wider cultural, economic, and demographic forces offset the impact of revivals on church growth. As elsewhere, and for similar reasons concerning associational and work patterns and cultural constructions of gender, women were more likely than men to join evangelical churches. Although some commentators were concerned that pressure to contribute financially deterred the poor from membership, churches used flexible fundraising methods, and preliminary research suggests that members were socially diverse.[32]

The most obvious constraints on the effects of revivals on church growth were high rates of transiency. In northern New England and Atlantic Canada, this included outmigration from the region altogether, the pull of the west and the push of early rural decline. Of Wesleyan Methodist members between 1840 and 1881, only 27% were still members in 1881 and another 15% disappeared from the records without a clear explanation. Of the remainder – those known to have died, left the parish, or ceased their membership – 40% were listed as having left St Stephen, of whom only a small number moved to Calais. More precise records for nearly all Congregationalist members in Calais and St Stephen between 1825 and 1881 show that at least 35% had left these communities by 1881. In 1869, a Baptist minister noted

32 Lane, 'Evangelicals, Church Finance, and Wealth-holding in Mid-Nineteenth Century St Stephen, New Brunswick and Calais, Maine', in Michael Gauvreau and Ollivier Hubert, eds, *The Churches and Social Order in Nineteenth- and Twentieth-Century Canada* (Montreal, Que. and Kingston, Ont., 2006), 109–50.

that transiency offset revivalism in church growth, estimating that three times 'as many families have removed from among us within the last 8 years as are now connected with this congregation.'[33]

By the late 1870s, some commentators on Methodism in the region saw changes in revivalism. One lamented preferences for eloquent preaching over a 'rousing prayer meeting' and that 'Methodist shouts . . . are banished to lands less cultivated.' Another urged that traditional prayer meetings not be superseded by those featuring mainly the 'testimony' of the converted.[34] Some have argued that Methodism recovered John Wesley's original moderation while merging with the Romantic 'rhetoric of inspiration and heroic individualism'.[35] Similarly, evangelical discourse in New England moved through doctrinalism, moralism, and devotionalism or sentimentalism, focusing on religious feelings and the means of eliciting them.[36] Although late nineteenth-century revivals contained elements of all of these styles, these distinctions might have been recognizable to their observers.

Nevertheless, church records, newspaper accounts, and religious obituaries suggest that in St Stephen Wesleyan Methodist revivalism was stronger from the late 1850s on than it had been since the early 1840s.[37] This echoed trans-Atlantic patterns of church growth related to inter- and intra-denominational strife, migration patterns and trade cycles, but also reflected local church conflicts and hardship. Revivalism in St Stephen and Calais may have been stronger than in other communities; according to one 1879 writer on Methodism in the Maritimes, some places had not 'been religiously disturbed for ten, fifteen or twenty years'. Others argued that the holiness movement showed that 'experimental religion' and the 'witness of the spirit' were even more 'explicit' in the 1880s than they had been earlier.[38] One can speculate that Methodism in Atlantic Canada may have remained more

[33] See H. V. Dexter, 'Farewell Sermon', *St Croix Courier*, 22 April 1869.

[34] *Provincial Wesleyan*, 11 January 1879, 1 February 1879, 2 September 1881.

[35] Semple, *Lord's Dominion*; William Westfall, *Two Worlds: the Protestant Culture of Nineteenth-Century Ontario* (Montreal, Que. and Kingston, Ont., 1989), 76–89.

[36] Richard Rabinowitz, *The Spiritual Self in Everyday Life: the Transformation of Religious Experience in Nineteenth-Century New England* (Boston, MA, 1989).

[37] See also Calvin Clark, *History of the Congregational Churches in Maine*, 2 vols (Portland, ME, 1926), 1: 342–4.

[38] *Provincial Wesleyan*, 11 January 1879; Stephen F. Huestis, *Centenary of Methodism in Eastern British America 1782–1882* (Halifax, NS, 1882), 65; see also Ricker, *Personal Recollections*, 103, and Henry S. Burrage, *History of the Baptists in Maine* (Portland, ME, 1904), 470.

enthusiastic or more accommodating of its different strains, thus protecting itself from the divisions over styles of revivalism that occurred in larger denominational groups elsewhere, or at least delaying them until the formation of the United Church of Canada in 1925.

Overall, in St Stephen and Calais, revivalism was sometimes confined to only one church, sometimes shared by more than one church, but only in a few years by more than one denomination or community. A micro-history approach to the study of revivalism thus confirms the limitations of contextual or contagion theories of revivalism, and the importance of leaders and individuals' private reasons for their responses. The demographic analysis suggests that revival participation was not necessarily equivalent to formal church involvement, and shows the limitations of aggregate totals of church members as revival indicators, since these can conceal how transiency prevented the retention of those who did join churches.

This study also suggests that arguments for American or, more rarely, Canadian exceptionalism in the history of evangelicalism are more useful as speculative reflections on whole national histories, or concerning very historically specific questions,[39] than as models applicable to borderlands communities. Moreover, distinguishing revivalism as more or less British or American is more problematic for coastal, densely populated contiguous communities along the Canadian-American border than for inland settlement frontiers, such as the Eastern Townships in Quebec.[40] This essay's concentration on Wesleyan Methodism should not be take to imply that revivalism was absent in other traditions in St Stephen and Calais. Moreover, literary sources suggest that many of those who attended church services including revivals came from a variety of denominations, and quantitative analysis of adult Protestants linked to two New Brunswick census returns found considerable movement between denominations. Though local evangelicals could conflict

39 See William Westfall, 'Voices from the Attic: the Canadian Border and the Writing of American Religious History', in Thomas A. Tweed, ed., *Retelling U.S. Religious History* (Berkely and Los Angeles, CA, 1997), 181–99. Thus, Canadian-American differences seem sharper when the American South is included. In contrast, see David Bell's nuanced analysis of non-Calvinist Baptists in Maine and New Brunswick, 'Yankee Preachers and the Struggle for the New Brunswick Christian Conference, 1828–1838', in Daniel C. Goodwin, ed., *Revivals, Baptists, and George Rawlyk* (Wolfville, NS, 2000), 93–112.

40 J. I. Little, *Borderland Religion: the Emergence of an English-Canadian Identity, 1792–1852* (Toronto, Ont., 2004).

on some points, they co-operated on others, a balance perhaps more typical of the northeast than elsewhere. In St Stephen and Calais, revivalism was multi-denominational and borderless, reflecting these communities' broad and fluid evangelicalism.[41]

Mount Allison University

41 See Lane, 'Tribalism, Proselytism, and Pluralism', and Richard Carwardine, 'Unity, Pluralism, and the Spiritual Market-Place: Interdenominational Competition in the Early American Republic', in R. N. Swanson, ed., *Unity and Diversity in the Church*, SCH 32 (Oxford, 1996), 297–335.

THE PLEASANT SUNDAY AFTERNOON MOVEMENT: REVIVAL IN THE WEST MIDLANDS, 1875–90?

by DAVID KILLINGRAY

IN January 1875 John Blackham, a West Bromwich draper, a deacon and Sunday school teacher from the Ebenezer Congregational Church, went to Birmingham intent on hearing the American evangelist Dwight D. Moody. So large was the crowd that Blackham was turned away from the meeting. He then went to look for an alternative Christian gathering and, in his own words,

> I came across a room where about 30 fine young fellows were assembled listening to their teacher, a magnificent man, with a marvellous store of information. His address was *so long and so good* that my head and back ached with the prolonged attention. ... I wondered how it was that Moody could get 4,000, while this splendid Bible class leader could only draw about thirty, and as I thought on this *the first light broke in*, and I saw clearly why we had failed. I learnt also *how not to do it*. I realised that if the men were to be won, we must give them a service neither too long nor too learned, we must avoid dullness, gloom, and constraint.[1]

Blackham's deep concern was that most young men ceased to attend church. His solution to help 'reclaim the lapsed masses' to Christian faith was first to call the Ebenezer congregation to pray. He then went out into the streets of West Bromwich to seek young men, former Sunday school scholars who did not attend a religious service, and invite them to a 'a pleasant Sunday afternoon class' that 'will be short and bright' and 'only last three-quarters of an hour.'[2] Within a few weeks 120 men were attending a class in the Ebenezer schoolroom, but as numbers rapidly increased it moved into the church.[3] Within a few

1 *The P.S.A. Reporter & Record for Stockport and District*, No. 1, March 1892, 1–7. *The P.S.A. Leader*, June 1898, 98. John Richards, 'On a Sunday Afternoon', *The Blackcountryman* 2: 4 (1969), 38–42.

2 *P.S.A. Leader*, June 1898, 98.

3 A. Holden Byles said that the PSA 'sprang out of the Adult Bible-Class movement originated in Birmingham forty-five years ago by the late Mr. Joseph Sturge. . . . The P.S.A. Movement – started by Mr. Blackham in West Bromwich fifteen years ago – is a further

months other local nonconformist churches in the Black Country had established Pleasant Sunday Afternoon (PSA) classes, and ten years later there were more than a dozen classes in West Bromwich and a total of 35,000 men regularly meeting each Sunday afternoon for Gospel services within a radius of eight miles of the town.[4]

Although the PSA is mentioned briefly in studies of late nineteenth-century nonconformity there is no detailed study of the movement.[5] This paper, initial research in a joint study of the PSA and Brotherhood being undertaken by the author and Dr Mark Smith of Oxford, examines the early years of the PSA and places it in the context of the various attempts made by various denominations and non-denominational bodies, such as the Salvation Army, to evangelize the working classes. The early purpose of the PSA was primarily evangelical, conceiving spiritual change allied to ideas of self-improvement as an answer to prevailing acute social and economic distress.

In 1885 the PSA spread first to Derby, then to Nottingham, and thereafter throughout the British Isles and overseas. By the early twentieth century regional and national federations had been created, some classes being more intent on social reform than spiritual transformation. Under its new title 'PSA and Brotherhood' it increasingly attracted the support of leading figures of the Labour parties and the trade unions. By 1910 it had half a million members in the United Kingdom and abroad. There are certain problems in researching the history of the early PSA classes. Each class was autonomous and met in church, chapel, or a convenient public hall. The 'movement' in the early years lacked a regional and national structure. Records for individual classes do exist but these are scattered and often incorporated within the records of the churches to which they were attached. It was not until 1888 that the Nottingham class began producing a regular monthly

effort in the same direction, but on somewhat different lines'. Byles, *The P.S.A. What it is, and How to Start* it (London, 1891), 4. See, further, S. Lees, 'History of Ebenezer Chapel, West Bromwich' (1906 ms., copy in William Salt Library, Stafford).

4 *P.S.A. Reporter & Record*, No.1, March 1892, 5. Of course, this figure needs to be properly investigated; even if halved, to exclude those who attended occasionally, it is a remarkable figure.

5 K. S. Inglis, *Churches and the Working Classes in Victorian England* (London, 1963), 79–85. Two brief works written by officials of the Brotherhood Movement are J. W. Tuffley, *The Sowers* (London, 1937), and A. E. H. Gregory, *Romance and Revolution: the Story of the Brotherhood Movement 1875–1975* (Sevenoaks, n.d. *c.*1975). The Brotherhood and Sisterhood Movement continues today with about 2,000 members, run from Penge Congregational Church in south-east London.

magazine for members. (No surviving copies of this publication have yet been identified). Perhaps more surprising is that the spectacular growth in the number of PSA classes in the Black Country and beyond by 1890 was rarely mentioned in the contemporary ecclesiastical press. For example, an article in *The Congregationalist*, edited by J. Guinness Rogers, in 1886, discussed the work of the Salvation Army, and how working men might be reached for the church, but there is no mention of the PSA.[6] When John Blackham addressed the fiftieth autumnal meeting of the Congregational Union meeting in Hull on 'The PSA movements' this received a one-line mention in the *Congregational Year Book 1890*.[7] Two years later John Blackham commented in the *P.S.A. Reporter & Record* that 'the P.S.A. has spread over England faster than that other great movement of our times, the Salvation Army, and is spreading still, quicker than ever'.[8] But the PSA did not have a central organization or a uniform, nor did it project a high public profile by aggressive evangelistic and social activity.

Attempts by nonconformists, mainly of evangelical persuasion, to promote the Gospel among working-class men by a variety of means were not new. Similar meetings had been organized for men earlier in the century. In 1854, the politically radical Baptist pastor, Revd Hugh Stowell Brown (1828–86) of Myrtle St Chapel, Liverpool, began a PSA-style meeting for working men, mainly skilled labourers, in the Concert Hall, and in 1861 he established a workman's bank.[9] The interest of another Baptist, John Clifford, in reaching working men began at Praed Street Chapel, London in 1859,[10] while Harper Twelvetrees, an industrialist with dye and chemical factories in the East End of London, a supporter of abolitionism and temperance, in an attempt to

6 J. Guinness Rogers, 'The Churches and the Working Classes', *The Congregationalist*, May 1886, 329–36. Rogers does point to the 'special services for working men on Sunday afternoons' that he established when minister at Ashton-under-Lyne, which he describes as a 'denominational class'.

7 Blackham (1834–1923), was a linen draper in West Bromwich, in partnership with William Eld, a fellow member of Ebenezer Congregational Church. He and Eld, from 1892–1900, traded as 'linen drapers, booksellers and publishers', supplying books to the PSA; from 1900 the two men 'ran "The PSA Bookshop", 63 & 64 Moor Street., Birmingham'. Blackham opposed the idea of a PSA federation and declined to become its first president. He is not mentioned in any of the standard biographical works. For obituaries, see the Liberal *West Bromwich Free Press*, 8 June 1923, 6, and the *West Bromwich Weekly News*, 8 June 1923, 5.

8 *P.S.A. Reporter & Record*, No. 1, March 1892, 7.

9 H. Stowell Brown, *Lectures to the Men of Liverpool*, 3 vols (Liverpool, 1858, 1859, 1860).

10 D. Thompson, 'John Clifford's Social Gospel', *Baptist Quarterly* 31: 5 (1986), 199–217.

elevate his work force, built a hall next to his factory in 1861, and organized temperance and choral societies, literary and mechanics institutes, lectures and concerts.[11] F. B. Meyer, following his encounter with D. L. Moody in the 1870s, made the evangelism of the 'submerged masses' one of his major goals, and later founded a PSA class at Christ Church Lambeth.[12] And at Ashton-under-Lyne the PSA meeting, so it was reported, was 'a very old class that had been in existence for fifty years and was doing PSA work before the PSA was started'.[13]

Revival?

Can the growth of the PSA classes in the West Midlands, and in certain other localities, be described as 'revival' or 'awakening'? Certainly any minister of a church, finding that over 1,000 unchurched men were regularly turning up each Sunday afternoon for a Gospel service would count this to be so. PSA origins in West Bromwich may owe something to the revivalist meetings of Moody and Sankey, but to what extent is not clear. The early PSA classes soon adopted Sankey's *Sacred Songs and Solos*, and class meetings included ingredients copied from the large revival meetings. Revival was in the air but its development requires further research. However, the growth in numbers of men, and women, attending PSA meetings from a specific geographical area, and with many becoming Christians would seem strongly to indicate that this was revival

Blackham had a background in Adult School work and he was all too aware of the failure of the churches to appeal to the needs of working-class men. Many nonconformist churches had become the preserves of the middle classes, financed in part by pew rents, and

[11] R. J. M. Blackett, *Beating against the Barriers: the Lives of Six Nineteenth-Century Afro-Americans* (Ithaca, NY, 1986), 210.

[12] Ian M. Randall, *Spirituality and Social Change: the Contribution of F.B. Meyer* (Carlisle, 2003), 233.

[13] *The P.S.A. Leader*, March 1906, 33. According to J. Guinness Rogers, *An Autobiography* (London, 1903), whose second pastorate was at Old Albion Chapel, Ashton-under-Lyne (Congregational), the Sunday School was 'a mighty force, not only in promoting the work of the congregation, but in the influence which it exerted upon the town' (109). Rogers formed a Working Men's Class 'which itself was a remarkable power for good in a stratum of the social life of the town where such influence was sadly needed. It grew partly out of a series of lectures delivered by me on Sunday afternoons addressed to the working classes' (200 men, met week days and on Sundays); 'one of the most conspicuous members' soundly converted from a ' blackguardly life', became a stalwart supporter of Rogers and the Class (110).

offering sermons in an environment that helped emphasize the educational and social inferiority of working-class men. Providing a different form of service was hardly inspired, and yet it worked. Men came regularly and consistently in large numbers to meetings, often held in a non-church setting, which were designed to be 'bright, brief and brotherly' with hymns, solos, a Bible reading, and a short Gospel address. 'Best' clothes were not required, the structure of most classes was democratic and informal, clapping and cheering were often permitted, and tea provided. At the same time, the whole needs of men were catered for with help in literacy and numeracy, a penny savings banks, sick provident funds, and books offered as prizes and as an incentive to regular attendance, although the men paid for the books. What occurred in the West Midlands and elsewhere was certainly not 'spontaneous and unstructured'. Blackham's approach to evangelism was carefully organized and planned, although it is doubtful if he ever thought that it would be met by such a large response. He was not planning for revival although intent on 'regaining the lapsed masses'. His object was confined to the locality of the Ebenezer church, at least to start with, and not to the whole of West Bromwich.

Blackham's methods provided a pattern for others planning similar classes. In Nottingham, Hanley, Batley, and elsewhere, Bible class members or church congregations were mobilized, weeks of prayer arranged, door-to-door visitation carried out, leaflets distributed, and the town covered with large posters. In 1890, when the Revd A. Holden Byles began a society at Tabernacle Church, Hanley, Staffordshire, he required the support of the whole congregation, a preliminary visit to, or meeting with representatives from, a PSA class, followed by a week of prayer so that 'Faith will be strengthened and vision enlarged'. Next, he argued, 'catch the hare' by extensive advertising such as was used by 'commercial undertakings' and theatres which in his case involved 'big flaming advertisements to secure attention and awaken interest'. For ten days members of the congregation distributed 10,000 handbills to homes and to workshops.[14] This had become a standard formula for local evangelism, but it was not always effective, even for the PSA.[15]

[14] Byles, *The P.S.A.*, 19, 21–4. *P.S.A. Leader*, November 1902, 166. See also Theodore Taylor's account of starting a PSA class in Batley, quoted in George A. Greenwood, *Taylor of Batley: a Story of 102 Years* (London, 1957), 48–9. Taylor (1850–1952), was president of the Batley Congregational Church PSA from 1891–1922 when he became a Labour M.P.

[15] *The Congregationalist*, January 1883, 83, reported that several thousand listened to Moody at Southampton but that Archibald Brown, of East London Tabernacle, 'records with

So why did it meet with such a positive response in the West Midlands and in other localities? At this stage of the research it is difficult to be specific. Most members of PSA classes seem to have come from a common background or area. Men worked in similar forms of employment and lived in an environment that bred some sense of communal identity. But in many areas where the PSA flourished there was not a common sense of shared hardship in dangerous employment to enhance an awareness of mortality, which, it has been suggested, may have influenced religious revival in fishing communities in Scotland and Cornwall.[16] As was pointed out by many observers, most areas of London, with growing and constantly shifting populations, lacked a strong sense of communal identity and as a result PSA classes were not so easy to form and sustain in the capital.

Early PSA meetings drew on the methods of Moody and Sankey but without the manipulation of audiences and devoid of emotionalism or sentimentalism; they were direct and practical. As meetings were held every week and attended by a solid core of members, it was difficult to sustain interest by recourse to gimmicks and theatricals. As far as can be seen for the period 1875 to 1890, the vast majority of PSA gatherings were pointedly evangelistic, intent on 'winning men for Christ'. Revivals that were 'spontaneous' were invariably attended by dramatic conversion experiences. Other revivals, where there was a pronounced growth of interest in Christian faith, were more gradual, especially for men, and attended by what Parsons describes as 'a more prolonged experience of apprehension, conversion and then the sense of forgiveness'.[17] Moody did not keep statistics of conversions at his meetings; what is available is estimates of numbers who attended and accounts of people who went forward to make 'decisions for Christ.[18] Because their primary purpose was conversion, individual PSA classes *did* take note of conversions in one way or another, although statistical records are few and without any sense of triumphalism. It may be that the PSA, with its mix of Gospel message and social help, came at just the right time to

heaviness of heart his conviction that the reverse of the picture is true, and *getting daily more so*. . . . Last week some 10,000 homes were visited, and the inhabitants pressed to come to some services being held in this neighbourhood. Result: a congregation of 120.'

16 This is mentioned by David Bebbington, *Evangelicalism in Modern Britain: a History from the 1730s to the 1980s* (1989; London, 1993), 116–17.

17 Gerald Parsons, 'Emotion and Piety: Revivalism and Ritualism in Victorian Christianity', idem, ed., *Religion in Victorian Britain, vol. 1: Traditions* (Manchester, 1988), 213–34, at 218.

18 John Kent, *Hold the Fort: Studies in Victorian Revivalism* (London, 1978), 161.

meet the needs and aspirations of working men. Undoubtedly the social service aspect of the PSA was valued and welcomed by working men. So also was the environment that encouraged masculine comradeship with its spirit of the brotherly 'helping hand'.[19] Undoubtedly, as Luker says of Cornish Methodism, PSA classes 'provided religious and social fellowship' and for many who attended they offered 'fluidity and flexibility to be utilized for a wide range of objectives: as entertainment, social protest or support in times of particular communal or personal crisis, as well as satisfying basic needs of "primary religion"'.[20] But beyond this is the clear fact that PSA classes were also successful places of evangelism and that many men became Christians with transformed lives, new attitudes, and improved households.

'Revival' raises questions not only of immediate personal experience but of enduring impact and geographical extent. Individual conversion and its consequences is standard fare in Christian literature. Measuring the evidence of change in lives and consequent impact on communities is more difficult to compute. As will be argued below, this was perceived to have happened both for individuals and on a noticeable scale as a result of PSA work. Men, and also women gathering in parallel meetings, were revived in their Christian faith or converted to become church members; they took part in door-to-door visiting and open air evangelism, and were publicly seen by acute observers to have transformed lives and family relationships.

The Spread of the PSA

Until the mid-1880s PSA classes were largely confined to part of the West Midlands. A few classes had been started as a result of members moving to other parts of the country, or as clergy and church members caught the vision of how working men might be contacted and held by the Church. The first significant shift came in 1885 when a PSA class began in Derby as a result of initiatives taken by Blackham, George Müller, and YMCA staff in Derby.[21] Seven years later there were

19 The badge of the PSA and the subsequent Brotherhood movement showed clasped hands. The PSA class at Belgrave Chapel, Leeds, produced a weekly magazine called *The Helping Hand*, 1896–8.

20 David Luker, 'Revivalism in Theory and Practice: the Case of Cornish Methodism', *JEH* 37 (1986), 603–19, at 619.

21 *P.S.A. Reporter & Record*, No. 1, March 1892, 5; and No. 2, April 1892, 17.

twenty-six PSA classes meeting in Derby and, so it was reported, the town had spawned eighty other classes in England and several in America. From there PSA work extended to Nottingham, in 1887, and also to Leicester.

The PSA in Nottingham developed in a similar way to that in Derby.[22] In the Albert Hall every Sunday afternoon between 500–1700 men aged 'from 18 to 84' assembled, 'each man with a Sankey hymn book for which they have paid 3d'.[23] Those who attended the Nottingham class were 'all working men, [some] are educated, some otherwise; they are of every variety of trade. Some appear comfortably off, while the dress of others indicates poverty.' On arrival men were greeted by 'Welcomers' who shook hands and directed them to seats. Attendance was registered if men wished to subscribe for a book, 'as many do' by paying one penny per week. Contributions could also be made to a Sick Provident Fund and 'good penny books' could be bought from a stall, between 300 and 500 being sold each week. The meeting included hymns, prayer, a solo by a man or woman, an 'earnest, faithful and telling Gospel Address', a duet or quartet, a second Gospel address lasting ten minutes, followed by a third Solo or chorus and a closing hymn, all taking no more than one hour.[24] This seems to be very much the pattern of PSA meetings in the years 1875–90.

Robert Mellors, the Nottingham class leader, addressing the obvious questions posed as to the effectiveness of these classes, asked: 'What is it that draws them together?' and more importantly from the point of view of religious revival, 'By what means have these men been won?' and 'has it been secured?' The appeal did not rest on 'amusement, nor on entertainment. Every meeting is a religious meeting; nearly every

22 Robert Mellors, *How Two Thousand Men Have Been Won* (Nottingham, 1889). Mellors (1835–1931) was president of the PSA class begun in the Albert Hall in October 1887; he was a member of the new Nottinghamshire County Council, and his account was given at the World's Sunday School Convention, London, 4 July 1889.

23 As A. Holden Byles was later to comment about the music at his own Hanley class, 'The solo may be made one of the most profitable parts of the service. . . . Mr. Sankey has taught us that a sermon which is sung may be quite as effective as one that is spoken'. Byles, *The P.S.A.*, 26–7.

24 Mellors, *Two Thousand Men*, 3–5. The 'United Gospel Mission is an evangelistic agency, designed to aid and supplement the work of the Churches. It includes, as workers, many persons who are connected with various Churches. The persons rent the largest Hall in the town for Evangelistic purposes. A part of the work carried on was a Bible Class of thirty or forty men. The members of that Bible Class determined, God helping them, they would largely increase their numbers; they sent a deputation over to Derby to see Mr. Hodder's Class; they sought for additional workers, and so set the Class a going.' Ibid., 12.

address is a Gospel Address; sometimes temperance, or thrift, or good habits, will form the theme; never politics.' Men, Mellors said, were drawn 'by an earnest religious service', but also 'partly by means of various benevolent agencies'. One outcome was that 'The Evangelistic Choir sing the Gospel in the Market Place, and a number of the members join in out-door preaching'.

Planning of the first PSA class in Nottingham used many strategies common in local evangelism. According to Mellors, men were 'won' for Christ by carrying 'the Gospel into the hearts and homes of those who are not usually reached'. The ingredients of the success of the Class were the personal welcome into a public hall, not a 'sacred' church, the social concern, the use of a variety of talent, and the brevity of the service.

> An earnest Gospel is approved. Men care nothing for speeches on Church government, theological essays, intellectual doubts and disputes, but they do care for and appreciate the Truth as to God's Infinite Love, as to Christ's example and sacrifice, as to the provision God has made in the Gospel for making bad men good, and miserable men happy. . . . When conversion has been secured and rightly directed, all other good will follow; for with 'new birth' and proper guidance, come also cleanliness, thrift, better clothes, happy homes, kindness to women and children, industry and conscientiousness in the discharge of every-day duties, amiability and cheerfulness, with a desire to promote the good of others; these are sure evidences that the Life of God has begun: for what is the Life of God but the life of faith, of goodness, of truth, or righteousness?[25]

Mellors listed, without naming, various men who had been transformed by the Gospel, stating categorically that 'a large number' had been converted. His regret was the indifference of the churches and of many Christian workers. 'When will the Church realize that the masses are to be laid hold of for Christ . . . and that the present indifference among Christian workers – the class distinctions, the pew rent exclusiveness, the sectarian bitterness, the set forms of service, and other similar impediments are, rightly or wrongly, through the prejudices or otherwise, the means that occasion the alienation of the masses from the Gospel?'[26]

25 Mellors, *Two Thousand Men*, 14–15.
26 Ibid., 17–18.

Other witnesses wrote of the conversion of men, of how the PSA 'meeting has been a stepping stone to other religious services' and has helped to bring men 'back';

> Young men . . . have found our Class a Haven of Refuge. . . . They have been converted and have been admitted to Church fellowship . . . and in some cases old men have been converted under the agencies brought into operation by our Class. . . . We want words of cheer, comfort, warning, that Christ be preached and that souls be saved.[27]

A further class began in Nottingham, at Mayfield, in the autumn of 1889, which, within two years, had 1250 members on its books and a packed chapel each Sunday afternoon.

> The spiritual success of this class . . . is marked, and proves that the churches are doing what is right in removing those barriers which have rendered weak their efforts at reaching the masses and in giving to them something which, whilst it rings out the clarion notes of the Gospel message in the ear, yet is stripped of that which would embitter the mind against religion.[28]

At Hanley, said Byles, 'thousands of working-men who, until these meetings were started, attended no religious service of any kind, are now regular worshippers in many of our churches'. And he could point to cases of men once 'notoriously bad characters in the district' who are now 'clothed and in their right mind', and to wives who tell of 'new joy and brightness in their homes; masters of better and more reliable workmen; fellow workmen of the cessation of bad language and bad habits. There are scores of homes and workshops in our own district of which it may be said, that "Old things have passed away, and all things have become new".'[29]

The first Stockport PSA class began in similar way. Alfred Hopwood, who ran a Bible class for men on a Sunday afternoon, visited Derby and, encouraged by what he saw, set about creating a new class in the town. 'For months we quietly worked in visitation from house to house', using twenty visitors. The class started with seventy-two men

27 W. Higginbottom, 'Paper Read at the Conference of P.S.A. Classes Held October 1st 1891', *P.S.A. Magazine*, No. 1, 1 December 1891, 3.
28 Ibid., 6.
29 Byles, *The P.S.A*, 40–1.

on 1 January 1890; by the end of the year the number had grown to 278, and to 500 by late 1891. Another class was established at Trinity in 1890, growing in two years to have 620 'contributing members', and other classes followed in a variety of Stockport's churches and chapels.[30]

The PSA had many imitators that did not necessarily use the title adopted by Blackham. In London's East End, the Revd W. E. Hurndall, after the Sunday evening service, went to the Bromley and Bow Institute accompanied with a forty-strong 'evangelistic choir' where he 'conducts an hour's service for the benefit of those who will not come to church'. The form was five hymns, one short prayer, an exposition of ten minutes, plus a fifteen minute sermon. 'All is bright, rousing and telling. The building, holding 1,200, is invariably filled, and with the class desired. Mr. Hurndall's own church is strengthened and immense good done.'[31] Among the first PSAs in London were those founded by Thomas Barnardo and John Clifford in the mid-1880s. One class where there was solid evidence of 'revived' faith among working class men was that led by the Revd F. B. Meyer at Christ Church, Lambeth, 'Meyer's Lambs' as they were called. A collection of fifty-one letters of appreciation from men addressed to or about Meyer, covering a period of two to three years, speak of personal redemption in Christ and changed lives. Some use formulaic evangelical language and it is also clear that many are written by men unused to writing letters; one was written by an amanuensis and marked by a cross.[32]

John Blackham, asked in early 1892 to explain the 'marvellous success the movement has achieved', provided an answer which D. L. Moody would readily have given to his revival meetings. 'It was . . .

30 *P.S.A. Reporter & Record*, No. 1, March 1892, 12.

31 *The Congregationalist*, March 1883, 269.

32 London, Congregational Library/Dr Williams's Library, MS II.a.52. Collection of letters 'To the Revd F. B. Meyer B. A., Septr 1895'. For example, 'Bro W. Wallin' wrote that 'I have given up gambling and evere (sic) thing that was bad. And give my heart to god and now I am in the right Path. And I mean to go on fighting the good fight that he has given me to do and bring others to the fold . . .' H. Newton, in a badly spelled and constructed letter thanked Meyer: 'I was a black sinner I was a blackslider (sic) I had wandered so far in sin through my unpure actions many and time . . . and at last I was running the drunkards and gamblers path often I was playing cards all day on Sunday . . . and a long time after that I gave up drink and about 9 months later when in the p.s.a. I gave my heart to God 12 months last july and now in stead of taking my wife in the pubs we booth (sic) get on our nees (sic) every night by our bed side to ? & live happy prayerful lives with his love I abide very close to my saviours side'. G. E. Johnson, of Waterloo Road, recounted his conversion in the PSA meeting and that afterwards he had been 'through the summer engaged in outdoor work for the Master'.

conceived in prayer, nurtured in prayer . . . and sustained in prayer by the prayer of thousands of women'.[33] His emphasis on the role of women, which is also mentioned by other PSA class leaders, acknowledged that many working-class women urged their husbands to attend PSA classes. They were feminine allies perhaps more for the cause of domestic peace and economy than for Christian salvation.

There were evangelical and High Anglican critics of the PSA who questioned its spiritual value, stating that it destroyed Bible Classes, enticed teachers and elder scholars from Sunday schools, and took the place of Sunday services. In December 1898, John Blackham spoke at the Belgrave Chapel PSA: he answered criticisms that the PSA interfered with existing methods and existing school. Citing the example of Ebenezer Church, West Bromwich, where the Sunday School was never very strong, he said:

> In the long run the P.S.A. greatly helps the Sunday School, but when it is first started at a church, it often attracts a few of the elder scholars who would probably have drifted away from school and church if they had not been attracted and retained by the P.S.A. There was abundant evidence that the P.S.A. greatly develops and augments the Sunday School.[34]

A number of evangelicals condemned the movement claiming that it was insufficiently Christocentric, that it abused the Sabbath by permitting clapping and cheering, and that by focusing on 'pleasantness' it reduced the seriousness of Christian faith. Other evangelicals reacted to the idea of a 'pleasant Sunday afternoon', not because they were against enjoyable worship but because they feared that the social activities of the PSA inclined towards liberal theology. Widespread use of phrases such as 'the brotherhood of all under the fatherhood of God' as the goal of Christianity only helped confirm their fears that this was a slippery theological slope.[35]

33 *P.S.A. Reporter & Record*, No. 1, March 1892, 7.

34 John Blackham answered these criticisms in the Belgrave Chapel, Leeds, PSA magazine, *Helping Hand*, 4 December 1898.

35 Typical of a PSA that moved in this direction was the class started by the Revd Richard Westrope at Belgrave Chapel, Leeds in 1890, which by 1895–6 was involved in supporting various trade union disputes, in part reflecting Westrope's own political radicalism. This divided the congregation of the Chapel, possibly the PSA as well, and resulted in Westrope's resignation in early 1896. See J. W. Dixon, *Pledged to the People: a Sketch of Rev. Richard Westrope and Congregational Aggressive Work in Leeds* (Leeds, 1896), and issues of *Helping Hand*, the Belgrave PSA magazine 1896–8.

Some conclusions

The PSA movement was an important late nineteenth-century nonconformist activity that attempted to reach the working classes alienated from the Church and its practices, to arrest the decline in church attendance, and also to find answers to widespread acute social and economic distress. It was similar in aim to other contemporary institutions and ideas, for example the Salvation Army, the city Settlements, and Hugh Price Hughes 'Forward Movement' at West London Mission.[36] The attraction of the PSA was its informality, often meeting not in the church of the parson and the pew but in a hall or a custom-built institute. Men attired in working clothes could gather in warm friendly surroundings, not forbidden to cheer and laugh at free entertainment attended by cheap tea and food. It offered, as was intended, an alternative to the pub and the music hall and provided a range of social welfare and educational services that encouraged working men into thrift, healthy activities, and learning. Early PSA class meetings drew inspiration from Moody's revival meetings of the mid-1870s and, likewise, the primary aim was the proclamation of the Gospel. But PSA classes were autonomous and had to sustain work for many years among working-class men within a specific locality. The opening of other classes resulted from example and contact. This is not the kind of movement that is usually thought of in terms of 'revival', and yet the large numbers of working-class men attracted to the classes, many of whom were also converted and became church members, suggests a significant work that deserves to be considered, if not as 'revival', then as something very like it.

Goldsmiths College, University of London

36 For example, the Revd R. F. Horton argued in the *British Weekly*, 9 February 1893, 259, that the 'Forward Movement' was 'to bring the vast uncared for masses back to God', while his fellow Congregationalist, Dr J. Guinness Rogers wrote that 'What I understand ... by the Forward Movement is some action inspired by devoted loyalty to the Master for bringing men to faith in Him ... [with] one aim ... the conversion of souls to Jesus Christ ... *The process of change is from within outward, not from the outside inward.*' Rogers, *The Forward Movement and the Christian Church* (London, 1893), 4, 8, 12, 14 (his italics). See further C. Oldstone-Moore, *Hugh Price Hughes: Founder of a New Methodism, Conscience of a New Nonconformity* (Cardiff, 1999), ch. 5; Inglis, *Churches and the Working Classes*, 70–1.

REVIVAL AS CULTURAL SPOTLIGHT: THE STRANGE CASE OF RUGBY FOOTBALL AND THE WELSH REVIVAL OF 1904–5

by DOMINIC ERDOZAIN

HISTORIANS of religion should be used to seeing phenomena such as revivals 'reduced' to some other social or cultural phenomenon. Fifty years ago, Perry Miller was exasperated by attempts to explain the American Great Awakening in terms of 'debtors against creditors', 'the common man against the gentry' or any other such social relations. The Great Awakening, he insisted, was its own event and one that both illuminated and moulded the society that witnessed it.[1] The Welsh Revival of 1904–5 was not as far-reaching in its consequences but it shares a stubborn irreducibility with other great revivals and, as I will argue, it provides vital perspectives on non-religious phenomena. The bold suggestion here is that, rather than looking to social phenomena to explain revival, we use the coruscating clarity of revival to explore 'secular' social phenomena – in this case, the powerful threads of sporting affiliation that had been insinuating themselves in the cultural pattern since the 1870s.

It might be countered that such a sudden tear in sensibility represents a dubious basis on which to generalize about social life, but it was the very exceptionalism of the revival that makes it so illuminating. For a generation, Christian leaders in Wales had criticized and often condemned rugby football, yet it took the altogether more benign atmosphere of the revival to substantiate a sense of sport's challenge to Christianity. It demonstrated at once the depth of sporting zeal and the weaknesses of both the conventional Welsh evangelical opposition to sport and the English encouragement of it. It showed how seriously people took their sport but also how futile the traditional policy of denunciation had been. In the 1820s, the Scottish evangelical, Thomas Chalmers had rhapsodized upon 'The Expulsive Power of a New Affection', arguing that worldly affections would not be unseated by bullying the conscience but by a positive appeal to Christianity's own

[1] Perry Miller, *Errand into the Wilderness* (Cambridge, MA, 1956), 153.

charms.[2] Contrary to most accounts, this was precisely what the revival demonstrated – even if it lacked some of Chalmers' eloquence.

The argument here is that the largely spontaneous manner in which young converts exchanged 'old' affections such as sport for a rekindled spirituality tells us more about the depth of sporting commitments than almost any other source. The revival tells us much about contemporary religious life but it also sheds light on wider cultural trends. The bubbling to the surface of so many submerged anxieties over sport and leisure was perhaps the biggest compliment the revival could pay the new culture of Welsh rugby. Rugby's centrality in the revival confirmed its cultural centrality. Whereas in England sport had meshed strongly (if not always neatly) with late-Victorian Christianity – to the point that many people regarded religion and healthy recreation as two sides of the same coin – in Wales the relationship had always been more tense, and the sudden crisis of this relationship in 1904 demonstrated both the potency of sporting identities and the fragility of the English-style compromise that claimed sport all-too-comfortably 'for Christ'. When it came to a moment of intense religious decision many individuals regarded sport as a counter-religious influence on their lives. Scholars have belittled the narrow-mindedness of the rugby-renouncing zealots whose pious statements filled newspaper columns throughout the revival, and they have blamed the leaders of the revival for encouraging such extreme positions.[3] Yet the phenomenon of youths 'confessing' and 'renouncing' interests as apparently innocent as playing games demands greater scrutiny, especially when we recognize that very few of the revival leaders ever preached against sport.

Tension between Nonconformity and rugby had been simmering, with occasional flashes of confrontation, for thirty years before the revival. Such had been the penetration of the Evangelical sects in the eighteenth and earlier nineteenth century, it was not unusual to hear Welshmen claim to live in 'the most religious country in the world'.[4] It was certainly one of the most religious parts of the British Isles. The 1851 religious census report described the Principality as 'basking in an

2 Thomas Chalmers, *The Expulsive Power of a New Affection* (2nd edn, London, 1861).

3 E. T. Davies, *Religion in the Industrial Revolution in South Wales* (Cardiff, 1965), 173; D. Smith and G. Williams, *Fields of Praise: the Official History of the Welsh Rugby Union, 1881–1981* (Cardiff, 1980), 120, 126.

4 *South Wales Daily News*, 6 February 1899.

excess of spiritual privileges',[5] and the 1847 Royal Commission on Education in Wales affirmed that 'Dissent has a firm hold on the affections of the people'. It noted that in a population of over eight thousand surrounding the Varteg iron works, for example, only 24.4% did not go to any church or chapel.[6] Wales seemed to prove that Christianity and the 'mind forg'd manacles' of industrialism could coexist. At its most effective, Nonconformity did not so much mould Welsh social life as constitute it. Salvation religion was supplemented by extensive community structures, and Evan Roberts' experience of the 1890s when he spent five nights a week involved in chapel meetings and societies was not exceptional.[7] Nonconformity has been characterized as a de facto Welsh 'establishment' but the truth was that it reached parts that established religions rarely could. The Royal Commission on Trade Unions in 1867 quoted one witness who said, 'I believe the dissenting minister to have more influence with the Welshman than any man living'.[8]

So it was understandable that the chapels were jealous of their social territory. C. B. Turner remarked that in the heady days after the 1859 Revival, congregational discipline was tightened to the point where you could be excommunicated for as little as wearing a benefit society badge or 'violating' the Sabbath. Nonconformity then entered, as he put it, 'a phase of consolidation'[9] in which customary suspicion of secular pursuits hardened into official condemnation. The latter decades of the nineteenth century witnessed the social upheaval of massive population increase in south Wales and the cultural challenge of new, 'imported' leisure forms. Anxieties over benefit societies would start to look quaint. The progress of Rugby football, an English public-school game unknown in the valleys in the 1870s but described by the *South Wales Daily News* in 1891 as 'the one great pastime of the people', alarmed the chapels.[10] Clubs clustered around pubs, workplaces, streets and the Anglican colleges that first introduced the game to Wales. Indeed, the contrast between Nonconformist puritanism and Anglican 'muscularity' could not have been starker. Wales' first semi-official rugby side

5 Horace Mann, *Religious Worship in England and Wales* (London, 1854), 73.

6 Quoted in Davies, *Religion in the Industrial Revolution,* 22.

7 *Western Mail*, 22 January 1905.

8 Davies, *Religion in the Industrial Revolution*, 65.

9 C. B. Turner, 'Revivals and Popular Religion in Victorian and Edwardian Wales', unpublished Ph.D. thesis, University of Wales, Aberystwyth, 1971, 35.

10 Smith and Williams, *Fields of Praise*, 17.

was that of St David's College, Lampeter, launched by Revd Rowland Williams who had been at Cambridge when rugby was introduced in the 1850s. It was all in the tradition of 'sporting parsons', though a newspaper delighted in branding the Lampeter XV 'Fighting Parsons' after one on-field punch-up.[11]

Nonconformists drew graver comparisons with the era of the Book of Sports, arguing that, once again, national religion was being profaned by an ecclesiastical campaign for sport.[12] More interesting than the re-opening of this ancient cleavage, however, was the fact that rugby soon developed a culture of its own – inside or outside the Anglican schools or colleges. It broke free from the moralizing precepts of muscular Christianity and 'rational recreation' and became its own excuse. People played because they wanted to, and if the game served to integrate communities this was incidental. As Smith and Williams note, in towns like Barry, a place 'conjured out of sea-air and sand-dunes' in the 1880s, the rugby club provided a focus of community life in an environment otherwise devoid of social institutions.[13] The charm of the game seemed to be its very freedom from social, religious and work-centred disciplines. And this was what upset the chapel hierarchies as much as conventional complaints relating to 'the associations' of the new sport – i.e. drink, bad language, violence and Sabbath-breaking. Sport was not just problematic when entangled with 'vice': even in its purest form it represented a rival to traditional spirituality.

Welsh rugby was a new tradition, perhaps even a new source of transcendence. In 1887 the *Llanelli and County Guardian* asserted that 'the winter pastime' had become 'interwoven with the social life' of the community;[14] others wrote of 'the prowess of the national team permeating every corner of the land'. A. J. Gould, the game's first real star, explained the appeal as follows: 'The life of the toiling thousands is hard and uninteresting enough, the mind of the professional and business man is vexed with the cares of his occupation, and it is good that football should come once a week *to take them out of themselves*.' Another international described playing rugby as the experience of 'living life at its most intoxicating' – there was 'movement, energy, grace, strength,

11 Ibid., 7.

12 E. W. Davies, *Spirit and Sport: Church and Cheer* (London, 1902), 57.

13 Smith and Williams, *Fields of Praise*, 102.

14 Quoted ibid., 6.

fear, intelligence, competition, everything'.[15] Though it was a different sport, the sentiment of a cross-country runner could probably be applied to rugby: he described running as a source of 'unalloyed pleasure', producing sensations 'almost like flying'. 'Here was indeed freedom', he concluded, 'only, alas, for one short hour a week'.[16] Richard Niebuhr once wrote of eighteenth-century Methodism providing 'a psychologically effective escape from the drudgeries of an unromantic aesthetic life';[17] it is clear that sport was starting to provide something analogous at the end of the nineteenth, and Christian leaders worried about it. However it was not until the revival came that individual testimonies substantiated such concerns.

While rugby supporters boasted that the Welsh had 'intellectualized' the game with their sophisticated three-quarter play, critics focused on its brutality. Preachers unacquainted with the subtleties of the sport decried it as a kind of rekindled barbarism. Others detected a heathen quality in the new phenomenon of 'spectatorism', with one Baptist lamenting the 'pitiable sight' of men 'endeavouring to satisfy their immortal cravings with the poor husks of the Football Edition'.[18] Writing in 1902, he said he feared the day when the 'games of England and Wales' would be 'deified, like the games of Greece, when men were found with such warped judgements as to erect the enormous buildings of the Stadium to hold 60,000 spectators.'[19] Attitudes to the game became increasingly belligerent. Church members were threatened with excommunication in one Baptist church, while, in 1890, the community of Ystradgynlais in the upper Swansea valley held a public debate on whether a club should be established in the area. It was reported that 'the gamesters' had won the debate by four votes, but, lacking the public-school quality of stoicism in defeat, the indignant ministers arranged for the goalposts to be delivered to the police station.[20]

It is tempting, then, to see the events of 1904–5 as an extension of this tradition of obdurate resistance to 'the game of the Welshman'. In their otherwise brilliant account of rugby's progress in Wales, Smith

15 Quoted ibid., 84–5.

16 *South Wales Daily News*, 26 November 1904.

17 Niebuhr, *The Social Sources of Denominationalism* (New York, 1960), 62.

18 Davies, *Spirit and Sport*, 18.

19 Ibid., 21–2.

20 *Welsh Rugby Magazine*, December 1967; *South Wales Daily Post*, 24 January 1953.

and Williams suggest that the revival 'singled out' the game for particular 'condemnation',[21] and they quoted a French account that spoke of rugby being 'strongly abused at the height of the Revival'.[22] A more recent account asks whether the game was 'fortunate to survive the revivalist onslaught'.[23] Yet, the interesting thing is that there were few incidents that could be described as confrontational. There is certainly no evidence of an 'implacable war' waged by the 'Revivalists' against the game.[24] On the contrary, the revival leaders went out of their way to avoid negative comment on the habits and lifestyles of the young. This is why the abandonment of the game, however briefly, is so significant. As a contemporary wrote of the severance of leisure-ties during the revival months, 'It was not the result of thunderous denunciations by some preacher. Neither was it in consequence of anyone aggressively demanding the giving up of such carnal pursuits'.[25] Even if we account for the fact that many of the young converts inherited a certain scepticism towards sport, there was something novel about the way many of them felt the need to confess and discard the game as a sign of regeneration. After twenty years of distrust bordering on condemnation from the pulpit, it was only when religious leaders refused to condemn the sport that its true hold on the minds of the young was revealed. If conversion became 'the one thing needful' for thousands in these months, it is striking how many new or would-be converts regarded sporting 'idols' as the one thing to be discarded. All this occurred at the very point when official opposition was actually muted.

The revival took off when the intense emotions experienced in a series of prayer meetings in Loughour, west Wales, started to reverberate throughout the area. Word spread of a young preacher, Evan Roberts, and his band of 'Lady Evangelists', whose simple message of total consecration seemed to electrify whole communities. There was little preaching as such, but much singing and earnest intercession, as people expressed a sense of inadequacy before God. Roberts, who seemed to have a gift of 'delivering' converts, was immediately in demand. His visits were anticipated with curiosity, excitement and, very

21 Smith and Williams, *Fields of Praise*, 126, 120.

22 J. R. De Fursac, *Un mouvement mystique contemporain: le reveil religieux du Pays de Galles 1904–5* (Paris, 1907), 52.

23 G. Morgan, 'Rugby and Revivalism: Sport and Religion in Edwardian Wales', *International Journal of the History of Sport* 22 (2005), 434–56, at 440.

24 De Fursac, *Mouvement Mystique*, 52.

25 D. Matthews, *I Saw the Welsh Revival* (Chicago, IL, 1951), 50.

often, desperation. In some areas, work gave way to spontaneous gatherings. Suddenly, it seemed, the Spirit was penetrating what Roberts termed 'the paralysis of formalism' in the chapels – cutting through the conventions of established piety.[26]

There was naturally a determination to keep the movement fresh and responsive, rather than to emulate the 'machine-made Christianity' of the contemporary Torrey-Alexander mission from America. Revival and revival*ism* were understood to be different phenomena, and Roberts was explicit that this spiritual surge should not be trammelled by structures and agendas. He declined invitations to visit 'English' Cardiff, fearing the publicity might smother the revival, and it was in a similar spirit that he advised co-workers *not* to pronounce anathemas on popular pleasures. 'You need not say anything about the theatre and the public-house. You preach of the love of Christ to them, and if His love will not constrain people to lead a better life nothing else will.'[27] Reference to rugby, when it was made, was often good-humoured, such as the time when Annie Rees saw 'men rush through the streets in order to have good places in the stands' for the international against England. She prayed that the eagerness to rush to the Saviour should be equally prevalent in Cardiff, for 'there is another international match proceeding just now – Wales against the devil, and the land of the leek is going to win'.[28] Out of hundreds of references to rugby only a handful came from revival leaders themselves, and only one that equates to the 'accusatory finger' alluded to by Smith and Williams. It is surely significant that their examples of clerical opposition come from incidents several years before the revival.[29]

What the revival leaders did preach was 'the doctrine of the doubtful thing' – that peace with God could not be found until every barrier to prayer or needless encumbrance had been discarded.[30] This was where rugby suffered. H. E. Lewis cited a 'typical instance' of a young man who had lived for sport before he started attending revival meetings. He had attended Sunday school but played little part in church life. Before twelve months had passed, however, 'there was no one in the church more active than he': '[his] Bible took the place of the

26 Quoted in Turner, *Revivals and Popular Religion*, 354.
27 *Western Mail*, 20 December 1904.
28 *The Cambrian*, 20 January 1905.
29 Smith and Williams, *Fields of Praise*, 120, 101.
30 H. E. Lewis, *With Christ Among the Miners* (London, 1906), 189.

evening edition, the service of Christ became a substitute for the football ground.' 'Multiply that one instance by a thousand', Lewis suggested, and the full impact of the revival could be grasped.[31] Awstin's reports on the revival for the *Western Mail* were full of examples of converts publicly eschewing sport – often it was a case of 're-conversion' in which sport was identified as a cause of spiritual indifference. The *South Wales Daily News* ran articles under the headline, 'Revival versus Football', noting the cancellation of fixtures as people rushed to attend the meetings, and the more serious phenomena of clubs disbanding and players giving up the game.[32] Sometimes clubs suffered just a reduced 'gate' but in towns such as Ammanford, Morriston, Crynant and Loughour, rugby was stopped for up to four years.[33] Elsewhere it was reported that a number of players from Pontardulais had taken up work as missionaries, while the conversion of players at Bettws was expected to 'mean the end of their football days'.[34] General interest in the sport also waned, especially in the revival heartlands of west Wales. Under the incredulous headline, 'No one knew the result', the *South Wales Daily News* quoted a pastor in Ammanford who, on the afternoon of 16 January 1905, asked whether Wales had beaten England, and addressed the same question to an audience that evening. Before the revival, the article noted, 'scores of young people would have gone to see the game, and the result would have been generally known in the town', but eyes were now fixed on another prize.[35]

One of the most striking aspects of the revival was the repeated impulse to seal the moment of commitment with a sacrificial gesture. As individuals came to see rugby as an idol, there were scenes of iconoclasm as shirts, balls, and other paraphernalia were symbolically destroyed. One convert, who clearly did not think rugby sinful in itself, burned his own kit but gave his season ticket to his brother, presumably so he could still use it to watch matches. But his brother was also converted so he burned it.[36] Such displays often embarrassed friends of the revival, but as Lewis argued, '[i]n the revulsion of feeling produced

31 Ibid., 183.
32 *South Wales Daily News*, 12 December 1904.
33 Smith and Williams, *Fields of Praise*, 127.
34 *The Cambrian*, 6 January 1905; 25 November 1904.
35 Ibid., 18 January 1905.
36 *Western Mail*, 28 November 1904.

by the thought of wasted time, of duties neglected, of unchristlike companionships, one can understand the zeal that threw costume and ball into the fire.'[37]

Betting slips, 'dance cards' and drinking paraphernalia were also sacrificed but these were regarded as unambiguous evils. Rugby, like smoking, was not in that category so its sudden rejection was remarkable. But as a series of prominent players publicly washed their hands of the sport,[38] it fell to a member of the Penrhiwceiber team to produce one of the revival's defining sentiments: 'although he had been a church member for years he had not done any work for the Master in seeking the lost. "I am", he add[ed] "determined this shall not be the case any longer. I used to be full-back in the football field, but in future I am going to be full-forward for Jesus Christ" '.[39]

Such testimonies indicate that sport and normal Christian profession had coexisted for some time, but when the spiritual temperature was raised significantly, many felt the compromise unworthy. The captain of a student side in Bangor gave up the game, explaining that the decision was 'based not so much on any conviction that play was in itself evil, but that he now realised that life possessed for him some higher duty than athletics'. Another student, at Aberystwyth, swapped sport for 'mission-work', an act reminiscent of C. T. Studd and the 'Cambridge Seven' of the 1880s.[40] These were not the intemperate, ignorant decisions that they have been seen to be, and whatever one may think of their polarized logic, they say more about the depth of feeling associated with sport than anything I have found in the sports history literature. Sports history has looked to religious institutions and 'muscular Christianity' to explain the origins of modern games, but it often dismisses religious perspectives as representing essentially a dying past. The often glib sense that the future was with sport[41] understates the degree to which individuals struggled over sporting and spiritual identities. It took the crisis of the revival to expose such struggles and they were no less real for slipping out of view so soon after this great effusion of religious energy.

37 Lewis, *With Christ Among the Miners*, 189.

38 See, for example, *The Cambrian*, 30 December 1904; *South Wales Daily News*, 23 November 1904; 5 December 1904; 15 December 1904; 26 December 1904.

39 *South Wales Daily News*, 31 December 1904.

40 Ibid., 14 December 1904.

41 See, for example, Richard Holt, *Sport and the British: a Modern History* (Oxford, 1989), 74.

The English journalist W. T. Stead was no uncritical friend of the revival but he identified it as a useful mirror in which to examine some important contemporary trends. It took the 'Revival in the West' to demonstrate just how far the British had gone towards a vacuous hedonism whereby 'even the healthy game of football has become little better than a modern substitute for the gladiatorial sports of ancient Rome'.[42] Stead found himself defending the revival's lack of intellectual substance in the *Methodist Times*. 'The Revival', he insisted, was 'a rouser rather than a teacher'.[43] The sense was that the raw intensity of the Welsh revival said more about current values than the neat synergies of modern theology. In theory, rugby and Evangelical Christianity could form two sides of a rounded life, and in theory the singing of hymns at rugby matches could reflect mutual esteem, but the reality was that rugby – like many sports in this period – was becoming a significant rival to the churches. Whatever its advocates claimed, there was no real *modus vivendi* on the ground.

Yet for all the revival's powers to expose the muddled optimism of contemporary religious thought, its leaders were almost certainly culpable for not recognizing the need for some sort of social life beyond the spiritual. There was an understandable suspicion of English-style Guilds which seemed to overdo the social side of church life, but the idea that the young converts could live on a pure diet of prayer meetings was unrealistic. Resistance to the idea of resuscitating junior teams on a more moderate basis was perhaps unwise.[44] The danger was that after the fires of revival had lost their intensity, social life would slide back into the same channels – and this it did. Moreover, it was in December 1905 that Welsh Rugby enjoyed perhaps its finest hour – subduing the all-conquering New Zealand national side by one try to nil. *The Cambrian* reported strangers stopping one another in the street to discuss the marvellous deeds of the Welsh XV;[45] others likened the euphoria to 'Mafeking night'.[46] Similar things had been said at the height of the revival.[47] However, it is important that the apparent brevity of the revival does not diminish its historical significance. It

42 Stead, *The Revival in the West: a Narrative of Facts* (London, 1905), 13–14.
43 *Methodist Times*, 15 December 1904.
44 See, for example, *South Wales Daily News*, 16 March 1905.
45 *The Cambrian*, 22 December 1905.
46 *South Wales Daily News*, 18 December 1905.
47 Turner, *Revivals and Popular Religion*, 357.

may not have provided structured solutions, but it brought to light real, lived tensions between the spheres of religion and leisure. The wider implication is that historians should not see the jolting work of revivals as extreme or detached religious activity but as an invaluable spotlight on terrain too often smoothed by more cultured perspectives.

King's College, University of London

RENEWING METHODIST EVANGELICALISM: THE ORIGINS AND DEVELOPMENT OF THE METHODIST REVIVAL FELLOWSHIP

by MARTIN WELLINGS

WHEN the Wesleyan, Primitive and United Methodist Connexions combined in 1932 to form the Methodist Church of Great Britain, much was made of their shared evangelical heritage. The doctrinal clause of the founding Deed of Union affirmed that the Connexion 'ever remembers that in the Providence of God Methodism was raised up to spread Scriptural Holiness through the land by the proclamation of the Evangelical Faith and declares its unfaltering resolve to be true to its Divinely appointed mission.'[1]

Connexional rhetoric, however, masked two realities about Methodist evangelicalism in the early 1930s. First, in each of the three denominations which united in 1932 the previous forty years had witnessed a gradual accommodation to critical biblical scholarship, a retreat from traditional doctrinal shibboleths and a change of ethos in response to cultural developments. Methodist evangelicalism had thus been transposed into a liberal evangelical key. Second, complementing this development, traditional evangelicals in Methodism often felt out of step, isolated or even persecuted within their Church.[2] A few eminent but elderly conservatives, like Dinsdale Young, were able to continue much as they always had, but their position was untypical. After two decades of fruitless campaigning, the militant fundamentalists of the Wesley Bible Union effectively gave up on Methodism by renaming their organization the British Bible Union in 1931, while two younger ministers, J. Wesley Walker and John H. J. Barker, abandoned an attempt to launch a fellowship of 'fully evangelical' ministers in 1936 when fewer than six were prepared to declare public adherence to

1 *Minutes of the Uniting Conference* (London, 1932), 302.

2 Martin Wellings, *Evangelicals in Methodism: Mainstream, Marginalised or Misunderstood?* (Ilkeston, 2005), 23–31.

such a group. John Barker recalled that 'to take such a stand was regarded as a tactical blunder.'[3]

Twenty years later, however, the Methodist Conference agreed, without discussion or dissent, 'to grant the request of the Revival Fellowship to use the title "Methodist Revival Fellowship"' (MRF).[4] A group committed to prayer for revival was thus establishing itself with a measure of official sanction as an organized expression of conservative evangelicalism within the Methodist Church. This essay explores the origins and early history of the MRF, seeking to show how it developed from traditional Methodist evangelical emphases, drew on the broader evangelical resurgence of the 1940s and 1950s and won acceptance in the context of post-war revivalism, epitomized most strikingly by the Billy Graham crusades of 1954–5. A shared evangelical emphasis was expressed in a distinctively Methodist idiom, thus illustrating some of the variety, as well as the similarity or family resemblance, characteristic of mid-twentieth century evangelicalism.[5]

The principal architect and guiding spirit of the MRF, undeterred by the tactical timidity of his fellow evangelicals in 1936, was J. H. J. Barker (1903–76). John Barker gained a science degree from Leeds University and studied theology at Victoria Park College, Manchester, entering the ministry of the United Methodist Church five years before Methodist Union.[6] His father Henry (1874–1958) was also a United Methodist minister, and both Barkers had connections with a range of non-denominational evangelical organizations of distinctly conservative hue: Henry Barker, for instance, spoke at the Keswick Convention,

3 For Young, see *Methodist Recorder* (London), 27 January 1938, 4; Martin Wellings, 'The Wesley Bible Union', *Proceedings of the Wesley Historical Society* 53 (2002), 157–68; British Bible Union (BBU) committee minutes, 14 June 1951, in the BBU archive, now held by the Prophetic Witness Movement International, Leyland, Lancs.; J. H. J. Barker letter, 20 July 1975 (lent by the Revd Robert J. Kitching). For wider context, see D. W. Bebbington, 'Martyrs for the Truth: Fundamentalists in Britain', in Diana Wood, ed., *Martyrs and Martyrologies*, SCH 30 (Oxford, 1993), 417–51.

4 *Methodist Recorder*, 7 July 1955, 6.

5 There is one published history of the MRF: A. Skevington Wood, *The Kindled Flame* (Ilkeston, 1987). The Fellowship is also discussed in Robert J. Kitching, 'The Conservative-Evangelical Influence in Methodism, 1900–76', unpublished MA thesis, University of Birmingham, 1976, chs 3 and 4. I am grateful to the Revd Bob Kitching for the loan of this dissertation and of letters upon which his research was based.

6 From 1919 Victoria Park shared tutorial staff with the Primitive Methodists' Hartley College, where A. S. Peake (1865–1929) was the most eminent tutor. Peake was an enthusiastic advocate of 'higher criticism'; no record survives of J. H. J. Barker's opinion of Peake as a tutor.

was President of the BBU and spent the last five years of his active ministry seconded to the Bible Testimony Fellowship.[7] John Barker served as an Army chaplain from 1943 until 1945 and was then given permission by the Conference of 1946 to work for two years as a travelling secretary for the Inter-Varsity Fellowship (IVF). The IVF role brought Barker into contact with ex-service university students of conservative beliefs; these links, reinforced by a consultation with Methodist circuit ministers at the 1946 Fellowship of the Kingdom conference, led Barker to convene a meeting in Oxford later that same year to discuss the condition of the Methodist Church. A follow-up conference planned for 1947 had to be postponed, and the next gathering took place at Caterham in Surrey in July 1948.[8] A group of some twenty people met for four days at the Southwark Diocesan Holiday and Training House. Eighteen of the twenty were Methodist ministers or theological college students; the most senior people present were J. Baines Atkinson (1889–1963), a supernumerary minister,[9] Cliff College lecturer and Southport Convention speaker, and Barker himself. Among the younger participants were Howard Belben, Ron Taylor, Harry Stringer and Robin Catlin, all of whom were to play leading parts in the subsequent history of the MRF.[10]

As will be seen later, Barker and his colleagues were not unique in their burden for revival, even within their own denomination. One distinguishing feature, however, was the definite conservative theology of the Caterham group. The letter of invitation, signed by Barker, Belben and Lieut. Colonel Leon Dale, made the aim of the gathering clear:

> The purpose of the conference is to determine what contribution men of the evangelical and conservative position should be making to our Methodist Church. We believe that in our general attitude we are in direct line with the early Methodists. It will strengthen

7 *Minutes of Conference 1958* [hereafter: *Minutes*], 184–5; BBU committee minutes, 16 October 1951. Methodist involvement with Keswick was not unprecedented, but it was unusual: Charles Price and Ian Randall, *Transforming Keswick* (Carlisle, 2000), 44.

8 Wood, *Kindled Flame*, 6–8; *Sound of Revival*, September 1976, 2, 3, 10. Several later accounts 'remembered' the Caterham gathering as taking place in 1947; the extant correspondence makes it clear that it was 1948.

9 Methodist terminology for retired ministers.

10 Atkinson: *Minutes 1964*, 201–2; Stringer: *Minutes 1978*, 94; Belben: *Minutes 2000*, 25–6. Photograph of participants and some names supplied by the Revd David Lawrence in letter to author, 20 February 2006.

> our hands to gather together for prayer, study and discussion. We believe there would be a great response in the churches to the message of men ministering the Word from hearts that have been revived and who preach with a clear definite note.

Participants in the conference were expected to agree 'at least . . . in substance' with an eight point 'doctrinal summary' appended to the invitation. The summary affirmed belief, *inter alia*, in the infallibility of Scripture, a substitutionary interpretation of the atonement and the personal return of Christ. It was both significantly more conservative and markedly less Methodist than the section expounding 'The Methodist Witness' in the 1946 official report *The Message and Mission of Methodism*: not surprisingly, since it was taken not from a Methodist publication, but verbatim from the IVF's constitution of 1924.[11]

The programme of the Caterham conference included 'Bible readings' on salvation by faith, assurance and fellowship, papers on the authority of the Bible and the relevance of the Pentateuch, devotional talks and time for 'united prayer' and three sessions on revival: 'The New Testament pattern – where have we failed?', 'Towards revival – the next step' and 'Practical Suggestions'.[12] The revival emphasis was significant. Barker later reflected that 'We speedily saw that a call for orthodoxy and a mere return to the Bible was insufficient. There was too much *dead* orthodoxy in some areas, and too much of what we might call bibliolatry. We were led to define revival and put revival, prayer and preparation for revival as our priorities, and also the "Four Alls" of classical Methodism.'[13]

The Caterham group formed themselves into a body called 'The Aldersgate Fellowship', but this name seems to have been short lived.[14] By the beginning of 1952 Barker and a small group of colleagues were prepared to launch a more formal organization, and so the 'Revival Fellowship' came into being. A circular letter sent in January 1952 invited support; by the summer a second letter indicated that the Fellowship had sufficient backing to proceed; by the end of the year a

11 Material lent by Peter Barker; Douglas Johnson, *Contending for the Faith* (Leicester, 1979), 359.

12 Programme of Caterham conference, lent by Peter Barker.

13 *Sound of Revival*, September 1976, 10. The 'four alls' were a summary of Methodist doctrine, published by W. B. Fitzgerald in *The Roots of Methodism* (London, 1903), 173.

14 David Lawrence, letter to author, 20 February 2006.

quarterly newsletter was being circulated to 102 members and prayer associates.[15]

The new Fellowship established three important characteristics from the outset, and maintained them steadfastly throughout its history. First, its theological presuppositions and its constituency were conservative and evangelical. It has already been seen that the Caterham conference looked to the IVF for a summary statement of doctrine. The Fellowship was rooted in the traditional Methodist evangelicalism of Cliff College and the Southport Convention, with a leavening of IVF and CSSM influence and some unacknowledged debts to the Wesley Bible Union.[16] Fellowship members assumed a conservative doctrine of Scripture, although this does not seem to have been stated explicitly in the MRF's aims or basis until the early 1960s. The December 1952 newsletter included an article on the authority of the Bible by Stringer, praising 'the fundamentalists of our local churches in our youth, saintly folk, most of them, who set our feet on a sure basis for belief and conduct – the Bible'. In the same issue Roland Lamb quoted John Wesley in support of the infallibility of the Bible.[17] These comments appeared in the context of a debate in the correspondence columns of the *Methodist Recorder* provoked by a series of articles by Vincent Taylor under the heading 'Doctrine and Evangelism'. Taylor's articles were designed to prepare the Church for the 1953 World Methodist Campaign of evangelism, but the third in the series, 'Authority and Belief', published on 30 October 1952, antagonized conservatives by appealing to the combined authority of Church, Bible and Holy Spirit. Frank Ockenden, a member of the Fellowship, wrote to protest that Taylor's article 'illustrates how far responsible leadership has departed from our recognised Methodist Standards'.[18] This debate developed into a broader controversy about 'Fundamentalism' during the Billy Graham mission of 1954–5.

Second, the Revival Fellowship gave careful thought to the defini-

15 Circular letter, undated (probably spring 1952), and *Quarterly Newsletter*, December 1952, lent by Ron Taylor.

16 See n. 6 above on Henry Barker. Wellings, 'Wesley Bible Union', 166, places the Wesley Bible Union in the context of a broader Protestant/Fundamentalist movement. The MRF *Quarterly Newsletter* in the 1950s was printed by the Protestant Truth Society's Wickliffe Press.

17 *Quarterly Newsletter*, December 1952, 3, 10, 11.

18 'Authority and Belief', *Methodist Recorder*, 30 October 1952, 13; Revd F. Ockenden to editor, *Methodist Recorder*, 13 November 1952, 11.

tion of 'revival'. In one of the first newsletters, Barker asked: 'What is revival?' and then answered his own question:

> Primarily it is NOT the regeneration of sinners, although this is a common concomitant, but the quickening of God's People by the Holy Spirit. The very word 'Revival' indicates a renewal of life which has been dormant or diseased. Revival results in a greater consciousness of God, and this leads on to a greater consciousness of sin and lack of holiness, followed by its confession. Revival is indicated by increased activity of God's people in worship, in the study of His Word and in witness to the outside world. The latter results in conversions which often are the chief evidence of Revival to the outsider.[19]

This understanding, echoed by Roland Lamb in December 1952, distinguished the revival theology of the Fellowship from three other ways in which the terminology of revival was used in this period. In the religious press, the vocabulary was not infrequently loosely employed to indicate a new lease of life for a struggling local congregation: thus the *Methodist Recorder* reported fresh activity in the society at Little Houghton under the headline 'Northampton Policeman Revives Village Chapel'.[20] With greater justification, the term was also used to describe a new turning to the Church by a largely indifferent population, prompted by the Holy Spirit: this was the theme of the *Recorder*'s leading article 'Revival and Evangelism' in April 1952.[21] Thirdly, for advocates of the 1953 World Methodist Campaign, particularly W. E. Sangster, thoughtful, prayerful and energetic evangelism could itself produce revival. Sangster quoted Finney: 'the Holy Spirit was longing to break through all the time and we could have a revival whenever we wished, *if we would fulfil the conditions*'.[22] This struck a quite different note from that of the Revival Fellowship, with its anguished waiting upon God.

The third characteristic of the Fellowship followed on from its understanding of revival. Given the theology outlined by Barker, the Fellowship was committed to fervent and intensive prayer. Although at

19 Undated circular, probably spring/summer 1952.

20 *Methodist Recorder*, 27 May 1948, 3.

21 *Methodist Recorder*, 24 April 1952, 8.

22 'Motives in Evangelism', *Methodist Recorder*, 3 April 1952, 4 (emphasis in original). Compare W. E. Sangster, *Let Me Commend* (London, 1949), 41–4.

times it entered into theological debate, as will be seen later, and even became embroiled in Connexional politics, the principal emphasis of the Fellowship remained prayer for that spiritual renewal which Barker identified as the essence of revival. To that end the quarterly newsletter regularly carried articles on prayer and requests for prayer. The first organized activity planned by the Fellowship was a prayer conference in April 1953, and this remained the core event in the annual programme through to the 1980s.[23] Even when the Fellowship became something of a meeting place for opponents of modern theology or ecumenism in Methodism, the positive commitment to prayer for revival retained its place at the centre of the movement. John Barker's advocacy and personal example here were crucial in ensuring that the Fellowship continued to emphasize prayer for revival and did not become an association of campaigning Fundamentalists.[24]

The MRF's defining emphasis on prayer for revival brought the fledgling organization several significant benefits. From the outset it gave the Fellowship a thoroughly positive image, in clear contrast to the 'fighting Fundamentalism' of the Wesley Bible Union. No doubt Methodists were well aware that the MRF was a conservative evangelical body, but nonetheless it had a constructive purpose and therefore a greater appeal than its polemical predecessor. Furthermore, the theme of revival had a strong resonance for Methodists. The myths of Methodist origins, whether around the conversion of the Wesleys in the 1730s or in the story of the birth of Primitive Methodism at Mow Cop in 1807, were told and retold, celebrated and proclaimed, explained and analysed, throughout the nineteenth and twentieth centuries.[25] The annual commemoration of Wesley Day (24 May) prompted reflection (often uncritical) on the Aldersgate story and on Methodism's claim to be the finest product of the Evangelical Revival. Memories of nineteenth-century revivalism, moreover, were still alive in 1950s Methodism, and even those who were not nostalgic about former glories hoped that Britain might be on the verge of a fresh outpouring of the Spirit. The report on *The Message and Mission of Methodism*, produced by a committee of influential theologians and denomi-

23 *Quarterly Newsletter*, December 1952, 2.

24 See, for example, Barker's paper 'Where are the Intercessors?', published in the *Quarterly Newsletter* in April 1957 and reprinted as a pamphlet, in several editions.

25 See Timothy S. A. Macquiban, 'Dialogue with the Wesleys', in Clive Marsh, Brian Beck, Angela Shier-Jones, and Helen Wareing, eds, *Unmasking Methodist Theology* (London, 2004), 17–28.

national leaders, looked forward to 'a revival of religion' through 'a rediscovery by every individual Methodist of the Gospel as the power of God unto salvation'. The authors were sure that '[i]f Methodism is baptized anew into the fullness of the Christian Faith, it will be enabled to speak the authentic word to this generation. . . . We may, then, with confidence lift up our heads and look for a moral and spiritual awakening on a scale that is commensurate with the eternal purpose of God for mankind.'[26] W. E. Farndale, President of the Conference of 1947, addressing a District convention in Lincolnshire in April 1948 witnessed sixty to seventy people responding to a call to reconsecration and commented: 'The unexpected has happened again. I am beginning to wonder whether we are at the point of a break-through of spiritual power which is going to lead Methodism into a real revival.'[27] Four years later, the *Methodist Recorder* headlined a report on an address to Bournemouth District Local Preachers by the Revd Greville Lewis: 'Britain is on verge of greatest religious revival, says Connexional Local Preachers' Secretary'. Although Lewis pointed out that his address was much more nuanced than the headline suggested, Connexional leaders like Sangster, Colin Roberts and Cecil Pawson were upbeat about the prospects for revival during the year of preparation for the 1953 world campaign.[28]

This background and these expectations made it difficult even for sceptical Methodists to oppose the MRF. Beyond the legacy of Wesley hagiography and nineteenth century revivalism, moreover, the MRF came into being at a time when revival was firmly on the agenda of the British Churches, when confidence in evangelism was growing and when conservative expressions of Christianity were recovering from the nadir of the inter-war years. The Baptist Revival Fellowship began in the late 1930s and a Congregational Evangelical Revival Fellowship was formed in 1947.[29] A commitment to evangelism, evidenced in the Church of England by the report *Towards the Conversion of England* and in Methodism by the Christian Commando Campaigns of the 1940s, joined hands with the innovative methods of Youth for Christ and the

26 *The Message and Mission of Methodism* (London, 1946), 82.

27 *Methodist Recorder*, 22 April 1948, 5.

28 Ibid., 21 February 1952, 6; Revd G. Lewis to editor, 28 February 1952, 10; 19 June 1952, 3 (Pawson); 17 July 1952, 3–4 (Roberts' presidential address to Conference).

29 David M. Thompson, 'The Older Free Churches', in Rupert Davies, ed., *The Testing of the Churches, 1932–1982* (London, 1982), 87–115, at 93.

evangelistic endeavours of Tom Rees to create the conditions for the impact of Billy Graham.[30] Meanwhile, the theological climate had changed, as early twentieth-century liberalism gave way to Barthian biblical theology, while the dissection of the canonical books in biblical studies was replaced by a new emphasis on the unity of the Scriptures. Writing in the *Methodist Recorder* in 1955, F. F. Bruce argued that works such as H. H. Rowley's *The Unity of the Bible* and Norman Snaith's *The Distinctive Ideas of the Old Testament* justified Billy Graham's celebrated catch-phrase, 'The Bible says'.[31] They also allowed John Barker to pen a sharp retort to Donald Soper's attack on the 'spiritual fascism' of the IVF: Soper, wrote Barker, was 'many years behind the times' and manifested 'a closed mind to the weighty scholarship which now stands behind the IVF position.'[32] MRF, then, was a part, albeit a small part, of the conservative evangelical renaissance of the 1950s.

This conservative revival brought together the surviving adherents of traditional evangelicalism and those attracted by newer evangelical groups, of which the IVF was the most significant. Within Methodism, the MRF illustrated this combination. Among the founder-members of the Fellowship, David Lawrence and Howard Belben first met at a CSSM beach mission in 1935 or 1936; Belben, Stringer, D. W. Lambert and Baines Atkinson served on the staff of Cliff College, where other MRF members were students; Stringer and Atkinson were involved with the Southport Convention. As well as these links to and through traditional evangelical groups, Barker, Belben, Lamb and Donald English all had strong IVF connections: in his response to Donald Soper, John Barker mentioned his own involvement with the IVF, noting that he had joined the Fellowship in 1923 and had attended its second conference.[33] The MRF was able to revive and to begin to

30 Ian M. Randall, 'Conservative Constructionist: the Early Influence of Billy Graham in Britain', *Evangelical Quarterly* (Carlisle) 67 (1995), 309–33; Jean A. Rees, *His Name was Tom: the Biography of Tom Rees* (London, 1971), 86–92.

31 F. F. Bruce, 'The Bible and Evangelism', *Methodist Recorder*, 31 March 1955, 11.

32 Donald Soper to editor, *Methodist Recorder*, 14 October 1954, 11; J. H. J. Barker to editor, *Methodist Recorder*, 21 October 1954, 13.

33 David Lawrence to author, 20 February 2006; G. Howard Mellor, *Cliff: More than a College* (Calver, 2005), 554–5; *Minutes 1964*, 201; Roland Lamb was given permission to serve the IVF from 1952 to 1955, as indicated in successive editions of *Minutes*; D. W. Bebbington, *Evangelicalism in Modern Britain: a History from the 1730s to the 1980s* (London, 1989), 260; Brian Hoare, 'Profile: Donald English', *Epworth Review* (Peterborough), 25 (1998), 28–9; J. H. J. Barker to editor, *Methodist Recorder*, 21 October 1954, 13, and 'Fifty Years a Conservative Evangelical', *Conservative Evangelicals in Methodism Newsletter*, Summer 1973, 8–12.

reshape Methodist evangelicalism partly because it acted as a point of contact between different strands in the Methodist evangelical constituency and also because it served as a bridge between Methodist evangelicals and the wider evangelical world.

The MRF was not a large organization. The 102 members and prayer associates of 1952 formed a very small fraction of the Methodist Church's total membership of 741,000, and the Fellowship claimed the adherence of just twenty-seven of Methodism's 4600 ministers. The quarterly newsletter through the 1950s reported steady rather than spectacular growth, listing twenty to thirty new members, perhaps half a dozen of whom were ministers or lay pastors, in a typical issue. There were about six hundred members by spring 1956 and 1100 by 1962, by which time the infrastructure and programme of the Fellowship had also expanded.[34]

Although it was neither numerically strong nor connexionally influential, the MRF in its early years was not without significance. It provided a supportive network for Methodist evangelicals who might otherwise have lost hope or left the denomination. In a Church which set great store by unity, which was inclined to see acceptance of majority opinion as evidence of 'fellowship' and which was suspicious of parties and pressure groups, it managed to establish itself as a recognized organization representing a distinctive and unfashionable point of view. With the advent of debate over the Anglican-Methodist 'Conversations' in the 1960s the MRF took on a greater role as the voice of an evangelical critique of the proposals. In the same decade the Fellowship also provided a conduit for charismatic renewal to enter Methodism.[35] Both ecumenism and renewal proved controversial, and here, as in the first decade of its life, the MRF experienced and exemplified on a small scale developments in the wider evangelical world.

MRF, then, drew on the revival tradition which was embedded in the history, memory and psyche of Methodism. This shaped its particular emphases and also gave it credibility in a Church which had moved a long way from its revivalist roots. MRF grew out of the survival of conservative theology and spirituality in Methodism, articulating the beliefs and concerns of a constituency often overlooked or dismissed by Connexional leaders, but it was able to establish itself

34 *Quarterly Newsletter*, December 1952, 6–9 (listing members); March 1956, 8; January 1962, 2. Compare the statistics for Methodist members and ministers in *Minutes 1952*, 193.

35 These developments are treated briefly in Wood, *Kindled Flame*, 21–3 and 29.

because of a broader and deeper revival of conservative evangelicalism in post-war British Christianity. In the particular context of British Methodism the MRF demonstrated the complex interplay of survival, revival, renewal and reshaping which are characteristic of the phenomenon of evangelicalism.

Kidlington, Oxfordshire

THE 'REVIVAL' IN THE VISUAL ARTS IN THE CHURCH OF ENGLAND, c.1935–c.1956

by PETER WEBSTER

ONE fruitful organizing theme around which to write the history of the worship of the Church of England in the early part of the twentieth century might be that of the revival of ancient practice. In church music, for instance, the early years of the century saw the gradual readoption of plainsong, the rediscovery of the repertoire of the Tudor and Stuart Church, and the adoption of English folk-song, most visibly in the *English Hymnal* of 1907.[1] In the placing of contemporary visual art in churches, however, the contrast is marked. Recent analysis of this period has tended to posit a Church largely indifferent to the visual arts, except for the activities of isolated individuals, and of two men in particular: George Bell, Bishop of Chichester, and Walter Hussey, Dean of Chichester and formerly Vicar of St Matthew's, Northampton.[2] This sense was shared by Sir Kenneth Clark, former Director of the National Gallery, in a retirement tribute to Hussey, with whose patronage Clark had collaborated since the early 1940s. 'What' he asked 'has the Church done in the way of enlightened patronage of contemporary art in the present century?' Only one man, Hussey, 'has had the courage and insight to maintain – I wish I could say revive – the great tradition of patronage by individual churchmen'.[3]

1 Brief surveys include Erik Routley, *Twentieth-Century Church Music* (London, 1964) 13–31: Nicholas Temperley, *The Music of the English Parish Church*, 2 vols (Cambridge, 1979), 1: 315–38.

2 The literature on the subject is very much in its infancy. For a brief general survey, see Michael Day, *Modern Art in English Churches* (London, 1984), 1–39. On Walter Hussey in particular, see Garth Turner, '"Aesthete, Impressario and Indomitable Persuader": Walter Hussey and St Matthew's Northampton and Chichester Cathedral', in Diana Wood, ed., *The Church and the Arts*, SCH 28 (Oxford, 1992), 523–35; George Pattison, 'The Achievement of Walter Hussey: a Reflection', in Tom Devonshire Jones, ed., *Images of Christ: Religious Iconography in Twentieth-Century British Art* (Northampton, 1993), 13–16; David Coke with Robert J. Potter, 'The Cathedral and Modern Art', in Mary Hobbs, ed., *Chichester Cathedral: an Historical Survey* (Chichester, 1994), 267–82. On Bell, see Giles Watson, '"In a filial and obedient spirit": George Bell and the Anglican Response to Crisis, 1937–49', *Humanitas* 1 (1999), 4–24.

3 Clark, 'Dean Walter Hussey: a Tribute to his Patronage of the Arts', in Walter Hussey, ed., *Chichester 900* (Chichester, 1975), 68–72, at 69.

Many and various voices in the period saw a need for a revival in ecclesiastical art. George Bell passed a faculty for a mural painting by Hans Feibusch in a Sussex church in 1954, to the approval of the architectural historian Alec Clifton-Taylor. In a letter to the *Times*, he praised Bell's 'courageous decision' that 'will have given much satisfaction to those who are concerned that the Church shall once again become what it was all through the Middle Ages, and to a less extent [*sic*] in the Stuart and Georgian periods too, a major patron of living art.'[4] The sculptor Henry Moore noted to Hussey that Christianity had been 'the inspiration of most of Europe's greatest painting and sculpture – and the Church in the past has encouraged and employed the greatest artists'. However, this great tradition had become lost in recent years, and church art was often afflicted with an 'affected and sentimental prettiness'.[5] John Rothenstein, Director of the Tate Gallery, argued that 'for a well-known artist to make a painting or a piece of sculpture for a church is news so startling as to be announced in headlines.' This was a recent phenomenon, rather than the norm, since 'in earlier ages the paintings and sculpture made to communicate the Christian message were amongst the supreme works of man.'[6]

This essay makes two distinct but related points. It sets aside the degree to which this attempted revival was a success, however defined, and also the veracity of Clark's sense of the uniqueness of Hussey's role in it. It seeks firstly to begin to sketch the web of connections between the clerical and artistic worlds, and to suggest that the impetus for and shape of this putative 'revival from above' derived in large part from an informal yet determined alliance of interested clergy, artists, and critics. Secondly, by examining both the similarities and differences of motivation among the constituent parts of this informal church-artistic 'establishment', it will suggest that the anticipated shape of this 'revival' depended on whose revival it was to be.

* * *

The period immediately before, during and after the Second World War was characterized by a particular set of conditions under which debate on religious art was conducted within and on the periphery of

4 *Times*, 8 June 1954. On the Goring judgement, see Paul Foster, 'The Goring Judgement: Is it Still Valid?', *Theology* 102 (1999), 253–61.

5 Henry Moore to Walter Hussey, 26 August 1943, as quoted in Hussey, *Patron of Art: the Revival of a Great Tradition among Modern Artists* (London, 1985), 32.

6 John Rothenstein, 'Art in our Churches', *Picture Post* (19 May 1956), 27–9, at 27–8.

the Church of England; conditions which, whilst not unique to the Church of England, were uniquely operative within it. In 1944 George Bell convened a conference on the Church and the artist, to be held at the episcopal palace in Chichester, with the express intention of 'mutual interpretation' between the Church and the artist. Unsurprisingly, the conference was attended by local clergy and by Bell's Dean, Arthur Stuart Duncan Jones, but also by the Jesuit Martin D'Arcy of Campion Hall, Oxford, well known for his interest in the arts.[7] The visual arts were well represented, with relatively conservative figures such as Charles Wheeler and W. T. Monnington rubbing shoulders with the more controversial Henry Moore and Duncan Grant. As well as architects Sir Herbert Baker, Edward Maufe and Francis Xavier Velarde, the critics T. S. Eliot and Eric Newton and the writer and Christian apologist Dorothy L. Sayers were also present.[8] The list of attendees could scarcely have been bettered in range and eminence.

The present author has, with Ian Jones, elsewhere posited the existence of an informal church musical 'establishment', in which clergy and professional church musicians met, corresponded and debated with a concerned network of musicologists, professional musicians in secular contexts and other musical and cultural critics.[9] Although considerably less well developed, the diversity and eminence of the assembled delegates at the Chichester conference suggest that a similar network for the visual arts existed in and around the Church of England. This network functioned in several ways. Both Bell and Hussey were assiduous correspondents and worked hard to ensure the involvement of the most influential voices in decision-making. A proposed painting by Duncan Grant and Vanessa Bell in the parish church of Berwick in East

[7] On Duncan Jones' membership of the Alcuin Club, see S. C. Carpenter, *Duncan Jones of Chichester* (London, 1956), 67. The new Campion Hall was furnished with a number of 'objets d'arcy': Edward Yarnold, 'D'Arcy, Martin Cyril (1888–1976)', *ODNB*.

[8] London, Lambeth Palace Library [hereafter: LPL], Bell MS 151, fol. 186 (Bell's opening address to the conference); LPL, MS Bell 151, fol. 184 (programme and list of attendees). The Bell Papers are cited by kind permission of the Librarian of Lambeth Palace. A copy of Bell's summary of proceedings found its way to Hussey, probably through Moore. Chichester, West Sussex Record Office [hereafter: WSRO], MS Hussey 180. The Hussey Papers are cited by permission of the Very Reverend the Dean of Chichester and with acknowledgments to the West Sussex Record Office and the County Archivist.

[9] Jones and Webster, 'Anglican "Establishment" Reactions to "Pop" Church Music, 1956–c.1990', in Kate Cooper and Jeremy Gregory, eds, *Elite and Popular Religion*, SCH 42 (Woodbridge, 2006), 429–41, at 430. On the idea of a Christian elite, see Matthew Grimley, 'Civil Society and the Clerisy: Christian Elites and National Culture, c.1930–1950', in Jose Harris, ed., *Civil Society in British History: Ideas, Identities, Institutions* (Oxford, 2003), 231–47.

Sussex went to a consistory court hearing in 1941, and Bell mustered, as witnesses in favour, Kenneth Clark and T. A. Fennemore of the Central Institute of Art and Design.[10] Hussey's most prominent commissions of the 1940s, by Henry Moore and Graham Sutherland, were unveiled by Kenneth Clark in the case of the Moore, and Sir Eric Maclagan, Director of the Victoria and Albert Museum, for Sutherland.[11]

It was also the case that channels of communication were available for members of this network to communicate with each other and with the wider public. Periodicals such as *Theology* carried pieces on the relationship between the Church and the arts by clergy and theologians, but also by critics (Eric Newton of the *Manchester Guardian*) and art historians (T. S. R. Boase, director of the Courtauld Institute).[12] *The Student Movement*, a university term-time periodical from the press of the Student Christian Movement, carried a series of reproductions of modern works of art with accompanying commentary from (amongst others) Nikolaus Pevsner.[13] Although the discussions were dominated by those within the established Church, they were not confined within it. Hussey corresponded in March 1944 with Iris Conlay, art editor of the *New Catholic Herald*, over her coverage of the Moore 'Madonna and Child'.[14] John Rothenstein, as well as his work as Director of the Tate Gallery, sat on the advisory committee on decoration for Westminster Cathedral.[15]

This discussion was not confined to the religious press. Both Bell and Hussey were to be published in the artistic periodical *The Studio*, and *Vogue* carried a series of pieces on religious art in 1947–8.[16] The *Architectural Review* published a debate on Henry Moore between the Christian critic Eric Newton and the self-confessed 'pagan' Geoffrey

10 Schedule of fees for consistory court hearing. WSRO, Episcopal Records, MS Ep.II/27, Berwick, Series B.

11 The text of Clark's address is at WSRO, MS Hussey 335, and that of Maclagan at WSRO, MS Hussey 346.

12 T. S. R. Boase, 'Religion and Art', *Theology* 46 (1943), 241–8; Newton, 'The Church and the Artist', *Theology* 48 (1945), 36–9.

13 The series ran monthly between 1946 and 1948, and included Moore's Northampton 'Madonna', and works by Georges Rouault, John Piper, Marc Chagall, Eric Gill and David Jones.

14 Conlay to Hussey (16 March 1944), and C. G. Mortlock (British Council) to Hussey (17 July 1944), both at WSRO, MS Hussey 333.

15 Jennifer Booth, 'Rothenstein, Sir John Knewstub Maurice (1901–1992)', *ODNB*.

16 Edward Sackville-West, 'Art and the Christian Church', *Vogue* (March 1947), 64, 114, 120; 'Modern Church Art at Assy', *Vogue* (April 1948), 58–61.

Grigson, under the chairmanship of Nikolaus Pevsner, as well as comment on the early plans for the new Coventry Cathedral.[17] The message was also carried overseas, with articles appearing in *London Calling* (part of the BBC's overseas work), the *Near East Post*, and the New York-based *Magazine of Art*.[18]

There was also a period in the 1940s and early 1950s when this discussion spread from the specialist press into the mainstream media. Hussey's work at Northampton was reported very widely in the local and national press, and John Rothenstein's article, noted above, was published by the mass circulation *Picture Post*.[19] Broadcast media also took note, with Bell more than once appearing in *The Listener*.[20] Hussey was to take part in a television broadcast in 1948, alongside the artist Mary Kessel and the Keeper of Sculptures at the V&A, H. D. Molesworth, and chaired by the Archdeacon of London, O. H. Gibbs-Smith.[21]

What, then, were to be the features of this 'revival'? One vision, closest to the hearts of critics, was that of the clergyman as an enlightened individual patron. Kenneth Clark's tribute to Walter Hussey described the history of the Church's interaction with the artist as a highly personalized one, rather than one conducted through institutional structures. For Clark, 'the notion that Christian art at its best was the product of an institution is not borne out by history.' It was Hussey's qualities as 'aesthete, impressario and indomitable persuader' that had made him 'the last great patron of art in the Church of England.'[22] For Eric Newton, Hussey had been successful in his commissioning of Henry Moore, a sculptor without a track record in religious art, because Hussey possessed the two necessary requirements: 'a courageous unprejudiced view of the theme . . . and a real understanding of the artist.'[23]

17 '[Untitled article on Moore] *Architectural Review* (May 1944), 189–90; J. M. Richards, 'Coventry', *Architectural Review* 111 (January 1952), 3–7.

18 Eric Newton, 'Art and the Church Today', *London Calling* 283 (1945), 11–12; Iris Conlay, 'Modern Art Comes to Church', *Near East Post* (17 September 1944), 2; Benedict Nicolson, 'Graham Sutherland's *Crucifixion*', *Magazine of Art* (November 1947), 279–81; Kenneth Clark, 'A Madonna by Henry Moore', *Magazine of Art* (November 1944), 247–9.

19 See, *inter alia*, on the Moore 'Madonna', *Times* (21 February 1944), 6; for Rothenstein, see note 6 above.

20 'The Church as Patron of Art', *The Listener* (14 September 1944), 298; 'The Church and the Artist', *The Listener* (13 January 1955), 65–6.

21 Broadcast running order and script at WSRO, MS Hussey 205.

22 Clark, 'Walter Hussey', 68–9, 72.

23 Newton, 'Art and the Church Today', 12.

A tension between the personal and the institutional can be seen in the different approaches of Bell and Hussey. Hussey worked on a highly personal level, becoming on several occasions a friend and confidante to those he commissioned, but leaving little institutional framework behind him at his retirement. Bell, by contrast, repeatedly attempted to put in place structures that might maintain the work of fostering art in the Church. He attempted to set up a guild of church craftsmen attached to Chichester cathedral, under clerical direction but functioning on a semi-commercial basis.[24] He also attempted to remodel the office of Treasurer at the cathedral to take on a diocese-wide role of fostering artistic work.[25]

If an emphasis on reviving the patron-client relationship was one more characteristic of lay and art-critical voices, clerical commentators tended to invest the revival of Christian art with wider significance. A frequent theme in the discussion was the need to reverse the alienation of the worker from his labour, and the disconnection of the world of work from the Christian life. Much thought had been given in the early part of the period to the place of the worker in industrial civilization and how to make concrete the principle of '*laborare est orare*'.[26] John Betjeman told a congregation at Northampton of a state of 'mechanical barbarism' in which 'we let machines run our lives. We listen but we do not sing; we read, but we do not write; we feel, but we do not think; we buy, but we do not make; we judge things by money standards because money buys us escape from the roaring lunacy around us.'[27] For Bell, the engagement of artists in work for the Church was part of a wider vision of the nature of the church community and its relationship with its environs. 'Man's life, man's interests, man's gifts, should be brought there for a special consecration. . . . And in the offering of a man's gifts, his labour and his sacrifice, the art not only of the architect, but of the sculptor, the painter and the craftsman has each its peculiar signifi-

[24] See the leaflet 'A Guild Workshop for the Diocese of Chichester' (undated, but probably 1947) at LPL, MS Bell 152, fols 16–17. On the influence of guild socialism, see Grimley, 'Civil Society', 238–9.

[25] Hussey was Bell's preferred candidate for the vacancy that arose in 1948. Bell laid out his vision of the new post in a letter to Hussey of 16 November 1948: WSRO, MS Hussey 96.

[26] See, for example, the contributions of J. M. Heron and Philip Mairet in M. B. Reckitt, ed., *Prospect for Christendom* (London, 1945), 70–84 and 114–26.

[27] Sermon, preached 5 May 1946 at Hussey's invitation, and privately printed by St Matthew's: WSRO, MS Hussey 114, printed pamphlet *Five Sermons by Laymen*, 7–11, at 9–10.

cance.'[28] Sir Eric Maclagan, in the same sermon series as Betjeman, meditated on the words of the catechism on the duty to 'learn and labour truly to get mine own living, and to do my duty in that state of life, unto which it shall please God to call me.' It was thus for the artists to 'devote themselves to their Art . . . all serving God, certainly not only (perhaps in some cases, not at all) in specifically religious work.'[29] In this scheme, the artist had as clear a vocation to serve as the priest.

So it was that artists, critics and clergy saw a need for change at an individual, microcosmic level, but with different stresses placed on component parts of the synthesis. It was also the case that the 'establishment' pursued change at the national level. That there was a natural and inevitable causal connection between the life of a nation or civilization and its reflection and embodiment in the arts was deeply ingrained in much of the artistic thought of this period. The period under discussion here was more characterized by attempts to communicate and popularize that connection, utilizing theological work already in place from the 1920s.[30] John Rothenstein argued that, if the contents of twentieth-century British churches were the only evidence available to a later observer, 'our civilisation would be found shallow, vulgar, timid and complacent, the meanest there has ever been.'[31] A. G. Hebert saw that in architecture 'the design expresses the spirit of a period and a civilization' and so 'sin likewise expresses itself in ugliness: the meanness and sordidness of modern commercialism has stamped its image on [parts of] Bristol and Birmingham.'[32]

When handled by artists and critics, the importance of this organic relation between art and society tended to lead to an emphasis on the precise relation with *modern* art. Was a revival in the arts one that should draw on authentic roots (and that was therefore necessarily stylistically archaic) or one that should in contrast reflect the spirit of the age, and be therefore expressed in the most contemporary style of the day? For the critic Benedict Nicolson, Graham Sutherland, through

28 Bell, 'The Church and the Artist', *The Studio* 124, no. 594 (1942), 81–92, at 87, 90.

29 Sermon given on 26 May 1946. WSRO, MS Hussey 114, *Five Sermons by Laymen*. The connection may have been due to Maclagan's acquaintance with Earl Spencer, with whom Hussey was on good terms. Hussey, *Patron of Art*, 58–9.

30 See, *inter alia*, Percy Dearmer, ed., *The Necessity of Art* (London, 1924) and his *Art and Religion* (London, 1924).

31 Rothenstein, 'Art in our Churches', 27–8.

32 A. G. Hebert, *Liturgy and Society: the Function of the Church in the Modern World* (London, 1935), 239.

his highly contemporary Northampton Crucifixion, 'voices the present crisis in civilisation.'[33] The mural painter Hans Feibusch identified a strong tendency in the Church to 'shirk the question of style and cling to long-established forms and symbols.' This was for Feibusch a dangerous policy of isolation, which 'tends to separate the Church and all it stands for still more from the rest of modern life and put it into a remote corner. The ordinary man who easily takes the Church for a relic from the past, does so not least for its appearance.'[34]

Bell often stressed the necessary connection between art and contemporary culture. Religious art 'is not a thing which can be isolated from the general artistic movement of an age. Confine it and it becomes corrupted, its expression a dead letter.'[35] However, if critics and artists tended to express a rather static sense of the connection between a society and its art, it was the case that clergy and theologians viewed the arts as more instrumental in a dynamic process by which the Church was to revive and transform society at a national level. At its lowest pitch, this was expressed as a hope that the arts might provide a means of communication with the unchurched. Hussey suggested that a revived association between the Church and the artist 'would mean that Christian truth would be proclaimed in fresh voices, of increasing and lasting range, audible to many with whom the Church has unfortunately grown out of touch in recent years.'[36] Even if pictorial art was no longer the only means of educating an illiterate laity, as (it was often noted) had been the case in medieval England, it still had a role in communicating Christian truth.

This generalized missionary theme was transposed to a higher key by the general sense of societal crisis as the 1930s progressed, and during the war years. Bell, amongst others on the episcopal bench, was acutely aware that the sickness that had afflicted Europe could only be cured through a reconnection of European civilization with its Christian roots.[37] For Bell and others, the arts were both symptom of the

33 Benedict Nicolson, 'Religious Painting in England', *New Statesman and Nation* (12 July 1947), 29.

34 Feibusch, *Mural Painting* (London, 1946), 90–1.

35 Bell, 'The Church and the Artist', 65–6.

36 Hussey, 'A Churchman Discusses Art in the Church', *The Studio* 138 (1949), 80–1 and 95, at 95.

37 On responses to crisis in this period, see Giles C. Watson, 'Catholicism in Anglican Culture and Theology: Responses to Crisis in England (1937–49)', unpublished Ph.D. thesis, Australian National University, 1998. See also Keith Robbins, 'Britain, 1940 and "Christian

malaise and part of its cure, for behind the actual war of 1939 there 'lies the spiritual war. There is a totalitarianism of democracy as well as of dictatorship. The life of the spirit is no less gravely threatened by the mechanisation of culture which the former causes than by the brutal tyranny of the latter.' Fundamentally, European civilization had fallen out of communion with its source. However, a hopeful sense that all was not lost became stronger in Bell's thinking as the outcome of the war became gradually clearer. 'Religion and art, the Church and the artist, may yet do something together again to transform the spiritual life of Europe. . . . There is a void in the human soul, crying out to be filled.'[38] The correspondence between Bell and Hans Feibusch suggests that the latter caught some of Bell's vision.[39] The horrors of the war meant that the naive and childish language of past religious art would not do in the new world of 1946: 'Only the most profound, tragic, moving, sublime vision can redeem us.'[40]

* * *

Strikingly absent from the voices that could be heard in connection with religious art in this period were those of the non-specialist laity. Hussey stressed on several occasions that the congregation of St Matthew's had, with a little perseverance on their part, come to accept and indeed love Moore's 'Madonna and Child', despite the opprobrium heaped upon it by the local press.[41] However, despite this, the prevailing sense was that this was a revival that would require leadership, and that would attract lay opposition. Kenneth Clark told the Northampton congregation that the Moore sculpture 'may worry some simple people, it may raise indignation in the minds of self-centred people, and it may lead arrogant people to protest.'[42] The work of Robert Hewison has described a wider project of cultural elevation in the post-war years, in which the masses, so sorely tested during the war, should share in the treasures of high culture, disseminated by a national cultural bureau-

Civilisation"', in Robbins, *History, Religion and Identity in Modern Britain* (London, 1993), 195–213; Philip Williamson, 'Christian Conservatives and the Totalitarian Challenge, 1933–40', *EHR* 115 (2000), 607–42.

38 Bell, 'The Church and the Artist', 90, 81.

39 Watson, '"In a filial and obedient spirit"', 12–13.

40 Feibusch, *Mural Painting*, 92.

41 Hussey, *Patron of Art*, 47–8, 73.

42 Printed in the *St Matthew's Magazine*, copy at WSRO, MS Hussey 335.

cracy.[43] The picture that emerges from an examination of this attempted revival in Christian art was of a movement dominated by a determined coalition of religious, artistic and cultural experts. This essay has eschewed direct consideration of the actual success or otherwise of the attempt. However, as Kenneth Clark's tribute to Walter Hussey (quoted at the beginning of this essay) suggests, there was little sense among the members of this coalition that anything more than a start had been made. Much fundamental research remains to be done on the period after 1955, but it may be suggested that the ubiquity of the visual arts in the cathedrals at the time of writing should be viewed as a more recent achievement.

It is also the case that the varying standpoints of the stakeholders in this process account for the differences in emphasis. Critics and artists, and the cultural bureaucrats who supported them, tended to analyse the situation in static terms. It was simply in the nature of things that the national Church should be a major patron of the contemporary artist, both for the sake of the artist at local level, and to reflect the natural connection of religious art and national culture. Clergy were more likely to be proactive, and to view the arts as instrumental in a revival of Christian thought and practice both personal and collective, particularly under conditions of perceived crisis during the war years. In beginning to understand this attempted revival, then, it is necessary both to consider precisely what it was that was to be revived, and also whose revival it was to be.

Institute of Historical Research, University of London

43 Robert Hewison, *In Anger: Culture and the Cold War, 1945–60* (London, 1981).

ANGLICAN EVANGELICALS AND REVIVAL, 1945–59

by ALISTER CHAPMAN

THIS essay is a study of the religious revival that didn't quite happen in Britain after the Second World War. It focuses on conservative evangelical Anglicans, whose own renaissance during these years puts them at the centre of discussions about the post-war increase in churchgoing. Its central contention is that human agency and cultural peculiarities are just as important for understanding this chapter of English religious history as any seemingly inexorable, broad-based social changes inimical to religious practice. More particularly, the chapter focuses on Anglican evangelical clergy and their attitudes to religious revival. In so doing, it highlights the fact that the practices and prejudices of church people are an essential part of the story of post-war English religious life. Scholars looking to explain religious malaise in post-war Britain have frequently looked everywhere except the decisions made by the churches and their leaders, the assumption seeming to be that because decline was unavoidable there was nothing pastors, priests or their congregations could do to stem the tide. This chapter seeks to redress the balance by examining the ways in which evangelical Anglican clergy pursued revival in England, some of the obstacles they faced in this pursuit, and how they responded when they felt they had failed. Among the things they discovered was that 'revival' was a word to be handled with care.

I

In October 1949, Hugh Gough, Bishop of Barking and a leading Anglican evangelical, expressed his hope for an evangelical revival in England similar to the one associated with the Wesley brothers and George Whitefield in the eighteenth century.[1] A little over six years

[1] 'Bishop Gough on the "A" Bomb Threat – Sees Hope for Evangelical Revival', *Church of England Newspaper*, 7 October 1949, 5. Ian Randall has commented on the widespread nature of such hopes in Britain in the late-1940s; Ian M. Randall, 'Conservative Constructionist: the Early Influence of Billy Graham in Britain', *Evangelical Quarterly* 67 (1995), 309–33, at 325–6.

later, Gough addressed the Islington Clerical Conference and affirmed: 'We are witnessing the beginning of another Evangelical Revival. I am sure we are.'[2] Later that year, Maurice Wood, another prominent figure on the evangelical wing of the Church of England, expressed his conviction that 'when the books are opened we shall find that 1954 and 1955 are the dates which Church historians note as the days when the next great evangelical revival began.'[3] Indeed, expressions of optimism from Christian leaders during the mid-1950s could be multiplied almost at will. Christianity was 'taking the offensive' in Britain, according to the editor of *The Churchman*; 'the tide is turning', wrote the Bishop of Lichfield; and American evangelist Billy Graham declared that Britain was on the verge of revival.[4]

So was there a religious revival in England in the 1950s? There was an observable increase in the number of people participating in churches and their services. Statistical indices went up for many churches in the ten years after the Second World War. But in most instances the figures did nothing more than return to pre-war levels.[5] Did this constitute a revival? Richard Weight uses the word in his excellent history of post-war British culture, and Callum Brown has spoken of 'surges' of church membership, baptisms, communicants and so on.[6] But there was no explosion of church attendance of the sort dreamed of by Gough, Wood and others, and by the end of the 1950s it was clear that they had not experienced anything comparable to the stories of the 1730s. Nevertheless, during the 1950s church leaders were greatly heartened – such increases in religious observance had not happened for generations, and were a cause for joy and hope.

In the Church of England, most joyful of all were the evangelicals. Their fortunes had been rather depressing for almost all of living

2 Hugh Gough, 'Modern Trends in Evangelism', in *The Church Extends Her Frontiers: the 121st Islington Clerical Conference* (London, 1955), 40–50, at 50.

3 M. A. P. Wood, 'The Essence of Evangelicalism: a Symposium: III', *The Churchman* 59 (1955), 15.

4 'Editorial', *The Churchman* 59 (1955), 195; 'The Bishop's Letter', *Lichfield Diocesan Magazine*, June 1954, 58; and 'On the Verge of a Spiritual Awakening?', *English Churchman*, 28 May 1954, 255.

5 Robert Currie, Alan Gilbert, and Lee Horsley, *Churches and Churchgoers: Patterns of Church Growth in the British Isles Since 1700* (Oxford, 1977), appendix.

6 Richard Weight, *Patriots: National Identity in Britain, 1940–2000* (corr. edn, London, 2003), 223–4; Callum G. Brown, *The Death of Christian Britain: Understanding Secularisation, 1800–2000* (London, 2001), 5, 187. Brown, 233–47 provides the best recent bibliography on Christianity in post-war Britain.

memory. But as early as 1946, Max Warren, evangelical statesman and general secretary of the Church Missionary Society, could say: 'We live at a time when the wind of the Spirit of God is reviving the dry bones of Evangelicalism'.[7] Ten years later, this sentiment had been repeated so often as to become a truism.[8] Contemporary discussion of the revival of conservative evangelical fortunes (it was the growing success of the conservative wing of the evangelical movement in the Church of England that attracted the most comment) focused on their evangelistic successes among public schoolboys and university students and on the growing numbers of conservative evangelicals coming forward for ordination.[9] And although there were no aggregate statistics to measure their success across the country, there was certainly evidence on the parish level that the number of evangelical congregants was swelling.[10] It is hardly surprising that the word revival came easily to the lips of people like Gough and Wood.

II

So why were conservative evangelical Anglicans doing so well after the Second World War? Existing scholarship on the religious boom of the 1940s and 1950s has stressed the conservative nature of these years, as seen in attitudes towards everything from communism to biblical studies to women, and this climate was clearly a friendly one for evangelicals whose conservatism was usually social as well as theological.[11] It

[7] Max Warren, *Strange Victory: a Study of the Holy Communion Service* (London, 1946), 119.

[8] See, for example, '"Evangelicals Affirm": a New Alternative – Replies and Criticisms', *The Record*, 17 September 1948, 527; 'Whither Islington', *Church of England Newspaper*, 14 January 1949, 8; 'Evangelicalism – Party or School of Thought?', *Church of England Newspaper*, 25 March 1949, 8; and 'Preface', in *Crockford's Clerical Directory 1955–6* (Oxford, 1956), xi.

[9] See, for example, Michael Ramsey, 'The Menace of Fundamentalism', *The Bishoprick*, February 1956, 24; 'Preface', *Crockford's Clerical Directory 1953–4* (Oxford, 1954), xx; and Eric Kemp, 'Our Glorious Heritage', *Church Times*, 8 July 1955, 3.

[10] For evidence of this, see the statistics collected in Alister Chapman, 'Secularisation and the Ministry of John R. W. Stott at All Souls, Langham Place, 1950–70', *JEH* 56: 3 (2005), 496–513, at 511–13. The first attempt to quantify churchgoers by different, trans-denominational traditions such as 'evangelical' did not take place until the late 1980s. See Peter Brierley, *'Christian' England: What the 1989 English Church Census Reveals* (London, 1991), especially 161–5.

[11] For example, Brown, *Death of Christian Britain*, 170–5; Weight, *Patriots*, 223–4; D. W. Bebbington, *Evangelicalism in Modern Britain: a History from the 1730s to the 1980s* (London, 1989), 253–5.

is important not to push this argument too far, however. It tends to overlook what Weight rightly identifies as the 'accelerating social change' of the period, symbolized above all by the television set.[12] Brown's suggestion that one of the keys to the church growth of these years was the fact that it was 'the age of austerity' ignores the fact that the time when the flames of revival appeared the brightest in the mid-1950s was in fact a time of a marked decrease in austerity, as people threw out their ration books and many moved into one of the hundreds of thousands of newly-built houses.[13] As an argument, then, the link between a conservative era and the return to the churches is generally persuasive but imprecise.

The rest of this essay will analyze the use of the word revival in this period as a step towards greater precision. For one of the aspects of British culture during these years that was particularly congenial for evangelicals was the widespread talk of the need for revival in national life. As the Second World War progressed, more and more people expressed a desire to see not only victory but also a new, better social order. The famous symbol of this was Beveridge's *Report on Social Insurance* of 1942, the classic Christian statement, William Temple's *Christianity and Social Order* of the same year, but these were only the most obvious examples of a whole variety of war-time dreams and plans for a renewed kingdom. And in 1945 people were taking up one of the evangelicals' favourite words in order to name what they believed British society needed: revival. In 1945, *The Times* spoke of 'the administrative burdens imposed by peace-time revival and the new social programmes'.[14] In the same year, one of its columns reported '[t]he general sense of revival which has been stirring in Cambridge this academical year', going on to describe returning dons, windows being uncovered and fresh lecture series.[15]

The general use of the word revival, even with obviously secular referents, surely meant that evangelicals were more likely to gain a hearing when they used the word. They had participated in the war-time dreaming and scheming, most notably in the Church of England's 1945 report, *Towards the Conversion of England*, produced

12 Weight, *Patriots*, 223.

13 Brown, *Death of Christian Britain*, 170; Peter Clarke, *Hope and Glory: Britain 1900–2000* (2nd edn, London, 2004), 240–3.

14 'A Key Commission', *The Times*, 6 June 1945, 5.

15 'Easter Term at Cambridge', *The Times*, 22 May 1945, 6.

under the chairmanship of evangelical bishop Christopher Chavasse.[16] As the title of this report implies, their hopes focused, predictably, on the spread of the gospel, but evangelicals were also interested in the sort of national revitalization longed for by the broader population. Indeed, they argued that a revival in Christian belief was a precondition for this broader revitalization. Of particular significance here was a book published in 1938 by J. Wesley Bready, entitled *England: Before and After Wesley*, which argued that England was a desperate place before the eighteenth-century evangelical revivals ushered in an age of humanitarian action and enlightened reform.[17] For people such as Hugh Gough who read this book, it made sense to suggest that the new dawn for which so many longed would not arrive without a prior religious awakening.[18] Whether people accepted this argument or not, it was a boon for English evangelicals that they were living in a country where their desires for revival had clear resonance in the wider culture.

Post-war hopes of national rejuvenation were given a new lease of life by the protracted preparations for the coronation of 1953. The prospect of a new Elizabeth on the throne conjured up fantasies of what every English schoolchild had been taught was one of the greatest periods of the country's history. The editor of *The Times* wrote of an '"Elizabethan age"' with 'Christian values re-established, morals reasserted, conscientiousness revived, energy renewed, and national unity restored', while a correspondent for the *Evening Standard* dreamed of 'a new age . . . [of] greater glory and greater power than . . . ever known before'.[19] This cultural moment has a twofold significance for the present argument. Firstly, the coronation was a quintessentially Anglican event, which may help to explain why it was Anglican evangelicals who were in especially good spirits during these years.[20] Secondly, it was right at the time when evangelicals were beginning to use the word revival more frequently than at any other time in the

16 *Towards the Conversion of England* (London, 1945). See also A. Rendle Short, 'The Place of the I.V.F. in the World of Tomorrow', *The Inter-Varsity Magazine*, Lent Term 1944, 2–3, and B. Godfrey Buxton, 'Let us Prepare Now', *The Inter-Varsity Magazine*, Lent Term 1944, 7.

17 J. Wesley Bready, *England: Before and After Wesley* (London, 1938).

18 See Gough, 'Modern Trends', 49–50; and Hugh Gough, 'The Church of England (Evangelical)', in Hugh Gough *et al.*, *Our Churches & Why We Believe in Them* (London, 1961), 11–37, at 22–3.

19 'And After?', *The Times*, 3 June 1953, 13; 'Onward to Glory', *Evening Standard*, 2 June 1953, 4.

20 On the Anglican nature of the coronation, see Hastings, *A History of English Christianity, 1920–2000* (4th edn, London, 2001), 424–5.

twentieth century. The reason was the impending Billy Graham crusade at the Harringay arena in north London, preparations for which were already well under way by June 1953. For one evangelical at least, it was no coincidence that 'the Queen's Coronation, the 150th anniversary of the Bible Society, the explosion of the hydrogen bomb and the Billy Graham crusade all took place within one year.'[21]

III

Revival, then, was in the air, and on face value it seems that Anglican evangelical clergy were all for it. In reality, however, talk of revival sent shivers of apprehension as well as of excitement up the spines of evangelical Anglicans. For them, 'revival' was a two-edged word, evoking memories of both the wondrous conversions and the emotional excesses of previous revivals. The idea of thousands being added to the Church thrilled evangelical Anglicans, but many of the clergy who had been educated at the public schools and Oxbridge shared longstanding upper-class and Anglican fears of religious enthusiasm. In a sermon in 1959, the leading Anglican evangelical John Stott noted that many clergy were chary about revival because of 'fear of excess'. 'Perhaps the very word "revival" conjures up for us scenes of emotional exuberance', he went on, 'to which there is a deep-seated aversion in the British character. We are reserved and shy. Most of us are timid Timothys. We abhor fanaticism. We are lovers of decorum and the golden mean. Extremes and enthusiasms embarrass us.' But in his next breath he reassuring his listeners that God had given them 'the spirit of power, love and self-control'.[22]

This created a problem for those evangelical Anglicans who wanted to support Billy Graham, who was not only a revivalist preacher but also an American in an era when England's educated elites were prone to scorn anyone or anything that hailed from across the Atlantic.[23] Graham came in for some weighty criticism in the letter pages of *The Times*, and members of the English establishment who wanted to

[21] D. J. Wilson-Haffenden, in the foreword to Frank Colquhoun, *Harringay Story: the Official Record of the Billy Graham Greater London Crusade, 1954* (London, 1955), vii.

[22] John Stott, 'Rekindling the Inner Fire', in *All Souls* (the parish magazine of All Souls Church, Langham Place, London; hereafter *All Souls*), January 1960, 13–14. In the final part of the quotation, Stott was quoting from the text for the sermon, 2 Timothy 1:6–7.

[23] On anti-Americanism in England's middle classes, see Weight, *Patriots*, 175–6.

support him were always going to be on the back foot.[24] Gough and other Anglican evangelical leaders did give their support to Graham, but the way in which they frequently did so is telling. Before the 1954 London crusade began, Gough acknowledged that 'all our ordinary methods of evangelism are largely failing to reach the masses outside the Church', as he expressed the hope that Graham's would reach them.[25] And what was different about Graham's methods? According to Gough, it was that they were American. In a comment that both sounded snobbish and was designed to appeal to others who thought similarly, Gough wrote: 'We may not particularly like American methods but the vast numbers who are weekly fascinated by American films may well be attracted by them.'[26] John Stott made similar remarks.[27] As in the nineteenth century, revivalism was for most evangelical Anglicans something that Americans did – something which they hoped to profit from but would not dream of doing themselves.

Implicit in these comments was the difficulty that upper-middle class Anglican clergy faced in seeking to extend their churches' welcome to England's working classes. The evangelicals may have had more ordinands, but for them there could be no genuine national revival unless more people with blue collars decided to step inside their churches. From this perspective, Billy Graham was their best hope for genuine revival. The evidence suggests, however, that Graham's typical convert was not the sort of person who would previously have attended a boxing contest at the Harringay arena.[28] The testimonies collected in the official story of the crusade came overwhelmingly from the people in the middle and upper classes, including a lord and lady, an actress, a toy manufacturer, a company director and a doctor.[29] A 'large proportion' of those who responded were already 'respectable church people', while Chelsea football supporters 'jeered' Graham when he was invited to address the crowd at Stamford Bridge at half time.[30] Despite the claim that Graham was the talk of the town, the daily newspapers

24 See the collection of letters to the editor of *The Times* (some of which were supportive of Graham) collected in *Fundamentalism: a Religious Problem* (London, 1955).

25 Hugh Gough, 'Greater London Crusade', *All Souls*, November 1953, 16.

26 Ibid., 16.

27 John Stott, 'The Rector's Letter', *All Souls*, March 1954, 10.

28 On Harringay as a more usually working class venue for boxing, ice hockey and circuses, see Colquhoun, *Harringay Story*, 84.

29 Ibid., 205–19.

30 Ibid., 211, 142.

seemed convinced that people continued to be more interested in things like the build-up to the FA Cup Final between West Bromwich Albion and Preston North End. London's own *Evening Standard* gave the crusade scant coverage.[31]

Indeed, certain aspects of Graham's approach probably kept workers away. For one, Graham's well-publicized hostility to communism did little to win him any favours from the significant slice of the population with socialist and communist sympathies: just before Graham's arrival in England in 1954, a Communist candidate was only narrowly defeated in a vote in one of the country's largest unions.[32] Graham's political and cultural conservatism meshed well with evangelical Anglican visions for a green and pleasant land, but there is little evidence that he was able to make significant connections either with those who leaned further left or with those who were apathetic when it came to attending religious gatherings. This was a far cry from the nineteenth-century revival meetings of another American evangelist, D. L. Moody, which were much more democratic, populist, and anti-institutional.[33] Graham courted the support of bishops, archbishops and others as he sought the imprimatur of the establishment, but their presence on his platform diminished his ability to reach those more suspicious of or even hostile to the English establishment.

Anglican evangelicals therefore had the blessing of a revivalist who did not make them too uncomfortable but who for very much the same reasons was unable to win the ears of a large proportion of those who enjoyed American films. It was not surprising, then, that Graham's crusades failed to bring the revival for which he and his supporters had hoped. By the late 1950s, the mood among evangelicals had changed. The magazine *Crusade* was launched in 1955 in the wake of Billy Graham's British crusades, but four years later the editor made no bones about the fact that the 1954 crusade at Harringay in North London had not been 'the beginning, as some hoped, of imminent

31 In one of its very few mentions of the crusade, the paper reported on an open-air meeting on Streatham Common where the heavy rain meant Cliff Barrows was unable to continue playing his trombone and a sagging platform required the movement of heavier members of the platform party to the edges; 'Graham', *Evening Standard*, 17 May 1954, 5.

32 'Communist Defeated in Union Fight', *Evening Standard*, 23 February 1954, 10.

33 On the populist nature of Moody's revivalism, see John Coffey, 'Democracy and Popular Religion: Moody and Sankey's Mission to Britain, 1873–1875', in Eugenio F. Biagini, ed., *Citizenship and Community: Liberals, Radicals and Collective Identities in the British Isles, 1865–1931* (Cambridge, 1996), 93–119.

revival in the land.'[34] Gough was forced to backpedal: by 1961, revival was again an aspiration rather than a reality.[35] But if their own appeal was so limited, and even the great American could not bring the workers into the ecclesiastical fold, what hope was there? What was the way forward?

IV

Theoretically, one possibility was that some Anglican evangelicals would aspire to become mass evangelists themselves. In reality, however, for those who came from the public schools and Oxbridge, their grooming made such a role both unappealing and extraordinarily difficult to pull off. It would certainly have cut them off from the vast majority of the higher classes (including, in most cases, the majority of their friends and family) who saw revivalism as American and vulgar.[36] All the same, no one tried. Another possibility was to hope that people from other churches would take up the revivalist task. Some did, notably Tom Rees and Dick Saunders, and their efforts received significant support from British churches and bore fruit. But they failed to make any dramatic breakthroughs. For them too, the embrace of the establishment was attractive, with Rees enjoying a special commissioning service at St Paul's Cathedral before he embarked on a major evangelistic tour of the country.[37] It is interesting to speculate on what a populist, anti-establishment brand of revivalism might have achieved in twentieth-century Britain.

With no revival from any quarter, then, Anglican evangelicals had to decide what to do next. One option was to ask why God had not sent revival, and the easy answer was that his Church was not ready. The revival they needed, then, was first and foremost a revival of the Church.[38] Not coincidentally, this was the time when the charismatic movement sprang up within Anglican evangelicalism, and this offshoot claimed that it was the revival that people had been praying for.[39] After

34 'Anniversary', *Crusade*, March 1959, 5.

35 Gough, 'The Church of England', 35–6.

36 On anti-Americanism among Britain's elites, see Weight, *Patriots*, 176.

37 Jean Rees, *His Name was Tom* (London, 1973), 126.

38 This concern was very evident in John Stott's ministry in the early 1960s. See, for example, Stott, 'Rekindling the Inner Fire'; and idem, 'A Study of Revival', *All Souls*, March 1960, 12–14.

39 For example, Michael Harper, *None Can Guess* (London, 1971), 41. On the history of

1960, non-charismatic conservative evangelical Anglicans largely stopped talking about the possibility of a religious revival, partly because of diminished hope, partly because the charismatics had co-opted the term, and partly because many of them were increasingly intent on becoming committed participants in an established Church that remained suspicious of evangelicals and their enthusiasms.[40] They still talked about revival, but increasingly it was only used of the revival in evangelical fortunes within the Church of England, a revival which very few outside that body cared about.[41]

V

As dissatisfaction with secularization theory has increased, many historians of Christianity in modern Britain have been looking for an alternative narrative to explain religious decline.[42] Callum Brown's work is the best example of this trend.[43] This essay suggests that stories such as the one told here, with their focus on human decisions and particular cultures, point towards a more satisfying and sophisticated understanding of post-war British religious history than any single story. The point of this essay is therefore not that religious decline in post-war Britain was simply the result of the limited appeal of some Anglican evangelicals – a whole variety of other stories must be told if we are to have anything like a full picture, not least of the English working classes and how interested they were in the sort of faithful religious adherence that church leaders cared about.[44] But this essay does suggest that an

the charismatic movement in Britain, see Peter Hocken, *Streams of Renewal: the Origins and Early Development of the Charismatic Movement in Great Britain* (Exeter, 1986).

40 The National Evangelical Anglican Congress at Keele in 1967 was the defining moment. See Bebbington, *Evangelicalism*, 249–50.

41 For example, Gerald Bray, 'Anglo-Catholicism – Facing the Challenge of the '80s', *Church of England Newspaper*, 20 November 1981, 9; and Alister E. McGrath, *To Know and Serve God: a Life of J. I. Packer* (London, 1997), 133.

42 See Jeffrey Cox, 'Master Narratives of Long-term Religious Change', in H. McLeod and W. Ustorf, eds, *The Decline of Christendom in Western Europe, 1750–2000*, (Cambridge, 2003), 201–17, at 214.

43 See especially Brown, *Death of Christian Britian.*

44 For the best recent work on working class religious beliefs and practices, see S. C. Williams, *Religious Belief and Popular Culture in Southwark c.1880–1939* (Oxford, 1999). Mark Smith's essay 'The Roots of Resurgence: Evangelical Parish Ministry in the mid-Twentieth Century', 318–28, in this volume, provides an excellent example of the kind of story needed, and one that demonstrates that Anglican evangelicals for whom Oxbridge was a foreign country could flourish in a working-class community.

understanding of how Anglican evangelical leaders thought of revival in the 1950s is an instructive part of the puzzle. Among the things that they learned about revival was to be as chary of the word as of the reality, for it too was double-edged. At first, it functioned to situate their programme in a compelling cultural context and to rally the laity to support events such as the Harringay crusade with rhetoric of a repeat of the eighteenth-century revivals. But when their ongoing outreach whimpered rather than banged and there was still sitting as well as standing room in most of their churches, disappointment and even disillusionment set in. Crying revival, Anglican evangelicals discovered, could be a bit like crying wolf. It was a word to be used with caution, if at all.

Westmont College, Santa Barbara, California

THE ROOTS OF RESURGENCE: EVANGELICAL PARISH MINISTRY IN THE MID-TWENTIETH CENTURY

by MARK SMITH

HISTORICAL analyses of twentieth-century evangelicalism have rarely focused on the experience of the parish. In many respects this is unsurprising. The renaissance in the historiography of evangelicalism since the 1970s has concentrated primarily on the eighteenth and nineteenth centuries, leaving the twentieth – and especially the period after the Second World War – relatively unexplored. Where work has been done, it has tended to focus on ecclesiastical politics, activity in universities, and biographies of major leaders.[1] Nor are more general histories particularly illuminating in this respect. Roger Lloyd, for example, concentrates on Anglo-Catholics and modernists rather than evangelicals[2] and Paul Welsby, whose work devotes considerable space to pastoral ministry, is more concerned with its organization than with its practice.[3] The consequence of this historiographical gap has not been so much to create a vacuum in relation to mid-twentieth century Anglican evangelicalism as to leave an impression of a rather elitist movement, dominated by the products of Public Schools and the Inter-Varsity Fellowship (IVF) and therefore almost irremediably middle class. Ironically, this impression has been reinforced by the one substantial study of mid-twentieth century parish evangelicalism so far in print – Alister Chapman's study of the ministry of John Stott at All Souls, Langham Place: 'Evangelical Anglicans,' he notes, 'just as much if not more than other Anglicans, continued to be associated with the middle classes, and they had significant difficulties reaching people lower down the social scale.'[4] Though persistent, this

1 See, for example, R. Manwaring, *From Controversy to Co-existence: Evangelicals in the Church of England 1914–1980* (Cambridge, 1980); D. Goodhew, 'The Rise of the Cambridge Inter-Collegiate Christian Union, 1910–1971', *JEH* 54 (2003), 62–88; A. McGrath, *To Know and Serve God: a Biography of James I. Packer* (London, 1997).

2 R. Lloyd, *The Church of England 1900–1965* (London, 1966).

3 P. A. Welsby, *A History of the Church of England 1945–1980* (Oxford, 1994), 131–50.

4 A. Chapman, 'Secularisation and the Ministry of John R. W. Stott at All Souls, Langham Place, 1950–1970', *JEH* 56 (2005), 496–513, at 509.

image is as much a consequence of the direction in which observers have turned their gaze as of the reality they have sought to observe. This essay uses the example of Christ Church, Chadderton, an industrial parish in the north of England, to display a rather different face of mid-twentieth century evangelicalism and to suggest that no estimate of the reasons for evangelical resurgence can afford to ignore the work of ordinary parishes.

The parish of Christ Church was created in 1870 as a consciously evangelical enterprise. Although its founders included some wealthy individuals[5], the new district was overwhelmingly working class in nature – a state of affairs that persisted into the mid-twentieth century. Initially, cotton mills provided much the largest source of employment and in 1931 the vicar reported that most of his parishioners were cotton operatives.[6] After the Second World War, the decline of the textile industry produced a greater occupational diversity in the parish but a survey of baptisms in the mid-1950s reveals a continuing preponderance of working-class parishioners – making up over 88% of the total, with a heavy weighting (some 77% of the total) towards manual occupations.[7] The congregation at Christ Church was recruited almost entirely from the parish and thus, while there was always a handful of middle-class or professional members, the vast majority of workers and worshippers in the church tended to come from working-class backgrounds. The parish of the 1950s had developed considerably since its inception. The far western portion had been hived off into a new district in 1911[8] and in the remainder, services were held not only at the parish church but also at two other centres: one in a set of converted cottages at Butler Green and the other in a tin tabernacle, the St Saviours Mission church.

The parish not only began with a strong evangelical identity but also succeeded in maintaining it. Especially important in this regard was the vesting of the patronage of the living in the hands of a local trust whose members co-opted their own successors. The trust restricted the living

[5] S. F. Cornell, *The History of Christ Church Chadderton, 1870–1920* (Oldham, 1920), 10–25.

[6] Manchester Central Library, Christ Church, Diocesan Visitation Return 1931, M39/addnl/103.

[7] Christ Church Baptism Register 1934-57 (Unless otherwise stated all records relating to Christ Church and St Saviours are located on the church premises as is the collection of material relating to the Butler Green Mission formerly in the possession of Mr E. Turner).

[8] A. Dixon, *Christ Church Chadderton: the First Hundred Years* (Manchester, 1970), 12.

to avowed evangelicals and they, in turn, accepted only evangelical assistant curates. In the 1950s Christ Church had two incumbents, both of whom trained at Tyndale Hall, Bristol, and four curates, all products of Oak Hill Theological College. With the exception of one of the latter, who took a University of London BA from Birkbeck concurrently with his training at Oak Hill, none of the clergy had received a university education.[9] Both from the point of view of the congregation and that of the clergy, this was an Anglican evangelical experience as far removed from the world of 'Bash camps' and Oxbridge Christian Unions as could be imagined. It was, however, no less clear and conscious in its evangelicalism. In 1953, for example, the Parochial Church Council (PCC) rejected a proposal to support the Church of England Children's Society on the grounds that the bishop of London was President of its executive committee 'and that it was run by Anglo-Catholics.'[10] It was decided instead to channel the charitable energies of the congregation towards Dr Barnardo's Homes, 'a truly evangelical society . . . and worthy of our support.' At the same time, however, this evangelical identity was not excessively narrow – the church continued, for example, to support both the Church Missionary Society (CMS) and the Bible Churchmen's Missionary Society (BCMS) long after the split.[11] There are also signs that it had moved away from some of the more aggressive manifestations of popular Protestantism. One member of the congregation remembers the surprise that ensued when, on clearing out the vicarage for the arrival of the new incumbent, the attic was found to contain an Orange banner, formerly processed around the parish probably at Whitsuntide. The banner was subsequently stored under the floorboards of the church school and a somewhat anxious discussion opened with the headquarters of the Orange Order in Liverpool in an attempt to repatriate it.[12]

The evangelical tradition of the parish is also evident in the pattern of Sunday services, which varied little over the decade. At both Christ Church and St Saviours, the main services were Morning and Evening Prayer, with communion being added to each of these once in the month. A Sunday school met during the morning service and at 2.30 in

9 *The Manchester Diocesan Directory* (Altrincham, 1950–60).
10 PCC minutes, 16 December 1953.
11 Ibid.
12 Interview with Mr E. Smith, 19 May 2006; PCC minutes, 4 September 1951, 25 March 1952.

the afternoon. Most months also included a family service in the afternoon and, at the parish church, a celebration of communion at 8.00 am. Although congregations seem to have been respectable in the mornings, the evening services were much the most popular and the Butler Green mission provided services only at this time. Worship was plain, with communion celebrated from the north end, and though both Christ Church and St Saviours had a paid organist their choirs were recruited endogenously, sang voluntarily and were not robed.[13]

The services, however significant on a Sunday, represented only the tip of the iceberg in terms of the life of the parish. Indeed, perhaps the most striking feature of the surviving church records is the continuing high tempo of activity in a style most commonly associated with the late Victorian and Edwardian churches analysed by Simon Green.[14] At the Annual Church meeting in 1952, for example, the vicar paused to thank the voluntary workers in the Sunday schools, the Handicraft class, the Ladies Working Party, Ladies Sewing Class Tea, Scouts and Cubs, Girl Campaigners, Young Harvesters, Men's fellowship, Mothers Union, Guild of Fellowship, Ladies Home Mission Union, the Church Choirs, Young Ladies Class, Women's Meeting, Youth Fellowship, Men's Working Party, Wednesday evening class at St Saviours and all the others: this on an electoral roll of around three hundred.[15] Such a plethora of activity clearly reflected a high level of commitment for a congregation of working men and women with relatively limited leisure time. However, it also represented a considerable danger of diversion of effort and at the 1954 Annual Meeting the vicar, Osmond Peskett, a former BCMS missionary in China, articulated his criteria for organizational activity,

> I . . . am going to remind you of what should be the ultimate aim of all such activities. That aim, I believe, should be *threefold. Evangelistic* – the winning of men and women to Jesus Christ; *Fellowship* – promoting and building up the Christian fellowship of the members of the church; *showing forth the compassion of Jesus Christ* – the bringing of help and comfort to those in need. I measure the success and usefulness of our organisations and activities by the

13 Christ Church Preachers Book 1953–9; St Saviours Preachers Book 1953–61; Butler Green Service Register 1952–69; E. Smith interview.

14 S. J. D. Green, *Religion in the Age of Decline* (Cambridge, 1996).

15 PCC Minutes, 15 April 1952.

> contribution they are making towards these, the supreme objects of the church's activities.[16]

This relatively holistic view of mission may have been informed by Peskett's experience in China and certainly did not have to wait until Keele 1967 to discover that 'Evangelism and compassionate service belong together in the mission of God'.[17] Nevertheless, traditional evangelism had a high priority for Peskett and he readily responded to a call from the bishop of Manchester that a mission be held in each parish. In the case of Christ Church this 'Forward Movement' took place in the autumn of 1953 and comprised a two-week visit from a team of evangelists from the Church Army who visited people in their homes and work-places and held Guest Night services in the evenings of the first week and then sought to follow up the contacts thus made in the second week.[18] Although extensively supported by the clergy and parishioners, and seen to be productive both of a 'quickening of the spiritual life of the parish' and some 'definite conversions', the results of the mission were not felt to have matched the expectations of it. For Peskett,

> Perhaps the greatest lesson that we learnt from the Mission was the fact that the evangelisation of this parish will only take place through the witness and labours of the local church, the laity having the greatest opportunity and responsibility in this matter. We should not be surprised at this experience, for it is one which the church is gradually re-learning up and down the country at the present time.[19]

No time was lost in putting this conclusion into effect. Already, in January 1954, Peskett had established what he called an 'Action Team', a group of lay people drawn from all three of the congregations who were responsible for systematically visiting every home in the parish. At each house the visitors would first try to ascertain whether the family considered itself to be part of the Anglican community, since there were strong Methodist and Roman Catholic presences in the parish. If they were Anglicans who did not attend church, the visitors would try

16 Ibid., 20 April 1954.

17 O. F. Peskett, *To China For Love* (Whitstable, n.d.); P. Crowe, ed., *Keele '67: the National Evangelical Anglican Congress Statement* (London, 1967), 23.

18 PCC Minutes, 11 November 1952.

19 Ibid., 8 September 1953; 20 April 1954.

to find out why and report back the information to the vicar. They would also issue invitations to church – an effort which, it was hoped, would be made more effective by the introduction of special Guest Night services at each of the churches once a quarter.[20] The development of systematic domestic visitation was essentially a return to the 'aggressive approach' common to evangelical churches in the area in the previous century.[21] It represented a deliberate attempt to use perceived popular associations with the established Church and its parish system as a vehicle for mission and is clearly congruent with Callum Brown's representation of a Britain in the 1950s in which mainstream churches enjoyed considerable sympathy and a strong working-class base.[22] A similar perception underlay the traditional annual walks at Whitsuntide that brought all three congregations out of their church buildings in an act of witness to the parish at large[23] and occasional programmes of outdoor preaching in the summer which also seem to have met with a degree of public acceptance. As one participant recalled, 'people wouldn't ignore a sermon, they felt they had to stop and listen'.[24] Much of this might be seen as indigenous activity, therefore, but, in relation to the Guest Night services Peskett noted that, 'this idea has arisen partly out of the activities of the Action Group and partly out of my own experience of what my fellow clergy are doing at the present time'[25] and it is possible that he may have been influenced by similar measures being deployed by John Stott and promoted via the Islington Conference and the evangelical press.[26]

The priority placed on mission via the building of local relationships using local resources was not entirely exclusive, however, and the parish continued to seize the opportunity to use external resources where the prospects appeared to be promising. In 1955, for example, Christ Church hosted relays from Billy Graham rallies at the Kelvin Hall in Glasgow[27] and the vicar later remembered, 'long queues lined up

20 Ibid., 20 April 1954; E. Smith interview; Interview with Mrs V Smith 18 May 2006.

21 M. Smith, *Religion in Industrial Society: Oldham and Saddleworth, 1740–1865* (Oxford, 1994), 101–4.

22 C. Brown, *Religion and Society in Twentieth-Century Britain* (Harlow, 2006).

23 For example, PCC minutes, 9 September 1952.

24 E. Smith interview.

25 PCC Minutes, 20 April 1954.

26 Chapman, 'Secularisation', 502–3, Bebbington, *Evangelicalism in Modern Britain: a History from the 1730s to the 1980s* (London, 1989), 254.

27 PCC Minutes, 8 March 1955.

outside the church waiting for the doors to open.'[28] According to the local press, seven-hundred attended the first relay and 'many inquirers were received in the counselling room.'[29] Similarly, from 24 May to 10 June 1957 the church held a 'Tent Crusade' with special meetings for children led by a speaker from Liverpool.[30]

However, as indicated in 1954, there was more to the mission of Christ Church than evangelism alone. Much of the work of '*showing forth the compassion of Jesus Christ* – the bringing of help and comfort to those in need'[31] – was carried on quietly by the clergy and by church organizations. The Butler Green mission was especially notable in this regard, having a track record of providing free meals for children whose parents were on strike or locked out and a fund to help parents who were out of work.[32] However, through the 1950s the church remained alert to opportunities to play a more public role. It continued to invest substantially in primary education, running two separate day schools at different locations in the parish. It was also particularly prompt in both responding to an invitation from the local council to participate in a recently established Old People's Welfare Committee which aimed to coordinate statutory and voluntary provision, and in securing involvement in the old people's home which was eventually established in the parish.[33]

The range of institutions involved in the third aim of building up the fellowship of the church was very extensive. Many of these, like the Mother's Union and the Men's Fellowship aimed to draw together particular sections of the congregation and either (like the Ladies Home Mission Union) had a direct spiritual purpose, or (like the sewing class) a practical one. But each organization also tended to reinforce the dense social network that bound together individual members of the congregations and anchored them in the life of the church. This was the warm heart of evangelical religion which, however focused on an individual relationship with God, was always experienced in community. There was, therefore, also a range of events, such as congregational socials organized by the men and the great annual sale of work, organized by

28 Peskett, *China for Love*, 116.
29 News-cutting in collection of Mr E. Butterworth, Oldham, Lancs.
30 Handbill in Butterworth Collection; *Oldham Evening Chronicle*, 24 May 1957.
31 PCC Minutes, 20 April 1954.
32 S. Platt, 'The Mission' (MSs memoir in Turner collection).
33 PCC Minutes, 9 September 1952, 31 October 1955.

the women, that aimed to draw in and integrate the whole congregation.[34] The church's leadership was nevertheless determined that such sociability, though a perennial feature of congregational life, should not become an end in itself or detract from the priority of committed discipleship.[35] The importance of a regular personal devotional life was strongly emphasized and in 1957, for example, the church ran an 'enjoy your bible campaign', a 'school of prayer' a 'Church teaching campaign' and also, for recent converts a 'school of discipleship' – the last three taking place on Thursday evenings after the parish prayer meeting.[36]

Local evangelical culture remained in tension with popular mores throughout the 1950s with drinking, smoking, dancing and cinema-going all considered to be questionable activities and 'definitely wrong', concluded the communicants' fellowship in 1952, if they hindered the Christian faith.[37] Films were more of a grey area than most, however, because they might be used to propagate the faith and by 1956 the new incumbent, Charles Reed, was willing to propose that such films might be shown on church premises as part of the winter's social arrangements.[38] Another grey area was sport. The capacity for organized sport to encourage sociability and to serve as a point of contact with the population at large was well understood and the church provided a range of sporting activities including a tennis club, a football club and a cricket team. However, the clergy and PCC were also wary of the danger that the teams and activities could become detached from the spiritual life of the church and took steps to mitigate this problem. In 1953, for example, it was decided that cricket would be supervised by a committee charged with avoiding, 'the tendency, in the past, of drifting away from church' and, in the following year, it was decided to close down a football club whose members were no longer attending church or Sunday school and to start a new one.[39]

Concerns like these were perhaps all the more keenly felt because so much of the strategy of the church in the 1950s centred on older children and young adults. Although it would be difficult to identify any section of the congregation neglected by the church's organizational

34 Ibid., 14 July 1953; 31 October 1955.
35 Compare Green, *Age of Decline*, 387–90.
36 PCC Minutes, 10 September 1957.
37 Communicants fellowship minutes, 29 May 1952.
38 PCC minutes, 31 July 1956.
39 Ibid., 10 March 1953; 13 July 1954; 7 September 1954.

structure, most of the innovations of the 1950s were concerned with this particular age group. Substantial and thriving Sunday schools were a matter of course during this period, and their pattern of activity, from regular meetings, teacher's preparation classes and teas to anniversary services and annual trips to Heywood Park or Southport, was well established.[40] However, both incumbents in the 1950s proved anxious to supplement this regular round. One of Peskett's earliest initiatives was the beginning of a Friday evening meeting for 'Young Harvesters' – a junior branch of the BCMS – aimed at children in the Sunday school. It operated under lay leadership and had a fairly light touch: as the vicar explained, 'there would be half an hour given to handicrafts, quarter of an hour to devotion and then half an hour of games . . . it was hoped to stimulate a little more interest in the children.'[41] Potentially rather more contentious was Peskett's attitude to uniformed youth movements. For boys, the church already had established groups for cubs and scouts and these seem to have been left untouched; but for the girls, Guides and Brownies were eschewed in favour of Girl Campaigners, which were considered to be more straightforwardly Christian in ethos. The Campaigners meeting was one of the responsibilities of Miss Seddon, the 'Lady Worker', assisted by volunteer helpers. Despite doubts in some quarters, this work seems to have prospered and a junior branch – the 'Junos' was established for younger girls.[42] Youth organizations provided a clear opportunity to link the three churches in the parish together and this was part of the purpose behind the institution of special 'youth services' at both Christ Church and St Saviours in which the uniformed organizations would participate, showing 'to many in our Parish that we had a fine company of young people in the Church'.[43] There was a particular concern to integrate young people from the Butler Green Mission which, by virtue of its location, tended to recruit from the poorest sections of the parish: they seem to have participated fully in the Saturday evening 'Youth Fellowship' which catered for the under 30s[44] and in perhaps the most successful innovation of the period, the 'Youth Squash'. Squashes were held in the

40 Ibid., 15 April 1952; 8 September 1953; E. Smith interview.

41 PCC minutes 3 October 1951.

42 Ibid., 3 October 1952, 7 April 1953; V. Smith interview; Bebbington, *Evangelicalism in Modern Britain*, 226.

43 PCC minutes 9 March 1954.

44 Ibid., 9 December 1952; 20 April 1954.

vicarage following the Sunday evening service where sometimes as many as eighty young people from the three churches – it was literally a squash – gathered for an informal meeting. The meetings always included 'a right good sing' of traditional hymns supplemented by songs from the Young Life Campaign chorus book, opportunities for prayer and testimony and a talk – often by a guest speaker – followed by a discussion. It provided fellowship, encouragement and a nursery for talent. 'It really bound us all together . . . we really did enjoy them', remembered one former participant.[45] For a group of working-class young people, many of whom would have left school at fifteen, and most of whom could never have aspired to a university education, the squashes perhaps represented the closest approximation they might know to the experience of their more advantaged brethren at the Cambridge Inter-Collegiate Christian Union (CICCU). This heightened activity might be regarded as an early response to the gradual emergence of a teenage culture in the 1950s. There is certainly little sign of the exhaustion of churches, especially in relation to the young, described by Brown.[46] Two of these young people found themselves accepted for ordained ministry in the church in the next decade but crucially, many more – perhaps precisely because of their limited access to higher education – remained rooted in their local community.[47]

When measured by conventional statistical tools, the vibrant activity of the 1950s seems to have produced relatively little effect. Although annual reports often recorded growing congregations, especially at the parish church, Easter communicant figures remained essentially static over the decade and the electoral roll grew by only 10% from 300 at the beginning to 330 at the end.[48] In fact, the churches seemed to have enjoyed much stronger growth in the late 1960s and '70s, mustering a joint electoral roll of 470 in 1976, for example.[49] While the relative success of this later period owed much to the work of a new generation of clergy, its foundation was laid in the 1950s, in the maintenance of a

45 V. Smith interview.

46 Brown, *Religion and Society*, 216.

47 A reunion of this group held in 1994 attracted sixty surviving participants. The extent to which increasing access to higher education in the 1960s, by increasing the geographical and social mobility of potential lay leaders, may have undermined the community-based approach of many churches in Britain is an issue that deserves further attention.

48 Christ Church Preachers Book, St Saviours Preachers Book, *Manchester Diocesan Directory* (1950–60).

49 PCC minutes, 9 March 1976.

mission-oriented culture and in the nurture of a whole generation of young men and women who provided the lay leadership and active workforce of the church through the next two decades.[50] David Bebbington has noted that 'the remarkable resurgence symbolised by Keele demands explanation',[51] but in this parish, at least, its roots lay in the enterprise and creativity and the solid persistent work of the 1950s. How much that is true more widely – how many of the rank and file of the university Christian Unions of the 1970s and 80s, for example, came from just such ordinary parishes – is a question that would well repay further investigation.

University of Oxford

50 Ibid., 7 April 1953; E. Smith interview; V. Smith interview; Peskett, *China for Love*, 115.
51 Bebbington, *Evangelicalism in Modern Britain*, 252.

BOUNDARY CROSSING AND BOUNDARY MARKING: RADICAL REVIVAL IN CONGO AND UGANDA FROM 1948

by EMMA WILD-WOOD

DISSENTERS, whatever their cause, challenge the boundaries of their society. Revivalist dissenters are no exception. Their dissent has often been studied in terms of doctrinal nuance and generational tension. The slight variations of enthusiasm are bewildering to the outsider if dissent is understood simply as a 'second generation movement' attempting to ignite past passion in a revival that has become clerical and formulaic.[1] This essay places one particular instance of revivalist dissent within the wider context of a countercultural stance towards migration, disadvantage, local spirituality and ecclesiastical governance and suggests that the movement is better understood by this holistic approach.

Ubotha Marthe grew up in a 'pagan' household and married into the African Inland Church in Congo. She was later 'saved' through the preaching of Anglican radical revivalists from Uganda. Behind her conversion is a story of dissent within the East African revival. In an interview, Ubotha offered the following narrative:

> During the 1964 war, this [Simba] rebellion caused us to move to Mahagi-Port. There some evangelists from Arua had entered the country. Their teaching struck their listeners, particularly my husband and another, called Aloni. The preaching was centred around the confession of sin, '. . . if you teach that's good. But be assured that without conversion or confession of sin you are not real Christians. You teach with many iniquities reigning in your body, since your childhood until you entered your (own adult) homes.' And they confirmed the truth of it. When the evangelists returned to Arua, they took with them my husband and the other one who had publicly confessed their sins . . . my husband and his

1 Josiah Mlahagwa, 'Contending for the Faith: Spiritual Revival and the Fellowship Church in Tanzania', in Thomas Spear and Isaria Kimambo, eds, *East African Expressions of Christianity* (Oxford, 1999), 296–306, at 299.

> friend went to get this salvation in Arua. [Later, I] freely accepted to be converted . . .[2]

Ubotha's testimony suggests a number of things about the nature of this particular revivalist movement and its context: true believers have confessed their sins, they do not simply do church-related work: a point with which most revivalists could agree. Education, very much the work of the Church, was a source of false pride: a point with which mainstream revivalists would have had difficulty. In radical revival discourse, mainstream revivalists had lost their passion for spiritual renewal and for evangelism and were involved in worldly affairs. However, most revivalists had similar aims, theology and praxis. Derek Peterson has observed that revival in Kenya encompassed not only spiritual and moral issues but was, '. . . a way of interpreting social conflict'.[3] Ubotha's testimony situates these revival events in a time and place of dislocation. Mahagi-Port is a town on the border with Uganda. Arua is further north in Uganda. Congo had suffered internal upheaval since its independence in 1960. The Simba rebellion caused large numbers of people to take refuge in towns.[4] Soon after her conversion Ubotha and many others fled into Uganda and spent several years there before returning to Congo. Ubotha's radical revivalist Christianity was shaped by physical boundary crossings and the social marginalization such transience often entailed.[5]

This case-study provides a way of understanding revivalist dissent that may be pertinent to other contexts: dissent arises from the negotiation within a shared revivalist discourse of social boundaries by those felt to be marginalized. Revivalism can provide a language by which to challenge socio-religious inequalities. The study also supports an understanding of African Christianity which rejects the idea of a monolithic colonial religion imposed upon an oppressed people. The

2 Ubotha Marthe, interview, Alur, Mahagi, 28 August 2000. Tapes and transcripts of all interviews are available from the author or from L'Institut Superieur Théologique Anglican, Bunia, DR Congo.

3 Derek Peterson, 'Wordy Women: Gender Trouble and the Oral Politics of the East African Revival in Northern Gikuyuland', *Journal of African History* 42: 3 (2001), 469–89, at 478.

4 Mawa Lekeni, 'L'Exode des Lugbara vers Bunia de 1960 à nos Jours: les Facteurs determinants', unpublished Ph.D. thesis, Bunia University, 1990, 45.

5 Gender issues in revival are discussed in chapter six of my thesis, 'Migration and Identity: the Development of an Anglican Church in North-East Congo, 1960–2000', unpublished Ph.D. thesis, University of Edinburgh, 2005.

radical revivalists demonstrate what is apparent elsewhere on the continent: that Christian identity, belief and practice were intensely local and vernacular. Africans acted as autonomous agents in reviving and reforming western mission Christianity in order to engage with the immediate context.

The East African Revival was a regional experience of conversion and spiritual renewal.[6] It emerged in Rwanda and South and Central Uganda in the 1930s. It aimed to revive the Anglican Church from the inside, challenging nominal Christians to become 'saved ones' and to focus on spiritual rather than socio-political religious issues. The majority of the 'saved' remained faithful to the Church and an intrinsic part of it. It was a movement that effected society as a whole, not least in the areas of education and development. The Revival is well known but the corpus of scholarly work on it is relatively small.[7] Scholarship on the northern dissenters comprises for the most part unpublished dissertations, which supply the following chronology. The Revival was brought to North-west Uganda about 1948 and tensions developed almost immediately.[8] At times radical groups were so critical of the Church of Uganda that their continuing membership was burdensome, and some chose to break completely from the Church. Like the revivalists in the south, the northern revivalists called for public confession of sin, a commitment to fellowship and evangelism and a renunciation of local, traditional customs. However, an influential number of them also developed a suspicion of aspirations to improve one's education or socio-economic development, expressed in a condemnation of worldly achievement and wealth and a claim of greater reliance on the spontaneous guidance and provision of the Holy Spirit. Ajuku Dronyi, who led the team of evangelists to Mahagi Port in 1964, was particularly zealous.[9] After his conversion in 1949 he tore up his teacher's certificate claiming that the Holy Spirit would instruct him. He called on revival-

6 Steve Latham, '"God came from Teman": Revival and Contemporary Revivalism', in Andrew Walker and Kristin Aune, eds, *On Revival: a Critical Examination* (Carlisle, 2003), 171–86.

7 The most thorough examination remains in manuscript, C. E. Robins, '"Tukutendereza": a Study of Social Change and Sectarian Withdrawal in the Balokole Revival of Uganda', unpublished Ph.D. thesis, Columbia University, 1975.

8 A 'reawakened' group emerged in Central Uganda at the same time. They are usually considered less radical than the northern Chosen Evangelical Revival.

9 Nason Akamifwa, Rachel Opindu, and Revd Ruben, interview, English, Arua, 25 August 2000.

ists to abandon their teaching and nursing jobs and to eschew material reward in order to carry out vigorous evangelism.[10] The actions of Ajuku and his followers were seen by mainline Anglicans and revivalists as disruptive. However, discipline and even imprisonment were greeted by Ajuku as signs of success; persecution was expected for those who showed loyalty to Christ's command to preach salvation.[11]

An attempt was made to bring the northern movement under the norms of the southern and central Ugandan *Balokole* movement in 1954 but it failed and resulted in two distinct movements with parallel organizational structures. Ajuku's followers became known as Trumpeters (from their use of loud-speakers) or Strivers, and called themselves the Chosen Evangelical Revival (CER).[12] One observer, who described the Revival as 'a movement of the Spirit of God bringing people into an experience of Christ's power to save from sin, and into a new understanding of . . . Christian fellowship', described the CER as the 'lunatic fringe'.[13] The insults were not one sided: the CER called mainstream revivalists *Wapumzifu*, the resting ones. The next forty years saw violent division followed by painful reconciliation between the two movements and the Church of Uganda. Although the revivalist groups had split, most of them operated primarily within the Anglican Church of Uganda.[14] The entire West Nile Church and the Anglican Church in Congo were affected by one movement of revival or the other.[15] Mainstream revivalists were largely willing to accept the liturgical and clerical order of the Anglican Church. The CER, however, maintained a sectarian stance within (and occasionally outside) the Church and contested the validity of the dominant Anglican identity.

By the time the CER movement reached Congo in the 1960s it appealed to the socially disenfranchised, people who had been ill-served by modernity and yet felt dislocated from traditional life. They were uprooted by war, poverty or by the effects of colonialism and

10 Adraa Mokili, 'The Growth and Impact of Chosen Evangelical Revival (CER) in Ayivu County, Arua District, West Nile-Madi Diocese', unpublished Ph.D. thesis, Makerere University, 1986, 11–14.

11 Margaret Lloyd, *Wedge of Light: Revival in North West Uganda* (Rugby, n.d.), 20.

12 The Acholi and Teso also had CER movements in fellowship with the West Nile one. The north/south divide suggests the presence of cultural and social differences.

13 J. H. Dobson, *Daybreak in West Nile* (London, 1967), 36.

14 This included the Anglican Church of Congo/Zaire until 1981.

15 Alio Samweli, interview, English, Arua, 8 August 2000; Archbishops of Uganda, Rwanda, Burundi and Boga-Zaïre, Janani Luwum and Silvanus Wani were both mainstream Balokole from the north.

independence. Their testimonies suggest that they considered themselves victims of circumstance stuck in unhelpful behaviour patterns. Turning to revivalism provided their lives with a greater sense of purpose expressed in terms of repentance and salvation. Uketi Amos, founder of several churches, emphasizes the transformative power of conversion on his personal relationships. In a discourse similar to that of other revivalists, he understood confession of sins as changing his lifestyle beyond that expected of mere church-goers:

> Salvation helped me to leave the drink for ever . . . I went to my father and asked his forgiveness and to my wife who'd returned to her home. . . . I also went to my family-in-law declaring, 'Please forgive me. I acted foolishly.'[16]

The act of confession was often also an act of indirect evangelism. Uketi's wife, Uweka Marie, returned to him when she saw the difference in her husband and was herself converted.[17] All members of the CER were expected to participate in weekly evangelism and in fellowship meetings. Open-air evangelism often took place at markets using home-made loud-speakers and lively singing and dancing. Fellowship was provided by small close-knit spiritual groups. This new life was described as 'freedom', as Uketi explains,

> Since the day I knew Jesus and confessed my sins . . . and put them on the cross of Jesus . . . I was automatically freed and I had no desire to act like that again.[18]

Revivalists claimed freedom from sin, from the fear of death, from regular blood sacrifice, from anti-social living (drunkenness, lying, stealing, adultery), freedom to do the will of God, to itinerate, to improve family life.[19] The CER took the claim of freedom further than other revivalists, seeing it as freedom from constraining social boundaries, both modern and traditional, and the freedom to draw their own boundaries.

In adopting this stance they challenged the culture which had become acceptable to ordinary Christians and mainstream revivalists. In

16 Uketi Amos, interview, Alur, Mahagi, 29 August 2000.

17 Uwake Marie, interview, Alur, Mahagi, 28 August 2000.

18 Uketi Amos, 29 August 2000.

19 Ozua Samson, interview, Swahili, Aru, 10 August 2000; Adoroti Ombhabua, interview, Swahili, Kumuru, 17 August 2000.

his essay, 'Revival: Empirical Aspects', William Kay contends that '[r]evival is, at least initially, counter-cultural and rather than legitimating political and social authority, stands out against it'.[20] Dissent continues a counter-cultural stance when mainstream revival has become, to some extent, normative. Many mainstream revivalists still displayed great spiritual vitality but, in large part because their movement had already changed their culture, they were no longer counter cultural. The CER attracted converts who had alternative social and cultural perspectives. They had little to lose by alienating themselves from society and gaining notoriety. Indeed, the CER were proud to differentiate themselves from both nominal and 'saved' Christians, considering themselves to be the true followers of Jesus Christ. In this counter-cultural stance the CER can be seen as establishing a unique position within the Christian community. As has been said of revivalists in Namibia, 'Christians who lacked other forms of status had an interest in asserting a distinctive identity'.[21] In their counter-cultural identity the CER exhibited more zealous moral behaviour, more fervent evangelistic activities and a greater tendency to criticize authority and ultimately to fragment. They also demonstrated an ability to assign a divine purpose to both migration and other forms of dislocation.

Migration shaped the CER movement. Almost all radical revivalists in Congo had spent time in Uganda and many Ugandans fled into Congo when Idi Amin fell from power in 1979. During the 1950s, '60s and '70s crossing of physical borders was seen as inevitable for many of those attracted to the CER movement. Sometimes they were economic migrants, sometimes they were refugees. Revivalism enabled them to redefine the importance of travel into a new region or country. Forced migration was perceived to be part of God's greater purpose and deliberate crossing of national, ethnic or just parish boundaries was now done at the prompting of the Holy Spirit. The freedom gained through salvation included the freedom to travel in order to preach the gospel. Sometimes CER members felt prompted to leave good employment and return home to evangelize their own families. Some left home to evangelize neighbouring ethnic groups, while others used their migra-

20 William Kay, 'Revival: Empirical Aspects', in Walker and Aune, eds, *On Revival*, 187–204, at 198.

21 Meredith McKittrick, *To Dwell Secure: Generation, Christianity and Colonialism in Ovamboland* (Portsmouth, NH, 2002), 261.

tory networks to further their evangelism – perhaps staying with someone who had once worked on the same plantation. Uketi understands this as an obvious result of his conversion. He should not stay calm in church, like Christians or mainstream revivalists, rather, he maintains,

> My faith has given me strength to explore lots of unknown places. When I was saved I went by foot to Aru, everywhere . . . yesterday I was in Nebbi, Uganda. Following this faith I don't worry about my tiredness.[22]

The discourse of tireless itineration is a frequent one, overcoming check-points, border officials and language barriers to preach the gospel, striving to promote salvation rather than resting as other Christians did. In Congo the itineration of the CER resulted in the development of many small chapels from the 1970s onwards. The best itinerant evangelists could be responsible for the foundation and nurturing of ten to fifteen Anglican chapels.

CER members could also travel confidently to brothers and sisters in Christ. Like the mainstream revivalists, they developed international networks which included local and regional leaders, meetings and conventions, through which news could quickly be disseminated. They maintained transnational connections during the 1970s, when the Anglican Churches in Uganda and Congo were instead emphasizing national ecclesiastical structures.[23] The migratory paths taken previously for employment or security were followed again and again for spiritual fellowship with a wider network of revivalists. Physical boundaries now presented the CER with opportunities for fellowship and evangelism. They had gained a sense of greater control over their fragile circumstances. Furthermore, a settled, ordered and calm existence was considered to be less than ideal for someone who was truly 'saved'.

Modernity presented other barriers to the CER. Many members existed on the margins of a monetary economy. To address this they made poverty a social and spiritual virtue, ostentatiously refusing to wear ties, jewellery, or elaborate hair-styles, or to pursue wealth in any form: there was plenty of encouragement in the New Testament for this. These practices developed a new culture of the initiated which set

22 Uketi Amos, 29 August 2000.
23 Ibid.

them apart from the community – Christians and non-Christians alike – and earned them the criticism from mainstream revivalists for being legalistic. In taking this stance they were investing their sense of marginalization with value and purpose. The CER understood the Church not simply to have colluded with modernity, but – in its promotion of education and development projects – to be encouraging it. The Anglican Church expected a certain level of education and training for those it entrusted to preach and to teach. This education had to be paid for. The freedom to preach and to teach gained through CER confession was a freedom extended to those whom the western initiated churches considered as lacking the necessary qualifications. The CER made their lack of education a point of spiritual superiority, spurning opportunities for learning and claiming the inspiration of the Holy Spirit was the key to spiritual leadership. The CER drew its own boundaries on the issues of wealth, education and ministry. Mainstream revival had given people the opportunity to live a morally and spiritually upright life and thus take advantage of the further education and development available. The CER criticized them, believing that too much wealth and education would lead people away from a spiritual life.

As a result of moving the boundaries on modernity, the CER contested the respect for properly appointed authority within the Anglican Church. CER leaders were charismatic individuals who were able, zealous preachers and commanded great loyalty from group members. Belonging was primarily to the CER rather than the Church. The influence of the leadership was tempered by democratic voting systems for decisions on who the leader of open-air evangelism should be, or which theme was to be chosen for the Sunday afternoon meeting.[24] CER events were self-supporting. Their leaders received no financial remuneration. The CER were suspicious of the institutional Church and its desire for educated, salaried leaders who did not sufficiently challenge themselves or their congregations to repentance and right-living. Their loud, confident preaching outside churches directly after the Sunday services as worshippers left the building often criticized the content of the sermon and challenged the ecclesiastical authority of church leaders and the social complacency of their congregations. One pastor explained that they attacked the Church by saying,

24 CER meeting, Bunia, 17 September 2000.

'In the church there is sin, the church is full of sinners.'[25] The radical anti-development of the CER stance challenged the progressive developmental aspirations of mainstream revivalists who appreciated order and respect in church government, worship and social interaction.

Most CER members considered there to be a division of labour between them and the Church.[26] The Church's work centred around the sacraments but the work of the CER was evangelism and preaching with CER activity being of paramount importance. The issue which most threatened Anglican identity was the reversal in the minds of the CER of the importance of roles within the Church. The CER believed that this authority was rightfully and biblically theirs. The Mahagi archdeaconry evangelist and CER leader, Ndiritho Paulo, explained:

> We go about the country looking for other people outside. If we find people there we take them to the church worker . . . As the Bible says, 'We will chose seven people to stay here but we will go out to preach.'[27]

His understanding of the role of the diaconate in Acts 6: 2–4 and the role of the church workers put the CER in a position parallel with the first apostles and the official Anglican workers as those appointed by them to carry out tasks of secondary importance. The CER believed their activities to have priority over church activities; their group was pivotal, not an optional extra. By this approach, the CER effectively attempted to uproot the order of Prayer Book and episcopal hierarchy from their place of paramount importance for the Anglican Church and relegate them to a secondary place below the freedom of fellowship meetings and open-air evangelism important for CER identity. They inverted not only the dominant Anglican order but also mainstream revivalist order. The CER disliked the boundaries surrounding ecclesiastical authority and wanted to draw their own better to serve itinerant evangelism.

The CER also contested the value of the Anglican liturgy. Ubaya Ucaki explains the tension between Anglican order, to which most of the CER submitted on Sunday mornings, and CER worship:

> Well, in the morning service they follow the order of the church

25 Tabu Abembi, interview, French Bwakadi, 6 October 2000.
26 Sila Bileti, interview, Swahili, Aru, 10 August 2000.
27 Ndiritho Paulo, interview, Swahili, Mahagi, 29 August 2000.

> completely. They sing praises as well here at church but [at CER meetings], as it's evangelism, they really dance. At the church they only do order because it's the special place to respect God . . . There at the place of evangelism people really show Him, they really dance.[28]

Ubaya respected the Anglican service as displaying reverence for the Almighty. However, he considered CER meetings more engaging and, therefore, more likely to attract outsiders. Worship was exuberant, spontaneous and followed local dance and musical influences. The CER used their own compositions and also the hymn book, singing its songs with more gusto than was customary in church. They preferred their own style of worship to the formal, Prayer Book style. More importantly, at a lively evangelistic event, suggested Ubaya, God was revealed through dance and music in a way that God was not seen in the order of a church service. This striking claim clearly demands that attendance at the CER meeting take priority over the church service. The CER eschewed elite structures and condemned rites which upheld those structures, embracing instead a popular, pneumatological religiosity. These differences caused great strain as CER and non-CER members tried to co-exist within the one institution. In Congo, for example, the CER created new Anglican congregations, enlarging the Church numerically and geographically. They also created serious tensions between themselves and the Anglican leadership. Much energy went into mediation and resolving tension which hampered growth in other areas.

The CER considered their expression of Christian faith as liberating them not only from the marginalizing effects of modernity but also from the constraints of tradition. Radical revivalists were outspoken critics of traditional rites. They banned end-of-mourning ceremonies for their dead and the use of indigenous medicines and were implacable opponents of more widely-accepted prohibitions of alcohol and polygamy.[29] They were willing to confront rather than simply ignore traditional beliefs and practices, breaking up shrines and clearing sacred forests. Ironically, some of their activities was perceived by onlookers as

28 Ubaya Uchaki, interview, Swahili, Mahagi, 30 August 2000.

29 Ang'omoko Tek'akwo Upio, 'Mouvement des "Barokole" dans le diocèse de Boga-Congo; cas de l'archidiacone d'Aru', unpublished Ph.D. thesis, Bunia University, 1997, 12.

being close to traditional practice. When dissent developed into division the use of local cultural customs was one of the issues which caused a greater rift. Ajuku's strange behaviour was initially attributed by Ugandans to his falling under the influence of the Yakan spirit thrown by Rembe, a Kakwa prophet who had led a resistance to colonial occupation up until 1920.[30] The CER used local music, vertical jumping styles of dancing, exuberant drumming and all-night fellowships frowned upon by ordinary revivalists. Well-respected leaders of the Revival from Central Uganda, welcomed in this way by North-western revivalists in 1954, reprimanded the people and appealed to them for calm, an action which further soured relations amongst revivalists of different persuasions.[31] The CER was a local expression of revivalism which adapted certain aspects of northern culture. This is also reflected in attitudes to authority. The CER operated within a variety of traditionally segmentary cultures like the Kakwa, Lugbara, and Alur. Whereas peoples further south generally had greater centralization of power with a paramount ruler, in the northern area when someone contended for the position of elder it was not uncommon for families to fragment.[32] Dissent and division were therefore understood in the north as a normal stage of growth. In Uganda, the northerners were often disparaged by the southerners for their cultural differences and distanced from economic and political advantages in the colonial and post-colonial state. Whilst some northern revivalists were influenced by centralized southern models of authority, CER members tended to be less removed by education, work patterns or colonial privilege from decentralized patterns of power than were their mainstream counterparts.

The radical revivalists positioned themselves against other groups by rejecting the boundaries they had imposed and establishing their own boundaries instead. They negotiated a position for themselves as regards tradition and modernity which gave them greater cohesion and stronger expressions of identity than were available in the Church. A more radical form of the East African revival was satisfying for its adherents because it met their needs for freedom and confidence in a situation in which they often felt disadvantaged. The very things which gave CER members a sense of control over their lives were the things

30 Nason Akamifwa, Rachel Opindu, interview, Lugbara, Arua, 22 August 2000.
31 Mokili, 'Growth and Impact', 15.
32 Ibid., 3.

which caused dissent among revivalists. The discourse of revivalist dissent is often presented in terms of disagreement about internal issues of the revival movement. This essay has suggested that competing ideologies which emerge within the same broad categories of Christian experience are complex responses to a broad set of social situations which reach beyond issues of best belief and practice.

Cambridge Theological Federation

BAPTIST REVIVAL AND RENEWAL IN THE 1960s

by IAN M. RANDALL

ACCORDING to Callum Brown in *The Death of Christian Britain*, from 1963 Christianity in Britain went on a downward spiral. More generally, Brown sees the 1960s as the decade in which the Christian-centred culture that had conferred identity on Britain was rejected.[1] This claim, however, which has received much attention, needs to be set alongside David Bebbington's analysis of British Christianity in the 1960s. In *Evangelicalism in Modern Britain*, Bebbington notes that in 1963 charismatic renewal came to an Anglican parish in Beckenham, Kent, when the vicar, George Forester, and some parishioners received the 'baptism of the Holy Spirit' and began to speak in tongues. During the next quarter of a century, Bebbington continues, the charismatic movement became a powerful force in British Christianity.[2] Both Brown and Bebbington view the 1960s as a decade of significant cultural change. Out of that period of upheaval came the decline of cultural Christianity but also the emergence of a new expression of Christian spirituality – charismatic renewal. Within the evangelical section of the Church this new movement was an illustration of the ability of evangelicalism to engage in adaptation. To a large extent evangelical Anglicans were at the forefront of charismatic renewal in England. The Baptist denomination in England was, however, deeply affected from the mid-1960s onwards and it is this which will be examined here.

Baptist Revival: 'the power of the Holy Spirit'

Alan Gilbert, in *The Making of Post-Christian Britain*, notes that in 1964 the 'increasingly-active' Baptist Revival Fellowship (BRF) was seeking to alert the Baptist community to changes taking place in British Christian identity. A significant publication of the BRF in that year, *Liberty in the Lord*, considered that traditional denominational patterns were

[1] C. G. Brown, *The Death of Christian Britain* (London, 2001), 1, 193.

[2] D. W. Bebbington, *Evangelicalism in Modern Britain: a History from the 1730s to the 1980s* (London, 1993), 229.

being eroded.[3] The BRF dated from 1938 and its constitution spoke not only about revival but also maintaining a testimony in Baptist life to 'Biblical truths'.[4] The driving forces within the BRF, particularly in the later 1950s and 1960s, were disparate: a somewhat romantic view of past revivals in Christian history; a fear of a centralizing form of church government within the Baptist Union that would undermine the independence of local churches; antipathy towards the growing ecumenical and sacramental movements; and a deep anxiety among the strong body of conservative evangelicals in the denomination about what was seen as a dominant 'liberal' approach to the authority of scripture on the part of the Baptist Union leadership.[5] Similar, though smaller, Revival Fellowships functioned in Congregationalism and Methodism.[6]

The spiritual emphasis of the BRF was illustrated at its first major public meeting, in Bloomsbury Central Baptist Church, in April 1942. The large, predominantly young congregation heard Theo Bamber, the commanding leader of the BRF and minister of Rye Lane Baptist Chapel, Peckham, stressing in his address 'the power of the Holy Spirit'.[7] Bamber was not, however, advocating the view of Spirit-baptism and of gifts of tongues and prophecy that characterized Pentecostal denominations such as the Assemblies of God and the Elim Church. His primary concern, in keeping with traditional evangelical spirituality, was deeper spiritual dedication.[8] Later in 1942, calls to pray for wider revival were made at a meeting in London at which Colin Kerr, vicar of St Paul's Church, Portman Square, and Bamber, were major speakers.[9] The BRF was forging closer links with wider conservative evangelicalism. In the years after the Second World War, a period in which there was significant conservative evangelical growth in Britain and North America,[10] the BRF became more prominent and

3 A. D. Gilbert, *The Making of Post-Christian Britain* (London, 1980), 150–1. *Liberty in the Lord* (London, 1964), 33–4.

4 *The Baptist Revival Fellowship: Constitution and Rules* (London, n.d.): London, Spurgeon's College, BRF Archive [hereafter: BRF]. Correspondence is filed by year.

5 *Liberty in the Lord* deals with these issues.

6 Bebbington, *Evangelicalism in Modern Britain*, 251.

7 *The Christian*, 30 April 1942, 3.

8 See I. M. Randall, *Evangelical Experiences* (Carlisle, 1999), chs 2, 6 and 8.

9 *Christian Herald*, 13 August 1942, 108.

10 See D. W. Bebbington, 'Evangelicalism in its Settings: the British and American Movements since 1940', in M. A. Noll, D. W. Bebbington, and G. A. Rawlyk, eds, *Evangelicalism: Comparative Studies of Popular Protestantism in North America, the British Isles, and Beyond, 1700–1990* (Oxford, 1994), 365–88.

vocal. In 1949 it published a call to share in the 'Opening of the Door to Mid-Century Revival'.[11]

In the 1950s interdenominational Nights of Prayer for Revival were convened, some in St Paul's, Portman Square, with a strong conviction about the need to 'pray a revival down from heaven'.[12] The spiritual needs of the British nation were in view. The BRF *Bulletin* of January 1954 spoke about a new spiritual impetus and this was expressed in a BRF Ministers' Retreat in the following month which attracted forty-six ministers.[13] The numbers at BRF conferences thereafter grew steadily. This was associated with the sense of confidence felt by British evangelicals following the huge Billy Graham campaign in London in 1954.[14] In the late 1950s the emphasis on revival in Britain continued. Within the BRF there was also a widespread belief that – as Bamber put it in 1956, the year of the Suez crisis – the 'signs of the times' pointed to 'the appearing of our Blessed Lord'.[15] Premillennial Adventism, which had been a notable feature of evangelicalism,[16] was strong in the BRF. But it was pneumatology which was to attract more attention. Martyn-Lloyd Jones, minister of the Congregational Westminster Chapel, London, who had a powerful influence on several BRF leaders, preached a series of sermons in 1859 on one of his favourite themes – revival. He looked for an 'outpouring of the Spirit' which he termed, controversially, a 'baptism with the Spirit'.[17]

The scene was set, then, for the new emphases in the 1960s – among Baptists and others – not only on the familiar theme of revival but also on Spirit-baptism. Within Baptist circles the BRF annual conference, which in the early 1960s was attracting over one hundred participants (mainly ministers), was a crucial conduit for fresh spiritual experiences. Those present in 1960 heard two addresses from Martyn Lloyd-Jones. Ernest Payne, General Secretary of the Baptist Union, also spoke. As an ecumenical statesman, Payne was regarded with some suspicion in BRF

11 *Opening of the Door to Mid-Century Revival* (London, n.d.): BRF.

12 See P. Hocken, *Streams of Renewal* (Carlisle, 1997), 70–4.

13 *Baptist Revival Fellowship Bulletin*, No. 41, January 1954, 1, 3: BRF.

14 See I. M. Randall, 'Conservative Constructionist: the Early Influence of Billy Graham in Britain', *The Evangelical Quarterly* 67: 4 (1995).

15 *Baptist Times*, 13 December 1956, 7.

16 See D. W. Bebbington, 'The Advent Hope in British Evangelicalism since 1800', *Scottish Journal of Religious Studies* 9: 2 (1988), 103–14.

17 I. H. Murray, *David Martyn Lloyd-Jones: the Fight of Faith, 1939–1981* (Edinburgh, 1990), ch. 18.

circles.[18] Indeed, for a number of ministers connections made through the BRF took precedence over commitment to the Baptist Union. Thus in 1961 a Baptist minister in Gloucester, Douglas Jones, who would later leave the Union, wrote to Alec Steen, Secretary of the BRF, to say: 'It is a striking thing that my path has crossed with that of several others recently who share a longing that we might see the Hand of God moving in revival'.[19] The BRF was seeking in 1962 to work more closely with other revival-minded individuals and Fellowships, including the Anglican Prayer Fellowship for Revival, which met at All Souls, Langham Place, London. As well as receiving positive responses from these groups, Theo Bamber enjoyed personal encouragement from Lloyd-Jones.[20]

Theo Bamber's vision for 1963–4 was to hold BRF-related meetings across the country addressing themes such as 'fullness of life', and 'revival within our Churches'.[21] To some extent, however, his more traditional evangelical vision was overtaken in the early 1960s by the phenomenon of 'neo-Pentecostalism', or the charismatic movement. George Forester of St Paul's, Beckenham, shared his recent experience of the 'baptism of the Spirit' with a local ministers' fraternal, and Malcolm Piper, a member of the fraternal and also of the BRF, was deeply affected. Piper had recently completed training at Spurgeon's College and had started his first ministry, in New Addington, Croydon, in 1962. He was, therefore, typical of those Baptist ministers who would be drawn to charismatic renewal – young, evangelical and open to influences from outside Baptist life. Piper wrote to Alec Steen in April 1964 asking whether 'those responsible for booking speakers [for the forthcoming BRF conference] have considered asking any minister who has personally experienced the baptism of the Holy Spirit recently'.[22] This idea was to come to fruition in a way that neither Piper nor anyone else in the BRF anticipated.

18 *Baptist Revival Fellowship Bulletin*, No. 66, October/December 1960, 1–3: BRF.

19 Douglas Jones to Alec Steen, 7 December 1961: BRF.

20 Theo Bamber to Alec Steen, 18 January 1962: BRF.

21 *Baptist Revival Fellowship Bulletin*, No. 73, September/October 1962, 2. Letters from Theo Bamber to all BRF members, October 1962 and 28 March 1963: BRF.

22 Malcolm Piper to Alec Steen, 9 April 1964: BRF.

Charismatic renewal: 'the baptism of the Holy Spirit'

Malcolm Piper's letter referred to recent developments in America. It was in 1962 that British evangelicals became aware of the neo-Pentecostal phenomena – specifically speaking in tongues – that had been experienced in an Episcopal congregation in Van Nuys, California, in 1960. The interest of British evangelicals was stimulated partly through a visit to California in 1962 by Philip Hughes, a respected Anglican evangelical scholar and editor of the *Churchman*, who reported on what he called 'indications of a new movement of the Holy Spirit'.[23] The British Evangelical Alliance (EA), the influential umbrella organization that brought together evangelical Anglicans, Baptists, Methodists, Congregationalists and others, held a seminar in 1963 at which, the Alliance reported, 'scholarly papers have been read by evangelical theologians, dealing with different aspects of the work of the Holy Spirit'. Gilbert Kirby, the energetic General Secretary of the EA, hoped the discussions would 'clarify evangelical thinking on this vital matter'. Kirby described the tensions over Spirit-baptism and spiritual gifts, and raised the question as to whether the new emphases would lead to the formation of new groups and denominations (as had happened in earlier Pentecostalism) or whether renewal could come within the denominations.[24] In the event both these possibilities would become realities.

For Malcolm Piper it was experiential rather than denominational questions that were paramount. What Piper had heard from Forester and had witnessed in Beckenham evidenced, he believed, 'the unmistakeable mark of a work of God'. The BRF members who heard Forester's testimony wanted to know more about 'this work of the Spirit'. Of the speakers that Piper suggested to Steen for the BRF conference, three were Anglicans, including Michael Harper, a curate at All Souls, Langham Place (where evangelical Anglicanism's most influential leader, John Stott, was rector), and the fourth, Amos Edwards, was a Methodist minister in Stoke-on-Trent. Edwards had recently addressed the Methodist Revival Fellowship.[25] Harper, to his own surprise, had a powerful experience of the Holy Spirit in September

23 'Editorial', *Churchman*, September 1962, 131.

24 *The Evangelical Alliance Broadsheet*, Winter 1963, 2. For the EA see I. M. Randall and D. Hilborn, *One Body in Christ* (Carlisle, 2001).

25 Hocken, *Streams of Renewal*, 67.

1962. In the summer of 1963, through contact with an American Lutheran, Larry Christenson, he began to speak in tongues. Harper's experience was indicative of the trans-denominational nature of the new movement and his own influence began to be felt in Baptist as well as Anglican circles.[26] 'In our longing to know the increasing work of the Holy Spirit in our own lives and in the work of God's Church in these days', Malcolm Piper argued in his letter to Steen, 'I believe we should make the opportunity of hearing from one of these brethren'.[27] The reference to the 'longing for the increasing work of the Spirit' was classic BRF terminology.

Most evangelicals had little sympathy for traditional Pentecostal teaching about the necessity of a baptism of the Spirit evidenced by speaking in tongues. John Stott stoutly opposed it.[28] Martyn Lloyd-Jones, however, despite having serious questions about aspects of Pentecostalism, affirmed the longing for deeper spirituality.[29] Gilbert Kirby of the EA, who was a supporter of the Congregational Evangelical Revival Fellowship and a determined conciliator, was encouraged that evangelicals were studying 'the biblical doctrine of the Holy Spirit'.[30] In the spring and summer of 1964 Kirby, who had links with a number of BRF members, expressed his unhappiness about the view being promulgated that tongues was essential 'initial evidence' of Spirit-baptism, but he did not want to dismiss 'ecstatic utterances' since 'whenever and wherever God pours out His Spirit in abundance there are unusual manifestations'.[31] At this stage a few Baptist ministers had received the baptism of the Spirit. One was Frank Wilson of Willesborough, Kent, who worked for a time with Michael Harper.[32] Another was Douglas McBain, minister in Wishaw, Scotland, who was to become central to the charismatic movement in Baptist circles.[33] The movement was having an impact among Baptists as ministers entered into new experiences. The pattern in the 1960s was for ministers, as was the case with Malcolm Piper, to be attracted by hearing of the experi-

26 M. Harper, *None can Guess* (London, 1971), chs 3 and 6.
27 Malcolm Piper to Alec Steen, 9 April 1964: BRF.
28 See J. R. W. Stott, *Baptism and Fulness* (London, 1964).
29 Murray, *The Fight of Faith*, 480–2.
30 *The Evangelical Alliance Broadsheet*, Winter 1963, 2.
31 *Crusade*, February 1964, 33; cf. *Evangelical Alliance Broadsheet*, Summer 1964, 2–3.
32 Hocken, *Streams of Renewal*, 115–22, 258, n. 34.
33 D. McBain, *Fire over the Waters: Renewal among Baptists and Others from the 1960s to the 1990s* (London, 1997), 37–8.

ences of others. This was a sign of the growing impact of the experiential culture of the period.[34]

The most significant leader of the new movement was Michael Harper. In February and June 1964 he organized informal conferences at an Anglican retreat house in Stoke Poges, Buckinghamshire, to foster renewal. In the same year Harper left All Souls and became the first General Secretary of an interdenominational body set up to encourage renewal, the Fountain Trust.[35] At the second Stoke Poges conference a few Baptists were present, including David Pawson, who had recently entered Baptist ministry, having previously been a Methodist minister. His first Baptist pastorate was Gold Hill, Buckinghamshire, which was to become known as a centre of charismatic renewal. Pawson had already been impressed by charismatic spirituality through meeting (at an EA event) Mike Pusey, from Basingstoke Baptist Church, who had a Pentecostal background. At the Stoke Poges conference Pawson heard speaking in tongues and asked a conference participant to pray for him. Although no new experience happened at the time, Pawson began to preach a series of sermons on the Holy Spirit at Gold Hill. Part way through he began to pray privately in tongues.[36] Within a few months Pawson was to have a profound effect on the Baptist Revival Fellowship.

Revival and renewal

Over a five-year period from 1960 the numbers attending the BRF's annual conference grew from over 100 to approaching 300. Several BRF leaders were ministers of large congregations, such as E. G. Rudman at Holland Road Baptist Church, Hove, and Geoffrey King at West Croydon Baptist Tabernacle: both churches had over 500 members. Over 400 Baptist ministers were members of the BRF in the early 1960s, representing about one-third of the ministers in pastoral charge within the Baptist Union. The BRF conference was, therefore, a highly significant Baptist meeting point. Among the speakers booked for the 1964 conference was Leith Samuel, minister of Above Bar Chapel in Southampton, but he withdrew because of a minor operation. David Pawson, then little known in Baptist life, was asked to take

34 Bebbington, *Evangelicalism in Modern Britain*, ch. 7.

35 Harper, *None can Guess*, 62–4.

36 D. Pawson, *Not as Bad as the Truth* (London, 2006), ch. 9.

his place. Leith Samuel wrote to Alec Steen to say he felt Pawson had 'more to offer on the subject of revival than I have'.[37] One of those present at the 1964 conference, Harold Owen, minister of Carey Baptist Church, Reading, who was a BRF committee member, had heard Pawson speak a few months earlier on the baptism of the Spirit. There was eager anticipation among some of those attending in 1964 about what Pawson would say. On the way to the conference Owen was told by colleagues that several BRF members were now speaking in tongues.[38]

David Pawson did not disappoint those present (including Malcolm Piper) who were looking for a clear message about Spirit-baptism from someone with that experience. For Theo Bamber, as chairman of the BRF, Pawson's Bible study had 'got us all thinking'.[39] This guarded assessment came soon after the conference but seems to have represented Bamber's considered opinion. Other participants were much more deeply affected. Harold Owen, after hearing Pawson speak, said to him: 'So, it's happened to you, David.' Pawson, in an electric moment, replied, 'Yes'. Those ministers at the conference who had entered into charismatic experience, such as Mike Pusey from Basingstoke, prayed for those seeking the baptism of the Spirit. Several ministers, including Harold Owen and another BRF committee member, Henry Tyler, from Felixstowe, testified to receiving this experience during the conference.[40] The view was expressed by some enthusiasts that 'the Lord set aside Leith Samuel to make way for David Pawson'.[41] The sense that these Baptists leaders had of being caught up in an immediate way in the divine purposes was palpable.

Following the conference, discussion continued. A number of those present asked Alec Steen for tapes of what Pawson had said.[42] But Pawson had already written to Steen to say he wanted the recordings erased. 'I was speaking very frankly', he explained, 'and made a number of remarks in the context of the Conference which would not be suitable for wider circulation.'[43] Stanley Voke from Walton-on Thames, a

37 Leith Samuel to Alec Steen, 4 November 1964: BRF.

38 Hocken, *Streams of Renewal*, 133–4.

39 Theo Bamber to Alec Steen, 8 December 1964: BRF.

40 Hocken, *Streams of Renewal*, 134–5.

41 Bamber was doubtful about this interpretation: Theo Bamber to Alec Steen, 20 January 1965: BRF.

42 Stanley Jebb to Alec Steen, 7 December 1964: BRF.

43 David Pawson to Alec Steen, 4 December 1964: BRF.

BRF committee member, suggested that the BRF was 'on the verge of a new advance', and proposed that Pawson should write for the BRF on the subject of the Holy Spirit. However, Voke did not see the view of Spirit-baptism promulgated by Pawson as the only credible position. 'David Pawson, of course, stands strongly on the basis of the Spirit with signs' (especially tongues), Voke wrote, 'whereas others would not be so clear on this.' Voke's, hope, which was not to be fulfilled, was that the BRF could blend several spiritual emphases: he mentioned the Ruanda Revival, charismatic experience, Puritan spirituality, and 'the dear old Keswick and I.V.F. emphases' – a reference to the long-established evangelical spirituality of the Keswick Convention and the Inter-Varsity Fellowship in universities.[44] Those who wanted Pawson to return to the BRF conference in 1965 were disappointed: in response to an approach Pawson said he felt he had 'shared all that he should'.[45]

Tensions now began to be evident in the BRF. Those who considered that charismatic power was (at least in part) the fulfilment of traditional BRF concerns for revival pushed for speakers from the charismatic camp. Ron Luland, a minister in Bedford, wrote to Theo Bamber to suggest as a speaker for the 1965 BRF conference Arthur Wallis, who in the 1950s had written a book on revival entitled *In the Day of Thy Power*, and who had himself experienced the baptism of the Spirit. Luland wanted to have 'a clear line' at the conference.[46] But Luland's view was far from being dominant in the BRF. A major speaker at the 1965 conference was the Anglican theologian, James Packer. His allegiance was to the kind of robust Reformed and Puritan theology promoted by Martyn Lloyd-Jones and he was, as he put it to Steen, prepared to 'set lots of cats among lots of pigeons'.[47] A Reformed anti-charismatic stance would in fact attract a number of BRF members. However, at the 1965 conference talks on the Holy Spirit by Wallis, then attending a Baptist chapel near Exeter (his background was the Brethren movement), were well received. Before the 1966 conference Harold Owen, Voke and Pawson met to see how they could foster openness to the Spirit, and at the conference – which attracted 280 participants – Pawson gave addresses on the Church.[48] This was a

44 Stanley Voke to Alec Steen, 2 December 1964: BRF.
45 David Pawson to Alec Steen, 14 January 1965: BRF.
46 Ron Luland to Theo Bamber, 18 February 1965: BRF.
47 James Packer to Alec Steen, 15 March 1965: BRF.
48 Harold Owen to Alec Steen, 15 September 1966: BRF.

period of growth in BRF membership: during 1966, 120 new members joined, bringing the total membership to 1,200, with 440 being ministers.[49] Among younger Baptist ministers particularly, of whom there were many in the BRF, desire for spiritual renewal was wide-spread.

Baptists, renewal and bifurcation

In the period 1965–7 bifurcation was evident, however, among those who wanted to see Baptists embrace renewal. There had always been a section of the BRF on the fringe of Baptist denominational life and critical of the Union leadership, and this tendency became more pronounced. BRF publications opposed ecumenical bodies such as the World Council of Churches and applauded evangelical fellowship across denominational frontiers, citing as examples Martyn Lloyd-Jones's Westminster Fellowship for ministers, which a number of BRF members attended.[50] Speaking at the 1966 National Assembly organized by the EA, Lloyd-Jones famously called on evangelicals to stop being only a wing in what he believed would be a 'total, national, territorial Church', and instead to 'start afresh' and 'go back to the New Testament'.[51] This kind of call was not new, but it was taken up with fresh vigour, not least (although Lloyd-Jones had not anticipated this) by Baptists who saw charismatic experience as needing to be embodied in new 'Restorationist' churches – 'restoring' the New Testament model – under the authority of 'apostles'.[52]

Growing criticism within the BRF of the Baptist Union's ecumenical links and its apparent toleration of liberal theology – most controversially in an address in 1971 by Michael Taylor, Principal of the Baptist College in Manchester, which appeared to question traditional Christology – led to a number of BRF leaders, including some influenced by renewal and others who were anti-charismatic, distancing themselves from Baptist Union life.[53] Among the BRF committee members who left the Union and embraced the new Restorationist movement was Harold Owen, and a Bible Week in Surrey, run by a

[49] Minutes of Members Meeting of BRF, 22 November 1966; *Baptist Times*, 1 December 1966, 2.

[50] *Liberty in the Lord*, 33–4.

[51] Evangelical Alliance, *Unity in Diversity: Evangelicals, the Church and the World* (London, 1967), 11–13; Murray, *The Fight of Faith*, 523–5.

[52] See A. Walker, *Restoring the Kingdom* (rev. edn, Guildford, 1998).

[53] I. M. Randall, *The English Baptists of the Twentieth Century* (Didcot, 2005), 365–82.

committee which included Owen, became a platform for Restorationist leaders like Bryn Jones and Arthur Wallis. Jones then launched the Dales Bible Week, which grew to 8,000 participants, and this was replicated in the south of England by Terry Virgo, a former Baptist.[54] Andrew Walker considers that in the 1960s Wallis, who saw no future for denominational bodies, was hardly listened to, and that the stage was taken by those committed to renewal within denominations.[55] But this is to underestimate the sympathetic hearing Wallis received in BRF circles.

Tensions within the BRF over spirituality and ecclesiology grew from 1965 onwards. In March 1965 there was a suggestion that the BRF might produce a book on the Holy Spirit for use within the Baptist denomination, perhaps written by David Pawson. Stanley Voke suggested that George Beasley-Murray, the outstanding New Testament scholar and Principal of Spurgeon's College, could contribute, but there were objections on the grounds that Beasley-Murray did not distinguish baptism in the Spirit from water baptism.[56] It is clear that a significant number of leaders in the BRF, including Theo Bamber, had little belief in renewal within the Baptist Union. In July 1965 Bamber commented privately that although he had 'great respect for David Pawson' he believed that 'well meaning efforts endeavouring to find common ground with other views within the [Baptist] Denomination will come to nothing'.[57] Other BRF leaders, however, opposed Bamber's position. In 1967 Hugh Butt, a Baptist Area Superintendent, resigned from the BRF committee, and other well-known committee members subsequently followed suit. Hugh Butt's commitment was to 'revival and the outpouring of God's Spirit',[58] but he believed the BRF was losing the vision for that renewal to take place in Baptist life.

Yet an inclusive vision for renewal was in the longer term to have a considerable impact on Baptist life. In June 1965 a Fountain Trust conference at High Leigh drew together Anglicans, Baptists, Brethren, Presbyterians and Pentecostals.[59] The theme was 'The Holy Spirit and the Church'. Pawson gave three addresses and at least a dozen Baptist

54 Walker, *Restoring the Kingdom*, 84–5.
55 Ibid., 59.
56 BRF Memorandum, March 1965, on BRF Study Groups: BRF.
57 Theo Bamber to Alec Steen, 30 July 1965: BRF.
58 Hugh Butt to Alec Steen, 18 April 1967: BRF.
59 Hocken, *Streams of Renewal*, 115–22, 258, n. 34.

ministers were present, including A. Morgan Derham, the new EA General Secretary. For Douglas McBain this conference 'felt like the beginning of a movement of massive significance'.[60] Another notable event in 1965 was a Full Gospel Business Men's Fellowship International Conference in London, which several Baptists attended.[61] Amid debates about spiritual resurgence within historic churches, Pawson gave a paper to the 1966 EA National Assembly in which he commended a statement from Vatican II on charismatic gifts.[62] From 1967 Roman Catholics became significantly influenced by charismatic renewal.[63] Within the Free Church sector it was evident, as Peter Hocken argues, that Baptists were more affected by the charismatic movement than any other Free Church.[64] Stanley Voke argued in 1969 for a need 'to play a more constructive role together within the [Baptist] Union and not less'.[65] This view gained ground and led in the late 1970s to the launch of Mainstream, a movement committed to 'life and growth' within the Union,[66] by contrast to the oppositional stance of the BRF. From the mid-1970s, McBain suggests, the majority of Baptist ministers beginning ministry identified with what they viewed as the positive attributes of renewal.[67] In the late 1980s a survey of students at Spurgeon's College indicated that 80% saw themselves as charismatic.[68] By this time it was also evident that the Baptist denomination was the only mainline denomination in England that was experiencing growth.[69]

Conclusion

The mid-1960s saw significant new influences affecting Baptist life in England. Although the impact of the charismatic movement on Anglican life has received most attention, the Baptist story shows the

60 McBain, *Fire over the Waters*, 46–7. McBain gives the names of other Baptists present.

61 V. Fotherby, *Catching the Vision* (Eastbourne, 1989), ch. 3; McBain, *Fire over the Waters*, 40.

62 D. Pawson, *Fourth Wave* (London, 1993), Appendix C, 154–5.

63 N. Scotland, *Charismatics and the Next Millennium* (London, 1995), 8.

64 Hocken, *Streams of Renewal*, 133.

65 Stanley Voke to Theo Bamber, 13 November 1969 and 27 November 1969: BRF: Minutes of BRF Committee Meeting, 17 November 1969: BRF.

66 *Mainstream Newsletter*, No. 1, March 1979, 1.

67 D. McBain, 'Mainstream Charismatics', in S. Hunt, M. Hamilton, and T. Walker, eds, *Charismatic Christianity* (Basingstoke, 1997), 46.

68 *Baptist Times*, 21 December 1989, 10.

69 *Baptist Times*, 31 December 1987, 7.

complex outcome of charismatic renewal. There was fresh spiritual vitality and growth within denominational life, but also a loss of members and churches to Restorationist groups, and in addition a reaction against aspects of charismatic spirituality. The BRF, although not officially a channel for charismatic influence among Baptists, was crucial: BRF members were looking for revival. The openness to the new emphases within the BRF was such that one BRF commentator complained in 1970 that 'the B.R.F. was riddled with the tongues movement'.[70] This was an overstatement, since many in the BRF never associated with – indeed opposed – the charismatic movement; in any case by 1970 it was becoming clear that there were two new movements, not one. Commitment to renewal within denominational life was expressed at a major international charismatic conference organized by the Fountain Trust in 1971 in Guildford. The participation of Roman Catholics indicated its inclusive nature. McBain and Pawson were involved. Other more conservative Baptists, such as Harold Owen of the BRF, were suspicious of this inclusivism.[71] Following the conference *Crusade* magazine suggested that 'neo-Pentecostalism' had become 'the most important single development in British church life since the War; possibly this century'.[72] Although, as Callum Brown argues, an inherited Christian identity may have been undermined in the 1960s, there was also spiritual resurgence. Among Baptists, many local churches began to grow, particularly charismatic congregations.[73] From the 1960s onwards, Baptists in England were profoundly affected by this new movement of renewal.

Spurgeon's College, London, and International Baptist Theological Seminary, Prague

70 Letter from George Craig, 10 September 1970, to BRF committee: BRF.
71 McBain, *Fire over the Waters*, 53.
72 *Crusade*, September 1971, 1.
73 Randall, *English Baptists*, 402.

RESCUED FROM THE BRINK: THE COLLAPSE AND RESURGENCE OF WYCLIFFE HALL, OXFORD

by ANDREW ATHERSTONE

THE twenty-five theological colleges of the Church of England entered the 1960s in buoyant mood. Rooms were full, finances were steadily improving, expansion seemed inevitable. For four years in succession, from 1961 to 1964, ordinations exceeded six hundred a year, for the first time since before the First World War, and the peak was expected to rise still higher. In a famously misleading report, the sociologist Leslie Paul predicted that at a 'conservative estimate' there would be more than eight hundred ordinations a year by the 1970s.[1] In fact, the opposite occurred. The boom was followed by bust, and the early 1970s saw ordinations dip below four hundred. The dramatic plunge in the number of candidates offering themselves for Anglican ministry devastated the theological colleges. Many began running at a loss and faced imminent bankruptcy. In desperation the central Church authorities set about closing or merging colleges, but even their ruthless cutbacks could not keep pace with the fall in ordinands.[2]

Wycliffe Hall theological college in Oxford, the focus of this essay, was caught up in the disaster and suffered worse than most. It collapsed in the 1960s and teetered on the brink of closure, only to be revived under new leadership in the 1970s. It was a tale of two principals. When David Anderson took charge in 1962 the number of students entered freefall – 64, 51, 42, 36.[3] Although there was some fluctuation, the

1 Leslie Paul, *The Deployment and Payment of the Clergy: a Report* (London, 1964), 298.

2 For official reports dealing with the crisis, see *Theological Colleges for Tomorrow* (the de Bunsen report) (London, 1968); *First Report on the Reorganisation of the Theological Colleges*, 1968 (Church Assembly no. 1708); *Second Report on the Reorganisation of the Theological Colleges*, 1969 (Church Assembly no. 1766); *Reorganisation of the Theological Colleges: a Report of the House of Bishops*, 1971 (General Synod no. 20). For the unpublished report of the evangelical commission chaired by John Stott, to rival the official Runcie Commission, see *The Future of the Evangelical Theological Colleges*, 1970 (copy at London, Lambeth Palace Library, Ramsey Papers, vol. 193, fols 2–23).

3 David Anderson (b. 1919), principal of Melville Hall/Immanuel College, Ibadan,

general trend was downwards and after seven years Anderson was forced to resign. When Jim Hickinbotham took charge in 1970 there was immediate and dramatic resurgence.[4] Within two years he had more than doubled student numbers, back up to sixty-five, and the Hall was almost at capacity. The central authorities tried to restrain this sudden growth with a 'quota' system, but within five years there were seventy-seven students in residence, greater than at any time in the Hall's previous one hundred year history. Before Hickinbotham retired the eighty barrier had been broken more than once.

Several factors contributed to the sudden collapse and equally sudden resurgence of Wycliffe Hall. National trends played a part, as did the contrasting leadership styles and administrative abilities of the principals in question. Yet this essay will seek to demonstrate that one of the key factors was theological orientation. Wycliffe had been established in 1877 as an Anglican evangelical bastion against the twin threats within the Church of England and the Universities of 'ritualism' and 'rationalism'.[5] However, under Anderson the Hall drifted away from these historic evangelical roots, which led to a haemorrhaging of evangelical support. Under Hickinbotham there was a deliberate attempt to revive the founders' vision from the 1870s in order to stimulate a revival at the Hall in the 1970s, bringing students back in their droves. We shall first examine the collapse so that the resurgence is seen more starkly.

The Collapse

Two of the key motifs running through Anderson's teaching and public proclamations in the 1960s are 'relevance' and 'dialogue'. He aimed to free Wycliffe Hall from the redundant world-view of a previous generation and to throw off its Victorian heritage. He sought to bring the Hall, kicking and screaming if necessary, into the modern age, unencumbered by the presuppositions of its long-dead evangelical founders. This would involve a radical overhaul of college life: 'there is a real and partly justified feeling that our training simply isn't "with it" – that we plug on along the old by-ways from which the cavalcade of modern life

Nigeria 1956–62, of Wycliffe Hall 1962–9, lecturer in religious studies at Wall Hall College near Watford 1970–84.

4 James P. Hickinbotham (1914–90), principal of St John's College, Durham 1954–69, of Wycliffe Hall 1970–9.

5 See further, Andrew Atherstone, 'The Founding of Wycliffe Hall, Oxford', *Anglican and Episcopal History* 73 (March 2004), 78–102.

has long since been diverted.'[6] Early in his principalship Anderson was interrogated about Wycliffe Hall's relationship to its evangelical past, but responded with a call to look not backwards but forwards:

> Someone asked me a week or two ago whether Wycliffe was still an evangelical college. Of course it is – not only by tradition but by conviction. But I would like it also to be thought of as a 'dialogical' college (or should the word be 'dialogistical'?) – a place in which there is constant effort made to engage in dialogue in the Church and with the world. . . . I want us to be wide open to every confrontation, every discovery, every challenge, recognising that only so can our faith develop in vigour, comprehension, and relevance.[7]

For example, Anderson rejoiced when his students read the early chapters of Genesis in the light of Desmond Morris's *The Naked Ape*, because it involved 'a highly stimulating dialogue'.[8] Likewise he wanted his young theologians to learn from other aspects of contemporary science, particularly 'modern secular investigation of the human condition'.[9] The principal invited scientific specialists to the Hall to teach on medicine, psychology and sociology, showing how up-to-date research sheds light on moral responsibility and allows a modern understanding of 'sin'.[10] He also welcomed the insights of the latest radical theologians, as he afterwards recalled:

> the 1960s were a good time to be at Wycliffe. Our buildings might be frozen, but the theological climate was warming up: Bultmann was 'demythologising' the New Testament; Tillich was asking 'existential' questions; Robinson was being 'honest' to God; van Buren and Harvey Cox (following Bonhoeffer) were promoting a 'secular' interpretation of the gospel; and A. J. Ayer was telling us that religious language was meaningless. It was stirring stuff, and it instigated some warm debate at Wycliffe as elsewhere.[11]

Some argued that the collapse in ordinand numbers was directly linked to the Church of England's obsession with Robinson's *Honest to God*[12]

6 Oxford, Wycliffe Hall Archives [hereafter: WH], Ember Letter, Michaelmas 1963.
7 WH, Ember Letter, Advent 1963.
8 WH, Ember Letter, Trinity and Michaelmas 1969.
9 WH, Ember Letter, Michaelmas 1963.
10 WH, Ember Letters, Michaelmas 1964, Advent 1964.
11 WH, Newsletter, Spring 2002.
12 John A. T. Robinson, *Honest to God* (London, 1963).

and these new radical theologians. How is it possible to recruit ministers to a Church which has apparently lost its grip on the Christian verities and its sense of purpose? However, Anderson directly rebutted this criticism and argued that ordinand numbers were dropping because there was *not enough* radical questioning within the Church. He explained:

> *the questions were already there*, long before the new theology came along – they were there in the novels and the weeklies, in films and the theatre, in the university disciplines and the student societies, in almost every area of human creation and inquiry. There is a widespread feeling of relief among some young christians at the university that *at last* the Church has begun to recognise the existence of these questions. Have you ever thought how difficult it must be to engage in the rigorous linguistic discipline of modern philosophy with Professor Ayer (shall we say) during the week, and listen to the traditional language of theology on Sundays?[13]

The principal's personal interests were mainly on the philosophical side of theology, especially existentialism. He was most influenced by authors such as Søren Kierkegaard and twentieth-century existentialist philosophers like Nicholas Berdyaev and Gabriel Marcel. Amongst atheistic philosophers, Anderson rated Friedrich Nietzsche as 'the most important influence' upon his thought. He encouraged Wycliffe students to read Nietzsche, 'because if they could stand up to him, they could stand up to anything'.[14] He also read widely in Jean-Paul Sartre and expressed 'a strong sympathy' with the existentialism of Albert Camus.[15] Yet these were not typical evangelical heroes and numbers at the Hall continued to plummet as a result. When the church inspectors arrived in 1965 they urged the principal to make renewed efforts to reassure and recruit 'the more conservative Evangelicals'. They warned:

> It is clearly important that Evangelicals should in their training be helped to face the intellectual challenges of our world. At the same time it is vital that 'ecumenical encounter' and 'dialogue' with the present age should not become ends in themselves. They must be

13 WH, Ember Letter, Trinity 1965.

14 David Anderson to Andrew Atherstone, 3 October 2005.

15 David Anderson, 'Images of Man in Sartre and Camus', *Modern Churchman* 8 ns (October 1964), 44.

> founded on and spring from evangelical conviction and evangelistic emphasis.[16]

This theological trend at Wycliffe Hall was compounded by Anderson's most significant staff appointment. He recruited a young vicar, Alan Dunstan, to teach Church history and liturgy, yet it was Dunstan's outside interests, notably his membership of the Modern Churchmen's Union (MCU), which caused most concern.[17] Anderson naively believed that his colleague's involvement in the MCU was 'simply an irrelevance', under-estimating the abhorrence with which the MCU was viewed in traditional evangelical circles.[18] Dunstan was a member of the MCU council and in August 1964 he chaired the annual MCU conference, held that year at St Hilda's College, Oxford. The theme for the conference was 'Symbols for the Sixties', and speaker after speaker appealed for a church which was relevant to the modern technological and atomic age.[19] Dunstan set the tone with a sermon on Mark 7: 13, 'Thus by your own tradition, handed down among you, you make God's word null and void.' It was a blistering attack upon the anachronism, the obsolescence, the 'innate and distressing conservatism' of the Church of England, which appeared

> to have no real point in the modern world – much less any gospel to offer it. Such attempts as there are to communicate, to express, to speak to the condition of twentieth-century men and women are almost invariably thwarted by the traditions behind which we are buttressed.[20]

David Anderson also gave a paper, on Sartre and Camus – the only Wycliffe principal ever to lecture at an MCU conference.

Far from being an inconspicuous event in a secluded Oxford college, the MCU conference of 1964 achieved wide-spread attention and

[16] 'Central Advisory Committee on Training for the Ministry Inspection Report 1965', 4–5, available at the Church of England Record Centre (London) file ACCM/COLL/WYC/1.

[17] Alan L. Dunstan (1928–2004), vicar of St Mary's, Gravesend 1957–63, chaplain of Wycliffe Hall 1963–6, vice-principal 1966–70, vice-principal of Ripon Hall, Oxford 1971–4, vice-principal of Ripon College Cuddesdon 1975–8, precentor of Gloucester Cathedral 1978–93.

[18] Anderson to Atherstone, 3 October 2005. On the MCU see especially Alan M. G. Stephenson, *The Rise and Decline of English Modernism* (London, 1984).

[19] For the conference papers, see *Modern Churchman* 8 ns (October 1964), 1–92.

[20] Alan Dunstan, 'Conference Sermon', *Modern Churchman* 8 ns (October 1964), 2.

provoked a reaction as fierce as some of the notorious MCU conferences of the inter-war years. Dunstan was interviewed for the BBC's Radio Newsreel and there was daily coverage in the national press, much of it highly critical. Most damaging was a leader in the *Times* which launched a broadside on MCU principles. It questioned whether the new religious symbolism suggested by the conference could 'in any historical sense be called Christianity'. Traditional Anglicanism, the leader argued, was 'closer to Hinduism than to the particular form of religion adumbrated by the Bishop of Woolwich in *Honest to God*.'[21] Reflecting on the affair, Dunstan celebrated: 'This year's publicity was better than ever.'[22] However, good publicity for the MCU was damaging publicity for Wycliffe Hall. Their close identification confirmed in the minds of many that the Hall had cut loose from its evangelical moorings and was drifting inexorably towards liberalism and inevitable shipwreck. Was Wycliffe Hall now any different to Ripon Hall, that MCU hotbed? Former Wycliffe graduates were stirred into action and wrote horrified letters of protest to the Hall Council. The college continued its steep decline having irretrievably lost the confidence of the Anglican evangelical community, as Anderson recalls:

> The rumour that Wycliffe was no longer evangelical grew in a crescendo like Basilio's 'slander' aria in *The Barber of Seville*. Ordination candidates from evangelical parishes were advised to apply elsewhere for training, and there were even instances of men to whom I had already offered a place being diverted to other colleges. In the end, the Council had no alternative but to ask for my resignation, and I had no alternative but to give it.[23]

Many of Anderson's ordinands felt a sense of anger and betrayal at his summary dismissal. One of his keenest supporters protested that the principal had been 'virtually hounded out because he was not willing to run a "party" college'.[24] Anderson ended his last ember letter to former members with a thinly veiled attack upon those who would keep Wycliffe Hall imprisoned in the past:

> . . . not a few colleges are working out policies of a kind very different from those of the past, some with greater reluctance than

21 'Honest or Not', *Times*, 8 August 1964.
22 *Modern Churchman* 8 ns (October 1964), 1.
23 WH, Newsletter, Spring 2002.
24 Richard Syms, *Working Like the Rest of Us: an Alternative Ministry* (London, 1979), 67.

> others. I feel that fresher and younger minds are needed, men who do not think that God spoke once for all through the Founders of the Colleges a hundred years ago or whatever, men who are prepared to step out into uncertainty with the faith of Abraham . . . I hope that my successor will be such a man.[25]

The Resurgence

During the early months of 1969, the Wycliffe Hall Council came to the conclusion (far from unanimous) that for Wycliffe Hall to prosper there must be a radical shift in its theological perspective. Rejecting David Anderson's plea to forget the founders, they sought a renewed emphasis upon the original vision of the Hall. A conscious attempt was made to revive its evangelical heritage, as enshrined in its Victorian trust deed. Having forced Anderson's resignation, the council aimed to recruit a 'conservative evangelical' in his place – or at least a new principal who would have the confidence of the 'conservative evangelical' constituency. First on their list was John Stott, rector of All Souls, Langham Place in London, the pre-eminent figure amongst the Church of England's younger evangelical clergy. He had an international reputation as a Bible expositor, university evangelist, author, organizer and statesman.[26]

When an invitation to Stott was mooted, Canon Talbot Mohan, a senior member of the Hall Council, wrote to him excitedly:

> I have watched the sad decline over the years which I believe has resulted from the determination of the Council *not* to appoint a Conservative Evangelical as Principal. Now, however, prayer is being answered & the Council have realised and acknowledged at last that they must appoint such an Evangelical if Wycliffe is to be worthy of its founders' hopes. My faith has been small & I did not think I should live to see the day . . .

Mohan urged Stott: 'this is an immensely critical moment, with possibilities for the gospel & the glory of the Lord beyond our ability to conceive'.[27] When Stott was officially approached by Bishop Blanch

25 WH, Ember Letter, Trinity and Michaelmas 1969.

26 John R. W. Stott (b. 1921), rector of All Souls, Langham Place 1950–75. See further, Timothy Dudley-Smith, *John Stott: the Making of a Leader* (Leicester, 1999) and idem *John Stott: a Global Ministry* (Leicester, 2001).

27 Mohan to Stott, 27 March 1969, papers of John Stott.

(chairman of the Wycliffe council),[28] he described himself as *bouleversé* (overwhelmed) at the suggestion. He rejoiced at the council's willingness to appoint 'a man of "definite" or "conservative" evangelical conviction', and declared that there was 'no other way for Wycliffe to be re-established or to fulfil its founders' intentions'.[29] Nevertheless, after much heart-searching, Stott declined the invitation. Jim Packer, warden of Latimer House in Oxford, was seriously considered, but the council feared that his appointment would be too radical a swing in the other direction.[30] As Blanch explained, they wanted a man

> who can command the confidence of the Conservative Evangelicals and, at the same time, not deter Evangelicals of a different persuasion. At its best, Wycliffe has always combined these two elements and I hope it will be able to do so in future.[31]

Packer's desire to train 'reformed pastors' would certainly attract 'conservatives' but, unlike Stott, might not appeal to a sufficiently wide spectrum of evangelical churchmanship. Elsewhere Blanch reiterated:

> It seems not only desirable but essential that Wycliffe should be able to command the approval of clergy and ordinands in the Conservative Evangelical school and in the [Oxford] Pastorate without sacrificing those who feel themselves at home in a rather wider Evangelical atmosphere.[32]

Finally it was announced after a six-month search that the new principal of Wycliffe Hall from January 1970 would be Jim Hickinbotham, principal of St John's College, Durham. He was well-suited to the task before him and able to move comfortably within a broad range of evangelical and ecumenical contexts. Immediately Hickinbotham laid out his vision for a college with deep and unashamed evangelical roots but a warm welcome to those from other perspectives. He announced his conviction that

28 Stuart Y. Blanch (1918–94), bishop of Liverpool 1966–75, archbishop of York 1975–83.

29 Stott to Blanch, 3 April 1969, papers of John Stott.

30 James I. Packer (b. 1926), warden of Latimer House, Oxford 1962–9, associate principal of Trinity College, Bristol 1972–9, professor at Regent College, Vancouver from 1979. See further, Alister E. McGrath, *To Know and Serve God: a Biography of James I. Packer* (London, 1997).

31 Blanch to Stott, 8 April 1969, papers of John Stott.

32 Blanch to Hickinbotham, 1 October 1969, WH, Council Minutes.

> the Church needs colleges like Wycliffe – colleges gripped by a strong and full Evangelical faith, and marked by the sound doctrine and missionary spirit, the evangelistic and social concern, which such a Gospel creates; colleges where love for the sacraments and worship and corporate life of the Church, and also belief in the liberty of the Holy Spirit and His leading of us into new understandings of truth, are appreciated as part of a full and balanced evangelical conviction; colleges with an ecumenical spirit, welcoming students of varying outlooks and promoting fellowship with all who love the Lord.[33]

Elsewhere Hickinbotham reiterated that 'the Church needs colleges of the comprehensive and generous evangelical outlook which characterises Wycliffe'.[34] Likewise in the new Wycliffe prospectus the principal stressed these twin themes, emphasizing the Hall's evangelical origins:

> The Hall was founded within the evangelical movement in our Church, and has always [*sic*] had at the heart of its teaching and its fellowship the great insights which have specially characterized that movement, with its commitment to the full Gospel of redemption centred in the atoning Death and victorious Resurrection of Jesus Christ, to the authority of the Bible, to the need for personal faith in Jesus Christ as Saviour and Lord and for experience of new life through the Holy Spirit, and to the call to personal evangelism and world mission. This gives the Hall its unity, its distinctive character and its sense of direction; and this in turn enables it, without loss of cohesion and clarity of purpose, to try to appreciate the whole of the Church's spiritual inheritance and to have a generous and outward-looking attitude, to welcome among its students men of varying outlooks, and to seek to live in fellowship with all who love the Lord.[35]

Hickinbotham quickly identified the two key areas within the University where evangelical ordinands were to be found – primarily the Oxford Inter-Collegiate Christian Union (OICCU) and St Ebbe's church, secondly the Oxford Pastorate and St Aldate's church. He

33 WH, Ember Letter, Trinity 1970.

34 WH, Ember Letter, Lent 1971.

35 Wycliffe Hall Prospectus 1977, 3–4 available at the Church of England Record Centre (London) file ACCM/COLL/WYC/1.

worked hard to build up 'friendship and trust' with both these circles, preaching at St Aldate's, enjoying tea with the OICCU Executive Committee and mixing as much as possible with them in other ways. The explicit support given by Wycliffe Hall for the 1970 OICCU Mission did much to restore and cement confidence, and Hickinbotham hoped the word would quickly spread to other Universities.[36]

Yet if Wycliffe Hall was to regain the support of the evangelical movement, it would require not just encouragements from the principal but also a deliberate change of personnel. Hickinbotham urged the council to look 'for more adequate representation of the more conservative wing of the evangelical school of thought'.[37] The first new council member appointed under the new regime was David Fletcher, successor to E. J. H. Nash as head of the Scripture Union camps at Iwerne Minster, a fertile recruitment ground for young public-school educated 'conservative evangelicals' called to ordained Anglican ministry.[38] Hickinbotham also set out to recruit a new staff team which would revive Wycliffe's fortunes. David Anderson's side-kick, Alan Dunstan, found the reorientation of the Hall uncomfortable and soon moved on. He returned to Ripon Hall, as vice-principal, where his MCU credentials were better appreciated. In his place Hickinbotham head-hunted a young curate and biblical scholar, Peter Southwell, who had a vibrant ministry of discipleship and nurture amongst evangelical students at Oxford.[39] Southwell's appointment in October 1970 was received with delight in OICCU circles and he personally recruited many ordinands for Wycliffe Hall. Next came David Holloway to teach doctrine and ethics, succeeded on the staff in October 1972 by a young evangelical doctoral student, Oliver O'Donovan.[40] Demonstrating his entrepreneurial skills, Hickinbotham also persuaded senior evangelical scholars in the Oxford area to offer their services to Wycliffe Hall part-time. John Reynolds, rector of Dry Sandford and an authority on

36 Principal's Report, January–June 1970, WH, Council Minutes; WH, Ember Letter, Trinity 1970.

37 WH, Council Minutes, 5 February 1970.

38 David C. M. Fletcher (b. 1932), Scripture Union field worker 1962–86, rector of St Ebbe's, Oxford 1986–98.

39 Peter J. M. Southwell (b. 1943), senior tutor of Wycliffe Hall from 1970, chaplain of Queen's College, Oxford from 1982.

40 David R. J. Holloway (b. 1939), vicar of Jesmond, Newcastle-upon-Tyne from 1973; Oliver M. T. O'Donovan (b. 1945), tutor of Wycliffe Hall 1972–7, regius professor of moral and pastoral theology at Oxford 1982–2006, professor of Christian ethics and practical theology at New College, Edinburgh from 2006.

Oxford evangelicalism, taught church history.[41] Roger Beckwith, librarian (and later warden) of Latimer House, taught liturgy.[42]

As a direct result of these radical changes, demonstrating a renewed and explicit commitment to Wycliffe Hall's evangelical foundations, ordinands began to flood back. Within eighteen months accommodation was stretched and every room was in use.[43] Soon the Hall was breaking records for recruitment year upon year. The heart-felt support of the wider Anglican evangelical community was firmly restored. Writing in 1972, Hickinbotham described the broad range of churchmanship represented at the Hall and stressed that 'It has always been Wycliffe's tradition to combine a profound evangelical stance with a generous welcome to men of varied outlooks'. Yet he observed:

> The situation in the Church of England generally is reflected in the fact that most of those who have a deep evangelical type of Christian faith and experience tend to be conservative rather than liberal, and the Hall owes much of its vitality to the conservative evangelical element among the students which includes many of the men with the greatest gifts of personality and of pastoral and intellectual leadership.[44]

While the Church of England continued forcibly to close and merge its surplus of theological colleges, Wycliffe Hall won a reprieve. Its 'survival' and 'revival' were closely intertwined, indeed inseparable. Hickinbotham was rightly confident that the church authorities would 'recognize Wycliffe's potential as a spiritual growing-point in the life and mission of the Church'.[45] By the time of the Hall's centenary in 1977 its future was assured, and its resurgence was celebrated as a vindication for the founders' vision. The new evangelical archbishops of Canterbury and York (both Wycliffe alumni) joined the public festivities rejoicing in Wycliffe Hall as both a symbol of, and a contributor to, evangelicalism's revitalized influence within the Anglican Church.

Latimer Trust, Oxford

41 John S. Reynolds (b. 1919), rector of Dry Sandford near Oxford 1956–85.

42 Roger T. Beckwith (b. 1929), librarian of Latimer House, Oxford 1963–73, warden 1973–94.

43 WH, Ember Letter, Michaelmas 1971.

44 Principal's Report, June–December 1972, WH, Council Minutes.

45 WH, Ember Letter, Trinity 1970.

THE EAST AFRICAN REVIVAL OF THE TWENTIETH CENTURY: THE SEARCH FOR AN EVANGELICAL AFRICAN CHRISTIANITY

by KEVIN WARD

AFRICAN Christian history in the twentieth century furnishes many examples of what can justifiably be described as revival or renewal. To the extent that Christian evangelization in sub-Saharan Africa was propelled by the European missionary movement, it is not surprising that an important element in revival should be a concern to ground the Gospel in an African milieu, expressive of African cultures and sensibilities, and driven by an autonomous African agency.[1] The missionary forms in which Christianity was expressed came under critical scrutiny. This essay is an examination of the East African Revival, a movement which originated in the Protestant mission churches in the 1930s and which continues to be a major element in the contemporary religious life of Christian churches throughout the region. There has been considerable scholarly debate about whether the East African Revival should best be seen as an 'importation' and 'imposition' of a western Evangelical revival culture in an African setting, or as marking the emergence of a distinctive 'African' religious sensibility expressed within Christian forms. In endeavouring to avoid the implicit essentialism which such polarities often convey, the essay aims to show how the East African Revival can fruitfully be understood as belonging both to the larger Protestant revivalist tradition, while springing out of the distinctive responses of East Africans to the Christian message as they experienced it from within African cultures which were themselves being transformed by colonialism and modernity.

The great evangelistic campaigns of William Wade Harris along the coast of West Africa during 1914, the healing ministry initiated by Simon Kimbangu in the Congo in the 1920s, the Zionist churches

[1] For a recent theological statement about the 'Africanness' of Christianity, see Lamin Sanneh, *Whose Religion is Christianity? The Gospel beyond the West* (Grand Rapids, MI, 2003).

which proliferated in South Africa in the early years of the twentieth century, were all intended as expressions of a more 'African' Christianity. The Aladura of Nigeria began as a renewal movement within Yoruba Anglicanism in the 1920s. But it could not be contained within Anglicanism, and rapidly established a series of independent churches.[2] In East Africa there were protests, in the name of a more truly African Christianity, against the alliance between colonialism and Christianity. In 1914 in Uganda, Yoswa Kate Mugema accused the government hospital in Mulago and the Anglican cathedral at Namirembe of being the twin shrines of a European pagan religion which should be eschewed by Baganda. A decade later, Kate Mugema's compatriot, Reuben Mukasa Spartas, enjoined his fellow Christians to come out of their local Anglican Church, where they could only ever be 'houseboys in their own home', to join him in the search for a truly African Christianity. Spartas was influenced by Jamaican, Marcus Garvey, and the pan-Africanist movement. Spartas founded an African Orthodox Church in Uganda to achieve this goal.[3] What unites all these diverse protests against missionary Christianity was a critique of the alien dress in which Christianity was clothed, or the subordinate position to which Africans were relegated.

In the 1960s, in the period when most African countries achieved independence, the claim of independent churches to enshrine an authentic African Christianity gave these movements particular interest to historians and to students of religion. Nevertheless the vast majority of African Christians continued to belong to Christian churches. Simplistic divisions between 'resisters' and 'collaborators', and critiques of the essentialism which so often lurks behind the use of 'European', 'African', 'authentically African' etc., have led to re-evaluations of the importance and role of Africans in shaping and reshaping Catholic and Protestant Christianity in Africa.[4] The East African Revival offers a particularly interesting example of the way in which African Christians

2 These issues are discussed in the three comprehensive histories of Africa published in the 1990s: Adrian Hastings, *The Church in Africa* (Oxford, 1994), Elizabeth Isichei, *A History of African Christianity* (London, 1995), and Bengt Sundkler and Christopher Steed, *A History of the Church in Africa* (Cambridge, 2000). Sundkler was a pioneer in the serious study of independent Christianity in Africa: *Bantu Prophets in South Africa* (London, 1948) and *Zulu Zion and Some Swazi Zionists* (Oxford, 1976).

3 F. B. Welbourn, *East African Rebels* (London, 1961).

4 For diverse discussions of these issues, see David Maxwell with Ingrid Lawrie, eds, *Christianity and the African Imagination: Essays in Honour of Adrian Hastings* (Leiden, 2002).

have fashioned the historical Protestant churches. The East African Revival has always presented itself both as an African movement of renewal within historic Christianity, and a means of reinforcing Evangelical values and norms within mission-founded churches, where the marks of Evangelicalism have, in the opinion of the revivalists, been lost or compromised.

The origins of the East African Revival lie in the condition of the Church of Uganda (the Native Anglican Church as it was called in colonial times) in the 1920s and 1930s. As a movement of popular evangelistic power it first became evident in Gahini, Ruanda, a mission field of the Church of Uganda, but situated in the Belgian administered territory of Ruanda-Urundi. Revival spread back to Uganda itself and by the 1940s was a force within the Anglican churches of Kenya and Tanganyika, Southern Sudan and the Congo. Its impact was also impinging on Presbyterian, Methodist, Lutheran and Mennonite churches in the region. The Revival was at the height of its power and influence in the 1950s and the early years of independence. In these years it counted martyrs whose deaths were related to their Christian faith and espousal of revival – in Kenya during the Mau Mau struggle of the 1950s, in Rwanda, during the revolution of the late 1950s and early 1960s which overthrew Tutsi power, in Uganda, during the Amin period in the 1970s, during which the Archbishop of Uganda, Janani Luwum, was murdered.[5]

Revival began as an opposition to ecclesiastical institutions and structures of power, perceived as rigid and inimical to the Gospel, within the churches, and indeed within the wider society. But by the 1960s, revivalists had come to dominate the church leadership in many Protestant churches, and particularly within the Anglican episcopates throughout East Africa. The Revival decisively shaped the spirituality and self-understanding of these churches. The Revival has, however, always stressed its independence of church structures as such. It has strenuously resisted its own institutionalization, and its continuing vitality consists in its ability to create informal communities of fellowship. Its pre-eminence in shaping the ethos of East African Protestantism varies from place to place, denomination to denomination, and its influence has changed over time. The East African Revival as *the* authentic expression of revival in this region is now facing a strong

5 Kevin Ward, 'Archbishop Janani Luwum: the Dilemmas of Loyalty, Opposition and Witness in Amin's Uganda', in Maxwell and Lawrie, eds, *The Christian Imagination*, 199–224.

challenge from Pentecostalism, which spread across East Africa in the 1980s and 1990s in ways parallel to the revival of the 1930s, but with radically different consequences for the established churches.[6] From the perspective of a global Christian history, the East African Revival combines elements of the Methodist movement in its evangelistic zeal and German Pietism in its ability radically to transform the official Church with its ethos, while remaining distinct from ecclesiastical structures. It is the inheritor of nineteenth-century forms of popular revivalism dating back to Charles Finney and has been profoundly (though not uncritically) influenced by the Keswick movement.

The Basic Grammar of the East African Revival

It is clear that the East African Revival understands itself to stand in a long tradition of Evangelical revivalism. As with many reform movements within the Church, it has been subject of a variety of epithets. Its most distinctive name, and the one most commonly used to this day in East Africa itself, is *Balokole.* This is a Luganda word meaning 'Saved People'. The term was first used by outsiders, often to mock or criticize, but it was also an accurate designation of a central tenet of the Revival – the offer of salvation (*kulokoka*), and as such has become a widely accepted term used widely by revivalists themselves, church people as a whole, and society generally. Nevertheless, revivalists are suspicious of the use of the term *Balokole* to suggest that the movement is a particular party within the Church, or a sect. I once made the mistake of asking a Ugandan revivalist 'When did you became a Mulokole?'[7] What I should have asked is 'When did you get saved?' By framing the question as I did, the interviewee understood me to be implicitly demeaning salvation, by likening it to joining a club, making revival into just an optional way of being a Christian, rather than the only possible response to the invitation of salvation. Revivalists prefer to call themselves *Ab'oluganda* – brethren, or, more accurately, brothers and sisters (the term in Luganda is not gender specific). In English this has tended to be translated as *Fellowship.* Again to talk of the Revival as 'the Fellow-

[6] Allan Anderson, *Zion and Pentecost: the Spirituality and Experience of Pentecostal and Zionist/Apostolic Churches in South Africa* (Pretoria, 2000), idem, *An Introduction to Pentecostalism* (Cambridge, 2004).

[7] Luganda is a Bantu language, with a system of noun prefixes. *Balokole*: saved people; *Mulokole*: a (single) saved person. *Kulokoka* is an active verb: to get saved; and also an abstract noun: salvation.

ship' is a useful descriptor. Anyone who does not meet in fellowship with those who have been saved, or who ceases so to meet, is a backslider, whose salvation is in doubt. This emphasis on constant and active participation in the fellowship group effectively prevents the Revival from simply being identified with the Church as a whole, however much revival may seem to influence the general ethos of Protestantism in East Africa. Meeting in fellowship means first membership of a particular local fellowship. But it also connects one with a wider network of Brethren. Revivalists are characterized by their mobility, incessantly on the move – attending the monthly fellowship meetings at strategic points in a region, journeying to annual and decennial Conventions, but also constantly visiting the brethren in an informal way. The big Conventions, in their hey-day in the 1950s and 1960s, attracted crowds of thousands, enquirers as well as brethren, and were a major factor in the transmission of the Revival. A sense of belonging is reinforced by the repeated singing, during all these meetings, and indeed whenever two or three are gathered together or meet each other in the street, of the revival anthem, *Tukutendereza Jesu* ('We Praise You, Jesus'), sung in its original Luganda by all Balokole throughout East Africa, though also sung in vernacular translations, and in Kiswahili, in areas where Luganda is not understood. The *Tukutendereza* anthem constitutes a basic confession of faith in the cleansing power of the 'blood of the Lamb'. It acts as an absolution of sin by the community, each time a personal confessions is made. Traditionally such individual confessions have constituted the chief act of worship within the fellowship meetings. Specific greetings (including the use of the word, *Tukutendereza*), exuberant handshakes and embraces, addressing each other as 'brother' and 'sister', all reinforce the sense of being a special people of God. Basic constituents of Balokole identity are: a sense of 'brokenness' at the Cross, repentance of sin, the personal appropriation of salvation through the blood of Christ, the public confession of sin to the brethren not only after initial conversion but continually, 'walking in the light' – that is, an honesty about oneself and an unwillingness to keep quiet about the sins which are discerned in others (whether fellow brethren or the population at large). Being a revivalist is a life-changing experience of personal responsibility before God mediated through fellowship in the community of the saved.[8]

[8] For a good recent account of the salient characteristics of the Balokole, see Medad Birungi, 'The Glory of the East African Revival in its Characteristics', in William Rukirande

Origins

The origins of the East African Revival are situated in two distinct but intertwined geographical places and historical situations. The first locus was Namirembe in Buganda, and related to the spiritual life of the Church of Uganda, which in 1927 celebrated its jubilee, and where the Church was a well-established institution of enormous significance in the colonial life of Uganda. The second locus was Gahini in Rwanda, where the Church Mission Society (CMS) mission hospital was an outpost of the diocese of Uganda, and still in the pioneering stages of missionary work.

The Gospel had first been preached in the independent kingdom of Buganda by missionaries of the Anglican CMS in 1877. The arrival eighteen months later of French Roman Catholics had engendered a religious rivalry between Protestant and Catholic. This was further compounded by a rivalry between Christianity and Islam, which had arrived in Buganda a generation before, in the 1840s. All these new religions (they were called by the Arabic loan word, *diini*, in Luganda) were opposed to the traditional Balubaale cult and other traditional expressions of religion. The struggle which was inaugurated by the advent of the forces of international colonialism produced martyrs in all three communities, a bitter war of religion in the 1880s and 1890s, and the eventual triumph of the Protestant (i.e. Anglican) religion, which occurred at the same time and was not unconnected with the imposition of British colonial rule in the 1890s. The Anglican faith became a quasi-establishment in Buganda and throughout the larger Uganda Protectorate of which Buganda was the core. However, British policy protected the rights of the other religious communities to exist and to propagate. In the immediate aftermath of the wars of religion, Anglican evangelistic zeal had been given even greater impetus by a revival associated with the missionary George Pilkington. Influenced as a student at Cambridge by the Keswick movement, he had experienced the infilling of the Holy Spirit after a period of mental and physical exhaustion during a turbulent period in Buganda's history. This led him to a personal sense of 'entire sanctification' and a message of the 'victorious Christian life' which met with a response from young converts, many

et al. eds, *The East African Revival Through Seventy Years (1935–2005): Testimonies and Reflections* (Kabale, 2005), 49–64.

of whom had been soldiers in the wars.[9] In the years before 1914, Christianity in both its Anglican and Catholic forms was spread to most other parts of the Uganda protectorate. The success of the Protestants was predicated on two vital but potentially conflicting factors: the quasi-established status of the Anglican Church in the new Uganda Protectorate, which made it attractive to indigenous rulers and which led to its wide-spread dissemination among the peasantry, who naturally followed the example of their leaders; and the ethical and spiritual demands of a revivalist commitment to an experience of salvation expressed in a disciplined personal life. Being a 'folk Church' and espousing Evangelical values of a revivalist tendency were not incompatible, but the combination did produce tensions.[10] On the one hand, there were manifestations of a grass-roots political opposition to the Anglican elite which dominated Church and state (and this was expressed in the movements inaugurated by the Mugema and Spartas mentioned above); on the other hand, there was a longing for a more purely spiritual form of Christianity. The key figure in this latter tendency was Simeoni Nsibambi, a member of one of the Protestant elite families of Buganda, and a landowner with a home on Namirembe hill (where the Anglican cathedral was situated, and where the bishop of Uganda lived). From the early 1920s, though still a young man, he retired from employment in government service to devote himself to purely spiritual pursuits. A familiar figure on Namirembe, he walked bare foot and wearing the traditional kanzu (a loose-fitting white garment) rather than European clothes. He was critical of the formalism of his Church and its ethical compromises. He gathered around him a small pietistic circle, a network of family members and like-minded Anglicans from the 'traditional' Buganda landowning families, and aspiring members of a new 'middle class' educated in Protestant schools.[11] The spiritual aspirations of the Nsibambi circle in the 1920s were to find a productive outlet in its relationship to the most recent

9 Charles Harford-Battersby, *Pilkington of Uganda* (London, 1898), 221–39.

10 There is a large literature on the origins of Christianity in Buganda. For the turbulent political events of the late nineteenth century, see M. S. M. Kiwanuka, *A History of Buganda* (London, 1971). For the institutional life of the Anglican Church and its relationship to the state in the early twentieth century, see H. B. Hansen, *Mission, Church and State in a Colonial Setting, Uganda 1890–1925* (London, 1984).

11 I am grateful to the late E. M. K. Mulira of Namirembe, a historian of great acumen, for details of Nsibambi's early life. See the account in J. C. Church, *Quest for the Highest* (Exeter, 1981).

mission field of Ugandan Anglicanism, in the Belgian League of Nations mandated colony of Ruanda-Urundi.

Gahini was the first station established by the Ruanda Mission of the CMS in Belgian territory in 1925. The existence of the Ruanda Mission was the result of the vision and stubborn determination of two medical doctors, who first arrived to work as volunteers at the CMS Mengo hospital in Kampala in 1914. Leonard Sharp and Algie Stanley Smith had been students in Cambridge and in the London hospitals at the period when CICCU, the Cambridge Inter-Collegiate Christian Union, had split from the Student Christian Movement over questions of biblical authority and 'modernist' theology.[12] Convinced that the practice of medicine could be a vital evangelistic tool, and critical of mission work which concentrated on institutional consolidation rather than pioneer evangelism, they used their time in Kampala to identify an area in East Africa which could be the field for missionary work to 'unreached people'. The Banyarwanda[13] emerged as the target for evangelistic medical missionary work; populous and potentially receptive to the Gospel, Protestant missionary work had only just begun in the area at the end of the period of German colonialism, and with the expulsion of the Germans and German missionaries during the First World war, it was waiting to be 'occupied'. With difficulty, but by dint of stubborn perseverance, the doctors persuaded the CMS, all too conscious of financial constraints in the post-war economic recession, to sanction the establishment of a self-supporting mission linked to, but separate from, the Uganda Mission of the CMS. It was to be self-supporting in the sense that the doctors pledged to find the money from supporters in England. The first difficulty in realizing their vision lay in the political consequences of the First World War: the League of Nations mandate of the territory of Ruanda-Urundi to the Belgians. The Belgians were initially reluctant to allow British missionaries into their new territory, partly because of British disappointment at not receiving the mandate themselves. The other major set-back for the mission erupted when the CMS experienced a major schism over the very issues which had led to the emergence of the CICCU in the pre-war years: the struggle over

12 For the history of this split see Douglas Johnson, *Contending for the Faith* (Leicester, 1979).

13 During the Belgian period, the independent states of Rwanda and Burundi were ruled jointly as the territory of Ruanda-Urundi. The people of Rwanda are known as Banyarwanda (singular Munyarwanda) and the language is Kinyarwanda.

biblical inspiration and the opposition to a liberal Evangelical theology, which was seen as modernist. All the instincts of the doctors led them to sympathize with the dissidents who created the rival Bible Churchmen's Missionary Society (BCMS) in 1922. Sharp and Stanley Smith made the decision to remain within the CMS fold, on the assurance that their distinctive theological emphases would be respected and that missionaries appointed to the Ruanda Mission would similarly espouse conservative Evangelical biblical principles and a 'Keswick' spirituality.[14] The Ruanda Mission had first established a mission station in Kabale in southern Uganda, an area which contained a significant number of Banyarwanda, who occupied the Bufumbira district of Uganda, bordering Rwanda. The first mission in Rwanda was established in 1924 at Gahini, where a hospital was built and where the new medical missionary, Joe Church, was located in 1928. It was the meeting between Dr Church and Nsibambi at Namirembe in 1929 which Joe Church remembers as decisive for the birth of the Revival. Joe Church was tired and spiritually exhausted from his initial exposure to pioneering work in difficult conditions – he was responsible for medical care during one of the severest famines for a generation in the Gahini area. He found in Nsibambi a kindred spirit, as they together read the scriptures illuminated by the marginal references provided by the Schofield Bible. The experience of renewal, which parallels that of Pilkington, lit a spark which eventually ignited the fire of the East African Revival. Gahini hospital recruited Baganda medical 'dressers' and school teachers, many from Nsibambi's circle. In 1933, a revival broke out in Gahini, with many of the manifestations commonly associated with revivalism. Joe Church's gifts as an organizer (it is no accident that he was particularly attracted to John Wesley) meant that he quickly became involved in the establishment of evangelistic missions in other parts of the Ruanda Mission territory and back into the heartlands of the Church of Uganda. The union of heart and mind which Church had experienced with Nsibambi became a model for revival missions, which included both a missionary and an African as joint speakers. The 'team' principle was of fundamental importance both as an assertion of the communal nature of the faith into which people were invited, and of the fundamental equality between Euro-

14 For details of the negotiations with Belgian authorities, and with CMS over the crisis over biblical inspiration, see the CMS Archives (Birmingham), particularly G3/A7/o, letters from 1919, 1920, 1921, 1922, 1923.

pean and African, which was such a feature of the Revival, and which contrasted with the racial and cultural segregation which was such a feature of the colonial Church.[15]

The radical message of the Revival, and even more its style of operation, caused severe commotion within both the Church of Uganda and within the Ruanda Mission. There was a strong possibility that the Revival would cause a permanent schism within the Church, a fragmentation of the Ruanda Mission, and a rift between the Ruanda Mission and its supporters in England, not to mention its parent body, the CMS. The message of revival was always conceived as a challenge to the institutional Church: 'Zukuka' –Awake – was the message of Blasio Kigozi, in his address to the Synod of the Church of Uganda in 1936, shortly before his early death. Kigozi was Nsibambi's younger brother, who had gone to Gahini in 1929 to supervise the development of schools in the mission. He was an important promoter of the Gahini revival. In 1935 he had been ordained deacon by Bishop Stuart, the Bishop of Uganda, who wanted to encourage educated revivalists like Kigozi to become clergy. One feature of the early revival was, however, a trenchant criticism of the existing clergy, the *bakulu* (literally elders), whether they were Ugandan clergy, missionaries, or the Bishop himself. Bishop C. E. Stuart had known Joe Church when Stuart was chaplain of Ridley Hall in Cambridge. He worked for a reconciliation of the tensions within Evangelicalism between conservatives and liberals. In the battle which the Revival engendered in Uganda, Joe Church saw him as a representative of the compromise against which revival must fight. Forces of liberal Evangelicalism were seen to be particularly at work in the teaching at Bishop Tucker Theological College, at Mukono, under the Wardenship of a Welsh CMS missionary of considerable stature, J. C. Jones.

The lack of politeness among both missionary and young African revival enthusiasts was particularly offensive to the authorities. It offended both English and African norms and sensibilities. A major criticism focused on the way in which revivalists spoke out against sexual immorality and participation in 'pagan' practices – consultation with ancestral spirits, the reliance on diviners for healing, beliefs in witchcraft – which revivalists confessed on their own account, and denounced in others, directing their attacks to particular individuals.

15 See Church, *Question for the Highest.*

Yet the Balokole themselves were accused of transgression in this regard. The mobility of revivalist speakers led to accusations of sexual immorality.[16] The emphasis on the 'blood' was itself seen as a reversion to superstitious forms of religious practice.[17] On the other hand, their inability to preserve the bounds of decency, in particular their exposure of sexual sin, either in confessing their pre-conversion life or in criticizing the hypocrisy of seemingly respectable Christians, was widely seen as fundamentally un-African.

Fear of these 'excesses' created a crisis within the Ruanda Mission itself, both in the field and in England. Committed to a revivalist Keswick-style Evangelicalism, the mission prayed for revival but found the actual forms of revival hard to take. The founders of the mission, particularly Dr Sharp, felt apprehensive. The blunt, often insensitive criticism of missionaries was difficult to accept. Particularly hurtful was the tendency of revivalists to discount any religious experience which predated the East African Revival or diverged from the pattern of repentance and confession which had become the norm in the Revival. The Keswick piety of the Ruanda Mission led missionaries to look for and expect a 'second blessing' experience, but they rejected, at least at first, the call to conversion, as if they were not yet Christians at all. For a number of years in the late 1930s and 1940s tensions between those missionaries who had made that decisive step of confession and were now accepted as brethren and those who did not do so polarized the mission. The tension was exemplified by the book which Dr Leonard Sharp produced in the late 1930s or early 1940s entitled *Great Truths from God's Word*, a kind of systematic itinerary of biblical quotations organized around the great themes of Evangelical doctrine. It was compiled as a counter-weight to Joe Church's influential *Every Man a Bible Student*, structured similarly as a catena of scripture quotes, but based on a revivalist, experiential schema.[18]

16 The Irish CMS missionary Mabel Ensor, herself a critic of the spiritual 'deadness' of the Church of Uganda, was as forthright as any Mulokole in her attacks in a pamphlet entitled 'Some Plain reasons why the movement called Balokole is injurious and retrograde'. See Joe Church Papers, File: New Way. The Papers are held in the Henry Martyn Collection at Westminster College, Cambridge.

17 Archdeacon Herbert felt that the emphasis on 'blood' indicated a superstitious faith in a new kind of 'nsiriba' – charm. Joe Church Papers, File: Call to Mukono 1935–40. Also interview, June 1984, with Erasto Kato (a student at Mukono in the 1930s, and a Revivalist).

18 J. C. Church, *Every Man a Bible Student* (London, 1938; 2nd edn, Exeter, 1976). Leonard E. S. Sharp, *Real Truths from God's Word* (Secunderabad, 2004). This is a reprint. The original publication details are not given.

In 1941, the expulsion of Balokole ordinands from Bishop Tucker College, Mukono, brought to a head a crisis in relations between revival and both Church and Mission.[19] For a few years it seemed likely that the Revival and the Anglican Church would part company, and that the Ruanda Mission might become an independent mission outside the Anglican fold. But revivalists themselves were deeply attached to the Church, even if they were ruthlessly critical of it. William Nagenda, a Muganda landowner related to Nsibambi, and the leader of the expelled dissidents, never did get ordained. He embarked on a career as an international evangelist, part of a two-man team with Joe Church. Their missions in the 1950s and 1960s included England, India, South Africa and Brazil. By the late 1940s, the Revival was becoming an accepted part of the life of the Church in Uganda. It formed the backbone of the Church in Rwanda and Burundi.[20]

The expansion to Tanganyika, Kenya and Sudan tended to replicate the situation in Uganda – initial hostility, from African clergy and missionaries, tended to give way to welcome and incorporation into the life of the Church. Only in the Africa Inland Mission (AIM), an American based interdenominational faith mission, strongly revivalist in spirit, was the East African Revival effectively excluded. In Nandi, in western Kenya, those AIM adherents who were influenced by the Revival eventually left the Africa Inland Church and became Anglican.

The Historiography of the Revival

Formal sermons at Conventions, confession in the fellowship, testimony in the market place and on buses, individual conversation – these are the characteristic and defining modes of communicating the message of the East African Revival. It was above all a movement of face-to-face communication. Writing was a secondary activity. Moreover the Revival eschewed formal minute taking, the paper trails generated by committees and church council meetings, which frequently provides the staple sources for historical scholarship. Revivalists have

[19] A full account of these events and their consequences is given in Kevin Ward, '"Obedient Rebels": the Mukono Crisis of 1941', in *Journal of Religion in Africa* 19: 3 (1989), 194–227.

[20] For a detailed account of the Revival in Uganda see Kevin Ward, '*"Tukutendereza Yesu"*: the Balokole Revival in Uganda', in Zablon Nthamburi, ed., *From Mission to Church: a Handbook of Christianity in East Africa* (Nairobi, 1991), 113–44.

themselves been keen to write down their personal testimonies and develop a narrative of the outward progress of revival in time and place. They have shown enthusiasm to co-operate with others in writing down these accounts – first of all fellow revivalists, in the spirit of the 'team', but also outsiders: historians, social scientists and students of religion, who have demonstrated an interest in understanding the movement. One reason for this openness to outsiders is the opportunity it gives for witness, even if the researchers are not themselves viewed as 'saved' people, and their subsequent accounts may diverge from the shared understandings of revivalists themselves. Despite the priority of oral material (especially for uncovering African perspectives), there is also a large amount of written material dating from the early days of the Revival. Yet Joe Church was assiduous in maintaining a correspondence with the brethren over a forty-year period, particularly with the highly literate leaders such as William Nagenda and Erika Sabiti (the first African Archbishop of Uganda). Joe Church was also a most careful and methodical archivist of his own collection. Much of this material is now deposited in the Henry Martyn Library at Westminster College in Cambridge, and is an essential resource for studies of the East African Revival. The CMS archives at Birmingham University include much Revival material, as well as correspondence relating to the Ruanda Mission. Towards the end of his life, in 1981, Joe Church published an autobiographical account of the Revival, *Quest for the Highest.* Even before that the overwhelming stamp which he had put on the Revival within East Africa, the assiduousness with which he acted as a spokesperson for and a promoter of the Revival outside Africa, has meant that his interpretation of the Revival has become the standard one, reflected in a score of accounts written by insiders or sympathizers. Patricia St John's, *Breath of Life* (1971) remains the standard work.[21] The tendency in works geared towards the core English-speaking Evangelical constituency in Britain has been to play down the intensity of the early conflicts within the Ruanda Mission; Revival and Mission become synonymous.[22]

A significant milestone in the study of the Revival, from historical and sociological perspectives, was Catherine Robins's Columbia

21 Patricia St John, *Breath of Life: the Story of the Ruanda Mission* (London, 1971).

22 This is not entirely the case. There are books which are more geared to the history of the mission as a whole, rather than simply the Revival, e.g. L. Guillebaud, *A Grain of Mustard Seed: the Growth of the Ruanda Mission* (London, [1959]).

University Ph.D. thesis of 1975, *Tukutendereza: a Social Study of Social Change and Sectarian Withdrawal in the Balokole Revival.*[23] This is the first sustained attempt by an outsider systematically to examine Balokole self-understanding and theology, but to interpret these within a sociological framework. Her thesis is particularly important for its attempt to explain the divisions within the Revival which had emerged in the 1960s between the more outward looking and inclusive forms it had taken in Kigezi and Ankole (in South West Uganda) and the rather narrow and inward orientation of the brethren in Buganda itself. In this Robins discerned a reflection of the disquiet running through Buganda society as a whole, as their traditions and autonomy as a kingdom came under remorseless attack from the first independence regime of Milton Obote, and later under Amin's dictatorship. An emphasis on Buganda exceptionalism was seen as essential to political and cultural survival.

My own studies of the Mukono crisis and historical account of the revival in Uganda in the 1980s were attempts to position the Revival movement within a wider context of Ugandan church history. In the study of the Mukono crisis I was concerned to allow both the dissident case and that of their accusers to be made in a non-partisan fashion, as well as to explore the processes by which the Balokole movement eventually became acceptable within the Church.[24]

What might be called the official history of the Balokole is still overwhelmingly the story of Joe Church's spiritual journey and his interaction with the educated African leadership of the movement. Unfortunately those first generation African leaders – Simeoni Nsibambi, William Nagenda, Erika Sabiiti – did not themselves leave memoirs or any substantial body of correspondence except that which survives within the Joe Church Papers. The story of ordinary Balokole, and particularly the impact of the Revival in specific localities, has, since the 1970s, been given detailed attention in unpublished work done particularly by theological students at Mukono.[25] Balokole leaders, particularly of the second generation such as Bishop Festo

23 Catherine E. Robins, 'Tukutendereza: a Study of Social Change and Sectarian Withdrawal in the Balokole Revival', unpublished Ph.D. thesis, Columbia University, New York, 1975.

24 See n. 18 above for full reference.

25 During my time as lecturer in Church History at Mukono (1976–90) I encouraged students to write such local histories, much of it related to Balokole themes., e.g. Daniel Kiggundu, Kefa Zoida, Kenneth Gong, Sam Kermu, George Kasangaki, John Magumba,

Kivengere, have themselves written memoirs, or their biographies have been written, largely by people from within the Revival fellowship.[26]

Dorothy Smoker, who collaborated with Kivengere in a number of the books he published in the 1970s and 1980s, is the compiler of Kenyan revival testimonies, which she published in 1994 under the title *Ambushed by Love*.[27] Smoker, an American Mennonite who became a revivalist when she worked for the Mennonite Church in Tanzania, had the full cooperation of the brethren in Gikuyuland (Kenya). Her collection focuses on their experiences during the Mau Mau independence struggle of the 1950s. The material is richly illuminating of Kenyan revivalists' uncompromising refusal to take up arms either on the side of the forest fighters or the Home Guards, the Gikuyu militia set up by the colonial authorities to combat Mau Mau. The stories are impressive in their detail, showing that revival testimonies are not unhistorical, unspecific accounts of the salvation of the soul, but evidence a deep participation in the life of the society, even in their criticism of the sinful world from which they have been saved. The Revival experience clearly enabled men and women to engage actively with the events through which they lived, whether it be the Mau Mau liberation struggle, living in Uganda under Amin, or coping with genocide in Rwanda. The critical loyalty which Balokole show in relation to the Church is mirrored in a similar commitment to the society in which they live. The peace witness revealed by the revivalists in Kenya is naturally an attractive trait for Mennonites. After the Anglicans, they are perhaps the missionary group most active in promoting the work of Revival within East Africa, and in spreading its message outside, particularly in America. Moreover the sense of community and the austerity and transparency of personal life are hallmarks of the Balokole in ways which echo the Mennonites' own history and experience. The recent historical study, *A Gentle Wind of God* (2006), by Mennonites is a thorough, judicious account of the mainstream revival, with a specific interest in the impact which revival has made in America itself since the 1950s.[28]

Samuel Tusuubira. Further details can be found in ch. 4 of Nthamburi (1991), cited in n. 20 above.

26 Festo Kivengere (with Dorothy Smoker), *I love Idi Amin: the Story of Triumph under Fire in the Midst of Persecution in Uganda* (London, 1977). Anne Coombes, *Festo Kivengere* (London, 1990).

27 Dorothy Smoker, *Ambushed by Love: God's Triumph in Kenya's Terror* (Fort Washington, PA, 1994).

28 Richard K. MacMaster with Donald R. Jacobs, *A Gentle Wind of God: the Influence of the East Africa Revival* (Scottdale, PA, 2006).

The weakness of Dorothy Smoker's book from an historical point of view lies in the absence of the critical apparatus recording the circumstances under which the interviews were conducted, the original language of the interviews, the larger context in which the stories were originally located and in which the interviewee is now situated, and the extent of editorial composition or recomposition. In this regard the American historian of Africa, Derek Peterson, is doing groundbreaking work in uncovering the local dynamic of revivalist history. His work among the early revivalists in the Presbyterian Church at Tumutumu in Kenya, shows the ways in which women saw in the Revival a means by which they could realize their humanity, with a decisive impact on their situation as women, wives, daughters, and agents of change within society. The outspokenness of women revivalists threatened male authority, both at a domestic level in their open, often blistering criticism of their husband's philandering, and in the Church and local society in their refusal to be quiet in the face of official dishonesty or oppression.[29]

> The rhetoric of conversion gave converts a grammar with which to apprehend the social world, a grammar also to condemn their opponents . . . Terrified by a morally inchoate world, converts . . . used the rhetoric of good and evil to conceptualize social disorder.[30]

A comprehensive history of the Revival has yet to be written. Jocelyn Murray (obit 2001), whose bibliography of works by East African Revivalists and on the Revival is an invaluable research tool, planned to write such an account, but was unable to complete the work.[31]

The Diversity of the Revival

The writings of the Mukono ordinands and Peterson are important for uncovering an aspect of the Balokole revival which differs significantly

29 Derek R. Peterson, *Creative Writing: Translation, Bookkeeping, and the Work of Imagination in Colonial Kenya* (Portsmouth, NH, 2004). Idem, 'Wordy Women: Gender and the Oral Politics of the East African Revival in Northern Gikuyuland', *Journal of African History*, 42: 3 (2001), 469–89.

30 Peterson, *Creative Writing*, 164.

31 Jocelyn Murray, 'A Bibliography of the East African Revival Movement', *Journal of Religion in Africa*, 3: 2 (1976), 144–7. Murray was both an Anglican missionary in Kenya during the Emergency and had Mennonite connections.

from the master narrative which the Joe Church legacy has given to studies of the East African Revival. This narrative may tend to over-emphasize the cohesion of the Revival. Joe Church's writings and papers cannot be accused of ignoring conflict and dissent within the Revival. But his tradition does tend to assume that there is a correct line of revival, an orthodox revival. To use the word 'orthodox' has difficulties in that the word was used by the early revivalists to refer to the dry, cerebral 'orthodoxy' of the official Church from which they were themselves dissenting. But revival itself was both intensely argumentative and centrifugal. By and large it did not establish rival churches, but it did create competing versions of revival.

There is a left-wing of the Revival, much less influenced by European norms, much less integrated into the life of the Church. This trend is particularly important in Northern Uganda, largely non-Bantu speaking and with a very different social, political and cultural traditions from the kingdoms of southern Uganda and Rwanda and Burundi. Here the Revival quarrelled early with the southern Ugandan leadership and developed forms of revival which diverged markedly over time from that of the main movement; it produced groups which remained for much longer, and more fundamentally, antagonistic towards the Church without, however, leaving it. These forms have been given various names at different times and do not necessarily constitute a single stream of tradition. In the 1950s and 1960s, the term Trumpeters was used for the practice of revivalists haranguing worshippers by preaching at them through megaphones during or after the official Anglican church service. Later, revival groups in the North of Uganda began to call themselves the Chosen Evangelical Revival (CER). They had a wide impact not only in Northern Uganda and West Nile Province, but in Southern Sudan and in the Congo Democratic Republic. Such groups have been more receptive to incorporating elements of traditional cultural practice (e.g. dance) into their meetings, and their singing diverges much more from traditional hymnody. Yet, even in Northern Uganda, there has always been a more 'orthodox' form of revival, which has produced a number of remarkable Archbishops of Uganda: Janani Luwum, Silvanus Wani, and the current primate, Henry Orombi.[32]

[32] For the CER in West Nile, see E. Azraa, 'The Growth and Impact of the Chosen Evangelical Revival in Ayivu County', unpublished Diploma in Theology thesis, Makerere University, 1986, held in Uganda Christian University Library, Mukono, Uganda.

In Buganda, the fount of the revival movement, the Church was already well established, with a pride in its history and its integration into Kiganda culture. The Balokole have always been somewhat resented, by Church people at large, for their attack on those traditions by the Church at large. But within the Fellowship, Baganda have remained decisive in defining what the 'mainstream' revival is. Buganda, also, has produced what may be called a 'right-wing' deviation from the mainstream: the *Bazukufu*, or Reawakened, a controversy which simmered throughout the 1960s, and which eventually led to the formation of a separate network of fellowships, with one of the early revivalists, Yona Mondo, as its Taata (Father). This movement argued that Balokole had 'gone to sleep' and needed to be awakened: an echo of Kigozi's original challenge to the Church, Awake (Zukuka!) The group argued that the old values of the movement were being diluted, a worldliness (*obw'ensi*) was creeping in. They were critical of the upward social mobility of many brethren, their concern for wealth and good clothes. The Bazukufu opposed taking loans, locking doors, or keeping guard dogs – all signs of a concern for material goods which distracted from spiritual matters.[33]

A similar history of conflict and accommodation between revival and Church, with the two remaining distinct, has been characteristic of other parts of East Africa where well-established churches already existed before the coming of revival: particularly the various Protestant denominations among the Gikuyu and Luo of Kenya. Here too, revival has produced remarkable leaders such as Bishop Obadiah Kariuki (one of the first generation of Kenyan brethren), Bishop Henry Okullu[34] and Archbishop David Gitari.[35] The stature of such Episcopal leaders has been enhanced by the sharpness of their social and political critique of government in independent Kenya. For them the apolitical pietism which was a strong element in the Revival of the 1950s has been gloriously transcended. This was also true of the Revival in Kigezi (Uganda), the first mission area of the Ruanda Mission. Bishop Festo Kivengere

33 John Magumba, 'The Bazukufu in Busoga', unpublished Diploma in Theology thesis, Makerere University, 1978, held in the library of the Uganda Christian University, Mukono, Uganda.

34 Bishop Okullu wrote a book on Church and politics which has become a standard text. Henry Okullu, *Church and Politics in East Africa* (Nairobi: Uzima, 1974). His autobiography is also an important account of the Revival in Uganda and Kenya: Henry Okullu, *Quest for Justice* (Kisumu, 1997).

35 David Gitari, *In Season and Out of Season: Sermons to a Nation* (Oxford, 1996).

(the first African Bishop of Kigezi) was able to combine leadership of the Revival with an acute awareness of the political implications of Christian discipleship.

The situation in Rwanda and Burundi has been more complicated. Kigezi had benefited from being incorporated into the pre-existing structures of the Church of Uganda. In Rwanda and Burundi the Revival more or less created the Anglican/Episcopal Churches. But how was revival to cope with the responsibility of constructing an institutional Church? The immensely complex and difficult political situation created by the conflict between Hutu and Tutsi in the independence era, and the insecurity of independent regimes, made this task extraordinarily problematic. It is an issue which some of the bishops, and missionaries, in post-genocide Rwanda and in the continuing ethnic divisions of Burundi are still wrestling with.[36] 'How could genocide occur in a land where revival has had such an impact?'. This unanswerable question causes deep self-searching in church and revival fellowship.

Theological Reflections on Revivalist Belief and Practice

The cross, repentance and salvation through being washed in the blood shed at Calvary – these central tenets of the East African Revival put it firmly within the world of the Reformation and the evangelical revivalist tradition of Europe and America. Elijah Gachanja, one of the first Gikuyu converts, put it this way, recalling in an interview I conducted in 1974 the decisive experience of his life:

> In 1937 . . . the Lord broke my heart. I accepted the Lord Jesus Christ to be my personal Saviour . . . The Lord showed me all the burden of sin – he opened my eye to see that I was a sinner and kneeling at the foot of the Cross. . . . I felt I would die because of my sins. . . . I said 'Lord, save me' and that moment I knew I was saved, and I went back to give my testimony. Before that I had been a keen preacher but I did not know about the lòve of God or what the Bible meant. I was very much surprised. I started to love God

36 Roger Bowen, 'Genocide in Rwanda 1994 – An Anglican Perspective', in Carol Rittner *et al.*, eds, *Genocide in Rwanda: Complicity of the Churches?* (St Paul, MN, 2004), 37–48. An earlier version of this article was published in *Anvil*, 13 January 1996. See also, Meg Guillebaud, *The Land God Forgot?* (London, 2002) and eadem, *After the Locusts* (Oxford, 2005).

> more and repented that I had been preaching for such a long time and had not been saved.[37]

The words are in tune with the emphases which Joe Church preached; they parallel the experience of Wesley – Gachanja was already a pastor. It was also a testimony completely personal to Gachanja. He had no doubt that salvation was a completely new experience which could only be described as totally different from what had gone before – indeed a negation of what had passed for his previous Christian life.

The Revival had a dynamic which meant that it could never be controlled by missionaries. It was not amenable to European supervision. Moreover, Brethren very decisively rejected the Oxford Group/Moral Rearmament (MRA) emphases which had influenced Joe Church, and whose influence can be seen in the importance of confession in the fellowships. The brethren felt that morality had become an end in itself for the MRA, divorced from the cross. The centrality of the cross could not be compromised by the East African brethren. Their break with the MRA in the early 1950s put a wedge between the Balokole and a number of missionaries, especially in Kenya, where the MRA was attracting support within the settler community. Although there was no break with the Keswick movement, the Revival has never endorsed the idea of a 'second blessing'.

The Revival equally had no wish to conform to African cultural expectations. They abandoned many of the accommodations which Christianity had made with the prevailing culture. They opposed bride price, challenged food taboos and avoidance practices between in-laws, and devalued clan loyalties, emphasizing instead their membership of a new clan of 'saved people'. Bishop Josiah Kibera, Lutheran bishop of Bukoba[38] in Tanzania, and a revivalist, has reflected on these emphases, showing how the practice of the Brethren conform to a very deep indigenous spirituality. There is a quest of enormous significance within African societies for reconciliation, particularly between people of different ethnicities, to overcome the rift between the community of the living and the world of the spirits. In Kibera's theological analysis, the emphasis on the blood of Jesus accords well with East African

[37] Kevin Ward, 'The Development of Protestant Christianity in Kenya 1910–1940', unpublished Ph.D. thesis, University of Cambridge, 1976, 352. The interview occurred on 18 February 1974 at Gachanja's home in Njumbe, Gikuyuland.

[38] For the Revival in Bukoba, see Bengt Sundkler, *Bara Bukoba: Church and Community in Tanzania* (London, 1980).

rituals of *Omukago* (blood brotherhood) by which hostility between rival clans or rival ethnicities are confronted and overcome.[39] It should be said, however, that for the Balokole the new relationship with Christ transcends and nullifies all such human covenants, just as Christ's sacrifice rendered obsolete the temple sacrifices. Balokole are unconcerned to make the Christian message fit into any humanly conceived cultural or spiritual need. Kibira's imaginative attempt to give Balokole an African theology is still somewhat exceptional.

It is clear that the Balokole have no interest in 'africanization' or 'indigenization' for their own sakes. Equally, though, they evidence a 'modern' sensibility in many ways – insisting on monogamy, putting high value on schooling for their children, rejecting traditional medicine in favour of hospital treatment, emphasizing hard-work, honesty, sobriety and the careful management of resources – they subordinate these to a concern for maintaining the consistency of their witness to Christ.[40] Max Warren's essay on the East African Revival, *Revival: an Enquiry*,[41] written in 1954, was important for showing the importance of the Balokole movement within a theological appraisal of African Christianity. But he was also a critical friend. Of William Nagenda he wrote:

> He seems to be a terribly insensitive person to any approach to God other than his own. Almost, if not actually, he doubts its validity. The very terms 'born again', 'cleansed in the blood', 'saved' must be given one precise meaning, and the results of the experience have to follow one pattern to be recognized as authentic. This is in many ways a noble and courageous creed but it is desperately impoverished and leaves wholly out of account a vast range of human need.[42]

The Future of the Revival

The East African Revival is now some three quarters of a century old. It is remarkable that a movement which has, to an overwhelming extent,

[39] Josiah Kibera, *Clan, Church and World* (Uppsala, 1974).

[40] Mark Winter, 'The Balokole and the Protestant Ethic', *Journal of Religion in Africa* 14: 1 (1983), 58–73.

[41] Max Warren, *Revival: an Enquiry* (London, 1954).

[42] Max Warren, 'Unpublished Diaries of a Uganda Journey'. I am grateful to Mrs Pat Hooker, Max Warren's daughter, for allowing me to see these diaries.

resisted becoming a church or taking on organizational expressions of any kind, has survived. The fellowship meeting, found at the local level in parishes, in regular meetings at central sites, and in occasional great Conventions, continues to be essential for the continuance of the Revival. But the membership of fellowships get old. Their natural conservatism, their opposition to fashion and personal adornment, and to innovations in worship (electronic music, for example), limit the ability of the Revival to attract contemporary youth, for whom Pentecostalism is more clearly the movement of the future. Organizations like the Africa Enterprise (founded by Bishop Kivengere), Youth for Christ and FOCUS (Christian Unions) see themselves as imbued with revival values. They work within Anglican and other mainline Protestant Churches. Equally, the Anglican Church in much of Uganda and Kenya can be seen as having taken the Balokole ethos into their systems. The early tensions between fellowship and Church are no longer evident. But as testimonies become more stereotyped and avoid really personal or conflictual issues, and even Balokole become too respectable to make a nuisance of themselves by denouncing sin in the marketplace or on the road, so there can come a nostalgia for the old confrontational spirit.[43] Others have notice the severe limitations of biblical understanding in the Balokole. The emphasis on testimony has often led to a subjectivism of isolated texts, or a text book of rules.

Conclusion

> It is clear that revival was a huge protest against one form of Africanization of Christianity and yet it can rightly be seen as a major wave of Africanization in itself – an appropriation of Christianity not through hierarchy or school but through something very typically African: a decentralized association unified by its singing and certain basic forms of behaviour.[44]

The genius of the East African Revival is rightly to be found in this very distinctive life in fellowship, over against both Church and society. The possibility that the whole Church should become revivalist, while attractive as an aspiration, may not be good for the Church. If revival is,

43 Medard Rugyendo, 'How to Keep the Revival Fire Burning: a Few Observations and Ideas', in Rukirande *et al.*, eds, *East African Revival* (2005), 81–91.

44 Adrian Hastings, *The Church in Africa 1450–1950* (Oxford, 1994), 599.

by its nature, a corrective to established religion, it loses its *raison d'être* if it becomes the established way of doing things. It seems to be basic to Revivalism that a distinction is made between the world (*eby'ensi* in Luganda) and the realm of the Spirit. A Church which is only revivalist is likely to be narrow, unsympathetic to creativity and unresponsive to dissent, intolerant of different theologies and spiritualities. The legacy of the East African Revival may not be to create the Church in its own image but to retain that critical solidarity with the larger Church which has been its particular, and outstanding gift to the East African Church and to African Evangelicalism generally.

University of Leeds

REVIVAL, CARIBBEAN STYLE: THE CASE OF THE SEVENTH-DAY ADVENTIST CHURCH IN GRENADA, 1983–2004

by KEITH A. FRANCIS

IN 1993, commenting on the changing proportion of Christians in the major regions of the world, John V. Taylor (1914–2001), a past General Secretary of the Church Missionary Society (1963–74) and later Anglican bishop of Winchester (1975–85), wrote:

> The most striking fact to emerge . . . is the speed with which the number of Christian adherents in Latin America, Africa, and Asia has overtaken that of Europe, North America, and the former USSR. For the first time since the seventh century, when there were large Nestorian and Syrian churches in parts of Asia, the majority of Christians in the world are not of European origin. . . . Moreover, this swing to the 'South' has, it would seem, only just got going, since the birth rate in those regions is at present so much higher than in the developed 'North', and lapses from religion are almost negligible compared with Europe. By the middle of the next century, therefore, Christianity as a world religion will patently have its centre of gravity in the Equatorial and Southern latitudes, and every major denomination, except possibly the Orthodox Church, will be bound to regard those areas as its heartlands, and embody that fact in its administration.[1]

Taylor was drawing attention to a phenomenon which has fascinated historians and sociologists of religion for more than a decade. The advance of Christianity in the Global South – and its relative decline in the 'North' – has been stated most forcefully and persuasively by Philip Jenkins in *The Next Christendom: the Coming of Global Christianity* published in 2002. As Jenkins notes:

> Although we might be tempted to despair about any attempt at

[1] John V. Taylor, 'The Future of Christianity', in John McManners, ed., *The Oxford History of Christianity* (Oxford, 1993), 651 and 653.

> prediction, we are still observing major trends in the development of Southern Christianity, and in every case, these suggest surging growth. . . . This trend is so marked any predictions offered . . . might be overly-conservative. The religious maps may change, the frontiers may shift, but Southern Christianity will be growing.[2]

Other commentators have drawn attention to this development,[3] but Jenkins's analysis is probably the best known. Voted one of the best religious books of the year by *Christianity Today* and *USA Today*, *The Next Christendom* has been the focus of numerous symposia and lectures.[4] The future growth of Christianity in the Global South could be entitled, quite appropriately, the Jenkins Thesis.

Like all theses in history, Jenkins's assertions will be tested by the passage of time. Only the future will reveal whether Jenkins and others are right. Jenkins himself has acknowledged the capacity of Christianity to surprise and only a bold (and foolish) historian would predict confidently that there will not be a revival of Christianity in the northern hemisphere. For Jenkins, that Christianity will survive is, perhaps, the only given.[5]

Leaving aside questions about the future direction of the growth of Christianity, it is possible to test the validity of the claims made by Jenkins and others about the present and the recent past. Perhaps the most interesting characteristic of the analysis of Jenkins and others is the micro-examples they use to demonstrate the macro-development of the rapid growth of Southern Christianity. The confrontation between the burgeoning faiths of Christianity and Islam with the added, and incendiary, mix of tribalism and petro-politics in Nigeria is one such example of these micro-phenomena.[6]

An equally intriguing, but much less commented on, example is

2 Jenkins, *The Next Christendom: the Coming of Global Christianity* (Oxford, 2002), 89.

3 See David Aikman, *Jesus in Beijing: How Christianity is Transforming China and Changing the Global Balance of Power* (Washington, DC, 2003); Samuel Escobar, *A Time for Mission: the Challenge for Global Christianity* (Leicester, 2003); and Lamin O. Sanneh, *Whose Religion is Christianity? The Gospel Beyond the West* (Grand Rapids, MI, 2003).

4 The following are examples: 'Next Christendom: the Coming of Global Christianity' in March 2004, sponsored by the Center for Free Inquiry at Hanover College, Indiana; the G. Arthur Keogh Lectures in April 2005, given by Jenkins at Columbia Union College, Maryland; the Pruit Symposium 'Global Christianity: Challenging Modernity and the West' in November 2005, held at Baylor University, Texas.

5 Jenkins, *Next Christendom*, 220.

6 Ibid., 172–5. See also Brian Murphy, 'Christianity's Second Wave? – Close Up', *The Seattle Times*, 26 March 2006, A3 and A14.

found in the developments in the West Indies. Evangelical churches in particular are experiencing numerical expansion as well as revival among existing members. Foremost among these growing churches is the Seventh-day Adventist Church, a Church which originated in the North-East of the United States in the mid-nineteenth century and whose most distinctive doctrine is keeping the Sabbath on Saturday.[7] Until the 1960s, the preference given to the theology in the writings of Ellen G. White (1827–1915), one of its founders, and the emphasis on ideas such as the salvific efficacy of doing good works and a pre-Advent judgement led some commentators to label the Seventh-day Adventist Church a cult.[8] The changes in theology and practice begun in the 1950s have resulted in more recent commentators placing the Church in the mainstream of evangelical Protestantism.[9] Interestingly, these changes coincided with the growth of the Seventh-day Adventist Church in places such as the West Indies and Central America.

Although the Seventh-day Adventist Church has nothing like the numbers or global reach of the Roman Catholic Church,[10] the majority Church in the West Indies, the growth of the Seventh-day Adventist Church on the island of Grenada, one of the southernmost of the

[7] Using David Bebbington's definition, the Church is evangelical – Seventh-day Adventists emphasize conversion, Christ's atonement is central to their theology, they respect the text of the Bible, and expect members to be active in evangelism – but, like Jenkins's description of Southern Christianity, much of Seventh-day Adventist theology has an apocalyptic bent. See Bebbington, 'Evangelicalism in Its Settings: the British and American Movements since 1940', in Mark A. Noll, David W. Bebbington, and George A. Rawlyk, eds, *Evangelicalism: Comparative Studies of Popular Protestantism in North America, the British Isles, and Beyond, 1700–1990* (Oxford, 1994), 366–7 and 381 and Jenkins, 217–20. Useful sources on the early history and theology of the Seventh-day Adventist Church are: Ronald L. Numbers and Jonathan M. Butler, eds, *The Disappointed: Millerism and Millenarianism in the Nineteenth Century* (Indianapolis, IN, 1987); Richard W. Schwarz and Floyd Greenleaf, *Light Bearers: a History of the Seventh-day Adventist Church* (rev., Nampa, ID, 2000); Malcolm Bull and Keith Lockhart, *Seeking a Sanctuary: Seventh-day Adventism and the American Dream* (2nd edn, Bloomington, IN, 2006); Keith A. Francis, 'Adventists Discover the Seventh-day Sabbath: How to Deal with the Jewish "Problem"', in Diana Wood, ed., *Christianity and Judaism*, SCH 29 (Oxford, 1992), 373–8.

[8] See Anthony A. Hoekema, *The Four Major Cults* (Grand Rapids, MI, 1963), 89–169; Louis T. Talbot, *What's Wrong with Seventh-day Adventism?* (Findlay, OH, 1956); Jan K. Van Baalen, *The Chaos of the Cults: a Study of Present-Day Isms* (Grand Rapids, MI, 1956), 204–30.

[9] Mark A. Noll, *A History of Christianity in the United States and Canada* (Grand Rapids, MI, 1992), 465–6. For a list of characteristics which suggest the Seventh-day Adventist Church is part of mainstream Protestantism, see George M. Marsden, 'Defining American Fundamentalism', in Norman J. Cohen, ed., *The Fundamentalist Phenomenon* (Grand Rapids, MI, 1990), 22–37.

[10] See Table 1. There are more than a billion Catholics.

Windward Islands and approximately 150 miles off the coast of Venezuela, is typical of the growth experienced by evangelical Protestant churches throughout the West Indies.

The island of Grenada is approximately 133 square miles – slightly larger than the city of Birmingham[11] – twenty-five miles in length and ten miles in width at its maximum points. The population has been close to 100,000 for the last decade – about one-third of the city of Cardiff. Grenada's GDP and economy – which rely heavily on tourism and the sale of agricultural products such as bananas, cocoa, and nutmeg – place it squarely in the developing world.

Grenada may be a poor and small island but the church-growth statistics for the Seventh-day Adventist Church are impressive. In 1983 the number of Seventh-day Adventists on Grenada was 4,682; twenty years later the number was 10,227. In 1983 there were twenty-four Seventh-day Adventist churches on the island; in 2004 there were thirty-eight plus four companies, groups of members meeting regularly but not organized formally as a church with their own building.[12] The number of Seventh-day Adventists as a percentage of the population has increased steadily over the last twenty years: in 2004 it passed 10 percent.[13]

But Grenada is not a typical West Indian island. It is one of two islands – Cuba is the other[14] – which has experienced a one-person dictatorship since the Second World War, the rule of Eric Gairy (1922–97) between 1974 and 1979. It is the only island to experience a Marxist revolution in the last thirty years, the People's Revolution of March 1979. It is also the only island to be invaded by the United States or any major world power since the Second World War.[15] In September 2004 Hurricane Ivan struck the island; subsequent to the last hurricane to cause similar damage, Hurricane Janet in September 1955, Grenada experienced the largest migration in its history.[16]

To be specific, the growth of the Seventh-day Adventist Church has

11 London is 620 square miles and Cardiff is 54 square miles.

12 See Table 2.

13 See Tables 2 and 3.

14 The term West Indian is generally used by peoples in the Caribbean islands to refer to those islands which were former British colonies. Cuba is not usually referred to as West Indian.

15 The Bay of Pigs Invasion of Cuba in April 1961 was not an official invasion by the United States.

16 Beverley A. Steele, *Grenada: a History of Its People* (Oxford, 1983), 342–4.

occurred against a backdrop of political, economic, and social instability. Workers' riots in the 1950s, mass migration in the 1960s, political repression and revolution in the 1970s preceded the beginning of the period of accelerating growth. In the 1980s and 1990s Grenadians had to deal with war and its consequences, the difficulties of establishing an accountable parliamentary democracy, and the challenges of its 'Third World' economy.[17] For the Seventh-day Adventist Church it has been growth under duress.

Despite its recent history, should the growth of the Seventh-day Adventist Church in Grenada specifically, and the West Indies in general, be described as a revival? In a larger context, the growth of the Seventh-day Adventist Church in Grenada is a (small) part of the growth of Seventh-day Adventism in Central and South America. In Central America – the administrative term Seventh-day Adventists use for the area is Inter-America – the church membership in 1983 was little more than 100,000 greater than that of North America, the supposed home of Seventh-day Adventism.[18] By 2005, Seventh-day Adventists in Central America outnumbered those in the United States and Canada by more than a million and a half.[19] In South America, Brazil alone had more Seventh-day Adventists at the end of 2004 – 1,169,889 – than North America's 1,006,317 members.[20] Perhaps the term 'revival' would become meaningless if it had to be used for the growth of the Seventh-day Adventist Church in particular and Christianity in general throughout the Global South.

The best reason to consider developments in Grenada and the West Indies a revival is the uniqueness of the phenomenon. Jan Rogoziñski, in his indispensable book on the history of the islands, calls West

17 Apart from Steele's book, the best history of Grenada prior to 1983 is George Brizan's *Grenada: Island of Conflict* (London, 1998). The best histories of Grenada in the years just prior and after 1983 include: Anthony Payne, Paul Sutton, and Tony Thorndyke, *Grenada – Revolution and Invasion* (New York, 1984); Gregory Sandford and Richard Vigilante, *Grenada: the Untold Story* (London, 1984); and Eileen Gentle, *Before the Sunset* (Ste-Anne-de-Bellevue, Que., 1989).

18 The headquarters of the Church was in Washington, D.C. then and is in Silver Spring, Maryland now.

19 See Table 1.

20 Office of Archives and Statistics, General Conference of Seventh-day Adventists, Silver Spring, Maryland, *142nd Annual Statistical Report – 2004*, 18, 20 and 22. For Inter-America, the increase in membership represented the maintenance of same percentage of Seventh-day Adventists as compared to the Church in the rest of the world: 18.71% in 1983 and 18.12% in 2004. In North America the increase in membership reflected a drop in the percentage: 15.94% in 1983 and 7.22% in 2004.

Indians 'deeply religious' and the West Indian theologian, Noel Titus, notes that 'one of the most significant elements in Caribbean culture is religion'.[21] In other words, Christianity does not need to 'come to' Grenada or the West Indies: it is already ingrained in the culture. What is different about the growth of the Seventh-day Adventist Church is the adoption by significant numbers of Grenadians (and West Indians) of a new Church affiliation: Seventh-day Adventist as opposed to Roman Catholic or, in fewer cases, Anglican.[22]

In the *Evangelical Dictionary of Theology* 'revivalism' is defined as:

> A movement within the Christian tradition which emphasizes the appeal of religions to the emotional and affectional nature of individuals as well as to their intellectual and rational nature. It believes that vital Christianity begins with a response of the whole being to the gospel's call for repentance and spiritual rebirth by faith in Jesus Christ. This experience results in a personal relationship with God.[23]

While it may be difficult for a historian to assess whether a person or group had undergone spiritual rebirth using the critical tools of the discipline, personal commitment is much easier to analyse. One difference between a Grenadian Catholic and a Grenadian Seventh-day Adventist is the level of commitment required and given to the Church. For Seventh-day Adventists their commitment is a seven-day-a-week task. For the majority of Catholics their commitment is one day per week, generally less – at least, so Grenadians believe.[24] The Seventh-day Adventist Church in Grenada has found a way to persuade people whose adherence to the Christian Church is an important part of their culture to transform their membership into active and regular

[21] Jan Rogoziński, *A Brief History of the Caribbean: from the Arawak and Carib to the Present* (rev. edn, New York, 2000), 359; and Noel Titus, 'Our Caribbean Reality (1)', in Howard Gregory, ed., *Caribbean Theology: Preparing for the Challenges Ahead* (Kingston, Jamaica, 1995), 60.

[22] There is a strong strain of anti-Catholicism in Seventh-day Adventist theology; see P. Gerard Damsteegt, *Foundations of the Seventh-day Adventist Message and Mission* (Grand Rapids, MI, 1977), 179–213. Interestingly, in the oral interviews the author conducted, antipathy toward Catholicism was not mentioned as a motivating factor for new converts from the Roman Catholic Church nor by Seventh-day Adventists trying to convert Roman Catholics.

[23] Walter A. Elwell, ed., *Evangelical Dictionary of Theology* (Basingstoke, 1985), 948.

[24] Telfer Garcia, interview by author, 5 January 2004, Mt Nesbit, Grenada, tape recording, Baylor University Oral History Institute, Waco, Texas (hereafter: BUOHI).

participation.[25] Thus, while the percentage of Roman Catholics is just keeping pace with the population at about 60 per cent, the percentage of Seventh-day Adventists continues to rise.[26] This is revival Caribbean-style.

Can this revival be dated? In the case of Grenada the task is made more difficult by the lack of information. There is no membership information available for Grenada before 1983 because the island was simply a part of a larger administrative unit called the Caribbean Union Conference. In 1983 the Seventh-day Adventist Church was forced to create an independent administrative unit in Grenada, called the Grenada Mission Conference,[28] by the People's Revolutionary Government (PRG). The PRG saw the churches as a potential obstacle to the establishment of a Marxist state in Grenada; in order to observe the activities of the Seventh-day Adventists better, the PRG told the leaders of the Church in the United States that it wanted to deal with 'an administration it could relate to right on the island' and the Grenada Mission Conference was the result.

Leaving aside the historiographical difficulties, it can be argued that something was already occurring by 1983. The addition of 316 members in that year is not far from one per day. However, the political turmoil of the years 1983 to 1985 meant that the Church lost more than 380 members per year in those three years. About 1987, the membership gains started to outweigh the losses by more than two hundred in every year except 1990, the year of the second parliamentary election after the overthrow of the PRG. If the revival did not begin in 1987 it was certainly going by 1991.[29]

Why did this (ongoing) revival occur? From observations and oral

25 Clinton Lewis, President of the Grenada Conference of Seventh-day Adventists, interview by author, 5 January 2004, Grenville, Grenada, tape recording, BUOHI and Emmanuel Francis, interview by author, 6 January 2004, Mt Nesbit, Grenada.

26 See Paul Seabury and Walter A. McDougall, *The Grenada Papers* (San Francisco, CA, 1984), 136 and Secretaria Status Rationarum Generale Ecclesiae, *Statistical Yearbook of the Church 1996* (Città del Vaticano, 1998), 36.

27 A mission is the smallest unit of administration in the Seventh-day Adventist Church. A Mission can act independently of other administrative units in the Church – for example, institute policies specific to itself – but its officers are elected by the next largest administrative body, usually a Conference or a Division. See 'Mission', in Don F. Neufeld, ed., *Seventh-day Adventist Encyclopedia* (rev. edn, Washington, DC, 1976), 907.

28 See Seabury and McDougall, *Grenada Papers*, 128–49 and Clinton Lewis, interview by author, 5 January 2004.

29 See Table 2.

interviews conducted by the author, there are seven major reasons for the revival in the Seventh-day Adventist Church in Grenada. Some are exactly as suggested in the Jenkins Thesis; others, unsurprisingly, are unique to Grenada.

First, the Seventh-day Adventist Church is a young Church. The majority of members, particularly new ones, are under the age of forty. This has meant the inculcation of youth culture into church worship, for example, with West Indian styles of music such as reggae and calypso being used in conjunction with nineteenth-century hymns.[30]

Second, the Church emphasizes the social gospel. The majority of its members are poor but they learn frugality, partly through being encouraged to give fixed sums of their income to the Church and partly through being made responsible for their fellow-Grenadians in an even more penurious position than they. There is no Welfare State in Grenada and the Church acts like a charitable NGO to compensate for this. Like the Methodist Church and the Salvation Army in England in the nineteenth century, the Seventh-day Adventist Church is known in Grenada as the institution to turn to for anyone with economic needs.[31]

Related to the Church's social gospel is its social outreach. Seventh-day Adventists aim to convert their family and friends first: new converts, in particular, are encouraged to do this. The majority of evangelistic efforts are one-to-one between individuals who are familiar to each other, a much easier task on a small island.

More particular to Grenada (and the West Indies) is the impact of former immigrants to Britain. Having left the island in the 1950s and early 1960s, these Grenadians began returning in small numbers in the late 1970s and much larger numbers in the 1990s. A significant number of these returnees had become Seventh-day Adventists while in Britain: not only did they boost the membership numbers, particularly in 1997 and 1998,[32] but they brought organizational skills which they had learnt in Britain and extra money.[33]

The professional approach to evangelism is perhaps the most impor-

30 Joseph Bowen, pastor, interview by author, 1 January 2004, Mt Granby, Grenada, tape recording, BUOHI.

31 Joan Britton, interview by author, 31 December 2003, Hermitage, Grenada, tape recording, BUOHI and Agnes Francis, interview by author, 6 January 2004, Mt Nesbit, Grenada.

32 See Table 2.

33 Fred Francis, interview by author, 6 January 2004, Industry, Grenada, tape recording, BUOHI.

tant factor in the revival. With the support of the Church leadership, every local church is encouraged to have a least one evangelistic campaign per year. The Church provides money for lay members to learn preaching, how to give Bible studies, and administration. Each local church is expected to think of the pastor as a special-skilled leader but not the full-time leader of the church's evangelistic efforts: these are lay-driven. New churches are built by members with the appropriate expertise and located in prominent positions in the towns or villages.[34]

Much is expected of the Seventh-day Adventist laity: in complete contrast to the Catholic Church, for example. The Seventh-day Adventist Church seems to have filled a vacuum in the life of Grenadian society. While the Catholic Church lacks the priests to pastor the twenty parishes on the island, new converts to Seventh-day Adventism are encouraged to run their local church. The ennui of Grenadians – partly a characteristic of West Indian culture and partly due to the island's recent troubled history – is combated by the energy and direction of the rising number of Seventh-day Adventists on the island.[35] Rodney Stark's comment that religious groups with high growth rates demand greater commitment certainly applies.[36]

It is a young, poor, evangelical, and active Church. Remove the 'evangelical' and this description of the Seventh-day Adventist Church in Grenada could be applied to the whole of Christianity in the Global South. In the case of Grenada, and the West Indies, Philip Jenkins appears to be correct: this is the future of the Church. However, numbers are no guarantee of the future status of the Christian Church – a point the first two hundred years of the Church's history confirms. Furthermore, revivals cannot be sustained forever; they are, by their nature, transient.

Is the Caribbean-style revival in the Seventh-day Adventist Church in Grenada unique? Probably not. Some of the characteristics of Christianity in Africa and Asia described by Jenkins are similar to those of Seventh-day Adventism in Grenada. Wide-spread appeal to all ages, particularly the young, transforming Christianity by inculcating it with

34 Clinton Lewis, interview by author, 5 January 2004.

35 David Sinclair, interview by author, 4 January 2004, Mt. Nesbit, Grenada, tape recording, BUOHI.

36 Stark, *The Rise of Christianity: a Sociologist Reconsiders History* (Princeton, NJ, 1996), 177–9.

the local culture, evangelizing while society is in turmoil, a theology that emphasizes social concern as much as dogma: these factors have spurred the growth of the Seventh-day Adventist Church in Grenada and Christianity in the Global South. How ready the 'developed North' is for the changes in Christianity brought about by the South's new and active converts is one of the most intriguing questions in Christian history of the next half-century.

Baylor University, Waco, Texas

Table 1:[37] Seventh-day Adventist Membership in Central and North America, 1983–2004

Year	Inter-America	North America	World
1983	774,807	660,253	4,140,206
1984	832,908	676,204	4,424,612
1985	869,893	689,507	4,716,869
1986	953,982	704,515	5,038,871
1987	1,028,502	715,260	5,384,417
1988	1,094,557	727,561	5,749,735
1989	1,177,964	743,023	6,183,585
1990	1,251,266	760,148	6,661,462
1991	1,313,427	776,848	7,102,976
1992	1,385,517	793,594	7,498,853
1993	1,457,090	807,601	7,962,210
1994	1,520,588	822,150	8,382,558
1995	1,571,162	838,898	8,812,555
1996	1,654,683	858,364	9,296,127
1997	1,703,467	875,811	9,702,834
1998	1,817,431	891,176	10,163,414
1999	1,964,489	914,106	10,939,182
2000	2,078,226	933,935	11,687,239
2001	2,164,570	955,076	12,320,844
2002	2,291,583	974,271	12,894,015
2003	2,442,050	992,046	13,406,554
2004	2,525,557	1,006,317	13,936,932

37 Unless stated otherwise, statistical information in the tables is taken from: Office of Archives and Statistics, General Conference of Seventh-day Adventists, Washington, DC, *Annual Statistical Reports, 1983–1987* and Office of Archives and Statistics, General Conference of Seventh-day Adventists, Silver Spring, Maryland, *126th–142nd Annual Statistical Reports, 1988–2004*.

Table 2: Seventh-day Adventist Church Membership in Grenada, 1983–2004

Year	No. of Churches	Members Added	Members Lost[38]	Total
1983	24	316	209	4,682
1984	24	440	264	4,937
1985	28	263	692	4,668
1986	27	297	128	4,858
1987	27	562	127	5,316
1988	28	322	87	5,566
1989	28	413	118	5,898
1990	28	466	335	6,086
1991	28	517	262	6,359
1992	29	262	89	6,553
1993	28	373	163	6,781
1994	29	443	184	7,109
1995	29	328	136	7,330
1996	30	308	133	7,520
1997	33[39]	876[40]	168	8,228
1998	35[41]	717[42]	318	8,627
1999	35[43]	422	197	8,852
2000	37[44]	537	147	9,219
2001	35[45]	288	100	9,407

38 This figure includes members who died, were dropped from local church membership records, or sent letters asking for their membership to be removed. In the latter case, they might be attending another Seventh-day Adventist Church in Grenada or another country, or had left the Church entirely. Internal membership transfers are the reason why the membership at the end of a given year is not simply a combination of the additions and subtractions during the year plus the previous year's membership.

39 Includes three companies.

40 Includes seventy-seven members added by letter; that is, transferring their membership from one church to another – probably another country in most cases.

41 Includes six companies.

42 Includes 162 members added by letter.

43 Includes three companies.

44 Includes four companies.

45 Includes two companies.

Table 2: (cont.)

Year	No. of Churches	Members Added	Members Lost	Total
2002	38[46]	487	56	9,838
2003	39[47]	586	197	10,227
2004	42[48]	482	138	10,571

Table 3: Seventh-day Adventist Church Membership Compared to Total Population, 1983–2001[49]

Year	Membership	Population	Percentage of Population
1983	4,682	90,966	5.14
1984	4,937	94,148	5.24
1985	4,668	93,910	4.97
1986	4,858	90,400	5.37
1987	5,316	94,128	5.64
1988	5,566	93,900	5.93
1989	5,898	94,500	6.24
1990	6,086	95,000	6.40
1991	6,359	95,597	6.65
1995	7,330	98,540	7.43
1996	7,520	98,921	7.60
1997	8,228	99,516	8.26

46 Includes four companies.

47 Includes three companies.

48 Includes four companies.

49 Population statistics taken from: Central Statistical Office, Ministry of Finance, Grenada, *Annual Abstract of Statistics 1991* (St George's, Grenada, 1992), 10; Statistics Division, Ministry of Finance, Grenada, *Vital Statistics Report 1998* (St George's, Grenada, 1999), 8; Department of Economic and Social Affairs, United Nations, *2000 Demographic Yearbook* (New York, 2002), 144; Department of Economic and Social Affairs, United Nations, *Statistical Yearbook 2002–2004* (New York, 2005), 34. Statistics based on mid-year population estimates except in the census years 1991 and 2001.

Table 3: (cont.)

Year	Membership	Population	Percentage of Population
1998	8,627	100,100	8.61
1999	8,852	101,000	8.76
2000	9,219	101,000	9.13
2001	9,407	102,632	9.17